The publisher gratefully acknowledges the generous support of the Ahmanson Foundation Humanities Endowment Fund of the University of California Press Foundation.

Absolute Music, Mechanical Reproduction

Contents

Illustrations

Acknowledgments

This book was a joy to write—because of the importance and timeliness of its subject, certainly, but also because it brought me into contact with quite a few enthusiastic and very knowledgeable people. Book and author profited especially from the expert insights, assessments, and corrections, not to mention kind encouragement, of the anonymous readers selected by University of California Press; I hope they are satisfied with the final product. Mary Francis proved the most helpful of acquisitions editors, taking an interest in the book from the get-go, and then alternating carrots and sticks in such a way that the thing seemed to write itself all the more smoothly. Mary has my heartfelt thanks for bucking the publisher default option and being so proactive and personal. Cindy Fulton and Nick Arrivo at the Press were also very supportive in keeping things moving along. The book never would have left the ground without a half-year Faculty Professional Leave from The Ohio State University. I drafted several chapters in happy daytime seclusion in Hong Kong, where the Pun family was kind enough to put me up for an entire month. An Ohio State College of the Arts research grant, awarded through the offices of Associate Dean Mark Fullerton, made a preliminary cleanup of the entire manuscript possible at a critical time. For their astute readings of individual chapters at various points in the trajectory, I am grateful to Amy Bauer, Nicholas Cook, Kay Dickinson, Steve Jones, Karl Klug, Ralph Locke, Alejandro Madrid, Robert Morgan, Mark Obert-Thorn, and Philip Rupprecht. Jonathan Dunsby went far beyond the call of duty and read most of my first draft, and his many criticisms proved vital in giving the book focus. Joseph Panzner read through the entire final draft, and I am grateful for his many suggestions. It is a measure of Joe's extraordinary scope, insight, and all-round helpfulness that a few of his aperçus and thought-provoking turns of phrase remain detectable in my final prose, hard as I tried to avoid this for the sake of scholarly ethics and authorial self-respect. I also thank Stephen D. Franklin and Hyun Park for their shrewd commentary on matters of media and technology. Philip Rupprecht was, thank goodness, a tireless stickler for clarity and context in the Mahler discussions. Ilse Lehiste gave gracious counsel on intricacies of linguistics and German semantics. Alan Green was kind enough to point me to various resources regarding the digital library, particularly those from the Council on Library and Information Resources. Dmitry Sitkovetsky and Sergey Schepkin took hours from their busy schedules to talk about Glenn Gould and Bach, two subjects close to their own hearts. Richard Griscom—head of the Otto E. Albrecht Music Library at the University of Pennsylvania, and a curator of the Leopold Stokowski collection there—was kind enough to examine Stokie's markings in his Sibelius conducting scores and relay some fascinating discoveries. My friend Andrew Steinman worked doggedly to keep me abreast of developments in high-end audio and will, I hope, continue to do so. Alex Pun assisted with the graphics, and made the mad run through Blackwood Sheet Metal at closing time to help shoot pictures for figure 9. Andrew Martin pointed me to D. F. McKenzie and the broader subject of bibliography, which proved instrumental for chapter 1. I would like to thank not only Joe and Andrew but all of my students for teaching me so much over the years. They will never know just how much I've learned from them, and their influence on this book has taken various forms. Anthony Vine, not least among these scholars-to-watch, came through in a pinch and did a beautiful job with the musical examples. Finally, I am delighted to thank my own original teacher. Arved Ojamaa, my father, set the wheels in motion for this book when he played nonstop Chopin and Schubert on the stereo four decades ago, and he has now taken a keen interest in every line of what follows. If I've managed to avoid cant and jargon while showing love for my topic, it is because Dad has served, from start to finish, as my ideal reader.

Introduction

"When you buy a record there are always cuts that leave you cold. You skip them. You don't approach a record as a closed book that you have to take or leave. Other cuts you may listen to over and over again. They follow you. You find yourself humming them under your breath as you go about your daily business."[1] Brian Massumi urges readers to approach Gilles Deleuze and Félix Guattari's books *Anti-Oedipus* and *A Thousand Plateaus*, the two volumes comprising *Capitalism and Schizophrenia*, as if they were music albums. He presents the record as a metaphor for vernacular reading practices, as a practical way to reconcile an arcane study with everyday life.

For anyone working with art music, Massumi's suggestion becomes a disciplinarity matter: it seems odd that a philosopher and political theorist should find music recordings more useful, conceptually and practically, than many musicians do. Though the recording has been "serious" music's main vehicle of currency for at least twenty years now, American musicologists fail to give it or other mass media much ontological recognition beyond documentary functions. Such coverage as there is comes neither from musicians nor from musicologists, strictly speaking, but from media theorists and philosophers of aesthetics. Against the substantial work on recordings from nonmusicians like Michael Chanan, Kathleen Marie Higgins, Paul Thom, Stan Godlovitch, Lee B. Brown, and Theodore Gracyk, we need to place Simon Rattle's conviction—not unusual in his field—that "music was not meant to sound like gramophone records," music ontologist Roman Ingarden's distancing of the recording from the composition by invoking "a record of a work in performance and not of the work itself," and Harvard musicologist Lewis Lockwood's anger that Bernard Rose dared make his Beethoven movie *Immortal Beloved* as a Hollywood film and not as a history textbook.[2]

This intellectual neglect of recordings and other media is emblematic of a wider oversight in American musicology: to judge from the scholarly literature in this country, there would seem to be no vernacular practice for so-called classical music.[3] Recordings, films, and other media have enabled—or, more simply, *are*—vernacular practices with art music, and those music scholars who slight or ignore them are relics tending a relic discipline. If the same mind-set held sway in literary circles, we would be discussing the Bible as an object of oral transmission, Shakespeare's dramas would be analyzed exclusively as works for the playhouse with seminars devoted to his stage directions, and Coleridge's poems would be examined as inviolate wholes incapable of being excerpted or read in part, the final word immanent in the first. Musicologists speak enthusiastically of ethnography, the study of music "out in the field," as used and practiced by ordinary people in ordinary life, but—perhaps out of some unspoken condescension—they tend to restrict such perspectives to popular and folk musics.

Whence the discrepancy between literary critic and musician in attitudes toward media and colloquial practice? The differences must stem from contrary conceptions of the work, though in the end such an explanation raises more questions than it answers. For a literary critic like Massumi, the books by Deleuze and Guattari are latent or even "open" texts that are realized in the minds of their readers. In Massumi's view, there can be no difference between a private and a public reading. For Rattle, Ingarden, and Lockwood, the musical work floats timeless and free of any particular performers and listeners and is therefore open to no vernacular practice. Performance of a Beethoven symphony or a Brahms sonata consists of a historically substantiated reading of an authenticated text. By way of contrast, Massumi discusses the Deleuze and Guattari books as printed lexical texts requiring no interpretation as commonly defined, and urges us to order and define them for ourselves. One could say Massumi's representation is textually underdetermined, and Lockwood's and Rattle's textually overdetermined. Beyond this, Massumi encourages us actually to put these texts to use, and even instructs us how to do so.

Historical musicology is the most scientist of humanistic disciplines, and also the most inflexible with regard to textual conceptions. Musicologists like to build secure Euclidean universes out of paper and ink, or at least they do in the United States, and the record, CD, and MP3 file have suffered neglect because they can't be picked up and read as easily and factually as a book. As Richard Taruskin notes, musicologists, "better than any other group of humanistic scholars," have learned over their discipline's relatively short history "to distrust conjecture, indeed to deride it, and to regard as real only what can be seen and touched."[4] While comparative literature, say, sets great store on critical imagination and initiative, in historical musicology these same interpretive processes are beholden to more stringent ideas of work and text. In its defense, musicology must owe some of this mistrust and fear to a major uncertainty: the musical work, the center of its disciplinarity for a century, is fated to remain textually decentered. A notated musical score represents a set of often ambiguous instructions, while the prose text offers a highly determinate phonetic analogy to its message. As heard, a musical work does not map onto its printed score with nearly the same directness and precision. It requires the mediation of performance. Books, on the other hand, have moved in the opposite direction of nonmediation over about the past six centuries and benefited from increased literacy, dominance of the vernacular, and cultures of silent reading.

In this book I want to bring Massumian approaches to Beethoven, Brahms, and Mahler out of the closet and acknowledge them from a musician's perspective. I will focus not on those approaches themselves as much as the Massumian attitude's effect on the public cultural constructs that we call Beethoven, Brahms, and Mahler. These composers are now less likely to be heard in a concert hall than as a ringtone or in a video game, or paused, fast-forwarded, and shuffle-played on an MP3 player. With Freenet, iTunes, YouTube, and Amazon.com, the forces of individual eagerness, corporate luster, and cutthroat anti-ontologies have long since shoved aside reception-history apologia and constructivist wheedling. How many music-lovers still listen to the "Eroica" Symphony straight through from beginning to end, wiping the slate clean before each hearing and savoring the triumph of Beethoven's final coda in real time as a cumulative moment, a true teleology? Most of us—even, one imagines, Rattle, Ingarden, and Lockwood in their more private moments—no longer choose to hear Beethoven's String Quartet op. 131 "as a closed book that you have to take or leave." Certainly few current music-lovers—apart perhaps from literary critic Harold Bloom, provided he enjoys music as he does literature, as an experience of "the reader's solitude"—would find it possible to hear Beethoven as "entirely individual, extremely personal, subjective, and wholly divorced from the outside world" (to quote the nineteenth-century Viennese music critic Theodor Helm on the late quartets generally).[5]

Film, video, and various integrated-circuit media have had an immeasurable impact on various aspects of our lives. Describing the situation in terms redolent of Marshall McLuhan's media theory, Paul du Gay finds a fundamental connection "between the meanings and practices which form the basis of all modern culture and the technological means—the media— by which much (though not all) of that culture is now produced, circulated, used or appropriated."[6] In this book, I choose to address vernacular art-musical practice primarily through one medium, that of recordings. Thomas Edison announced his device for recording and playback in 1877, calling it a phonograph. The word literally means "that which writes in sound," and I present recordings as a chapter within the history of writing. The role of recordings in that age-old history has not been explained, at least as regards art music, largely because they play such an ambiguous role: do they really represent written transmission, or are they a subtype of performance and therefore accessories to oral transmission? One could think of recordings as being both: a recording is "written" in that it relies on technology to fix a particular musical expression into permanency, but it is also "oral" in that a listener learns directly and intuitively from it.

It is in part because of this duality that recordings have managed to change music in its every aspect. Their transformative powers can be seen not only in James Brown's originative importance for funk and hip-hop, say, but also in the streamlining of vibrato across the second half of the twentieth century, the global personality cult of singers both popular and operatic, and the role of music in commercial cultures and social interaction. Such causal phenomena have been thoroughly documented by—among others—Robert Philip in *Early Recordings and Musical Style: Changing Tastes in Instrumental Performance, 1900–1950*; Mark Katz in *Capturing Sound: How Technology Has Changed Music*; Timothy D. Taylor in *Strange Sounds: Music, Technology, and Culture*; and several contributors to Hans-Joachim Braun's compendium *Music and Technology in the Twentieth Century*.[7] Philip and Katz discuss recordings and audio equipment for the most part as performance vehicles or as musician-substitutes. Less often discussed, with any musical specificity and in a way that takes into account the deep and wide cultural import of recordings, is the impact that recording has had on aesthetics and on basic questions of ontology— on what sort of thing music *is*. I aver in this book that recordings have irrevocably changed notions of performance and the musical work, and that certain bodies of "classical" music have had as profound a symbiotic relationship with media as has some pop.

Several authors deserve mention for approaching classical music in its vernacular aspect. None of them, however, asks basic epistemological questions about how our musical expectations and music-historical understandings are shaped and colored by the recording formats themselves, or about how recording represents a textual endeavor and has in fact affected classical-music practice in a way that is less (or less directly) aesthetic than ontological. There are certainly ethnographic studies, focusing, for instance, on music consumption and interactions with the Walkman and iPod: such inquiries include du Gay et al.'s *Doing Cultural Studies: The Story of the Sony Walkman* and Tia DeNora's *Music in Everyday Life*, both of which explore the vernacular-everyday to such an extent that musical forms and genres disappear from view.[8] Colin Symes, in *Setting the Record Straight: A Material History of Classical Recording*, goes deep enough into the electronic listening experience to consider its material accoutrements—long thought irrelevant to "the music"—such as record jackets, magazines, and the equipment itself. In his own fine description, "the record has never been a medium sufficient unto itself but has always been extended and mediated by a number of 'off-the-record' practices, both material and discursive."[9] Symes interrogates these rituals but, exploring phonographic fetishism more than musical-ontological issues, doesn't avoid trivial detail. Quite the reverse approach is taken by Eric F. Clarke in his *Ways of Listening: An Ecological Approach to the Perception of Musical Meaning*. Clarke approaches listening from the most basic cognitive and epistemological standpoints, entertaining a vernacular approach in the way he takes us well past the score, as it were.[10] Despite his ecological matrices, however, Clarke barely distinguishes between live and electronic listening and gives almost no attention to the same materialities that Symes overemphasizes. This reader, in short, was disappointed that Clarke's notion of listening ecology barely encompasses the increasing mediatedness of the musical experience. Philip Auslander provides an innovative and crucial discussion of the increasingly permeable divide between live and mediated performance, but does not address art music, an area where the questions would be quite different, as would the answers.[11] Finally, there is the study that apparently gave phonography its name when it appeared in 1987—Evan Eisenberg's *The Recording Angel: Explorations in Phonography*.[12] Eisenberg's book originally defined the discipline, and in some ways remains the smartest phonographic study. Brilliant and frustrating and comedic by turns, Eisenberg takes a serious look at vernacular musical practice. His is an entertaining page-turner of a book, though scholars will regret the author's disinterest in deeper critical approaches and, indeed, in textual issues.

Even more reprehensible than disallowing classical music any real vernacular practice—or of ignoring such practice, which amounts to much the same thing—is the implication that vernacular customs are somehow synonymous with popular music, while classical music represents a kind of strict orthodoxy. Jonathan Goldman pointed out the "questionable . . . axiom that mass culture sides with pleasure—an axiom that reduces pleasure, in all its multiplicity, to a monolithic concept."[13] Goldman rejects lazy presumptions that the masses are basically concerned with having a good time, but the widely respected corollary—that high culture is about exclusion and forestalling pleasure—proves just as hollow. "Serious" music is no more limited to slide rules and hair shirts than popular culture is about bubble gum and testosterone. As Goldman notes, such suppositions only insult the idea of pleasure, which proves just as various as the people who experience pleasure.

WHY ABSOLUTE MUSIC?

Scholars have written much on the aesthetic and intellectual origins of absolute music while ignoring its latter-day history. My own book offers an account of absolute music in the second half of the twentieth century, providing a picture of its transformation—or societal assimilation, maybe?—at the hands of recording culture and consumer electronics.

What is absolute music? According to the nineteenth-century descriptions supplied by E. T. A. Hoffmann, Ludwig Tieck, Arthur Schopenhauer, and others, absolute music is music for music's sake—purely instrumental, structure oriented, untouched by extramusical elements, and with a purely aesthetic rather than social function. Supposedly ageless in its relevance, absolute music forms the cornerstone of the Western European classical tradition. One of the first writers to sketch the ethos of absolute music was E. T. A. Hoffmann. In plumbing the mysteries of Beethoven's Fifth in 1810, Hoffmann heard the symphony as "a world in which [man] leaves behind him all definite feelings to surrender himself to an inexpressible longing."[14] Such examples of absolute music are to be heard and paid obeisance to in rapt silence—what Immanuel Kant would call "disinterested" noiselessness, or Hoffmann would describe as a state of quiet untainted by any manner of "definite feeling." The absolute-music tradition emphasizes interiority and length of utterance and is epitomized by the Austro-German symphonic repertory stretching from Haydn and Mozart through Brahms, Bruckner, and some Mahler. In this tradition, music became a form of religion. In their profundity of meaning, absolute-musical works signified a philosophy of consecration in which wordless, sightless, and supposedly nonreferential art took on sacred meaning, and listening to the music became in itself a form of religious experience.

Why discuss absolute music at this point in history, when its pretenses to freedom from social condition and contingency—and therefore its very founding principles and *raisons d'être*—are discredited, and the construct itself looked upon as a cultural and historical relic?[15] Simply because its influence in the marketplace as an "aesthetic paradigm," to use Carl Dahlhaus's strategically imprecise phrase from intellectual history,[16] has only increased in direct proportion to its drop in intellectual and cultural capital. Like any number of other concepts—"the nuclear family" or "the sanctity of marriage," for instance—absolute music has gained rhetorical force by virtue of its empirical absence. The record critic asks if the latest disc of Beethoven string quartets emphasizes beauty at the expense of truth; the conductor decides to record an as-much-music-as-possible conflation of *Boris Godunov* versions, even though it would make no sense in the theater; Beatles fans cry "foul" when producer George Martin remixes the albums *Help!* and *Rubber Soul*.[17] And so the moralizing influence of absolute music continues in force—not in the concert hall, which isn't accorded nearly the cultural importance it once had, so much as in the recording studio and on the CD player. If we define absolute music as music that is heard without regard for the context surrounding its composition—whether that means actual, historical circumstances or the author-devised, programmatic day-in-the-life-of-an-artist context of, say, Berlioz's *Symphonie fantastique*—then intensifying and quickening commercial markets for recordings have forced more and more music to become "absolute" as a matter of course. But this is only to rephrase Dahlhaus's assertion from 1978, at least if his "day-to-day use of music" includes the utilitarianism of recordings: "The idea that instrumental music devoid of function or program is the 'true' music has since [the early nineteenth century] been eroded to a commonplace that determines the day-to-day use of music without our being aware of it, let alone doubting it."[18] Or we could step further back and assert more plainly, as Hanns Eisler did half a century ago in his essay "Musik und Politik," that absolute music is endemic to capitalist society.[19]

In discussing recordings as they relate to classical instrumental music, I don't mean to slight the vital links that have long existed between popular music and recording culture. Indeed, recordings never would have developed as they did without the wide commercial appeal of popular music generally and of singers, who have always crossed genre lines and audience divisions more easily than other musicians. A fine example is Enrico Caruso, of whom Compton Mackenzie wrote: "For years in the minds of nearly everybody there were records, and there were Caruso records."[20]

Caruso was getting rich from his records shortly after the turn of the century, but Edison's phonograph patent was already some thirty-five years in the past when the first commercial recording of a symphony was made— Artur Nikisch's interpretation of Beethoven's Fifth, recorded in 1913 with the Berlin Philharmonic.

But the collision—or collusion?—between a young and popular technology and an old, rationalist, high-art culture proved intensely interesting. Popular music and recording came together in symbiosis, while the meeting of concert art music and technology threw off sparks and left both the technology and the music irrevocably changed. The success of Haydn's, Mozart's, and Beethoven's symphonies with concert-hall listeners was no guarantee of popularity on record: the literal repetition introduced by recordings might even seem to undercut a culture of music that is "better than it can be performed " (as Artur Schnabel once described Beethoven's late music).[21] But symphonies and sonatas have taken readily to recording and recorded culture at just about every phase, and this alacrity can come as a surprise considering the aesthetic of abstraction and Kantian disinterestedness with which these genres were intertwined. Certainly the commercialism, utility, and easy access of recordings shouldn't necessarily befit a musical culture that "has nothing in common with the external sensual world," as Hoffmann described Beethoven's instrumental music in 1813.[22]

The associations between records and pop have been documented in studies too numerous to list here.[23] By comparison, two basic assumptions remain undiscussed relating to records and classical music: that recording by its very nature falsifies the art music experience; and that most popular music bears little or no connection with cultures of absolute music, or has even developed social and communal elements as de facto antitheses to absolute music.[24] Both these notions are questionable at best: the first I engage fully in the essays that follow, while the second is perhaps too large to interrogate in this introduction, apart from a few initial observations. There are several reasons recordings have been habitually downplayed when it comes to instrumental concert music. For one, recordings have not yet shaken their association with pop commercialism. Recording is especially open to accusations of mass-media commercialism because it is based on technology that stretches back only a hundred years rather than the millennia that underlie book culture. Of course, recording is not the only medium to bear the stigma of popularity. Defending photography in 1936, Walter Benjamin had to brush aside half a century of news photos and other commercialist traditions of photographic realism: "Much futile thought had been devoted to the question of whether photography is an art," he wrote. "The primary question—whether the very invention of photography had not transformed the entire nature of art—was not raised." Much the same wariness marked Gore Vidal's announcement in 1973 that the art of fiction had become thoroughly, perhaps irreparably, infected by film.[25]

THE FATE OF THE WORK

Absolute music has changed as an aesthetic paradigm over the century and a half following Richard Wagner's coining of the term—how could it not? We now see a strange, even schizoid split where the historical construct of absolute music still determines some aspects of concert-giving—though fewer nowadays than when Lydia Goehr stirred up discussion with her book *The Imaginary Museum of Musical Works*[26]—while it has also helped create lustrous new modes of commercialism and consumption. Absolute-musical culture has been transformed by recording, which has become the dominant form of musical transmission while "reducing" music to exchange value in a context of commodity capitalism. In short, the aesthetic-musical abstraction originating with absolute music has been widely influential as something relating vaguely to the work's composition: absolute music "names an ideal of musical purity," according to Roger Scruton, with the piece of absolute music "acquir[ing] objectivity through its structure."[27]

This defines absolute music much as Eduard Hanslick described it, decades before the experimental gramophones of Thomas Edison and Emil Berliner. Since the arrival of records, however, commercialism has co-opted the absolute aesthetic in order to invoke its own culture of objectivity. Recordings have helped break down the whole duality of creative and receptive, of poietic and esthesic, such that the mass-produced aesthetics of some popular music seem at least as distant from the circumstances of its creation as Brahms's symphonies supposedly are from theirs. To put this another way: there is at least as much aesthetic obfuscation surrounding a Coldplay song as there is accompanying a Mozart symphony, and one could trace a specific pop culture of misrepresentation and myth-making back at least as far as the Beatles' *Sgt. Pepper* and *Abbey Road* albums.

As common wisdom would have it, popular music—invoked broadly—is beholden to the contexts surrounding its creation and is more able than a Chopin sonata, say, to convey those contingencies. If that is consistently so, however, then how could complete mishearings—not isolated falsifications, but entire cultures of dogged misreading—emerge around Bruce Spring-steen's "Born in the U.S.A," Lynyrd Skynyrd's "Sweet Home Alabama," and Iron Maiden's "The Number of the Beast"? If the answer lies with audiences preferring to believe in ostensible musical style rather than lyrics whenever the two might contradict each other, that in itself says something about how objectively ("absolute-ly") people listen to songs that often strive to provoke a *subjective* hearing through their texts. Or, as already suggested, the answer could lie with the objectification that comes whenever the song is commodified and spins beyond its creator's influence and control—the mass-market record suggesting not a situation of oral transmission, but the more loosely held communities that Walter Ong attributed to written cultures.[28] It would indeed be difficult to imagine such misreadings happening in the smaller, close-knit communities surrounding acoustic American folk music in the 1940s and 1950s. In short, absolute-music aesthetics have had an influence well beyond absolute music itself, even on styles that are supposedly antithetical to instrumental art music and its supposed abstraction.

As its central project, this book addresses the strange fate of music at a point in history where recorded simulacra of performances of musical works are—contrary to the beliefs of Ingarden, Scruton, et al.—more relevant, accessible, and real than any lingering notion of the pieces themselves. While the musical work played an originative role in the past—acting as the source and origin of the musical experience—it now serves primarily an esthesic function, as a point of orientation and demarcation while the listener grapples with the departing landscape of the heard music. When Jonathan Sterne argues that heard events are no more transient than seen events, he ignores the fact that transience—the aural as distinct from the visual manifestation—has a particular poignancy for musicians.[29] The simple fact of musical notation offers testimony to this fact, for what other art form has developed such detailed notation-through-time as a way of counteracting its own evanescence?[30] The beautiful never-ending-ness of study and immersion in a musical composition stands in painful contrast to the fleeting and unstable nature of the thing studied. In one example of this striving for an elusive musical "truth," Robert Layton recalled Herbert von Karajan's 1980 Berlin recording sessions for Sibelius's First Symphony:

> After recording the Scherzo, however, Karajan remained unhappy with the results. There had been no want of virtuosity on the part of the Berlin Philharmonic, nor was there any lack of fire or excitement in the insistent pounding of the lower strings. But as he rightly said, it was

not up to speed—it did not represent the truth! A second take produced much more headlong, wilder playing even at the loss of some of the superbly controlled momentum of the earlier take. . . . When he heard this played back, Karajan remarked that Sibelius's metronome indication was probably a shade *too* fast. Yet the very act of striving after the letter of the truth enabled him to capture the spirit. . . . The very pursuit of Sibelius's metronome marking, impossible though it really is, ensured the right character.[31]

One could describe the musical work in terms of current practice as a real-time and connotative phenomenon that, prescribed within limited parameters, manifests itself differently in every case. These disparities—sometimes large, in other instances quite small—are what constitute interpretation and performance. Therein lies one difference, slighter than one might expect, between a musical composition and a film. A film resembles a music score in offering a kind of performative schematic across time, perhaps even the perfect "notation" that a formalist composer like Milton Babbitt might envy. But film diverges from musical notation in that the screenplay and its "performance" become one and the same thing: because a screenplay usually has no separate *raison d'être* or existence as a work unto itself, a film entails no performance, indeed nothing whatsoever, outside itself. Self-contained, it enshrines its own truth. The acceptance of films as works and texts may yet encourage acceptance of recorded performances of musical pieces as texts, or indeed works, unto themselves. The role of musical notation changes the more one hears the piece in question performed. When one is able to hear *the same exact performance* of a work repeated dozens or hundreds of times, the notated musical text inevitably changes for the listener. It is perhaps reduced to the importance that a screenplay has for a film by Jacques Tati or Luchino Visconti—a jumping-off point, a scaffolding, a heuristic, a pretense, a dimly remembered antecedent.[32]

Writing in 1966, at a time when Brahms symphonies still retained some of their old transcendental, Hanslickian significance, Ingarden showed his literary basis in declaring the composer's score primary in the ontology of the musical work. He spoke of "a record of a work in performance and not of the work itself," holding up both performance and recording as approximations of a Platonically idealized work. The score, however, had the upper hand in that its basic ambiguities instigated a variety of performances, and the work itself lay—always different, eternally latent—somewhere within that field of possibilities. In the decades after Ingarden, with new consideration of works as they might exist in popular music, consensus shifted away from the score and more toward questions of social and artistic value. In 2000, Michael Talbot offered an overdue update on Ingarden: "A work written according to the 'work-concept' aspires to possess not only objective features (authorship, finiteness, reproducibility) but also some subjective qualities such as status, originality and 'aura.'" Adding in post-Marxist views of the work as commodity, writers like Michael Chanan have described absolute music's place in an aesthetic economy of inactive and increasingly individualized consumption of commodities rather than as active, social involvement in performance.[33]

WHY TECHNOLOGY?

Technology is central to my discussion, but what has it got to do with music? Recordings have played a decisive role in both the dismantling and the perpetuation of absolute music, and as physical objects have even taken on the qualities of perfection, ineffability, and permanence once attributed to the musical work itself. In stating this conclusion in this particular way, I am flirting dangerously with the outmoded view of the technological determinist—the view that, to borrow Robert Heilbroner's recasting of a cold war catchphrase, machines make history.[34] A technological determinist ascribes historical or aesthetic significance to technology independent of any social considerations, making statements like "movable type helped bring about an international musical style" and "computers have prompted a re-prioritization in human memory."

Such assertions were common thirty or forty years ago, but current musicology—like recent cultural anthropology—is reluctant to give any social role to technology per se. Why, then, have I decided to emphasize the importance of recording in the twenty-first century, at a time when technological determinism is as démodé as absolute music and its abstractions? In my view, the current rejection of technology is a transparent political reaction, an implicit reprisal against the kind of technology-based generalizations made thirty or forty years ago by the likes of Ong and McLuhan. Or, more generally, it is a rebuff of the arrogant push-button culture in 1950s America. Or a renewed indictment of mechanized tyranny: Mitchell Morris stresses the machine aspect of Steve Reich's *Come Out* (1966) when he describes hearing this tape piece as "an actual human being . . . ground up in an infernal machine that resembles bureaucracy, administration, or any other incarnation of the principle of disengaged instrumental reason."[35] Because of such fears of dehumanization, technology has gradually supplanted non-Western colonial subjects as "the Other" of choice, beginning with the dystopian work of H. G. Wells, Lewis Mumford's notion of monotechnics, and the Hiroshima and Nagasaki bombs. But in the case of both the marauding machine and the ethnic Other, chauvinism stems from oversimplification and overgeneralization of the feared entity.

As cultural anthropologists and social researchers have tirelessly pointed out, to invoke technology is to risk isolating human expertise from its social contexts. Instead of discussing a dialectic between the two, however, writers now tend to squelch the former while investing the latter with vague and talismanic meaning. According to Sterne,

> At the most basic level—how they worked—tympanic sound-reproduction technologies are best understood as the *result* of a proliferation of a particular set of practices and practical understandings concerning sound and the ear, not as the *cause*. Of course new sound technologies had an impact on the nature of sound or hearing, but they were part of social and cultural currents that they themselves did not create.[36]

With its elevation of the social and cultural over the technological, the statement is one-sided and tendentious: to refuse sound technologies any causal connection with "social and cultural currents" is to oversimplify those currents. Sterne insists on giving technology the role of *result* rather than *cause*, and thus falls into line with so many now writing about Western culture from a humanist—as opposed to an industrial or pop-cultural—perspective.

Sterne constructs a burgeoning "audile technique," which he describes in very general terms as a practice that "articulated listening and the ear to logic, analytic thought, industry, professionalism, capitalism, individualism, and mastery." His examples—demonstrating a strictly rational and indeed domesticated notion of technology—stretch back to medical advocacy of the stethoscope in the early 1800s and forward to telegraphers' graduation from reading encoded messages to hearing them.[37] He implies that no ontology of repetition or documentation in sound could have existed before the audible technique that he mentions: while a McLuhan disciple would talk about the profound impact that the literal repetition of recordings had on music and hearing, Sterne turns the equation around and would insist that any such repetition was not conceptually possible before the repetitive audile techniques that precipitated the advent of recording. In other words, people needed a mental conception of verbatim auditory repetition before they could invent the phonograph. Sterne says that cultural understandings necessarily precede mechanical understandings, while McLuhan insists on the reverse. Neither thinker is particularly dialectical, nor does either do a good job explaining the "why" and "how" of invention.[38]

Sterne does not make the mistake of seeing recordings as impartial vehicles of transmission. In fact, he attacks the notion that "sound-reproduction technologies can function as neutral conduits," with such technologies functioning "as instrumental rather than substantive parts of social relationships." He refutes the long-held assumption that, in the case of recording and broadcasting, "technology vanishes, leaving as its by-product a source and a sound that is separated from it."[39] I agree with Sterne that recording is not a transparent process, but would go further and say recordings harbor certain agendas, subjectivities, and possible entropies, which aren't the same as what he calls "social and cultural currents." Sterne himself approaches my more technologically determinist frame of mind in a more recent study where he all but anthropomorphizes MP3 technology, linking that strategically reduced ("lossy") codec with the imperatives "Travel great distances frequently and with little effort! Accumulate on the hard drives of the middle class! Address a distracted listening subject!"[40]

In any event, Sterne's technological notions prove more constructive than the fallacies proffered by David Kusek and Gerd Leonhard in *The Future of Music: Manifesto for the Digital Music Revolution*. These authors present a utopianist *Aufhebung* of machines that solve many more problems than they cause. Haven't they ever seen a hard drive crash or an iPod battery fail, one wants to ask? Such techno-utopianism entertains what we might call the receding revolution cliché: a technology—increasingly powerful and music-amenable integrated circuits in Kusek and Leonhard's case—is described as bringing us to the point where life is about to change beyond all recognition. If anything outdoes the wonder to be experienced at that future time, it is the question of how we could possibly have failed to anticipate these seismic changes. Polemically minded social and media theorists usually cultivate these kinds of Hegelian visions as weapons, brickbats that—it must be admitted—can sometimes be put to good use. In Kusek and Leonhard's case, the wondrous revolution is invoked in order to undercut those who would stand in its way, specifically the dinosaur moguls of the record industry. Listeners of the world unite! Kusek and Leonhard's vision, contrasting with a deathly spectre of corporate dehumanization, almost seems to follow the Marxist account of the end of history.[41]

To summarize then, we have seen cultural anthropologists—inspired not infrequently by politics and revisionism—construct technology as

in flux. As a result, these lines of inquiry have become inseparable, or at least convergent. Last but not least, I return repeatedly to the question of what music performance means in the age of mechanical reproduction, and offer conclusions on this topic that can be placed alongside and contrasted with Robert Philip's more causal deductions in *Performing Music in the Age of Recording*.[54] I pursue these interconnected topics more as a cultural anthropologist than as a student of analytical philosophy or aesthetics, strictly speaking. Rules, definitions, and taxonomies—inductively reached and broadly applicable—hold less interest than critical approaches to individual examples.

Perhaps I should start with the book's title: in addressing the "problem" of art in a time of unlimited reproducibility, my project follows directly from Walter Benjamin's essay "The Work of Art in the Age of Mechanical Reproduction" ("Das Kunstwerk im Zeitalter seiner technischen Reproduzierbarkeit," 1936).[55] Benjamin describes a particular kind of aesthetic value, related to older ideas of ritual and religious significance, that he calls the *aura*. He then asks how people should relate to art—and more specifically to artworks themselves—at a time when it is easy to make multiple more-or-less identical copies of them, in short when the aura has dissipated or becomes irrelevant. Benjamin looked back to a time when art was, as a matter of course, explicitly or implicitly connected with religious observance and ideas of the sacred, and he asked what happens when such art not only survives into a secular age but is replicated at the demand of late capitalism. If the artwork is recent, its aesthetic capital comes from its indebtedness to those earlier ideals. Benjamin saw something similar to Kateb's madness in the "shattering" of custom and cultural notions of originality that is caused by technologically assisted reproduction:

> That which withers in the age of mechanical reproduction is the aura of the work of art. This is a symptomatic process whose significance points beyond the realm of art. One might generalize by saying: the technique of reproduction detaches the reproduced object from the domain of tradition. By making many reproductions it substitutes a plurality of copies for a unique existence. And in permitting the reproduction to meet the beholder or listener in his own particular situation, it reactivates the object reproduced. These two processes lead to a tremendous shattering of tradition which is the obverse of the contemporary crisis and renewal of mankind.[56]

But Benjamin's epochal essay represents no obvious, simplistic, black-and-white knee-jerk reaction to technology. He doesn't end by wringing his hands over the loss of aura seen in "the age of technological reproducibility," but in fact sees socially progressive possibilities in light of the technological change. It is important to mention here that Benjamin spends a good deal of time talking about film, describing it as both popular and progressive. Filmmakers managed to create an entirely new art form amid the collapse of the aura, and did so using the very sort of reproductive technology that had caused the breakdown in the first place: they developed a way to manufacture thousands upon thousands of images, link them into a new manner of narrative sequence that engages attention and awareness in a novel way, and then produce enough copies of the film to thoroughly pervade society with its message. In short, film is *the* art form designed by and for a time of cultural "overproduction."

Benjamin was a basic starting point for the present book. From my first reading of his famous essay, I was electrified by the author's faith in the transformative capabilities of technology, in its potential for necessary and beneficial change, especially as this informed Benjamin's belief in the necessity and instrumentality of art. In combining these views, Benjamin demonstrated great prescience. Scott Lash believes that "The Work of Art in the Age of Mechanical Reproduction" confirms its author's status as "critical theory's foremost sociologist of culture," and he even finds major connections with postmodernism.[57] With its exciting combination of technology, aesthetics, and social theory, Benjamin's inquiry became a cornerstone in the growing disciplines of media theory and media discourse analysis, laying the foundation for later work by McLuhan, Friedrich Kittler, Simon Frith, Nicholas Cook, Michael Chanan, and others. In looking into the original and creative aspects of performance, my study also follows specifically on the work of Cook and Jonathan Dunsby, and Peter Kivy to a lesser degree.[58] As a music-lover and stereophile of long standing, I introduce to these lines of thinking novel ideas that relate to canonic Western art music and contemporary recording technologies. These two perspectives prove all the more helpful because they bring together paradoxical concerns for the old and for the new. I believe this duality helps bridge gaps between the media theorists' understanding of technology, the critical thinkers' grasp of larger social questions, and the philosophers' interests in ontology and epistemology.

Though I hope to have kept techno-utopianism to an absolute minimum, the optimism of my book betrays its debt to Benjamin: I paint perhaps the first sanguine picture of art music as it connects—and will potentially connect in the future—with early twenty-first-century market technologies. I felt compelled to counter Julian Johnson's *Who Needs Classical Music? Cultural Choice and Musical Value* and Lawrence Kramer's *Why Classical Music Still Matters*, two protests against market forces, popular taste, and the corrosive forces of modern-day living.[59] Those authors and a good many others see a diminishing audience for classical music as emblematic of cultural malaise; I see this music as an ever-lively phenomenon that will always involve, if not a majority, then a vital and passionate set of listeners. Technology will neither save nor destroy classical music, or any art form for that matter. Innovations in audio electronics speed up the increase-decrease of a music's popularity, certainly, but in introducing sambas and sonatas to new cultures and manners of construal they also serve to broaden their significance. Some see the iPod as they saw the Walkman twenty-five years ago: as an instrument of aural wallpaper and mindless distraction. I hope that my fifth chapter, "Beethoven and the iPod Nation," will put some of those fears to rest; but then the book returns again and again to these thoughts of technology as an instrument for expansion as well as for "bringing forth." It is my belief, in the end, that the currency of classical music bears little if any connection to issues of education and commercialism; the only real concern is access to and distribution of the music, and that is now largely a technological concern.

Given such disavowals, one might well ask what sort of listener I have in mind: Is my listener an eager amateur? A tenured musicologist? A seasoned conductor? Or an amalgam of all three? In chapter 1, when I discuss the "verbatim repetition" of the recording as something distinguishable from hearing the same musician(s) twice in a row, I invoke a sensibility akin to T. W. Adorno's "expert listener."[60] Encountering Maurizio Pollini "live" in the same Schubert sonata on two consecutive nights, we hear the kind of small variants that will likely be terra incognita for the nonmusician since North Atlantic cultures don't emphasize this intensely localized kind of hearing. My readers are likely to have valid concerns about who pretends to be listening for whom here, and I would reply by saying that I am neither an ethnographer nor an authority on ear-training, and have chosen instead to interrogate classical music's dissemination through the ears and eyes of the cultural researcher. I can only speak for myself, especially as presenting "ordinary listeners" with Brahms and Lutosławski in a controlled listening study would create bizarre anomalies of its own. In any event, the "ordinary listener" is just as romanticized a concept as the "expert listener," and the two probably have more affinities—some of them subterranean—than people would willingly admit.

My array of intellectual sources—from Benjamin and Adorno to Henri Bergson, William James, D. F. McKenzie, Marshall McLuhan, Roland Barthes, Richard Rorty, Jacques Attali, Susan Sontag, and beyond—may seem chaotic, but these thinkers do have significant convergences when it comes to my subjects. The book, to return for a moment to the points suggested by its title, addresses the problem of unlimited reproducibility and the impact this has had on subjectivity, memory, and convention. Benjamin, Bergson, and Attali have each explored this area in their different but complementary ways, through notions of capitalism, repetition, epistemology, and the machine. Central to my inquiry into reproduction is the question of its effect on notions of art, authenticity, and reality. Here James and McKenzie—enemies of Platonistic, hierarchical notions of transcendent value—prove instrumental in their refusal to lower our material realities to second-order copies of meaning. They share a sense of radical empiricism, an approach to analysis that embraces the whole experience and excludes nothing sensible. This is especially valuable when it comes to discussing mass-mediated forms of "high art," where questions can arise concerning which salient aspects have been left out and which irrelevant or even corrupting elements have been introduced into the experience.

In this book I emphasize the roles of invention and technology in producing new intuitions and new manners of thought. In stressing the role of machines, and thereby parting ways with many social scientists, I found myself connecting early on with Bergson and McLuhan. These two theorists were more open than others to notions of mechanization, and to the potential instrumentality of human powers. Since both were concerned with externalizations of thought and memory, and their distribution between people, they almost seem to encourage discussion of recordings as documents and objects. Bergson developed a schematic understanding of the interaction between memory and present action, while McLuhan in *Understanding Media: The Extensions of Man* famously referred to the modern human as "an organism that now wears its brain outside its skull and its nerves outside its hide."[61] In both conceptions, intelligence is extended beyond persons to the point where it is no longer clear where the human aspect ends and the nonhuman, the technological, begins.

Changes in music technology and listening practices have wrought dramatic change in notions of work, text, and performance over past decades—which is to say, recording has had less an aesthetic influence on classical-musical practice than an ontological effect. In other words, it has helped shape and define the sort of thing that music is. Bergson, James, and Rorty count as three theorists who emphasize creative intervention in reality, with senses oriented to present action and creation rather than representation and reproduction. But a specifically textual question arises when the discussion turns to mechanical reproduction: What impact do reproduction and mediation have on the shared meanings, the conveyed "messages," that traditional aesthetics would place at the center of the musical experience? Three of my thinkers help answer this with their own instrumentalist and highly practical perspectives on communication and communicated significance: James, Barthes, and Rorty all helped in their own ways to end the structuralist insistence on shared meaning, and moved instead toward an interpretative practice of difference and local utility. Whether we refer in the end to James's notion of "cash value," Barthes's "tissue of quotations," or Rorty's "one more grid you can place on top of" what we hope to understand, each offers his own quasi materiality and individuality of approach, his own tangible-practical vernacular. All three thinkers are highly relevant to any discussion of recordings, as are all three of their metaphors for connection and significance.

This is not a history of recording and could not be mistaken for any kind of chronological survey. I believe enough histories of this kind have already been written.[62] Such historical perspectives also tend to encourage certain false causalities and conceptual limitations: historical narrative tends to imply influences and connections where none exist, and also encourages deceptive uniformity of terms and concepts across time. Over its 130-year history, recording has represented neither a single set of goals nor a single and continuous technology: to encompass the iPod, the radio, and the Victrola in a single prose account is to imply connections that are at best tenuous. If chronology is at all useful, it is in discussion of the recording as a commercial venture: the words "recording" and "recording technology" have proved powerful because the culture industry itself has used them, and the notion of music as a commodity is one element that has remained a constant for over a century. If we wish to understand a Brahms symphony or a Haydn quartet as a public resource across the twentieth and twenty-first centuries, we must discuss recordings, and talk about them as objects to be bought and sold.

MUSIC OR MEDIATION?

The term "media" is getting pretty dusty for the same sorts of reasons that the word "computer" is, and for the same reasons that the term "recording" itself verges on extinction: ours is a time of synesthesic electronic convergence, where video, audio, and whatever else are coming together on digital platforms and leaving the cultural theorist little choice but to adopt the lingo of the computer geek. Recordings have, over their century-long history, developed visual aspects—real and virtual—to compensate for their once-strict aurality. Conversely, all music has become a soundtrack in one way or another, regardless of whether it has ever appeared in a movie: films and their soundtracks have taken over stewardship of the long, parsed-out, attention-monopolizing time spans that were once the domain of art music. And this is the reason that traditional institutions of concert art music have declined so markedly in the past several decades: not because recordings have simply displaced concerts, by virtue of their convenience and economy, but because they have brought music more into line with the—increasingly inclusive, ever more invasive—cinematic experience. In comparison with the inflexible concert, the malleable recording allows the listener to see more, fantasize more, and do more mental spatiotemporal roaming. It has in a sense followed film's example as the primary model for sensual convergence, an influential metaphor for how we learn and make sense of the world, and not coincidentally a strong influence in designing the computers that now cue, parse, and monitor so many aspects of our lives.

Absolute music remains very much alive as an aesthetic model and cultural force, but as an exclusive aural paradigm it is dead and gone. Should we mourn musical works—as opposed to music in a less controlled and determinate sense—and the sorts of listening agendas that such works demanded 60 or 140 years ago? Lawrence Kramer, waxing lyrical in his recent book *Why Classical Music Still Matters*, answers with a resounding yes. "In today's media-saturated world," he suggests, "there are real concerns about [classical music's] viability." Presuming such a division, or indeed hostility, between music and media, Kramer can really only believe "classical music" to be in sharp decline. He expresses his concern for "the values made available by attentive listening and threatened by its erosion in contemporary society."[63] Old, common-practice music functions here as monad, as ethics, and as scripture, defying the corrosive effects of time while people themselves fall victim. Electronic media and technology more generally do not come to assimilate, translate, or otherwise mediate between old music and new contemporaneity; they work by nature to corrupt it. Bulwark-like, music epitomizes and upholds humanist ideals while technology militates just as single-mindedly against our humanity.

Kramer's technophobia seems a natural extension of Jonathan Sterne's, discussed earlier. But Kramer—impelled by mortal confrontation between "works" and modern "media," abstract instrumental music vying against information technology—astonishes with his dogged aural retrospection. He is far from an old school positivist, and this is one reason I single him out here: he has been in the vanguard of American critical musicology for several decades, making deep and eloquent excursions into poststructural issues of musical meaning and thick cultural description. All the more surprising, then, that Kramer thinks no listening transformations are inevitable, even as human sensibilities themselves become more and more fragmented: he entertains strong but selective subjectivities. Listening is for him an arcadian pursuit, one that stands to be "refreshed" in our own time. We should conform to it as a moral example, not the other way around: "The energies of this music are still vital; its value is still inestimable. The trick is to unlock the energies and recover the value."[64] Kramer allows no middle ground: we can either connect with the old music on its own old conditions, or suffer its loss and confront the full and utter corruption of modern life; the possibility of Bach, Chopin, or Ravel meaning something to us here, now, and on fresh terms never seems to have occurred to him.

I try to give an idea of what such terms might be in my final chapter, where I pull together the book's arguments under the rubric of one composer: Mahler the symphonist. If Beethoven helped define the grand and controversial Viennese symphonic tradition, Mahler is often said to mark its close. His idiosyncratic examples of absolute music achieved high popularity toward the end of art music's reign, injecting new life into that tradition by expanding symphonic discourse. Like the recording itself, or audio technologies more generally, a Mahler symphony problematizes the historical work–concept even as it offers a particular solution to those problems. Mahler created a strange, anti-Romantic disjunction between words and music, and the glut of video and web imagery in our own era has brought us closer to understanding his "meanings" without closing the hermeneutic circle. In saying this I challenge Kramer's belief, stated in the context of art music more generally, that "in a world that moves at digital speed, a world increasingly crowded by people, ideas, and agendas, a maelstrom of technological change . . . , the ability to listen deeply, to open the labyrinths of the ear and be sounded out by the voices that address us, may be the very ability we want the most."[65]

There has always been an imagistic or photographic aspect to Mahler's music, in my view, but it was the electronic media of the later twentieth century that helped listeners become literate, and then conversant, with this aspect. In short, Mahler's works are better assimilated precisely because the world has become "increasingly crowded," and not because of any developments in listening cognition or concentration. His symphonies press us urgently into a variety of roles, *except* that of listener. Or we might even say that Mahler's popularity is predicated upon listening "failures" of the later twentieth century—upon an inescapable, poststructural inability to focus "deeply" and "musically" in the way Kramer describes, thereby making room for other kinds of sense-memory, especially visual ones. But there's no room for this in Kramer's thinking, an ontology where meaning lies intrinsically, unchangingly, and synonymously with the work—the first and final determinant of significance. He believes this is true even of the mediated musical experience, where the machinery ultimately serves to focus our attention retrospectively on those musical meanings enshrined in aged works. He talks briefly about film and soundtracks, specifically Bach's G Major Cello Suite as it appears in both Peter Weir's *Master and Commander* and Roman Polanski's *The Pianist*. Kramer summarizes these episodes: "In their use of this music, these films provide a model of creative listening, listening with both music and meaning in mind. The films realize the meanings that lie like seeds in the music, eager to be disseminated."[66]

This scenario feels simply wrong to me, for music's pleasures of discovery are so scaldingly immediate, so of the moment and the marrow, that they could hardly depend on seeds and germination or hinge on triumphs of compositional meaning. If I were to cede Kramer his interest in works, I might reply with the assertion that compositions change alongside their manners of understandability, the two developing and aiming their own latencies toward the present. But this is a book about music and media, and I would prefer to say that technologies provide more kinds of access to common-practice works than Kramer can envision. To summarize my own sense of joyful, present-moment discoveries within old musical compositions, I turn to a marvelous aphorism from sexologist and author Havelock Ellis: "No other art tells us such old forgotten secrets about ourselves."[67] Ellis perfectly describes art music here as a layered, multichronological experience: the secret it imparts is simultaneously of past and present, and connecting with it gives a sense of both recovery and discovery. For well over a century, recordings and other media have helped us forget fewer and fewer secrets, and served to aid and amplify music in its telling.

1. The Recorded Musical Text

Just what is a musical performance? This is a difficult question, one that music scholars have been slow to ask and even slower to answer. We could begin our definition by saying a performance of Western art music transpires with a reading that is more or less normative and executed according to the composer's instructions. But such a description comes up short because it makes no room for interpretation and variance, leaving Furtwängler's view of Beethoven's Third Symphony much the same as Toscanini's, for example, while it is those very different approaches that make the "Eroica" the "Eroica," that make it so enticingly performable in the first place.

Drawing on ideas of Edward Said and Peter Kivy, Peter Johnson concludes that performances are important for what they do above and beyond the notated music. The observation has not been widely shared by scholars of Western art music, who, as Nicholas Cook observes, have been so intent on "locating the aesthetic centre of music in the written text"—in other words, on isolating musical invariance—that they have taken little notice of the variance that defines performance.[1] Johnson goes further to say that a performance, when heard as an aesthetic whole, in fact embodies "necessary otherness": it emerges as a function of the score only to the extent that it presents the right pitches at the right time and supplies appropriate articulations and dynamics. Its fidelity to the printed page might well enhance its value *qua* performance but by no necessity establishes such value.[2] I would add that the sounding rendition is "other" in that it can never be wholly comprised or predicted by the inner ear and the mind's eye: we are rarely surprised by a third or fifth visual, silent reading of a printed score in any circumstances, but acoustic happenstance or other unforeseen factors can have a considerable effect when we hear the same

score in performance. Unanticipated vibrato, variation of tempo, a reverberant performance space, or simply too much coffee are more likely to
change our impressions of a work than would irregularities of paper, ink,
or notation in a score.

If these thoughts get us a bit closer to understanding musical performance, the even more vexing questions remain: Just what is a recording,
and what is its relationship to the performance it contains? Is it a transparent vehicle, or a medium that recontextualizes or even transforms performance? Does it work for or against performers' concerns, or is it a neutral
conduit for interpretive thought? In the next chapter, we will address the
fate of a performance's "necessary otherness" when that particular foreign-
ness can be repeated—and therefore familiarized—ad infinitum. In this
chapter, I address performance of art music as a phenomenon unto itself,
and one that stands transformed when inscribed into permanency. But there
are also important questions to ask regarding the ontological role of recordings vis-à-vis performance: Does the recorded performance supplant the
musical work any more or less than the live performance, whether it is understood as a sounding entity ("Menuhin recorded a beautiful Beethoven
concerto") or as a physical or commercial object ("Menuhin's Beethoven
concerto is out of print and getting expensive on eBay")? Or does the
recording have the function of performing the performance? And how useful is the conventional notion of recording as documentation of a particular
musical "interpretation," at least in the basic sense that interpretation involves rendering a thought from one language to another?

THE RECORDING AS WORK OR TEXT?

Without referring to recordings, Peter Kivy emphasizes the permanence
of art music performance. He does this by describing the musical performance itself as a work, explaining, for example, that Artur Schnabel's rendition of Beethoven's "Waldstein" Sonata or Rudolf Kempe's particular
actualization of Brahms's Fourth Symphony is an aesthetic object that en-
dures through time much like the sonata or the symphony itself.[3] But how
would such a performance-work relate to the composition-work that is being performed? Adopting ideas from Paul Thom, Kivy says that the performance in essence "quotes" the work in an act of musical and declarative
assertion. It is because he emphasizes the work aspect of performance that
Kivy must invoke quotation rather than interpretation or rendering. The
former falls in line with the inviolate character of works in that it entails

based on their own predilections as readers—traits that Schnabel's and Gould's fans necessarily share with their favored pianist, since a musician can only connect with a listener who shares her textual beliefs. Those Schnabel and Gould textual perspectives are so different that we can never hope to hear the same musical work in their respective recordings of, say, Beethoven's Sonata op. 109—unless, that is, we take into account the varieties of textuality that Barthes and other literary theorists opened up in the 1960s and 1970s.

THE BIBLICAL PARADIGM

Recordings of art music represent mass distribution of so-called high culture, but they have proved more divisive and puzzling than, say, paperback editions of Shakespeare plays. We could summarize the strange ontological situation of recordings by saying that they are partly pornographic and partly biblical. They have become objects of depersonalized yet very individual pleasure, a peculiarly twentieth-century exercise in Kantian disinterestedness (*Uneigennützigkeit*). They have taken on a character more fetishistic than functional—thus the pornographic aspect. At the same time, like most written documents of "higher" cultural import, they are subject to the powerful textual-critical attitudes and ideologies that developed with Judeo-Christian scripture over the course of a millennium. Printed music scores have been subject to the same thinking, of course, but—to return to a persistent theme of this book—they have ceded more and more of that cultural and textual authority, more and more of that "biblicality," to recordings.

For Western societies, the Bible has served as the original and paradigmatic text—at least since the advent of Protestantism, the disappearance of an interceding *glossa ordinaria*, and the institutionalization of a vernacular. The first circumscribed and self-standing system of meaning after antiquity that demanded to be widely read in Europe, it served as a model for all later ideas of textual analysis and became the basis for the theories of interpretation called hermeneutics. The Bible represented a kind of victory of the written over the oral in Western civilization, its writing, compilation, and translation into the vernacular spanning two millennia. In the words of William M. Schniedewind, the Bible represents "an eyewitness to [an] epic shift in human consciousness, the shift from an oral world toward a textual world. Central to this shift [is] the encroachment of the text upon the authority of the teacher."[13] Before the general rise of literacy in

ancient Israel and again among the laity in modern Europe, writing had a
numinous aspect. For the Jews as well as the early Christians, the written
word was exclusivist and an instrument of government and empire, and
orality was populist and the domain of kinship relations. When literacy
emerged and literature flourished during King Josiah's reign in the seventh century B.C.E., there resulted—to quote Schniedewind once again—
"one of the most profound cultural revolutions in human history: the assertion of the orthodoxy of texts." Josianic religious reforms were based
upon the spread of literacy, and by enabling a widespread ability to read
scripture they facilitated "the religious authority of the written text." The
older ethos of the written text is suggested in the book of Isaiah (Isa. 1–39),
where writing is invoked in terms of magic and power.[14]

During the Protestant Reformation, however, the written text—or,
more accurately, the printed book—allowed the laity to evade the church's
textual authority and read God's word on salvation directly for themselves. The phrase *sola scriptura* (scripture alone) served as the reformers'
battle cry, emphasizing the individual's personal relationship with the text
over any kind of communal articulation of the authority wielded by that
text. Anyone wondering exactly *which* scripture was to be followed could
look to Erasmus, who in 1516 published a Latin translation of the New
Testament directly alongside the original Greek (which appeared in print
here for the first time). Erasmus's edition, and the so-called Compluten-
sian Polyglot published in Spain in 1522, allowed believers—at least those
who could read Greek—to see for themselves the mistakes Jerome made in
the Vulgate translation that had served the Roman Catholics for some seven
hundred years. The timing was bad for the Vatican, the new textual developments giving budding Protestants one more reason to circumvent the institutions of oral culture surrounding the scriptures and embrace the Bible
as a personal, readerly, written text.[15]

How to describe the "tipping point" between the suppressive and the
liberatory potential of texts as regards readers' *access* to such texts? Is a
situation where a text sits in the hands of a few a limiting situation, and
a scenario where a text is in the hands of many a liberating one? Though
simplistic, such an explanation does have some bearing on present art music communities, which are relatively small and relatively elite. The world
of art music has indeed been likened to a museum, with professional
curators preserving artifacts that have no direct cultural connection to the
present.[16] But we could just as well call it a postbiblical culture. This quasi-
religious basis is still seen in the aura that surrounds musical explanation and
interpretation, and in the zeal or even anger people show when defending

their own readings of a musical work. The scriptural paradigm also helps us understand why many musicologists and other scientistically inclined humanists believe that texts must involve writing on paper. The Western mind-set would be very different—and more music scholars would probably recognize performance as an intellectual discipline—if the Hebrew Old Testament and the Christian scriptures had come down to us in oral traditions rather than as a set of canonized writings. As it is, musicians speak of "the work" as a locus of authority in much the same way Christian ideologues refer to the Bible, and invoke "the work" as the seat of "divine" composerly intention. The very term "the Bible" is a clear misnomer for a collection of texts, even apocrypha, that cover a wide historical swathe, compiled from far-flung sources in several languages. In the case of both the musician and the Christian, then, the argument is really numerical: the singularity of the composition or book is contrasted with the multiplicity of interpreters, and the singularity must retain authority in order to prevent a breakdown of meaning. How might one react to the shocked report that "Friedrich Gulda played the 'Hammerklavier' with very slow tempos"? Probably by invoking the authority of the work, as invested in the definite article: "But that's a profanation against *the sonata!*" Borrowing a category from Kant's *Critique of Pure Reason*, Lydia Goehr describes the musical work-concept as regulative, meaning that it acts, by power of its own identifiable aesthetic weight and cultural authority, to rein in unorthodox readings and perhaps unorthodox musicality more generally. Goehr points out the quasi-ethical and even quasi-theistic aspect of the work's regulative power, but she might have gone further to say that someone making prohibitive statements on the basis of Beethoven's tempos also betrays textual, logocentric, paper-based thinking.[17] To the extent that they are even separable, the cultural authority of the work largely hinges on its connection with a specific written text, as is true of the Hebrew Old Testament, if not originally with the Jewish Torah.

Notions of textual authenticity—as manifest in the *Urtext*—formed the central nexus in an age where the recording was, at most, accessory to the performance. Now the best-selling recording has—as if in imitation of popular music practice—usurped the authority of the written text. Gunther Schuller has complained of exactly this, observing that the sheer multiplicity of recordings, and the marketplace thinking that produced them, have led to a collapse of musical authority:

> Conductors, battling it out in the fiercely competitive recording market, have now learned that they will stand out, will be reviewed and discussed more readily, and will thus attract more attention the more they

can interpret a work *differently* from the several dozen recordings of it that are already in the market place. This has become more than a trend in recent years: it has become an obsession and a specific skill, eagerly supported by managers and, of course, most record companies. At that point the composer's score becomes, alas, a total irrelevance, an annoying burden.[18]

The poststructural revolution was literary in orientation, its semiotic play representing, or at least springing from, reevaluation of the printed text and the reader's relationship to it. But if the poststructuralist turn had begun some twenty years later, one might well see it as a response specifically to a crisis of meaning in art-musical texts, induced by the exponential proliferation of recordings that began in the mid-1980s and slowed only at century's end; for devaluation of an authored text will inevitably result from proliferation of more or less permanent and more or less equally viable interpretations of that text, viable not in the sense of an original being amenable to the individual reading, but rather in the sense of surviving in the public mind. Literature has not faced such a situation the way classical music has, except to the degree that a set of competing performances of, say, *Hamlet* may have accumulated over the decades on film. For readings of *Twelfth Night*, Langston Hughes, or Emily Dickinson there is nothing like the kind of competitive marketplace that exists for the "Moonlight" Sonata (though such a statement of course begs the question of whether performances of a Beethoven sonata are indeed equivalent in any real sense to readings of a lyric poem or short story).

One could argue against Schuller by saying recordings have led neither to sacrilege nor to breakdowns of meaning but have, in essence, brought forth a musical "Reformation." They have fragmented authority invested in the work and inspired a kind of *sola musica* movement wherein "the word of Beethoven" became liberated from increasingly institutionalized and rule-driven ideas of performance. (In the statement above, Schuller does rather sound like a Roman prelate fighting to keep control of church texts during the Counter-Reformation.) According to such a recording-reformationist viewpoint, the question isn't whether a performer should observe a crescendo in the score, but instead centers on the issue of just what the crescendo means within the reality of a specific performance of a specific piece. Recordings have widened the field of possibility here, perhaps suppressing some attentiveness, as Schuller claims, but certainly doing more to make musicians sensitive to the question of just how many different ways a crescendo can unfold. Would a conductor from 1890 or a conductor today be more likely to know how a crescendo from Schubert's

"Unfinished" Symphony differs from one in Richard Strauss's *Don Juan?* Schuller's impractical and selectively Cartesian exhortation—to wipe all texts and all interpretations, except the composer's, from one's mind—can also be found in the philosophy of Artur Schnabel, to mention one like-minded musician-thinker. "All good composers mean each score to stand on its own," writes Schnabel student Konrad Wolff in conveying his master's textual philosophy, "as though there were no other music in existence."[19] Is such a scenario possible, one can only ask in disbelief, even hypothetically?

Neither Schuller nor our musical reformationist could explain the phenomenon of the so-called definitive performance, whether it be Toscanini's *Falstaff,* Callas and de Sabata's *Tosca,* Bruno Walter's Beethoven "Pastorale," or Martha Argerich's Prokofiev Third Concerto. The definitive performance epitomizes the recording as a textual function and is political and authoritative in that sense. It shows the public—the art-music-loving public, such as it is—"getting textual" with interpretation, and doing so in a way that most musicians refuse to do. The definitive recording is anathema to the more closed mind-sets of the academic, the connoisseur, and the working musician, three figures who are too busy teasing out and relishing music's many ambiguities to want to nail down a composition in such a way. "Getting textual" is usually not the public's wont outside of organized religion, since texts are really a private matter, an issue of reading and personal explanation. "Definitive" and "referential" are terms that music-lovers reserve for a vital recording, not necessarily the version they love and want to spend time with, but one that has proved influential, lasting, and worthy of respect. It is a version that has stood the test of time and promises to shape future tastes and judgments. Self-enclosed and in a sense tautological, it suggests centrality and endurance and seeks to establish the very interpretive criteria by which it is to be validated. Seemingly isolated from passing fashion, the definitive recording typifies the great interpreter's ability to imbue even the most improvisational music with a sense of decisiveness, and to convey a sense of musical understanding through performance. The definitive recording says what needs to be said about the music in question, even though the "what" only becomes clear after the performer in question has indeed said it. The definitive performance presumes a known work (there must be enough discourse behind the composition) and indeed entails a work that has a separate life and importance well beyond individual performance (for the definitive performance needs something larger than itself to be definitive of).

Here we come back to the question of performance-as-work. When Kivy describes Vladimir Horowitz's "Revolutionary" Étude as repeatable and enduring, he really characterizes it as definitive or paradigmatic. The paradigmatic rendition imposes a single and closed, what Mikhail Bakhtin might call centripetal, meaning on the composition: it presents an interpretation for immediate use. To grasp the meaning of these enduring artwork-performances, it would seem necessary also to understand their negative counterparts: those nonartwork-performances that do *not* endure. But Kivy is evasive when it comes to these, and to the questions of whether all performances are enduring artwork-performances, and if not, what that could mean for the others' qualities of endurance and aesthetic value. "Performances are events," Kivy avers. "Do they, or some of them, *endure?* They do not need to do so, on my view, to be 'art.' But some of them . . . are repeatable; they are types with tokens."[20] Glenn Gould's 1955 recording of Bach's Goldberg Variations is perhaps the preeminent example of a work-as-performance, or performance-as-work. With the arrival of this paradigmatic performance, the wider public saw a great musical work delivered from dormancy. This must be part of what Said meant when he said the release marked "a genuinely new stage in the history of virtuosity."[21]

It is worthy of fiction that such an international spectacle could emerge from an unknown musician essaying a then-obscure composition. But that relative obscurity served to enable this Bach-Gould paradigmatic text, and it is hard to imagine such an influential performance as the "Gouldbergs"—as the pianist himself jokingly dubbed the record—originating in different circumstances. Music and performer became indissolubly linked, perpetrator and perpetrated suddenly snapping into public view together, more like a political assassination than a musical performance. Intermittent repertoire for four internationally known pianists at most, the Goldberg Variations were unfamiliar enough in 1955 that they were still a malleable piece for the public. Then as now, they were also an unusually "open" work with regard to the manifold issues of repeats and tempos; indeed, there can be no other major work that entails performances ranging anywhere between 38 minutes (the time of Gould's 1955 version) and 104 (the duration of Rosalyn Tureck's 1957 recording).

Gould's 1955 *Goldberg Variations* demonstrate, in short, how textual fluidity of a composition allows fixity in its performance. This textual mutability opened Bach's work to Gouldian annexation, while the late Beethoven sonatas could not be thus opened. The pianist's very next recording, of Beethoven's opp. 109–111, enjoyed nothing like the sales and popularity of his *Goldberg Variations.* In fact, the recording of the sonatas was panned by the critics, fell out of print quickly, and wasn't reissued for almost forty years.[22] Gould's late Beethoven sonatas were a failure largely because Schnabel's centrist, centripetal performance-text had rendered superfluous, before the fact, Gould's attempt at a centrifugal performance of the same music. The paradigmatic performance-text either requires a blank slate or creates one, for it cannot tolerate the kind of split aural consciousness by which a listener hears the new continuously against the old. As Eric Clarke writes of conventional performance practice in art music, "Hearing expression, emotion, style and ideology in performance requires the listener to identify properties of the performance which stand out against an implicit background of neutrality—a kind of theoretical 'norm' in relation to which expression, emotion, style and ideology are marked."[23] In this sense, the paradigmatic text, and certainly the best-selling record of music from any era, are not to be related to traditional notions of art music performance, but to ontologies of popular song. In popular music, specifically, the cover version is synonymous with the paradigmatic performance to the extent that both have a parasitic relationship with an earlier text yet aim to obviate any such connection. The cover version must by definition effect a new and equally (if not more) viable rendering of an existing song, in essence a replacement of it, or it becomes a simple copy of the original. Cook's shrewd words about pop practice apply just as well to Gould's performances of Bach as to Led Zeppelin's covers of Willie Dixon: "The distinction between authorship and reproduction," Cook observes, "is a very slippery one."[24]

EMPOWERING THE READER/LISTENER

Conceptions of the text are still rooted in pre-Reformation biblical history in the sense that they are predicated on authority and centrality. The structuralist text represents a declaration of power, its consolidation of authority eliminating individual readerly freedoms. What does this mean for a specific body of music, exactly? Charles Rosen finds an example of such entrenchment with the Beethoven piano sonatas, induced by recordings. According to Rosen, recordings have all but eliminated the role the sonatas once played in amateur and domestic music-making. Recording introduced these sonatas to a wider public, which might suggest a fragmentation of textual authority. Rosen notes, however, that records did not create a grassroots movement of individual Beethoven performers but helped bring about a centralization and professionalization of these pieces. "Only when recordings finally dislodged the tradition of playing music at home,"

Rosen remarks, "did the Beethoven sonatas lose their special status in which the interests of the amateur and the professional were united."[25] In this instance, to upend a statement from Barthes, we could say entrenchment of the author necessitated the death of the reader. Rosen's conclusion holds true when we consider the number of individual Beethoven musician-interpreters, an eager population that—confronted by master interpreters on vinyl and CD—succumbed in a kind of intensifying Darwinist struggle. A person patiently wandering Leipzig in 1901 might have been able to catch thirty home-grown versions of the "Moonlight" Sonata filtering down into the street, not all of them of equal musical "competence" but all more or less peacefully coexisting. A century later, however, the number would probably be closer to five—not played at the piano, but mechanically reproduced from a specialist elite including the likes of Alfred Brendel, Maurizio Pollini, Evgeny Kissin, Vladimir Horowitz, and Artur Schnabel.

Rosen's is only one perspective on the role of the recording in textual authority, and it is probably a minority view. Others of a poststructuralist bent, citing numbers of nonperforming listener-readers, believe recordings of absolute music have helped loosen up conceptions of the text. Barthes described such dissolution of textual authority thus:

> Classic criticism has never paid any attention to the reader; for it, the writer is the only person in literature. We are now beginning to let ourselves be fooled no longer by the arrogant antiphrastical recriminations of good society in favor of the very thing it sets aside, ignores, smothers, or destroys; we know that to give writing its future, it is necessary to overthrow the myth: the birth of the reader must be at the cost of the death of the Author.[26]

Music, of course, has listeners (of recordings) as well as readers (of printed notation). These two demographics correspond in some ways, and in other ways do not: music is different from literature, though perhaps not from plays, in that the readership for its printed form—the score—has always been smaller than the listenership for its public performance. (Of course, questions arise regarding musical literacy and what form such literacy takes, questions that I address in chapter 5 and elsewhere.) To state this another way: art music requires translation, but translation of a written source that is largely unknown and irrelevant to the listener except to the degree that it is conveyed through performance.

Gould was passionately Barthesian in his views, largely because of his deep allegiance to the individual listener and his disregard for the printed text as a function of authorial intention and design. He anticipated something like Barthes's "birth of the reader" and saw it transpiring through recording. A recording could, in his view, provide the most readerly musical experience by giving the listener various takes, edits, and versions of the composition, allowing her to assemble her own optimal performance and thereby participate in the musical recreation. In this "*Hausmusik* activity of the future," as Gould described it, home editing would become "the prerogative of every reasonably conscientious consumer of recorded music."[27] You love the recording when it gets to the development section but don't like the performer's way with the coda? Simple substitutions will solve the problem and give the listener a new experience of creative participation going beyond conventional notions of musicality.

T. W. Adorno, Walter Benjamin, and Siegfried Kracauer described a culture of distraction—a disengagement of sensibility toward the work of art—as a condition immanent in the age of mechanical reproduction. Gould described such a condition in different terms. In one of his defenses of Richard Strauss as post-Romantic, Gould prophesied a devaluation of musical-compositional innovation, after recordings collapse the chronological sense that had supported notions of originality. Recordings disengage ideas of novelty, in short, by neutralizing historical philosophies:

> And there is little doubt that the inherent qualities of illusion in the art of recording—those features that make it a representation not so much of the known exterior world as of the idealized interior world—will eventually undermine that whole area of prejudice that has concerned itself with finding chronological justifications for artistic endeavors and which in the post-Renaissance world has so determinedly argued the case of a chronological originality that it has quite lost touch with the larger purposes of creativity.[28]

Gould foresaw audio technology turning music-lovers into "individuals capable of an unprecedented spontaneity of judgment," and to the degree that his Barthesian vision placed the listener at the level of composer and performer, or even above, it did indeed entail the archetypal author's death.[29] This kind of thinking could qualify Gould as a populist, an artist who enjoyed sales and wide popularity outside the usual markets for art music. But Edward Said came closer to the crux of the matter—namely, the delightful paradox of this pianist's insensible individuality—when he described Gould as every inch a humanist, a practitioner of "a critical model for a type of art that is rational and pleasurable at the same time," and also an artist who developed "an alternative argument to the prevailing conventions that so deaden and dehumanize and derationalize the human spirit."[30]

SUBSTANTIVES VS. ACCIDENTALS

A textual-critical stance, holding sway in English-language literary scholarship at least through the 1970s, emphasized authorial meaning over details of production. Writing in 1950, the influential Shakespeare scholar
W. W. Greg described this duality as

> a distinction between the significant, or as I shall call them 'substan-
> tive', readings of the text, those namely that affect the author's mean-
> ing or the essence of his expression, and others, such in general as
> spelling, punctuation, word-division, and the like, affecting mainly its
> formal presentation, which may be regarded as the accidents, or as I
> shall call them 'accidentals', of the text.[31]

If we wish to explain musicology's relative disinterest in performance, we
need look no further than the wide influence of such attitudes in textual criticism. In its basic division between substantive and accidental, Greg's duality
upholds the idea of information and information transmission in a way that
other potentially useful dualities—for instance Leonard Meyer's differentiation between "primary" musical characteristics like pitch and rhythm and
"secondary" aspects like timbre and dynamics—do not.[32]

Writing in 1977, bibliographer D. F. McKenzie lamented his colleagues'
disinterest in any material history of the book. He deplored Greg's
substantive-accidental duality and censured the "defeatist pragmatism" of
Hans Zeller and Morse Peckham, a scholar who insisted authorial intention is ultimately unknowable. "The book itself is an expressive means,"
McKenzie protested. "To the eye its pages offer an aggregation of meanings both verbal and typographic for translation to the ear." He accused
the inductivists of reading texts as nothing more than words and criticized
their self-limitation to trusted hermeneutic circles of meaning:

> Their sense of difficulty derives partly, I believe, from our commitment
> to inductive method and its use in the natural sciences. It is a method
> that tempts us to assume that the only evidence that counts is physical,
> not behavioural. Thus we are led to place undue emphasis on the sym-
> bolic images of manuscript or printed word-forms rather than on the
> interpretative act of responding to them.[33]

Shakespeare—the greatest writer in the English language and the classic
mainstay of twentieth-century English-language textual criticism—
unwittingly helped further such notions. By apparently taking a haphaz-
ard attitude in bringing his own stage works to print, the Bard encouraged
the attitude that words float free of the pages, ink, and bindings that carry

them to the reader—though even in the best of circumstances stage drama of the time had a tenuous relationship with the London book trade.

Across the first half of the twentieth century, such literary-critical disinterest in "presentation" and "the interpretative act" found a direct parallel in formalist composers' belittling of musical interpretation and its own "accidentals." A self-avowed *homo faber*, Stravinsky fetishized paper and pencil and invented a rastration gadget for drawing staff lines. Not coincidentally, he also cultivated dual aversions to musical interpretation and nebulous Romantic aesthetics, which he called a "ponderous heritage" that served as the basis for all bad musical breeding. In his *Poetics of Music*, Stravinsky proposed that "the musically extraneous elements that are strewn throughout [the Romantics'] works invite betrayal, whereas a page in which music seeks to express nothing outside of itself better resists attempts at literary deformation."[34]

These musical ontologies have followed in the footsteps of literary ontologies, and I attribute the formalist composers' denigration of "interpretation" to the same basic prejudice that caused the midcentury literary-critical disinterest in material "presentation." I am speaking of a stance that, under the influence of Saussurean linguistics, spread from literary studies to music hermeneutics. It's worth quoting at some length from McKenzie's 1985 protest against what he calls the synchronic bias in textual criticism:

> Saussure's insistence upon the primacy of speech has created a further problem for book-based bibliography by confining critical attention to verbal structures as an alphabetic transcription of what are conceived only as words to be spoken. Other formalized languages, or, more properly perhaps, dialects of written language—graphic, algebraic, hieroglyphic, and, most significantly for our purposes, typographic—have suffered an exclusion from critical debate about the interpretation of texts because they are not speech-related. They are instrumental of course to writing and printing, but given the close interdependence of linguistics, structuralism, and hermeneutics, and the intellectual dominance of those disciplines in recent years, it is not surprising perhaps that the history of non-verbal sign systems, including even punctuation, is still in its infancy, or that the history of typographic conventions as mediators of meaning has yet to be written.[35]

Acoustic space and ambience, equivalents to margins and white portions of the printed page, are typically considered "accidentals" to the recorded performance, if not irrelevant to it. Yet they become entirely different elements in a recording than they are in live performance. The liveness of an acoustic will affect tempos, of course, but beyond that the interaction of musical interpretation and acoustic—whether recorded or heard in concert—becomes more mysterious, personal, and perhaps arbitrary. While it is usually not very difficult to separate the sound production from the acoustic in the concert hall—depending of course on the hall and where one sits in it—it becomes much more difficult to do when making a recording or listening to one. Ambience and acoustic space become intrinsic to the sounding conception, indeed at times inseparable from it. Two significant factors that make a recording very different from a concert experience are directionality and what people in the stereo industry call imaging: with the help of the eyes, the ears are freer in concert to isolate and separate sound sources across 360 degrees than when they are confronted with a pair of speakers.

Technology has had a reductive and restrictive effect on books, serving to contrast that cultural form with calligraphic traditions—and specifically, as McKenzie notes concerning page layout, to "dull our sensitivity to space as an instrument of order."[36] While typography and white space were conscious aspects of *mise-en-page* in medieval scriptoria, most English-language books of the twentieth century are reductive in ways that make the fewest literacy demands. They hone texts down to stringently two-dimensional experiences of pure information, allowing the eye to move in only one direction, left to right. In contrast to the *mise-en-page* of medieval illuminated manuscripts, modern books also rarely cultivate any organic interrelation between text, white space, and—to mention another "accidental" aspect of textual history—illustrations. Image and information tend to be segregated, even in children's books, and the text is usually pure black against more-or-less pure white. Some of this segregation, endemic since Gutenberg, must be attributed to the limitations of printing and the habits brought about by those limitations. But technology has generally had the opposite effect in musical reproduction than it has with the printed word. To compensate for the quixotic properties of recording horns, engineers of acoustic (preelectric) recordings found it necessary to substitute instruments and rearrange musicians, placing the instruments without carrying power, like the strings, up front and relegating the brass to the back. Unable to capture and recreate any real sense of acoustic space or place, these old records are like books without margins, coherent layout, or typographical sense. But acoustic space became a significant aspect of recorded performance with the technological advances of electrical recording in the mid-1920s, digital playback in the early 1980s, and higher sampling techniques around the turn of the millennium.

One cannot say this of RCA's Toscanini issues, even those done at about the same time the company was making excellent early stereo tapes in Chicago and Boston. The Toscanini recordings still puzzle listeners with their dryness. We know this conductor emphasized textural clarity above all else, and after the introduction of tape insisted that instrumental lines—on occasion, even individual notes—be dubbed in if the orchestral textures weren't as clear as they were in his inner ear. Abetting that impression was NBC's infamously claustrophobic Studio 8H, originally designed for spoken radio productions. Toscanini's RCA records didn't present music resounding in a particular space so much as—to use Decca producer John Culshaw's description of other productions of the time—a "transcription of the notes" into acoustic terms.[37] The description Walter Toscanini gave of his father's recording philosophy recalls Greg's substantive-accidental dichotomy, perhaps no surprise considering the conductor and the textual critic belonged to the same generation. Walter Toscanini claimed that his father "liked the unresounding acoustics of Studio 8H in which the purity of orchestral tone was not marred by hall reverberations and echoes."[38]

But all this talk of aural aesthetics ignores the fact that Toscanini was a practical man working in an especially impractical profession. He owed his single-minded emphasis of the substantive over the accidental to his early life in the trenches—namely, his work in the 1890s with provincial Italian ensembles, where getting people to play clearly and together must have taken priority over sonic beauty. Studio 8H certainly exposed the kind of ensemble shortcomings that Toscanini had confronted in his home country: critic Olin Downes described how 8H gave the impression that "you listened to each instrument under a microscope" and that it thereby demanded the orchestra "be a particularly good one, exceptionally accurate."[39] The advent of the recorded acoustic *mise-en-scène* was thus a generational matter, a sensibility that followed standardization of instrument construction and playing styles, and the modern notion that mechanical reproduction could turn out art as well as documentation. Whatever its origin, Toscanini's basic disinterest in "sound for sound's sake" was aided and abetted by Studio 8H, according to Mortimer H. Frank. In this respect, we could contrast Toscanini with his slightly younger colleagues Leopold Stokowski and Sergey Koussevitzky, both of whom reorchestrated some scores for sonic effect. "Toscanini might alter a bowing to modify timbre or redistribute voices to enhance clarity," Frank points out, "but such changes were founded on a structural or expressive point that transcended sound for its own sake."[40]

RECORDING AS FACTUAL OR EXPRESSIVE MEANS?

Such Platonistic divisions between musical sound and musical acoustics soon disappeared, especially with the arrival of stereo techniques and virtuoso conductors who were not only record-savvy, but also good businessmen who understood the commercial potential of recording. Musicians take the performance acoustic into account both in concert and during recording, of course. But a few luminaries, Herbert von Karajan and Leopold Stokowski among them—men who stood in front of great orchestras while only in their twenties—consciously manipulated the sense of ambience in recording for musical as well as acoustic effect. For them, ambience became a substantive; or, to borrow McKenzie's statement on "the non-verbal elements of . . . typographic notations," Karajan and Stokowski used ambience as "an expressive function in conveying meaning."[41] Stokowski urged free bowing upon his orchestras, asking string players not to bow together as had been widely done in orchestral playing since Jean-Baptiste Lully, but to stagger their up-bows and down-bows inconsistently within sections, in accordance with their own individual instruments, bow grips, and musculatures. The resulting string tone, seamless and weighty, was Stokowski's attempt to build a kind of deep acoustic resonance into the orchestral sound itself, regardless of the actual space where the music-making took place. This distinctive, indeed ingenious, brand of sonic illusionism also had the practical benefit of making the smaller pickup ensembles that Stokowski took into the studio in the 1930s and 1940s sound considerably larger on record than they actually were.

Free bowing—and free breathing, its equivalent in wind sections—is but one example of Stokowski blurring Platonistic distinctions between "artificial" sound production techniques and ambience as a "natural" aspect. It shows him instituting a kind of preelectronic sound-enhancement technology, and therefore differs in quantitative rather than qualitative terms from the imaginative and unorthodox recording methods that he also developed. It would be hard to imagine a more non-Toscaninian approach to recording than Stokowski's: he "played" sound technologies as if they were musical instruments, from his presiding over the first American orchestral commercial radio broadcast in 1929 through his involvement with Bell Labs' stereo experiments in 1932, presiding over the sound mix at a three-channel Bell broadcast of the Philadelphia Orchestra in 1933, and his embrace of Decca's twenty-channel techniques on their "Phase Four" label in the 1960s.[42] Some of his more obviously interventionist RCA records of the 1940s and 1950s allow us to see what, if any, specifically "musical" goals such recording-studio techniques served. If each of the studio techniques could be substantiated in a specific aspect of the score, then Stokowski's uses of technology could be said to serve a composition-textual function. As my test cases, I choose his July 1950 recording of the Sibelius First Symphony and his September 1954 version of the Second Symphony, both recorded in New York, the first with "his orchestra" of hand-picked players, and the second with the NBC Symphony.[43]

Both these Sibelius recordings show, especially as clarified on CD, obvious multimiking and sound-level manipulations between the orchestral choirs. On both we hear the gain being raised and lowered, especially in tutti passages—creating an effect much like the swell pedal of an organ, another preelectronic sound-manipulation technology and one that Stokowski would have known from his earlier career as a church organist. These Sibelius recordings allow two generalizations about Stokowski's volume and balance maneuvers vis-à-vis the score: Stokowski enhances crescendos and decrescendos at strategic points in the compositional structures, and he points the listener's ear to particular textural details that would otherwise be lost—not always aspects that the composer himself chose to foreground in the score. The first of these practices now reminds one of old photo highlighting techniques: the gain knob flourished like India ink, an instrument for extracting half-buried truths that uncooperative reality had done its best to hide. Taken together, these techniques made Stokowski's records of the 1930s and 1940s electrifying at a time when it was common for orchestras and recording equipment to be set up without much thought, and then compensated for with frequent adjustments during actual recording—a process of "riding gain," as it was commonly called. While those other recordings tended to have a confusing sound, with no decisive sense of dynamic expression, Stokowski was able to spin out overwhelming crescendos that weren't even possible in the concert hall. The most obvious example on the two Sibelius records is the end of the Second Symphony, which begins quietly in G minor and unfolds gradually over a long scalewise vamp in the strings. With the gain turned far down eight measures before Fig.P, the orchestra is able to unleash an especially impressive crescendo as the volume is increased three pages later. More frequent and perhaps more interesting are those instances where Stokowski lifts the drama of transitional and developmental passages by exaggerating hairpin dynamics and making the confrontation of voices more acute within the texture.

Stokowski's reseatings of his orchestras, some of them boldly experimental, are another sign that he was happier creating new acoustic scenarios than conforming to existing ones. Recording gave him the liberty to do entirely as he wished in dividing the ensemble. An RCA photo of a 1955 session at Manhattan Center, New York, shows a common Stokowski setup: instrumental choirs separated by ten feet or more and each given its own microphones, the brass and strings at roughly a twenty-five-foot distance.[44] These distances and the sound baffles, preventing diffusion or bleed-over into the next section's microphone feed, are designed to isolate the audio tracks, allowing them to be easily manipulated at the mixing desk. This is really a pop recording setup, the kind of studio arrangement oriented to electric and electronic instruments fed directly into the mixing board, the acoustic elements like voices or drums, distinct enough that they can mixed alongside them. The arrangement shows just how Stokowski and producer Richard Mohr were able to adjust balances so quickly and easily on the Sibelius records and demonstrates how strict control—if not complete elimination—of ambient sound could allow the strictest control over the "accidentals" of a recorded musical text.

It is difficult to separate technology from musicianship in Stokowski's work and thinking: the two converge in service of beauty, expression, and convenience. In this way, his beliefs go far beyond the biblically oriented textual-critical attitudes discussed above. In Stokowski's sense of history and music-making, we can draw ever more meaning from the musical texts of the past, and the greater the music the more imperative it is to go beyond what the composer herself might have had in mind. As Stokowski wrote in 1943,

> Physicists, engineers, and musicians will combine to improve continually the recording of music. The first step is to make recorded music exactly like the original. The next is to surpass the original and, through future possibilities of recording, to achieve the dreams of musicians—of making music still more beautiful and eloquent—music they heard within themselves but which was unattainable in the past. . . . Everything will be possible in the realm of sound—and music will reach new heights of tonal quality, power, delicacy, beauty.[45]

Stokowski's sense of musical hermeneutics becomes twisted at times to his utopian vision, but in a way characteristic of technologically oriented musicians. In reference to recording Beethoven's "Pastorale," he suggests that studio-technological capabilities can help make the score truer to its own self: "Certain important features of the music only dimly heard or even inaudible in a concert hall can be brought out with the full eloquence and richness of tone which is their true nature." Problems of balance and scoring can be corrected in Beethoven's thunderstorm scherzo: "Because of the inherent lack of balance in the orchestration, I have never before heard these phrases [for bassoon, clarinet, and oboe] given their due prominence and tonal importance." But Stokowski's most interesting example of technology-based antifundamentalism concerns interpretive "impossibilities" in Musorgsky's *Night on the Bare Mountain* in the Rimsky-Korsakov edition. Here he laments that in concert performance the furious descending scale in the strings at Musorgsky's last big climax is never the decisive moment it "ideally" should be:

> These downward-rushing tones should sound like an avalanche—beginning loud and increasing in tonal volume the lower they go. In the concert hall this is impossible to achieve because the instruments have more strength of tone in their higher registers than in their lower, so that no matter how much the players try to increase the volume as the tones become deeper, exactly the opposite happens—the volume of the tone becomes less. In *Fantasia* we were for the first time able to achieve the ideal in this music—increasing the tone as the scale passage descended—because recording for motion pictures puts techniques at our disposal whereby the 'impossible' can sometimes be achieved. When these techniques are further developed the whole idea of 'impossible' will be forever set aside—because everything will be possible in the tonal sphere.[46]

Stokowski offers a marvelously contradictory Platonism where textual meanings ("these downward-rushing tones should sound like an avalanche") surface whenever and wherever technology allows them, or perhaps a form of radical Jamesian empiricism where no portion of lived experience is off-limits. The conductor's expressive palette widened here as a result of his conviction that nothing was "accidental," and everything "substantive," in the musical experience. Textual criticism here becomes a kind of game where meanings are incumbent upon the techniques used to ferret them out—a practice many critics would condemn as self-serving or at least tautological, and which pragmatically inclined minds would say simply embraces the hermeneutic circle for what it is. Stokowski needed recording technology to close his own hermeneutic circle in the Musorgsky, since—contrary to his assertion—both the composer's original score and Rimsky-Korsakov's edition indicate a *diminuendo* at this descending scale, not an "increase in tonal volume."[47] Whether this shows the conductor intentionally falsifying the score or simply misremembering it in pursuit of a personal *mise-en-scène* is ultimately irrelevant.

ACOUSTIC *MISE-EN-SCÈNE*

Karajan would just as likely claim ambience as a "substantive" part of the recorded performance in a way that it is not in concert. Like Stokowski, he had such firmly defined conceptions of musical sound that on records he bent any sense of acoustic space to the music making, and not vice versa. Starting in autumn 1973, he recorded with the Berlin Philharmonic in the Philharmonie, Hans Scharoun's hall in the round, which was a fairly radical design for its completion date of 1963. The increasingly dry sound of these Philharmonie records led many record critics to complain about the acoustic, when in fact some of the orchestra's tapings in this hall— usually with other conductors and record labels other than Deutsche Grammophon—enjoyed a wetter ambience. We can only conclude that Karajan made a conscious decision to control acoustic impressions for playback at home, as dictated by the music being played. Occasionally—in exceptions that proved the rule—Karajan made a record in the Philharmonie that ended up sounding just as "wet" as if it had been made in their earlier recording location, the reverberant Jesus-Christus-Kirche in the Berlin sub-urb of Dahlem. One such is the Philharmonie recording of the *Fountains of Rome* and *Pines of Rome*, where Respighi's luxurious and coloristic— perhaps "accidental-ridden"?—orchestration must have encouraged a pull-back of the microphones.

Karajan devoted part of his essay "Technische Musikwiedergabe"— written in 1974, shortly after he and the Berliners changed recording location—to a rather enigmatic concept that he called *Raumgefühl. Raumge-fühl* might be translated as "sense of space," "feeling of space," or "feeling *for a* space." In invoking a form of *Gefühl*, Karajan stressed sensibility over science, one's personal response to the sound of a space. He thereby used it in specific contradistinction to the more mainstream and institutional word "acoustic." So a *Raumgefühl* is—unlike an acoustic—subjective and immeasurable; a comparable linguistic term, *Sprachgefühl*, refers to the native speaker's internalized knowledge of what is right in an expression and what is not. One might expect an internationally known conductor to limit himself to concert halls when discussing sonics, but Karajan discusses a startling array of sound spaces in his essay. At one point he lists four un-usual electro-acoustic situations and describes their distinct *Raumgefühle* in affective terms: a voice heard in a resonant catacomb seems "strange and ghostly"; the same voice in a clothes closet will sound "like someone suffocating"; heard over a walkie-talkie with the high frequencies re-moved, it will become "incomprehensible noise"; hearing someone over a high-quality stereophonic telephone, "we experience the voice *and the actual person* with a warmth and nearness that seem almost physical."[48] Karajan's *Raumgefühl* is not ambience, which would be *Umwelt* or *Umgebung*. The conception might relate to *Akustik* but is not synonymous with it nor with the interior of any particular building: he mentions acoustics in the essay but declares it only one among many important factors and suggests he is less interested in such institutional and rationalized ideas than he is in an individual, subjective response to sound. The essential and fundamental acoustic, in short, is the one formed within the individual listener's ear and brain:

> The *Raumgefühl* that a hall lends to the music is very important. This depends greatly on the reverberation time. But many other factors contribute to the wonderful impression that the music supports itself [daß die Musik sich selbst trägt], that the space is boundless, and that for instance a wind solo seems not two meters distant but, embedded in a warm string sonority, as if coming from infinity.[49]

Three recordings will serve as examples of Karajan's subjective *Raumgefühl* taking priority over customary seating practices, Platonic notions of acoustics, or obeisance to "the listener's ear." In all three instances, the recording itself acts—to use a phrase from McKenzie—as a "determinant of meaning" equal to, or sometimes exceeding, the authority of the composer's score. The first example is Karajan's 1953 taping of Tchaikovsky's Fourth Symphony with the Philharmonia Orchestra in Kingsway Hall, London. Karajan dragged out these EMI sessions because he was unhappy with the way the opening motto on *forte* horns was sounding on the tape. He experimented moving the horns to various positions in the hall, to such an extent that the players decided to play a joke on him at one point and hid themselves up in the farthest gallery. The conductor was finally satisfied with leaving the players in their customary place but seated the wrong way round, with their backs to the conductor and the bells of their instruments aimed at the microphones.[50] The second recording is Karajan's 1981 version of Saint-Saëns's Symphony No. 3, where he, like a number of conductors before him, had a large cathedral organ dubbed over the orchestra in postproduction. This overdubbing practice has helped inflate the sonic vocabulary of the "Organ" Symphony in the public mind—inflated it above and beyond the score, which says nothing about the organ beyond thirty-two-foot pedal and *voix celeste* stops. Perhaps it is a symptom of this postrecording inflammation that everyone ignores the simple *forte* marking at the big C major and G chords that open Saint-Saëns's last Maestoso, and instead plays them at a towering *fortissimo*. Musicians playing the work in concert must now look wistfully at the composer's *forte* marking and remark to themselves how overplaying the chords on record has made anything quieter seem anticlimactic.[51]

The third example is Karajan's version of the Schoenberg Variations, op. 31, where the conductor reseated the orchestra from one variation to the next in the interests of realizing the composer's shifting orchestral balances or, as Karajan himself put it, "to create the acoustic that one sees and imagines when one looks at the score."[52] When he set about recording this score, he created his own text (or, perhaps more accurately, his own subtext to the printed score) and did it in acoustic terms. Adapting a term from film studies, one could speak of Karajan developing a specific acoustic *mise-en-scène* for Schoenberg's op. 31. Schoenberg scored the introduction, theme, nine variations, and finale of his op. 31 for a set of different ensembles, often breaking his large orchestra down into small chamber groups of one player per part. Variation 2 is for solo violin and solo cello against a set of between four and nine solo winds. The Variation 4 waltz begins with three solo strings and two solo winds accompanied by harp, celesta, mandolin, and tambourine. Variation 5 centers on full-section first and second violins doubling a line in octaves, beginning *fortissimo,* in full Romantic orchestral style. Karajan strongly believed in a chamber-music approach to orchestral performance and often required his players—and, in full orchestral situations, section leaders—to get their cues from each other rather than from him. In preparing operas, he was known to insist that the singers sit in on orchestral rehearsals—actually within the ensemble, and not in the auditorium or on stage. With a constantly changing orchestra like Schoenberg's, and the leading voices moving around within individual variations, such a listening-based approach would be difficult to institute, without the ensemble being rearranged variation by variation, which is what Karajan ended up doing for the microphones in 1974.

Karajan said he reseated the orchestra in direct response to Schoenberg's score, but his acoustic text for op. 31, and his reformulation of the Saint-Saëns symphony as well, go rather further than that. To borrow McKenzie's statement on page layout and typography, they show the conductor using "space as an instrument of order" and doing so in a way that reflects his own thinking at least as much as it does the composer's. One might think I am confusing the typographer's definition of space as a schematic margin, a background to cognition, with the musician's notion of space as a fundamental sonic arena, an acoustic palette for mixing musical timbres. Space on the printed page is blank, after all, while the musician's space is never empty. But I believe that these two ideas of space represent much the same thing, and propose that—in line with McKenzie's rebuttal of Greg—we are as wrong to suppose that the musician exercises as much control of space in recording as the author does in publishing. Karajan is of course the exception that proves the rule here. Note that he explains his retextualization of Schoenberg according to acoustics rather than musical substantives. He doesn't describe the differences between variations directly in ensemble terms, but according to the kinds of acoustics such ensembles would entail.

The particular subtext that Karajan establishes for Schoenberg's op. 31 is, in short, architectural—with each variation articulated according to its own distinct *Raumgefühl*, this one presuming a cavernous auditorium space, another a small room. One benefit is that this trades difficult, contentious taxonomies like "symphonic," "chamber," "orchestral," and "soloistic" for a less problematic series of aural acoustics, strung together in a personal vision that is, at most, accessory to the composer's conception. But this does some justice to Schoenberg, who aimed to continue Bach's example by transcending such compositional divisions. When we move from the *Raumgefühl* of Variation 5 (written for thirty-three players plus the strings) to that starting Variation 6 (an ensemble of nine soloists), the second cellist has to hear and perhaps see precisely what the first clarinet and other winds are doing, even though they don't usually sit near each other in the orchestra—and so Karajan followed a full concert hall acoustic with a large-ish salon.

I have no doubt that a listener could, if she worked at it, learn to hear Karajan's recording of op. 31 as a specific series of implied *Raumgefühle* rather than—or simultaneously with—a particular performance of a musical composition. I return here to my point that the recording by its nature overlays many texts, authored not only by the composer, but also by the performer, the recording engineer, the remastering producer, and so on. While none of these various texts usually crowds out any other, not all of them can be counted equally interesting or equally listenable. It must be possible to hear Martha Argerich's recording of the Chopin B-flat Minor Sonata in terms of the microphones used—something along the lines of "Did you hear how those Schoeps omnidirectionals give a pleasantly crisp-and-crunchy physicality to the finale's opaque textures?"—but one imagines even the most bookish engineer might tire of "reading" such a text.

ACOUSTIC CHOREOGRAPHY

The master of the recording as "determinant of meaning" was of course Glenn Gould. Like Karajan, Gould made drier and drier-sounding recordings as the years went by. Some were so determinedly arid and close that they seem to propagandize against sonic causes. Given his general need for control and his dislike for surprise, which even led him to script his own interviews, one might think Gould resisted ambience as an encroachment on his own domain as musical organizationist.[53] He wrote little about acoustics per se, though in his 1966 essay "The Prospects of Recording" he did invoke a "cathedral of the symphony" and hypothesized a link between quasi-religious conceptions of absolute music and classical music-lovers' interest in "acoustic splendor." But that was past practice, in Gould's view, a practice we have largely left behind "as our dependence upon [music] has increased." That increasing dependence has made it necessary for us not only to secularize music but also to domesticate it: "The more intimate terms of our experience with recordings have since suggested to us an acoustic with a direct and impartial presence, one with which we can live in our homes on rather casual terms." In a letter he wrote five years after those comments, Gould displays a more obviously substantivist philosophy as he refers to

> the relatively close-up, highly analytical sound which has been the hallmark of our recording at CBS and which reflects, not only my own predilection in regard to piano pick-up but, more significantly, a continuing persuasion as to the validity of the recording experience as a manifestation divorced from concert practice.[54]

Gould shows a Toscaninian anxiety over ambience as an uncontrolled variable, an aspect of the sounded musical performance that cannot be scored, perfectly predicted, or repaired in postproduction. Further details of Gould's acoustic apprehensions emerge in a short diatribe against Manhattan Center that he slipped into his 1978 essay "Stokowski in Six Scenes." Manhattan Center became a favorite recording locale for CBS Records in the 1950s and 1960s, Leonard Bernstein making most of his New York Philharmonic recordings there before Philharmonic Hall opened in 1962, and Stokowski and RCA using it in the 1950s. But Gould scarcely hid his sarcasm when he attributed "only one natural blessing" to the place, "a generous decay which adds ambient interest to music that is neither contrapuntally complex nor intellectually challenging." Strictly differentiating between music as conceived and music as sounded, Gould here declares himself a formalist and Platonist. He sees acoustics as accidentals: acoustic luxury, an accessory to music as a craft of substantives, might help compensate for compositional poverty. Other apologia for such an ample space, and the demands it placed on musicians, he dismissed as so much Romanticist mumbo jumbo: "One's natural tendency while playing there,

I felt, was to surrender to the Center's 'wet' sound and settle for a diffused and generalized approximation of ensemble—sometimes referred to in jacket notes as 'sweep and grandeur.' I had, in fact, vowed never to work there again."[55]

Gould's distaste for "sweep and grandeur" seems part and parcel of his disinterest in the "accidentals" of musical sound, as does his humming and singing while playing, making light of the quirks of his pianos, listening to and approving his final edited tapes over the telephone, showing apathy toward period performance practice, and, not least, emphasizing motivics over timbre and instrumentation in his own compositions. But in the 1970s Gould made quite a reversal when he turned acoustics to interpretive use in several studio projects, the only one released in his lifetime being the 1977 record of Sibelius's op. 67 Sonatinas and *Kyllikki*, op. 41. Several ranks of microphones, ranging from close-up to pointed toward the back wall of the hall, were cued in and out to reflect textural and harmonic changes in the scores. The published record was so avant-garde in this shifting aural perspective that producer Andrew Kazdin wrote a kind of *caveat auditor* on the sleeve, describing a technique of "acoustic choreography." In his jacket note, presumably written with Gould's consent and perhaps his encouragement, Kazdin justified this practice by appealing to acoustic authenticity: "The acoustic ambiance must be 'right' for the music," he writes. "Debussy seems to require a more reverberant surrounding than Bach. Rachmaninov should be bathed in more 'grandeur' than Scarlatti." Kazdin then introduces the "acoustic choreography" notion, saying it contravenes any assumption of aural-aesthetic unity for each musical composition—an idea that I would claim derives from nineteenth-century *werktreu* cultures. "No cognizance ever seems to have been paid to the variations of mood and texture which exist within an individual composition," writes Kazdin. "Why should the staccato articulation of an opening theme be wedded to the larger sense of space required by the lyrical second subject? Long intrigued by this subject, Glenn Gould offers here a bold and fascinating statement on the appropriateness of space to music."[56]

Such a division between music as conceived and music as sounded might seem to clash with Gould's embrace of recording—an embrace so passionate and progressive that he predicted concerts would disappear by the early twenty-first century. But any such contradictions seem lesser if one goes along with a basic assertion of the present book: that absolute music and its attendant cultures have in important respects been embodied—even encouraged—by recording. In the strange-bedfellow aspect of Gould's selective aesthetics, we find one key to this perpetuation.

Cued by what he saw in these Sibelius scores, then, Gould included ambience as part of his expressive means, a performance aspect alongside dynamics and phrasing. He rethought the recorded text as thoroughly as Karajan did several years earlier with his reseating of Schoenberg's op. 31. Stokowski did much the same with his creative use of multimiking and the mixing desk, techniques he had prophesied with typical zeal already in the early 1940s.[57] Karajan might well have spoken for all three musician-visionaries when he rejected shibboleths of "naturalness" and defended recordings from accusations of manipulation: "Manipulated? This is truly one of the most misused and misunderstood words of our time." He describes music making as a process of constant manipulation, from the composer's transcription of her thoughts to paper to the conductor's internalization of the piece, and the composer's and the musicians' interactions with the hall. "What in life is not manipulated?" Karajan asks. Indeed, he finds too much emphasis placed on imaginary and arbitrary conceptions of the listener's ear. "According to the ear of *which* listener?" he queries. "Even in a hall with a truly good acoustic, there are no two places with the same conditions." In a good hall with two or three thousand seats, Karajan continues, only about three or four hundred listeners will be able to enjoy the optimal acoustic—the quality of sound drops perceptibly beyond that number.[58]

Here Karajan touches on the central legacy of music's basis in scriptural ideals: the assumption that everyone "reads," or, better said, *hears*, the musical work in the same way. Recordings have grown out of and encouraged that idea, implicitly allowing new forms of auteurist control over musical "accidentals" and giving all listeners the same perspective—whether oriented to an idealized best seat in the hall or modeled on one specific musician's inner ear. Recordings, in other words, have been patterned more on an oral gospel model of transmission—the "Amen, I say unto you," Sermon on the Mount aspect—than on individualized modes of silent reading; they model themselves on the Mosaic Law before it was written down. But the three musicians discussed here were eager to get away from such centralized notions, and to develop new and individualized—written rather than oral, and post-Reformation rather than pre-Reformation—forms of literacy.

But a readerly and individuated document isn't necessarily made in an inclusive, open, and receptive atmosphere. What were the social rather than technological aspects of Stokowski's, Gould's, and Karajan's studio work? They were certainly more autocratic processes than when popular musicians entered the studio. In the 1960–1990 golden age of recording, many internationally known conductors tended to treat recording staff like musical subordinates and weren't very open to discussing studio practices. It's difficult to imagine even the most temperamental heavy metal guitar hero, not to mention a skilled studio auteur like Brian Wilson, doing what Fritz Reiner did at one of his first RCA sessions in Chicago, which was to announce to producer and engineer that he would hear correct balances on the first try or pack up and go home. According to his biographer Philip Hart, Reiner was "naïve about the recording process, unaware of the editing and technical capabilities of audio tape. . . . From playbacks in recording sessions or from edited masters, he listened for the musical result, unconcerned with how it was attained." But this didn't prevent him from being the dominant figure at his sessions: "Reiner applied to his recordings even more exacting standards than he set for his concert performances. . . . If balance or ensemble did not satisfy him, he consulted with Mohr on how to achieve what he wanted, preferably from the podium and only as a last resort at the control panel." It was not only conductors who tended to take such authoritarian approaches but, more generally, many classical musicians born before the 1930s. At one session, Emil Gilels proved just as imperious as Reiner—but even more naïve—when he absolutely insisted on a certain microphone he had heard about. The engineers obliged but then neglected to tell their pianist that the mike in question, though prominently stationed, never got turned on.[59]

In classical music-making, perhaps more than in popular musicianship with the exception of vocalists, sound per se is both highly personal and fiercely attended-to. When those musicians are conductors given music-director authority over large and heavily endowed ensembles, not to mention civic roles of some influence, the quest for individuality—and indeed singularity—of sound was pursued even more aggressively. I presume, on the basis of his interventionism and lifelong interest in sound technologies, that Stokowski was largely responsible for decision making in the studio. Richard Mohr was RCA producer for his records at this time, though Stokowski left the impression that their work was less cooperative than agreed-upon, and generally calculated and Machiavellian in a way that didn't always hinge upon the score.[60] Both Stokowski and Karajan had highly personal conceptions of orchestral sound that were based on a certain sense of *le son c'est moi*. Claudio Abbado offered an astute analysis of the Austrian conductor in 1988: "Herbert von Karajan has created an orchestral sound that is closely linked with his own personality, and unique in our century."[61] Considering the fact that "the Karajan sound" was as much a product of studio procedure as concert practice, Abbado was describing the visionary idealism of a studio auteur. The two memoirs of Michel Glotz, whom Karajan conscripted as his long-term producer for both Deutsche Grammophon and EMI, are unhelpfully quiet on the subjects of recording per se and Glotz's specific relationship with Karajan in the studio, beyond his job of insisting on retakes, which his boss resisted. Perhaps Erich Leinsdorf best accounted for Glotz by describing him as a functionary of Karajan's own sonic project, "an individual who was not furnished by any record company, who never became a producer for anyone else, and whose ear was evidently in tune with Karajan's own."[62]

Textual philosophies have changed dramatically over the decades since these three musicians passed from the scene. Developing audio technologies made acoustic space available to Stokowski, Karajan, and Gould as a substantive, a creative, tool. The recorded text, as it developed in the 1950s and 1960s, was able to liberate these individual musician-hermeneuticists from the authority of community-held tradition.[63] But the pendulum has now swung the other way, and more recent audio advances have—in tandem with new ideas of musical-cultural authenticity—taken audio space away again. A minimalist approach to recording first appeared in the early 1950s with Mercury engineer C. Robert Fine's single-microphone technique and led to an aural purist culture at about the same time popular music developed multitracking.[64] Several other classical labels, Telarc among them, took up this kind of purist approach and made it a house trademark. The audio-technological progressivism that once aided creativity has thus been pressed into serving transparency—and effectively underlined earlier brands of aural creativity in retrospect, isolating them, and making them sound mannered and perhaps even neurotic. At the same time, changed attitudes toward authorship and modernism have made written-ness and creative vision passé, to the point where Stokowski's, Karajan's, and Gould's freedoms with musical texts have somehow become conflated with their—what now sounds like—sonic arrogance. The risk is that their particular brand of textuality, as heard in our current time of objective and obsessive "atextuality," of authenticity and restoration, will sound only odd or defective.

The basic differences are again text-based and text-inspired. Earlier musicians like Artur Schnabel, Felix Weingartner, and Edwin Fischer approached Bach and Beethoven according to scriptural and exegetic traditions—the masters as godheads, their works as sacred writ, and the musician as mouthpiece for divine pronouncement. Gould, on the other hand, teased out a freer relationship—a musical equivalent to the popular 1966 Good News Bible, maybe—between the work and its representative texts. Those who raise their eyebrows when they hear Stokowski or Gould, or at least praise them as performers while denying them as interpreters, tend also to blame Barthes for the poststructuralist, Saussurean notion that "anything and everything can be a text." A textual argument hides under a dispute between authenticity and performance, and our three musicians—like Barthes himself—are implicitly linked with promiscuity and presumption.

2. Recording, Repetition, and Memory in Absolute Music

Edison's early cylinders wore out after only several plays, so aural history begins with one particular refinement of his invention: the electro-plated "phonogram" disk devised by Charles Sumner Tainter in 1881. Emil Berliner further developed this method for commercial markets, making multiple stampings from master discs onto a hard resin that could withstand repeat plays. By the late 1800s, then, people were able for the first time in history to hear the very same sequence of sounds not only once, but twice, four, seven, ten, a theoretically unlimited number of times. This marked an even more dramatic development in aural terms than photography did in the visual realm, since the visual world is more stable, less fleeting than the constantly, indeed restlessly departing landscape of sounds.[1] Photograph a singer or a church bell, and the visible object will remain more or less the same after the picture is snapped; record them, and you capture a fleeting moment within a state of continual flux.

Much has been written on the impact that the replayable record has had on popular music—transforming its textual aspect and, in the case of unpublished music transmitted orally, instituting a fixed text where none had existed.[2] But the replayable recording has had a deeper impact on the absolute-music construct, where works were once—before the proliferation of records—defined across time and through musical-aesthetic practice. Before the advent of recordings and the publicity agent's "world premiere performance," there was no conception of "this is, right here and right now, *the* real and singular Brahms Symphony No. 1." Indeed, the idea of a performance set down in permanent form conflicts directly with the absolute-music notion of an objective work that is "better than it can be performed" (to return to Artur Schnabel's thought-provoking phrase).[3] The carved-in-stone permanence of the one works to deny the elusiveness of the other, the diachronous performance threatening the synchronous nature of the masterwork. Walter Benjamin described modernity's destruction of the aura that once surrounded objects of deep cultural value; by this thinking, a Brahms symphony on CD or MP3 could be seen as eroding earlier concepts of performance and musical text. But we could also speak of today as a time where commodification creates cultural cachet, and say commodity prestige has far outdistanced any lingering cultural-musical value. In that sense, recording culture has mostly appropriated any ideas of auratic permanence and uniqueness for itself: the record has come to exist in a quid pro quo with the musical work, its carved-in-stone permanence salvaging the work in a time of ontological crisis.

We should step back for a moment and ask just what the listener listens to when she turns on the stereo, computer, or iPod to hear a symphony, sonata, or concerto—musical works that are still to some degree score-determined, but that by historical definition at least must remain open to multiple performances and interpretations. We can begin by saying that the repeatable aspect of recordings means that they function like substitute memories. But *how* do they relate—as instigations to remember, as memory stand-ins, as *aide-mémoire*, or perhaps all three? As regards aural recollection, recordings can represent several possibilities, which I list here in no particular order:

1. surrogate memories ("This is how Brahms's Third Symphony is to be remembered.")

2. experiences that are in and of themselves remembered ("Among the many ways of remembering Brahms's Third Symphony, here is Furtwängler's particular way.")

3. instigations to remember ("Oh yes, Brahms's Third Symphony . . . let's remember how it goes!")

4. specific preclusions to remembering ("Sorry, your memory of how Brahms's Third Symphony goes isn't right; let's remember that it proceeds like this.")

A given recording of Brahms's Third Symphony will fulfill several of these functions to varying degrees, depending on the listener (by sensibility "structural," "emotional," or "physical"?), her previous experience with this symphony (how "deep" and how recent?), and how the recorded performance finally affects her (disorienting? instructive? inspiring? supporting or challenging her memories of the work?). The listener likewise looks to a recording to satisfy different functions at different times, and might have different needs from one hour to the next. The function of the recording also naturally depends on the style, genre, and chronological context of the music that is being recorded and listened to: a Webern cantata will fulfill functions 1 and 3, a CD of Dvořák's "New World" Symphony functions 2 and 4, and a version of Berg's Violin Concerto possibly all four functions, provided the performance is distinctive enough in its own right to satisfy function 2. A recording of any piece that is new to the listener, whether written by Grieg or Gubaidulina, will likely be restricted to functions 1 and 2. But there are some first-hearing recordings that effect a quasi-imperialistic combination of 1 and 4, producing a first listen of a work that is immediately corrective as well as authorization.

In short, the recording serves not only to create new memories, but also to approximate, guide, or kick-start existing recollections. Any musical rendering, whether recorded or heard in concert, can perform such memory functions. But such functions become all the more intensely engaged when one listens to a recording—a form of supercharged recollection that facilitates and expedites our very act of remembrance, and goes further to extend the stylistic and chronological range of our immediate biological memories. Recordings, as one way of honing the listener's perception of interpretive individuality, allow immediate and interspersed comparison between performances: directly comparing Zino Francescatti with Arthur Grumiaux in Beethoven's "Kreutzer" Violin Sonata can help us understand just what makes Francescatti Francescatti and Grumiaux Grumiaux (and, as a corollary discovery, what separates Beethoven from more provincial composers like Louis Spohr and Joachim Raff). If there is a parallel for the memory function of a recording, it is music notation—a medium that can overlap with the recording in the way it serves to approximate, guide, or jar existing memories, or simply to create new ones. As the recording informs the listener in changeable symbiosis with her musical memory, so the notated page cues the performer: more or less ignored where recollection is strong, and engaged with full attention wherever the memory comes up short.

I have chosen three specific approaches to assist in sorting out these various functions of recordings as memory objects: in their different ways, Jacques Attali, Henri Bergson, and hermeneutics have addressed the difficult question of what impact infinite reproducibility has had on memory, habit, and subjectivity. To help understand recordings as commodified memories of specific time spans, I turn to Attali and his analysis of what he calls "the repetitive economy" of mechanical reproduction and its tendency toward stockpiling. Bergson assists with comprehending the complex dynamic between past, memory, and present moment, and with describing the different forms of remembrance that recordings represent. Finally, I discuss musical hermeneutics—interpretation not in the performance sense, but in the basic sense of construing what the music means—as a critical enterprise that has been deeply changed by the kinds of repetition that recordings allow. Memory is a large and multifaceted subject, clearly, and here we must consider it as a commercial-social construct, a historical resource, an everyday effort that humans accessorize more and more in the twenty-first century, and a participant in formation of musical texts.

REPETITION AND STOCKPILING

Jacques Attali developed a dualistic notion, as based on Marx's distinction between use-value and exchange-value, of an older economy based on "representation" giving way to a modern "repetition economy." Mechanical reproduction supplanted a music culture based on ritual and persuasion with one based on duplication and reiteration. As Attali sees it, power now lies less with capital and political influence than with controlling repetition as the means of production. In the representation economy, people consumed commodities as a way of becoming individualized, while in the repetition economy "one consumes in order to resemble." Attali associated the new culture of repetition and resemblance with two kinds of music: "popular music [that] is no longer hierarchically organized according to class" and what he called "learned music," described as "a kind of music that is limited to specialists in the aleatory, a spectacle organized by technicians for technocrats."[4] The duality sounds dated today, but other points of interest in his discussion—points that go beyond the usual, and by now tired, lament over apparent homogenization of music in the electronic age— illuminate recent realities of text and performance in mechanically reproduced classical music.

Attali attaches so much importance to music because it represents such a pure and transparent commodification of time: "Music remains a very unique commodity; to take on meaning, it requires an incompressible lapse of time, that of its own duration."[5] Time is the basic unit of human production and economy, and money—along with music—is the basic instrument for stockpiling time within the repetition economy. Indeed currencies, functioning as instruments of exchange, were the first augury of the repetition economy—coins and banknotes were reproduced in much the same way artworks are now, and like recordings their value depended on their exact equivalence to each other. In its most basic function, money enables a person to buy someone else's time: buy a pair of shoes from a shoemaker, and you purchase the time she took to make them, paid for with the money you earned selling your own time performing a service for someone else. In the repetition economy, we find stockpiling of time—where people run out of the time needed to experience the time that they are buying from others, and thereby lose both their own time and the time they are acquiring. Inhabitants of the repetition economy become locked into a rather dismal acceleration of material surplus and time deficits. "Stockpiling then becomes a substitute, not a preliminary condition, for use. *People buy more records than they can listen to. They stockpile what they want to find the time to hear.* Use-time and exchange-time destroy one another."[6]

In either popular or classical cultures, as Attali sees them, repetition causes alienation at the same time that it manages to cloak "the mode of power." Attali speaks of "the sacrificial relation" of the artwork, and relates this to the aura that Benjamin associated with singularity and originality. His term points to uniqueness, rareness, or even sanctity of access, qualities he sums up in *Parsifal*-esque terms as the "festive and religious character" of the work. In the representation economy, people had to make a sacrifice, an effort; while in the repetition economy, with its mass replication of goods, the sacrificial relation is folded into the commodity aspect of the work itself:

> A work that the author perhaps did not hear more than once in his lifetime (as was the case with Beethoven's Ninth Symphony and the majority of Mozart's works) becomes accessible to a multitude of people, and becomes repeatable outside the spectacle of its performance. It gains availability. It loses its festive and religious character as a simulacrum of sacrifice. It ceases to be a unique, exceptional event, heard once by a minority. The sacrificial relation becomes individualized, and people buy the individualized use of order, the personalized simulacrum of sacrifice.[7]

There isn't much difference, according to Attali, between commissioning a piece of music from a composer and buying a recording from the music store: both involve assigning prices to time spans and then selling them as entities to be repeated. Works of absolute music are in themselves memory objects comprising a specifically apportioned span of real time. It is tempting to say, at least for aficionados of classical music, that an appetite for new works—for spans of time parsed out in particular and individually novel ways—is now largely satisfied by new performances of old works. One might object that notated works are prescriptive, while recordings are descriptive. But to point to such a difference is to draw an unrealistically firm line between writing out music and recording it; certainly Bartók notated his scores so precisely—giving individual movement timings down to the second for his *Music for Strings, Percussion, and Celesta,* for instance—that they can seem less like sets of instructions *for performance* than transcriptions *of specific performances.*

After reading Attali, one begins to think there must have been more behind the mass distribution of classical music after World War II than white middle-class hunger for social and cultural prestige in a time of economic prosperity. Armed with the concepts provided by Attali, let's begin by looking at one project from 1957: the Book-of-the-Month Club's opening bid for classical record sales. The company entered this market with high ambitions, peddling the paragon of absolute music and indeed the very pinnacle of *Tonkunst:* the complete Beethoven String Quartets, as played by the Pascal Quartet. The Book-of-the-Month Club announced the project with a substantial and revealing preamble. Under the headline "A New Idea: The Classics Record Library," they proclaimed an ongoing subscription plan in which the Beethoven Quartets were the initial installment (see fig. 1).

Three themes emerge from the advertising prose of the Book-of-the-Month Club. First, there are promises of cultural prestige: the announcement assures subscribers to "this exciting cultural service" that they will rank among "the most cultivated families." Second, the wisdom and distinction of buying great music in subscription anthologies is promoted: "Undoubtedly most cultivated families are anxious to have the great masterpieces of music in their record libraries, just as they are pleased to own the works of great authors in sets." Third, potential subscribers are informed of the Book-of-the-Month Club's intention of offering the records to "moderate income" buyers: "Relatively few sets in albums, however, have been made available, *and invariably they are extremely expensive.* As one record dealer said, 'The companies seem to get these out for the carriage trade.'" The club's solution to the cost problem was to work with one-time pressing and one-time distribution.[8] Given the moderate price, this was an elite offering without becoming an extravagant one: "Compared with all recent and present opportunities to obtain these great masterpieces complete, the saving, at the very least, is more than 40 per cent!"

The subheading of the ad describes this subscription series as "a systematized plan to enable music-lovers to build up a record library of great music at a very low cost," and elsewhere the flyer says that the twelve records are "enclosed in a sturdy box for permanent protection." The library was originally associated with European royalty and aristocracy before

FIGURE 1. Book-of-the-Month Club ad for Beethoven String Quartets, 1957. Courtesy of Book-of-the-Month Club / Direct Brands, Inc.

becoming a civic concept: migrating from the Gonzagas' and Baron von Swieten's domain to a taxpayer resource in Grand Rapids and Boston. In the Book-of-the-Month Club announcement, the library becomes a more palatable word for what Attali calls stockpiling: libraries bank items as a resource against future utilization, casting a positive light on anticipatory disuse. The announcement at hand draws an analogy between the literary library and the home music collection—a connection that hinges on the culture of silent reading that I discussed in chapter 1, a culture entailing crossover from institutional or public instruction to private learning. In all cases, the material constitutes a reassuring surplus rather than an item for immediate use. The advertisement also offers a "divided-payment plan" of three monthly installments, revealing this as the very scenario described by Attali: the consumer using money she doesn't have to purchase spans of time that she will likely not get around to using.

Last, we come to alienation in the repetition economy—what Attali describes as the transmutation of "festive and religious character as a simulacrum of sacrifice." An intriguing message in the Book-of-the-Month Club advertising flyer—a "footnote from Mr. Conly about this album"—sums up the strangeness of offering such Beethovenian absolute-music abstractions in a popular market. This footnote seems an afterthought, a warning to the buyer that this might not be easy listening. At the same time, the rigorousness of the music becomes a marketing asset:

> Of all music, the Beethoven quartets may be the works best suited to
> the phonograph, since they are mainly personal communications,
> meant to be heard alone—and at need or desire. . . . Do not hearken
> here for prettiness, which would be an excrescence. Listen for substance
> and judgment, which you will find. This music was meant to last.

How many purchasers listened to each substance-laden minute of all ten discs, one wonders? But not to worry, the Beethoven quartets were "meant to last" just as the "sturdy box" would ensure "permanent protection" for the records that the BMC was offering. Losing the "unique, exceptional event" of the music, the listener would find honorable recompense in the cultural cachet of the library—the word evoking patrician splendor, old-world leather bindings, scholarly wisdom, and lost Alexandrine treasures. The library image certainly insinuates luxury and might even suggest a return to a pre-Enlightenment, aristocratic age when any "exceptional events" in art music were the property of the monied classes. Attali says power sits with control of the "repeatable molds" in the repetition economy, and the Beethoven advertising copy promises that as well: the quartet set is a limited edition, to be subscribed to "with as little delay as possible," and the ad mentions literary publishers' practice of destroying the plates for "limited editions of great works."

But the library idea proves wonderfully protean, since it invokes investment and sacrifice as well as opulence and control. If libraries hold material goods, they are not material*ist* goods: recordings are like books in that they represent portals, resources not to be limited, subsumed, or even represented by a cover price. But portals to what, exactly? In Attali's thinking, music's portal significance lies with its more-or-less direct linkage to earlier times. Music, in his description, represents

> an extremely effective exploration of the past, at a time when the present no longer answers to everyone's needs. . . . The use-value of the repeated object is thus the expression of lacks and manipulations in the political economy of the sign. Its exchange-value, approximately equal today for every work and every performer, has become disengaged from use-value.[9]

The library—whether musical or bibliographical—becomes a rare icon of use-value that has survived into the age of exchange-value. Intertwined with that use-value status is what we could call the library's burden of permanence: a library entails curatorship, responsibility, intransience, something not to be taken lightly in an increasingly disposable age. Mr. Conly presents the "simulacrum of sacrifice" up front, though none of the ad copy specifically connects the difficulty of Beethoven quartets with social and cultural prestige. Conly fixes the odds pretty well, since Beethoven lacks only "prettiness"—hardly a shortcoming when compared to the library values of permanence, substance, "judgment," and civic pride.

Attali discusses music in durational rather than informational terms, since the repetition economy has relegated it to that role: collecting music has become a form of collecting time, a culling of particular durational spans from the past. One could still ask Attali whether music is really the only commodity strictly measured in terms of time, in a kind of regressive persistence of use-value, a relation that makes it equivalent to hard currency. Aren't movies, TV shows, hired sex, church services, and cell-phone minutes also repeated time object-commodities? Perhaps, but a detailed taxonomy and structural logistics have been rationalized around music in a way they haven't around those other activities. Attali's conclusions seem particularly appropriate to classical music, which, since eighteenth-century Viennese Classicism and longer symphonic forms, has often been about carving out and apportioning time. In the later eighteenth century, musical discussions turned to balance, marking time, and long-range harmonic preparation. Symphonies, concertos, and string quartets in the Austro-German Classic tradition reached a standard length of about twenty-five minutes and thereby set that duration as a currency of musical time. Such objectivity, even severity, of time awareness was an aspect of the "disinterestedness" (*Uneigennützigkeit*) in Kantian aesthetics. What this means today—a conclusion that would seem to make Attali's ideas more relevant to classical than to popular music—is that purchasing Mozart's "Linz" Symphony makes for a more definite dollar-per-minute transaction than, say, buying the Beatles' *White Album*, the Stooges' *Fun House*, or Judy Garland's Carnegie Hall Concert. The query carries no value implications, just importance for questions of time awareness and currency: Would Beatles, Stooges, and Judy Garland fans be able to give durations for those albums, or the number of tracks they contain?

The composition, the "incompressible lapse of time" that Attali equates with the musical work, functions as an "effective exploration of the past" but also serves to exclude the present: it opens up a particular span of time, pushing aside less pleasurable matters like business deals, grocery shopping, house painting, visits to the auto mechanic, and doing the laundry. Were the musical duration to succeed in dominating the repetition economy, it would even supplant the labor time the music-lover needs in order to buy her next such experience.

MUSIC TREASURES

Attali and the Book-of-the-Month Club ad writers entertain no particular sense of the past, or even of past-ness; they speak of repetition and permanence, but these are not historical concepts. Their operative perspective sits firmly in the present, and instead of memories—personal or cultural— they wish to sell us prestigious time spans. Lack of an organic relation between past and present means that, among the four types of memory possibilities for recordings that I listed earlier, Attali and the BMC seem open only to what I called surrogate memories (type 1) and instigations to remember (type 3). These types of memory involve no synoptic bridging between past and present. Attali and the BMC see no sense of authenticity through history and grant old and distant things no special worth—they draw no linear value constructs.

Two other American record projects, *Music Treasures of the World* and *The Standard Treasury of the World's Great Music*, produced between about 1958 and 1960, intimate a greater gap between past and present. Both suggest ideas of value and authenticity that hinge upon rarity and oldness. Both call upon the past in powerful if also rather vague ways. *The Standard Treasury of the World's Great Music*, with an ancient Greek kithara on its label, evokes the distant and idealized past of antiquity. *Music*

FIGURE 2. *Music Treasures of the World* record sleeve, c. 1960. Courtesy of Francine Ringold.

Treasures of the World, with its keyhole image (see fig. 2), presents the masterpiece of instrumental music as a key for unlocking . . . prestige? the past? cultural knowledge? The image is telling, because the past becomes inaccessible to the present in much the same way that an object of value—thus the reference to treasure?—is locked away from larcenous hands. According to this kind of thinking, anything olden has automatic value. Historical thinking turns the past into a discrete concept—it aestheticizes past-ness—and *Music Treasures of the World* presents Western music for the space age, promising art as an accessory to the American Dream: "The supreme musical achievements of mankind, performed with magnificent artistry, recorded in the full range audible to the human ear." This is a meeting of the old and the new, cultural heirlooms preserved through progressive technology and New World chutzpah.

A treasure and treasury are, according to their most basic definitions, money and a place where money is stored: a nation's treasury is the equity storehouse that backs the value of its currency. But the words can also suggest, instead of hard assets, rarities that have no street value. The *Oxford English Dictionary* defines *treasury* as "a room or building in which precious or valuable objects are preserved," and *treasure* as "wealth or riches stored or accumulated; anything valued and preserved as precious." Though the financial connotations might be thought more relevant to these recordings' time and place—the *Music Treasures* key somehow giving access to upward social mobility—I would say the more salient implication is access to the past. A treasure, understood in the fantastical rather than financial sense—whether hidden treasure, a treasure chest, stolen treasure, or "the supreme musical achievements of mankind"—is something lost to the past that awaits discovery in the present.

These treasures may be hidden or lost, but they are valued according to linear historicist thinking where old is good and older is apparently even better. The paradox of this linearity in a market economy is that the treasure—the "rarity"—is prized according to its chronological distance from the present yet at the same time must be made available to the here and-now. How is this accomplished with a musical treasure? Directly, doubtless too unequivocally, it is encoded into notation or a stream of information. Whether written or recorded, the music takes the form of a groove or stroke that is inscribed continuously in one direction over time, in exact temporal proportion to the music being recorded. The methods of recorded inscription were variously devised and modified by Édouard-Léon Scott de Martinville, Charles Cros, Edison, and Tainter as a way of writing down a segment of the aural past for use in the future. (Scott might not belong on this list, since he devised his phonoautograph as a means of "writing" sound without seeing any need for "reading" those inscriptions back into audible form.) In essence, these men represented a segment of the past with a vectored line—or, insofar as the past is not directly recoverable, we could say Scott, Cros, and Edison drew lines in attempts to connect past with present. Why a line rather than, say, an oval, a zigzag, or a random scribble? Because time unfolds in linear fashion, and it is easiest and simplest to get the machines used to reading those sound-inscriptions to proceed in a linear direction—the line is analogous to time, and makes for good ergonomics. The stream of data is still linear in the age of microprocessors, because sound is represented as a set of instructions, and directives necessarily proceed in a linear fashion: do X, the microprocessor is told, and then do Y before doing Z.

If the linear aspect of the recording presents an illusion, it is one that the music itself betrays—or, indeed, lives to contradict. Encoding Beethoven's work in a more-or-less straight line might seem suitable to music that is marked by a fabled linearity: the history books tell us that this composer's long-range, goal-directed harmonic thinking and teleological aspect enabled him to expand instrumental forms. Scott Burnham refers to "the feeling of glorious consummation so singularly afforded by Beethoven's heroic style" and speaks of that composer's middle period in cosmological terms of universal causation: "Like the philosophical systems of the post-Kantian generation, the musical works of Beethoven's heroic style register as closed systems, self-generating, self-sustaining, and self-consuming. The musical process manifested in the heroic style is heard to share a similar sense of progressive development toward an immanent and transcendent telos."[10] As Burnham goes on to say, however, linearity is not especially interesting qua linearity; and what we are really drawn to as listeners is this composer's tantalizing manner of playing with that linearity, of both sustaining and threatening it.[11]

But just how linear is time—and, as a consequence, Western art music of the Austro-German symphonic tradition? Certainly relationships between events happening across time can appear linear in retrospect, after they have occurred. Making a bad driving decision, veering off the road, getting injured, seeing oneself whisked to the hospital, and then being saved by emergency surgery can seem unconnected and chaotic as they are happening, while after recovery the progression can seem causal and logical enough. But the question remains, as addressed for example by proponents of *cinema verité*, of whether such occurrences are accurately experienced in nonlinear, chaotic, firsthand form or—as the common expression would have it—as an ordered string of events.

BERGSON AND LINEARITY

Henri Bergson said we inscribe the past in simplistic, linear fashion not simply for convenience, but because we habitually misunderstand time. He argued that the tendency toward linear representations of past events—in the form of timelines, time-elapsed graphs, flowcharts—shows succession depicted as simultaneity, a privileging of space over time. These representations are, at best, symbolic of a past, immobile, and alienated chronology. Bergson thought time was embodied in consciousness, making it a process and not an object.[12] When we choose to understand time as linear, Bergson declared, we lock ourselves into a Euclidean conception not only of space but of history, and thereby prevent ourselves from understanding subjectivity. He claimed that we tend, because of a "bastard concept" of time as space, to confuse apparent duration for real duration: "As we are not accustomed to observing ourselves directly but instead perceive ourselves through forms borrowed from the external world, we end up thinking that real duration, the duration lived by consciousness, is the same as the duration that slips past inert atoms without changing anything."[13] One convincing way Bergson demonstrates the dissimilarity between apparent duration and real duration is by looking at the line and then at the span of time it is said to represent: the line, like physical movement in Newtonian theory, is unitary, repeatable, and potentially reversible, while time and consciousness are not.

Both the record and the CD organize data in linear form, in the form of a groove or a string of microscopic pits. But Bergson believes no linear depiction, or for that matter any ordinary graphic manner of representation, can accurately characterize time. He asks: "Can time adequately be represented by space?" And then responds: "The reply is: Yes, if it is a question of time already past. No, if you want to speak of the time that passes. Free action occurs in the time that passes and not the time already past."[14] To judge from this statement, the linearized time on a recording can represent only apparent duration—a closed, inert, and insensible chronological expanse. Bergson wrote nothing on the phonograph but claimed that another form of mechanical reproduction, the cinematograph, effected only the illusion of motion. The cinematograph merely juxtaposed static images, leaving any sense of time and movement to be produced by the only moving element in the equation, namely the projector itself:

> The process then consists in extracting from all the movements peculiar to all the figures an impersonal movement abstract and simple, *movement in general,* so to speak: we put this into the apparatus and we reconstitute the individuality of each particular movement by combining this nameless movement with the personal attitudes. Such is the contrivance of the cinematograph.[15]

Most music also continually requires that "we reconstitute the individuality of each particular movement," but requires this of a sentient human performer. Music, straddling notation conventions and aurally transmitted manners of interpretation, must also differ from film in that it regularly flouts its own semblance of real duration. In Beethoven's instrumental work, we could single out the six-bar, fermata-ridden cadential delay that threatens to derail the very end of the Fourth Symphony, the delightful diminished-seventh aporia of the E-flat Piano Sonata, op. 31, no. 3, or the disruptively avant-garde *piano* chords in the opening movement of the first "Razumovsky" quartet. Each of these Beethoven moments—and there are many more—persists as a "free action," unrepeatable moment, though doubly "of the past" and doubly rendered in linear, spatial terms, as written on the page and then written on the CD or computer hard disk. These are moments of real duration that somehow escape again and again from multiple enforcements of linearity. And so, when it comes to recordings we shouldn't ask about a lack of musical spontaneity but instead pose a different sort of question: How can a composed event still manage to surprise the listener, or bring the listener to construct a state of surprised-ness for herself, even when it is heard for the forty-second time?

We have arrived once more at the difficult question of the relation between the recorded information and the sounding music, and indeed beyond that, the problem of how to represent anything that happens diachronically. Just what kind of graphic representation of time does Bergson specifically deny? Concerned with questions of free will versus determinism, he presents a slightly irregular Y-shaped line as a graphic depiction of a free-choice situation, a person confronting a logistical "fork in the road" (see fig. 3). In this scenario, the subject makes a decision at point O between option X and possibility Y and moves in linear fashion from M to X or M to Y according to that decision. We could argue that this diagram represents Bergson's free-choice condition differently than a record or CD groove signifies a specific passage of music—the first being a schematic representation of a conceptual situation, and the second a prescriptive definition of a set of sounds, the first an iconic image and the second an indexical sign. And is the first self-enclosed—unitextual, maybe—in a way that the second is not? After all, the second has all manner of musicians, recording engineers, and microphone designers who—posing as prime movers or perhaps "ghosts in the machine"—pretend to have no initiative power but cause or at least influence each little jut and jag in the record groove. They are like the scribes in one of the less intuitive music notation systems of the late Middle Ages—say, from the monastery of St. Gall in what is now Switzerland. As a counter to these arguments, however, I would say that all the schemata mentioned here represent time-conditional, continuous, and causal situations. In both, we need to read the graphics in the linear sense in which they were intended, in which case point O in Bergson's diagram is immanent in point M, just as the eighteenth jag in the record groove is preconditioned by the sixteenth, and the fourth St. Gall neume was penned in a way that presumes the third.

FIGURE 3. Bergson's model for free choice. From *Matière et mémoire*, 1896.

So long as we find it necessary to record music in such a linear fashion—or to notate it on vellum, parchment, paper, or a computer display in a similar way—it seems inevitable that the habits we've developed of encoding music will stand in an alienated relation to the music thus encoded. Two persistent and conflicting demands have consigned us to this fate: the limitations of our technology, and the heavily determined nature of our music. We could choose to be less specific in what we require of our music in any given instance, as New York composer Earle Brown was with his *December 1952* and other "constellation" scores from the 1950s. These are nondirectional and nonlinear: the person playing the score can choose to follow the various strokes and rectangles upside-down, in a circular fashion, or in a random order of her own devising. Brown even suggested that the performer envision the markings in a three-dimensional space, and in performance imagine moving through the space while interpreting the indications. Or we could try to develop a device without moving parts that could instantaneously read a single image in its entirety and from that play back a performance of, say, Dvořák's Eighth Symphony. But both scenarios would fail, or would fail us in our current situation. In the first case, most lovers of Western art music would be left unsatisfied by the apparent lack of an organizing, subsuming intelligence. Indeed, that is largely the point of graphic scores like Earle Brown's, Morton Feldman's, or John Cage's: to preclude the omniscient, and in some minds suffocating, rationality that one finds with much Western art music. In the second situation, limitations of current technology would leave us with only a short span of music—two-dimensional matrix bar codes, looking something like an Earle Brown score, are often used today for tracking shipments. But these yield at most only some 2 KB of information—enough to encode a twelfth of a second of music at a barely tolerable bitrate—and in any event the information would have to be put back into linear order for playback.

So not only is it apparently impossible for us Western rationalists to avoid musical linearity at the local level, but it also seems unlikely at the intellectual level. I am speaking of another problematic kind of linearity, and another awkward understanding of time, and that is historicity. Can't we come up with some other way of understanding history than to force it into diachronic linearity, requiring it to conform to our understanding of the present? Perhaps complaints against narrative conceptions of history have begun to disassemble such thinking. But then Bergsonians and McLuhanians would agree that the various media we've devised across the centuries for understanding the world—from ancient scrolls to books, LP grooves, and data strings—have conditioned us to require such linearity and continuity, and indeed to supply it where none exists.

So what kind of relationship *should* we assume between past and present? Bergson says it should be a subjective and nonlinear relation. Because of our confusion between apparent duration and real duration, he says, "we do not see the absurdity of putting things back in their place once time has passed, or of believing that the same motivations repeatedly act on the same people, and concluding that these causes will always produce the same effect."[16] A specific example of such absurdity in music-historical terms might be the assumption that musical functions and the meaning of a work's constituent parts—cadenzas, for instance—remain the same across centuries. Before Beethoven began including his own cadenzas in published scores, the cadenzas in a Classical concerto were a place for the soloist's individuality and improvisational skills to emerge from the composition at hand. Perhaps the main source for information on the Classical German instrumental cadenza, D. G. Türk's *Clavierschule* (Leipzig and Halle, 1789), makes conflicting stipulations: Türk says the cadenza "should reinforce the impression made by the composition by providing a brief summary of it" and should also "express a unified sentiment"; but at the same time he calls it a passage of "novelty, wit and an abundance of ideas," a display of "ordered disorder" that "should be performed as though it had just occurred to the performer."[17] Cadenzas written for Beethoven's Fourth Piano Concerto by cognoscenti like Brahms, Clara Schumann, Anton Rubinstein, and Hans von Bülow would seem to satisfy Türk's requirements but have disappeared from performance—victims of the latter-day cults of historicity and compositional authenticity.

In our own historically fraught time, cadenzas create an insolvable dilemma that Türk had already hinted at long ago: Should the player create cadenzas in the style of the composer's time, present cadenzas in a present-day idiom, or play cadenzas that the composer wrote for her own performances? Bergson would say each solution is equally ridiculous, each an example of "the absurdity of putting things back in their place once time has passed." To play a cadenza in the manner of the composition, whether newly composed or from the composer's own pen, is to reify stylistic continuity over the historical purpose of the cadenza itself. On the other hand, it is just as strange to insist on the historical notion that a cadenza embodies the individual performer's world: to say that, we must hold onto a dictionary definition of a musical entity tooth and nail, even though more than two cataclysmic centuries have passed, and insisting on this definition will cause absurdities of another kind. This conundrum of the cadenza's modern-day absurdity follows inescapably from our current curatorial, museum-like relationship with instrumental art music.

We find an instructive example in the controversy over Alfred Schnittke's 1977 cadenzas for the Beethoven Violin Concerto, as championed by Gidon Kremer. Critic Harris Goldsmith found these unabashedly contemporary cadenzas "intrusive" and "disastrous" on record, taking exception to the way "these graffiti are blithely superimposed." Going further, he lambasted Schnittke for needlessly or even rudely attempting to update a canonical work: "It's too bad when gifted musicians like Kremer and Schnittke become so bored by the great masterpieces that they begin to seek out perverse ways of making them 'interesting.'"[18] To judge from several concert reviews, Schnittke's Beethoven cadenzas proved more welcome in the one-off experience of a concert than on disc. Attending a Carnegie Hall concert performance of Kremer playing Schnittke-Beethoven, Bernard Holland found no historical or stylistic grounds for offense:

> Mr. Schnittke's interpolations have kicked up a small critical fuss
> in American-music journalism, and the question has been whether
> Beethoven's Classical language can live easily alongside a more contemporary dialect—which is what Mr. Schnittke's cadenzas unashamedly
> speak. Judging from last night's performance, the answer is a clear, simple
> yes. Mr. Schnittke's cadenzas may venture far beyond Beethoven's harmonic vocabulary, but they are at the same time very true to his thematic

material. Everything is wonderfully condensed and organized, and the
cadential resolutions to Beethoven's dominant harmony at the end clev-
erly weld the two languages together with scarcely a hint of abrasion.[19]

In their divergent ways, Schnittke and Fritz Kreisler—composer of a conservative and much more popular set of Beethoven cadenzas—assumed a
historical constancy where none exists. Both presupposed a linearity, imposing a visual-spatial conception of history, and recordings have encouraged such a perspective: beholden to grooves and streams of data, they
have facilitated linear solutions to musical problems. The recording, possessed of a discrete and inviolate textuality, has encouraged historicism by
conditioning listeners to prefer stylistic continuity across the whole work
over any assertions of utility or individuality in the cadenza itself.

REPETITION, HISTORY, AND HERMENEUTICS

This cadenza problem seems insignificant compared to a more pervasive
"absurdity of putting things back in their place once time has passed."
This concerns the most powerful and deep-seated—yet unrecognized—of
all the influences wrought by recordings. The issue is phrased most simply
as a question: Can we presume, or even hope, to know how a piece of music sounded before Edison's invention? The neumes in manuscripts of
twelfth-century French St. Martial polyphony are still open to debate, to
the extent that a listener might not recognize a piece of music when confronted by two modern performances. This repertory obviously represents
an extreme example, but Chopin and Mahler haven't escaped such discussions. Basic differences of performance lessen as we go forward in time and
as musical notation becomes more detailed, but they never disappear. Nevertheless, recordings have helped us—or, it would be more accurate to say,
subconsciously encouraged us—to assume such uncertainties don't exist,
or to think that musical meaning rises above them. Recordings have
done this by instigating a largely imagined knowledge of the musical past
as a sounding—as opposed to written—phenomenon. How have they done
this while unrecorded performances have apparently contributed less to
such an imagined knowledge? By being fixed and more or less permanent
in themselves. And by creating a kind of self-perpetuating chain of presumption, something they achieve simply by being of the past rather than
of the present. Even if we find nothing specifically authentic about Arthur
Rubinstein's and Artur Schnabel's Brahms playing, the very sounding
presence of a Brahms *dolce* interpreted in the 1940s by a pianist born in

1887 can convince easily enough—again, through assumption rather than induction—that this is the right way.

Recordings have, with the help of such beliefs, served to telescope music history. That we can know how music sounded 200 or even 120 years ago is a historicist notion that did not exist before the 1950s. Even the interest in these questions is relatively recent. Such historicism becomes evident in an assertion by Michael White, who, writing on historically informed performance practice for the *New York Times,* referred to "the interventionist musical culture of the mid-19ᵗʰ century" as a set of obfuscations to be surmounted. More specifically, White believes it is possible to circumvent "ideas that had hardened into accepted norms" in order to reconnect with practices of a pristine past:

> Forty years ago there was not much of an issue about how you performed a Mozart symphony, a Bach cantata or a Handel oratorio. You played it the way Wilhelm Furtwängler, Thomas Beecham or Herbert von Karajan might have: with mid-19th-century ideas that had hardened into accepted norms and generally meant big symphonic forces, heavy textures, slow speeds and modern instruments. Then came 'early music,' also known as period performance. Early musicians researched period instruments, rediscovered forgotten composers, revived old performance practices and in effect declared war on the interventionist musical culture of the mid-19th century. They set out to make their case with fundamentalist fervor, espousing lighter forces, faster speeds and period instruments. And through the 1970's and 80's they multiplied and gathered force.[20]

Showing a similar mind-set, Christopher Hogwood tells us that attention to the specific ensembles used at Beethoven's premieres will help current listeners appreciate the differences between his individual symphonies and enable us to "make our starting point what the work *is*, not what we would, with hindsight, design or expect it to be."[21] Whence comes this idea that we can, in essence, erase time and return to a particular earlier *sounding* form of a piece of music? That we can rationalize our way through history as the crow flies, hewing a straight line in a world defined by curves, bends, and recursions? That we can hope to be any less interventionist than any other era, especially within a sensibility defined by that particular manner of inconsistency and predisposition that we call aurality?

Arnold Dolmetsch, a scholar who lived and opined before the repetition economy took hold, didn't subscribe to such "time warp" presumptions. We can contrast the Hogwood-White attitude with Dolmetsch's view, expressed in 1915, that performers would do justice to Frescobaldi by ignoring "modern methods" of interpreting seventeenth-century music—perhaps the same "stupid, mechanical practice of the present time" that he lamented in performances of mid-seventeenth-century English church music. According to Dolmetsch, "as soon as it is recognized that not only is it not 'wrong' to give the old music its natural expression, but, on the contrary, that the so-called traditional way of playing it is an insult to its beauty, the players will not be afraid to follow their own instinct, and the music will come to life again."[22] On the surface, Dolmetsch may sound like Hogwood and White in the way he decries a "traditional way of playing" and urges performers to seek a way of making the music "come to life again." But the "beauty" and "natural expression" that he aspires to are not specific manners of performance to be recovered by rationalizing our way back to pristine methods. The "natural expression" of the old music doesn't lie with a specific sound or a particular manner of playing. It doesn't even lie with "the music itself" or aspects of earlier practice, but sits instead with the performer's musical intuition—perhaps the element having the least direct effect on the way a piece of music will sound in performance.

What happened between Dolmetsch and the likes of Hogwood and White to cause such a change in views of aurality? Recording, primarily. Recordings have empowered us with entirely new kinds of surrogate musical memory, blurring distinctions between remembering and imagining, and allowing us to think we can hear and recollect far beyond the fickle recesses of the individual person's inner ear. Much of the difference between remembering and imagining lies with the variability of the person: if a listener attended a concert and then listened to a high-quality recording of the same performance in the same auditorium, she would not have anything like the same experience because the sounds are now preceded by different sensations and events, and the listener is in a different state of mind, body, and emotion. Part of the difference comes from innate processes of recollection. Bergson's contemporaries tended to understand memory as a present-to-past process where recollections are stored more or less precisely and can be retrieved or returned to. At the point where the sensation enters the memory, according to this perspective, the memory becomes free from the object that instigated the memory. Bergson reversed this view, saying that such conceptions represent an at best illusionary, surrogate, or prosthetic manner of recollection and force subjective memory to follow a graphical model of history. According to him, a person constantly verifies the memory-to-be against the object, and in that sense memory formation is a cooperative effort: "Any excitation which leaves from the object cannot stop *en route* in the depths of

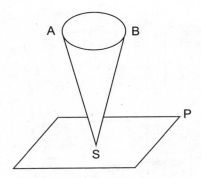

FIGURE 4. Bergson's model for the totality of memory. From *Matière et mémoire*, 1896.

the mind. It must always return to the object itself."[23] Instead of being a discrete entity that resides in the past, memory is a process of past to present where the recollection achieves actualization in the present moment in the form of current perception and bodily action. The memory resides in and lives for the present, where it shapes perception and physical action, and for that reason there can be no returning to a specific point or aspect that we might choose to "recall" from "the past."

The only discrete form of memory recognized by Bergson is what he called Pure Memory—a virtual construct, a heuristic that has nothing to do with the brain or any other part of the body. If there could be no physical aspect to memory as he saw it, what would he say of the recording, which seems to embody memory and even comes to replace our own "real" recollections? It is a physical object containing precise aural information and in that sense really cannot have much to do with the past as Bergson understood it, as a state of inaction, powerlessness, and the rule of the unconscious. Might Bergson have understood the recording as, paradoxically enough, a site of action? "For a memory to reappear to consciousness," he writes, "it would have to descend from the heights of pure memory to the precise point where action occurs."[24] In the totality of accumulated memories, graphically symbolized by Bergson as an inverted cone, which resembles the laser pickup that focuses on a CD, the tip S becomes the point where the memory AB enters the present and cuts forward into the future (see fig. 4). "The point of the cone, S, makes contact with a plane P. The point S figures my present, but it is to be thought as a moving point, always advancing in time."[25] Bergson's cone model points down rather than up to contact the present, suggesting that memory is a necessary, natural, and indeed passive process.

EXAMPLE 1.   Tchaikovsky, Symphony No. 4, first movement, second theme (mm. 114–120).

The very power of recordings, doubly strong because hidden, resides in their relationship with the musical work as "text" and as "act"—to borrow Richard Taruskin's description of the duality. The recording pretends to offer the work, more or less transparently, as musical act, while it is in fact textual in important ways. In his disquisition into notions of authenticity in performance practice Taruskin says we are hell-bent on imputing our own modern agendas to our Baroque and Classical predecessors.[26] As he describes them, notation and notational practices have their own ways of allowing, perhaps encouraging, such historicist attributions. I would say recordings have a similar effect. As an example, let us take Susan McClary's provocative discussion of the second theme in Tchaikovsky's Fourth Symphony, first movement (see ex. 1). McClary observes: "This is no simple 'feminine' theme. Like Carmen [in Bizet's opera], it is sultry, seductive, and slinky. . . . Moreover, unlike the obsessively goal-oriented protagonist, this theme manages to be at the same time both utterly static (even stagnant) and also irrational with respect to its unexpected twists and turns: precisely as is Carmen when she is seducing José."[27] McClary's discussion is contentious, though no less important and instructive for that: she wishes to show the gendered codings of themes in an "absolute" work written at a time of crisis for a composer who was probably conflicted over his homosexuality.

But how much of this characterization of Tchaikovsky's A-flat minor theme—presuming McClary's interpretation to be appropriate—is to be attributed to the composer, and how much to the symphony's interpreters? The music was written half a century before its first recording and, between publication of the score and that first appearance on discs, Freud caused a sea change in discussions of desire. Tchaikovsky composed his Fourth Symphony between 1877 and early 1878, at exactly the same time Edison completed his phonograph and prepared to patent the device. But it took half a century for the music to meet the machine.[28] Leopold Stokowski recorded the complete score with the Philadelphia Orchestra, in a 1928 Victor release, and then Willem Mengelberg did the same with the Amsterdam Concertgebouw Orchestra in 1929, for British Columbia.[29] These were influential recordings, and we can still hear Mengelberg's and Stokowski's influences on early twenty-first-century conductors, though between their lifetimes and the present Michel Foucault added yet another wrinkle of sexual interpretation. So I would ask McClary how much of the "sultry, seductive, and slinky" quality of Tchaikovsky's theme, its "utterly static" and even "irrational" aspect, its "sinister, slippery, potentially lethal" character, is the work of Mengelberg, the imperious—and heterosexual— Dutch conductor whose virtuosic and often willful vocabulary of rubato and phrasing effects are a big part of Tchaikovsky performance traditions? Certainly there are interpretive aspects to many later records of this music that seem to owe at least as much to Mengelberg as they do to Tchaikovsky's score, which at the entry of the theme in question simply stipulates a *ritard* and *diminuendo* to "Moderato assai, quasi Andante." (John Warrack disagrees with McClary's interpretation here, pronouncing "the second subject group, with its little woodwind scales and its lulling string theme" to have "an artificial prettiness touchingly remote from the first theme."[30] Can anyone be seduced by "artificial prettiness"? Perhaps Warrack had been listening to Igor Markevitch's 1965 recording: that conductor makes the smallest of *ritards* for the second theme, bringing us to a sprightly Andante where Tchaikovsky's chromaticism seems less heavy and his 9/8 meter more suggestive of the dance.)

I'm not pursuing White's or Hogwood's kind of reasoning here to suggest that McClary has been prevented by nineteenth-century obstructionism from understanding the "real" nature of Tchaikovsky's theme, and that we could counter her with a more authentic or historically valid under-standing of the melody. To try to construct a hypothetical, pre-Mengelberg and pre-Stokowski Tchaikovsky would be—and this is precisely Taruskin's point—to attempt an artificial manner of interpretation bearing little or no connection to any musical traditions, least of all Tchaikovsky's. No, I'm making the opposite declaration, and saying that McClary's confident im-putation of very specific affective qualities of the second theme to Tchaikovsky himself—and, more specifically, to the composer's sexual anxieties—is akin to the time-warp idea that we can confidently recreate a pre-Edison performance style. McClary demonstrates a kind of inverse au-thenticism.[31] The leap of faith she takes here is to link these specific emo-tional aspects not with the written score so much as with Tchaikovsky's own compositional project. It's therefore difficult to understand her ra-tionale for rejecting David Brown's readings of the Fourth: she finds it "crucial that inferences such as these be carefully grounded so that per-nicious essentialist stereotypes of homosexuals (excessively emotional, hysterical, self-loathing, etc.) are not unwittingly drawn upon and re-inscribed." If McClary were unaware of any performance tradition impu-tations, that would in itself serve as a measure of Mengelberg's substantial influence on Tchaikovsky interpretational practice, so universal that quiet chromaticism and scalar motion played "Moderato assai, quasi Andante" have come to signify "sultry, seductive, and slinky." So McClary has not been prevented from hearing the "real" character of Tchaikovsky's theme, whatever that might be, by some historical interregnum; rather, with her disquisition into Tchaikovsky's theme she embarks on a convenient linear-ity of thought borne of musical empathy and an implicitly phonographic sense of music history.

REPETITION AND PERFORMANCE

What of performers, who have been largely absent from my discussion so far? The long nineteenth century still influences today's musical aesthet-ics, and Romanticism remains the musical *lingua franca*. In such a context, recordings tend to wield less of a musical-stylistic influence than the abil-ity to sew up certain historical distances, for instance placing our current notions of sexuality and emotion closer to Tchaikovsky's than to Luigi Dallapiccola's, Stefan Wolpe's, or Ned Rorem's. But it is really only musi-cologists and listeners who have allowed recordings to function as surrogate memories, to the point of precluding their own and connecting historical then directly to current now. One example can be found in the illusion I mention above of direct communication and empathy between listeners and some composers of the distant past. For performers, however, the repetition economy has widened gaps and alienated musical interpreters from the musical text. Performers seem to be automatons in Attali's repetition economy—as much a part of mechanical reproduction as the recordings they produce, less readers of texts than mechanisms for keeping earlier readings in circulation.

In short, recordings have intensified the differences in the ways that performers, listeners, and musicologists "read" music. Recordings have enabled musicologists and listeners and allowed them to presume more. McClary permitted herself to overlook the fact that music of the pre-Edison past must be brought into sounding terms—*some* kind of aural form—before we can interrogate its psychosexual meanings. For where precisely does Tchaikovsky's chromaticism prove seductive, in the ear or on the page? By contrast, the repetition economy has caused the performer to feel restricted, less capable of presuming things of the musical text. She was once required as a matter of course to presume connection with the musical, cultural, and psychosexual matrices of the composer and work being played. In fact, for a performer to "read" the text that she was performing "aloud"—to question the presumption and directness with which interpreters connect with their text—would have been taken as a sign of bad faith, lack of musicality, or an overintellectual approach. But such distanced "reading" has now become the norm, and the aesthetic aspect of musical interpretation is largely undiscussed.

The immediate result of the performer's newly straitened relationship with the music was emotional alienation and dislocation. "The image of the machine in its impassive efficiency gained power over many minds," notes Alfred Brendel. "It became an obsession to strive for perfection. *In mistrusting their own nature, artists denied themselves access to the nature of music.* The usual symptoms of this are that emotions become either completely dried up or willfully superimposed. Often, both extremes are to be found in the same person; the vital area between them remains largely unfrequented."[32] We could take Brendel's assertion in a rather different direction and say that recordings, like filmed pornography, have turned us into musical voyeurs, external witnesses of our own most private, intimate experiences. Just as the repetition economy made sex something watched rather than experienced, even—especially?—by its active participants, music has become a manifestation of alienated subjectivity, something most actively experienced while in a state of passivity. This is less a commercial co-option of intimacy and inwardness, as Attali and T. W. Adorno might have it, than a willed phenomenon.

While Brendel thinks mechanical reproduction has alienated the musician from belief in her own musical emotions, Gunther Schuller thinks it is the composer's text that the repetition economy has forced from memory. Schuller sees originality as a nefarious impulse in performance, one that has been exacerbated by competition in the record market. In an unexpected twist of logic, he finds that this increase in variety of performances has actually brought about a stultifying uniformity:

> When several hundred conductors impose their interpretive whims and fancies on the works of, say, Beethoven, Brahms, Tchaikovsky, Schumann, or Dvořák, all those pieces begin to sound alike; they are covered by a blanket of subverting interpretations, which make it impossible to hear the true, dramatic, often startling differences between and among those composers. Beethoven sounds like Brahms; Brahms sounds like Beethoven, and both of them sound like Tchaikovsky, and so on. The extraordinary discipline, economy, terseness of construction—in a sense even the simplicity and directness—of Beethoven are lost and made to sound like the more luxuriant, effusive, romantic emotionality of Brahms or Tchaikovsky. He who has not heard that intrinsic difference between Beethoven and Brahms—their occasional similarities and close idiomatic relationship notwithstanding—can probably not imagine the considerable gulf between the two. And that distinctiveness, the work, after all, of two totally different personalities originating in two totally different periods, can be brought to life only through the most scrupulous, admiring and respectful realization—not interpretation—of the text, the score.[33]

How could Schuller hear sameness in such musical variety? If Amazon and eBay have come to represent cultural memory, we have a mind-boggling number of performances to think upon. There are now some 150 interpretations of Beethoven's Fifth Symphony on the market, reproduced and repeated in Attali's repetition economy: encased in durable polycarbonate plastic, they circulate in the tens of thousands; they enter library collections, get downloaded to MP3 players, are copied to try to convert students to the music or colleagues to a particular manner of its performance, are sent to friends through instant messaging, and find themselves resold on the Internet. True, basic laws of economics would suggest that 99 percent of these Fifths ultimately mean very little as individual performances. Conductor Christian Thielemann has confronted the crowded field of common-practice symphony recordings with a certain desperation, pleading in a liner note to his Bruckner Fifth disc that "at some point there has to be an end to all these comparisons. The public today often talks about Günter Wand, who was born almost half a century before me, or about Wilhelm Furtwängler, who's been dead for more than half a century. If as a young conductor you listened to these voices, you'd hardly ever dare to pick up a baton again."[34] This is a startling and presumptuous assertion, in response to which one would like to ask: Exactly how does your chronological recentness allow you to be any less original as an interpreter? But there seems to be no connection between such intimidating interpretive comparisons and Schuller's homogeneity-through-originality, unless Thielemann is protesting that he should be allowed to interpret music just as unexceptionally and conventionally as he wants.

Having heard a musical passage in ten variant readings rather than in ten repetitions of the same reading, as is common today, listeners a century ago would be less likely than today's to attribute any one meaning to that passage. If listeners confront Tchaikovsky performances as aural texts unto themselves, then a variety of such texts—some fast, others slow, some smooth, others heavily articulated—likely led to a variety of musicological and listened-to interpretations, or at least a less dogmatic approach to interpretation. Freudian psychology speaks of repetition in terms of compulsion, while Roland Barthes tells us in *The Pleasure of the Text* that a pleasure known in advance to the reader amounts to a perversion.[35] The listener who heard a dozen different construals of chromaticism and quiet scalar motion at a "Moderato assai, quasi Andante" tempo was less likely to attribute any single meaning to them. It is perhaps more than anything the varieties in performance that he heard—the executive inconsistencies, large and small, of his time—that encouraged Eduard Hanslick to insist a century and a half ago that instrumental music can only be indistinct in its subject and must therefore remain flexible in its interpretation:

> Though a single leak will sink a ship, those who are not content with that, are at liberty to knock out the whole bottom. Let them play the theme of a Symphony by Mozart or Haydn, an Adagio by Beethoven, a Scherzo by Mendelssohn, one of Schumann's or Chopin's compositions for the piano, anything, in short, from the stock of our standard music; or again, the most popular themes from Overtures of Auber, Donizetti, and Flotow. Who would be bold enough to point out a definite feeling as the subject of any of these themes? One will say "love." He may be right. Another thinks it is "longing." Perhaps so. A third feels it to be "religious fervour." Who can contradict him? Now, how can we talk of a definite feeling being *represented*, when nobody really knows *what* is represented? Probably all will agree about the beauty or beauties of the composition, whereas all will differ regarding its subject.[36]

Hanslick is of very different mind than McClary on the subject of musical interpretation, in part because he had no access to recorded repetition and the sense of interpretive empowerment it induces. Variable repetition makes for hermeneutic uncertainty, while a literal reiteration of musical affect implies a possible one-to-one connection between a specific phrase or group of notes and a specific emotion. Recordings have, in short, simplified and ossified musical hermeneutics, and I believe—contrary to Schuller—that this has raised the stakes for performance. Would it be easier for a musician to ascribe meaning to a Tchaikovsky symphonic theme in Hanslick's time, or in McClary's? Repetition has caused present-day audiences to demand interpretive originality but to reject it when it becomes extreme enough to forestall memory (instigation to remember, recording memory function 3, as described above). The line separating acceptable and unacceptable seems to grow narrower and narrower as the years go by, such that an individual performer can now stimulate in one phrase and offend in the next.

Just as the new institution of recording began to usurp the value of the notated score, literal repetition has had, in addition to an entrenching effect on musical meaning, the final consequence of deepening the "absoluteness" and transcendent aspect of the Brahms symphony and thereby challenging its interpreters even further. This is part of what Brendel means when he says recordings have encouraged musicians to "deny themselves access to the nature of music." Nicholas Cook describes a similar process in which the passive and increasingly private consumption of commodified products "has helped entrench the idea of autonomous musical texts, intellectual properties that are to be delivered from composer to performer."[37] Neither of these two interpretations is far from Carl Dahlhaus's view that "the idea of 'absolute music' . . . consists of the conviction that instrumental music purely and clearly expresses the true nature of music by its very lack of concept, object, and purpose. Not its existence, but what it stands for, is decisive. Instrumental music, as pure 'structure,' represents itself."[38]

Such a hermeneutic view probably depends too much on a stringent, Attali-esque understanding of repetition and effect. Attali had a rather simplistic conception of reiteration as brute repetition, the same stimulus always causing the same effect, and music clearly doesn't work that way. For Bergson, on the other hand, repetition becomes a way of experiencing difference: the same cause needn't have the same effect, resulting in a *compounding* rather than a *repetition* of past-ness. With his freer perspective on reiteration, Gilles Deleuze reads Bergson in a way that permits us a more realistic relationship between musical past and musical now. Returning to the Bergson inverted cone model, as represented in figure 4 above, Deleuze allows a broad view of the temporal complexity that attends hearing old musical works in past performances on present-day media, involving technology designed to suggest that the past is indeed the present, or at least coexistent with it. Deleuze emphasizes the cumulative nature of memory, the presence of past as "the whole, integral past; it is *all* our past, which coexists with each present." He also sees two linked types of memory, what he calls recollection-memory and contraction-memory—the moment either as it contains the memory that the preceding moment left to it, or as it contracts with the impending moment, the memory-to-be.[39] In expressing misgivings over the agglomeration of symphony interpretations over time, Thielemann and Schuller are Deleuzians insofar as they hear the memory embodied in recordings not as a selective form of memory, but as "the whole, integral past . . . *all* our past": a new Beethoven "Eroica" CD necessarily drags in its wake all those that preceded. But these two conductors have different ideas of how that "whole, integral past" should connect with the present: Thielemann seems Attali-esque in seeing the musical past as a culture of repetition rather than variance, and therefore wants a severing of past from present; Schuller suggests Deleuze in thinking that cumulative memory should lead to musical (compositional-stylistic) difference, an active expunging of similarity and repetition.

The aura surrounding a Brahms symphony—its cultural cachet—is commonly assumed to lie with its originality and uniqueness and self-sufficiency, and thus with its elusiveness. But as Michelle Henning reminds us, Walter Benjamin himself understood the aura specifically as memory—as the object rather than the function of recall, as "the associations which, at home in the *mémoire involontaire*, tend to cluster around the object of a perception."[40] Benjamin took the term "involuntary memory" from Proust, who used it in a celebrated passage of *À la recherche du temps perdu* to describe the buried childhood memories that return when he tastes a madeleine cake. Since the aura sits with memory, it might seem that the recording—as a form of memory both written and unwritten, clear and indistinct—is itself somehow "auratic" and therefore party to the absolute-music experience. The transcendent aspect lies with the *mémoire involontaire* itself, with that part of the music that is not to be grasped or consciously recalled but is embodied—in Proust's sense—in a physical thing that incites memory. Having tasted the madeleine offered by his mother, Proust loses himself in the mental and psychic search for its lost object, for "this memory, this old, dead moment which the magnetism of an identical moment has traveled so far to importune, to disturb, to raise up out of the very depths of my being."[41]

What does the recording represent, exactly? We listeners are like Proust, the recording like his madeleine: we audition a span of time that, residing in a physical entity, importunes and thereby rescues another that itself lay buried in the past. Is the one more important or higher than the other? This has long been the question hovering over recordings and their significance within an ontology of the musical work. As Roman Ingarden presents the choice, are we to have a recording of the performed composition or "the work itself"? Proust, music-lover and recordist before his time, is unable to make any such separation between past memory and the present's incitation to remember. Arriving at the key word of his interrogation of memory, he says the two are identical—the one a repetition of the other.

3. Schnabel's Rationalism, Gould's Pragmatism

To judge from their recordings, Artur Schnabel and Glenn Gould were extraordinarily different musicians. Their most obvious points of contrast concern keyboard address. Gould is commonly faulted for emphasizing pianism over service to the composer: "Gould had total command of his instrument," reads one review, "through which he projected his studiously considered and entirely personal view of Bach's musical firmament. One must, I think, be primarily interested in masterly pianism to want this . . . disc, one that shines more light on the performer than on the composer."[1] At the same time, Schnabel is criticized for attending more to abstract notions of musicality than to realities of musical execution: "Schnabel sounds as though he had not prepared this demanding sonata sufficiently," says one critique, "this brusquely insensitive performance [of Beethoven's "Hammerklavier"] . . . is an unqualified failure."[2]

Comparisons of Schnabel and Gould soon come to touch upon much deeper textual and historiographical differences: it becomes clear that Schnabel oriented himself, if I may borrow a literary duality developed by Umberto Eco, to the intention of the author, while Gould was concerned with the intention of the work. The second, Eco-Gouldian notion is not equivalent to the common textual-performative idea of *Werktreue*, which in the literal sense simply stipulates a faithfulness "to the work." According to Alfred Brendel, *Werktreue* is a vague notion that has served only to aggrandize, politicize, and confuse ideas of *Texttreue*, or fidelity "to the text."[3] But with his idea of the intention of the work, Eco didn't refer to the musical piece as an idealized and Platonistic entity, as a regulative principle, but rather as something that negotiates the readerly strategies by which it is to be approached and understood. The *intentio auctoris* involves old-fashioned exegesis of markings on paper that are read according to a reasonably hypothesized sense of the author, while the *intentio operis* floats free of any single author's intention. The first is a hermeneutic act, and the second is hypothesized on notions of consistency and genre.[4] This divides musical-interpretive authenticities between the past—what did the composer want when she wrote this?—and up-front immediacies of the present—what does the work want here and now? Schnabel and his fans subscribe to the Platonist belief that composer and work reign eternal as central, guiding principles, while Gould aficionados can become so mesmerized by his performance mechanism that the work seems contingent on the performance rather than the other way around. If Schnabel was very much the intentionalist—believing Beethoven the man specifically meant such-and-such with score indication X and had this-and-that in mind when he wrote indication Y—Gould was no deconstructionist but justified his performance decisions according to specific aspects of the work as he saw it.

Paul Myers, producer for many of Gould's later recordings, recalled an interview in which the pianist declared his own fidelity to the *intentio operis*: "I'm interested in Beethoven because I'm interested in the structure of composers," Gould confided in the dialogue remembered by Myers, "but if you want to hear Beethoven Sonatas played as they should be, listen to Schnabel, don't listen to me."[5] So Schnabel recordings and Gould recordings diverge not only in manner of interpretation, but even in their apparent purpose—the particular use they make of the recording's literal and unchanging repeatability. The Schnabel recording represents a kind of sounding *Urtext*, one painstaking attempt at the best real-world approximation of a work inhabiting what this pianist himself called "an irrational reality beyond and above natural occurrence."[6] In this sense, Schnabel took the unchanging aspect of the recording and—in spite of himself, for he professed to hating records—gave it high-cultural cachet. Gould was much less concerned with ideas of faithfulness and authenticity, rarely criticizing performances other than his own—and when he did, for instance when he complained about what he called Horowitz's showy "faked" octaves, the grounds for condemnation were pianistic rather than stylistic or textual.

As we pursue our comparison, the question arises: Can a Schnabel fan straddle this divide and listen with any empathy to Gould, or the Gould aficionado attend sympathetically to Schnabel? These pianists' performance aesthetics are distinct enough to suggest not only specific musical domains—which cannot be mutually exclusive, according to definitions of musical performance—but also distinct intellectual paradigms—which are discrete and absolute by nature. Edward Said suggested as much when he averred that Gould's "lifelong association with the great contrapuntal genius [Bach] establishes a unique and interestingly plastic aesthetic space essentially created by Gould himself as intellectual and virtuoso."[7] Said's unique analysis helps explain why the Gould phenomenon was not a matter of simple originality or what several unhappy critics heard as "Frankenstein" performances. According to Said, Gould pushed music performance into argumentative realms that had previously been reserved for verbal discourse. In that sense, the Gouldian "aesthetic space" proves to be "plastic" because it is neither specifically verbal nor specifically musical, but somewhere in-between. Gould's virtuosity, to quote Said, proved able "to draw the audience in by provocation, the dislocation of expectation, and the creation of new kinds of thinking based in large measure on his reading of Bach's music."[8]

This starts to make Gould sound like an intellectual, but Schnabel was the pianist so dubbed by critics of his time. The description was inspired by Schnabel's stylistic poise, rare for his time, and his fastidious approach to musical texts. Edward Sackville-West and Desmond Shawe-Taylor, writing in the 1955 *Record Guide,* discussed his famous Beethoven performances in such terms:

> When he made his first appearance in Great Britain in the late twenties,
> his performances were acclaimed for their authenticity of style, and
> their superb dynamic and rhythmic control; and since that time the
> playing of Beethoven's piano music has come increasingly to be associ-
> ated with the intellectual standards which Schnabel imposed.[9]

As a musician who came to maturity in central Europe around the time of World War I, Schnabel was caught up in some of the same aesthetic and intellectual currents as his contemporaries Schoenberg, Stravinsky, Bartók, and Ludwig Wittgenstein. Influential cultures of executive and compositional virtuosity—the Liszt school of pianism, Richard Strauss's orchestral mastery—had ended or were drawing to a close. Schnabel's was a time of theorizing antilogocentrists: emphasis shifted from speech and the mind to the inviolate written word. A *Zeitgeist* of what might loosely be called classically inclined modernism, as opposed to avant-gardism, reassigned authority from deeds to objects—from acts to texts, to use Richard Taruskin's duality.[10] One modus operandi of this reattribution involved discarding the emotional and aesthetic criteria that had defined so much late nineteenth-century thought, a changeover that can be seen in Wittgenstein's *Tractatus,* Stravinsky's *Pulcinella,* and Schnabel's readings of Beethoven and Schubert. All three substituted thing-ishness for person-ishness, concreteness for subjectivity.

RATIONALISM AND PRAGMATISM

Given the "intellectual" differences between Schnabel's and Gould's performances, as mechanically reproduced at least, the question even arises of whether one musician might somehow invalidate the other. Has Gould now come to eclipse Schnabel by reason of his tactile immediacy and sheer omnipresence through recordings and video, or has Schnabel perhaps precluded Gould by aligning more neatly with today's "authentic" performance aesthetics? Clearly, differentiating between Schnabel and Gould doesn't mean having to "decide" between structuralism and poststructuralism— that would be too rough a reduction of their dissimilarities. Schnabel's intellectualism offered, in contrast to Gould's "provocation" and "dislocation," a centralizing and stabilizing influence on Beethoven performance. He held a traditional, partisan attraction to the elitism of absolute music, as did Gould, but at the same time Schnabel developed a streamlined performance style that some have called modern. In contrast to Schnabel, Gould defined what might be called a Bach keyboard vernacular: a nonscholarly style that just about every young would-be Bach pianist, reeling from the sheer impact of his recordings, soon found coming irrepressibly to her fingers. Schnabel's Beethoven is considered definitive because his readings have come down as authoritative and essential. Gould's Bach, on the other hand, is almost invariably greeted with the "brilliant but not to be imitated" verdict. The great differences between Schnabel's and Gould's recordings help us explore the full impact of recordings and, more specifically, tease out Peter Kivy's statement that great performances have a work aspect: for Gould felt as liberated from the printed music as Schnabel felt obligated to it, and Gould's performances might therefore seem the more emancipatedly "work-like," the more "necessarily other."

Fortunately for anyone trying to "decide" between these two iconic pianists, philosophy has already traveled these paths. Specifically, the Schnabel-Gould divide is subsumed within a broader confrontation between rationalism and—to use the term formulated by C. S. Peirce and popularized by William James—pragmatism. Schnabel was less an intellectual, someone with an internal ability to know and understand, than he was a rationalist—a person who believes in a truth-out-there and emphasizes thought over intuition in getting closer to it.[11] The rationalist program has nothing to do with interpretation or understanding the self, and everything to do with understanding truth as the correct correspondence with an external reality. Gould, on the other hand, given his unwillingness to believe in objective and transcendent truths above and beyond daily practice, qualifies as a pragmatist in the philosophical lineage of James, F. C. S. Schiller, and Richard Rorty. If we were to change just a few words in James's articulation of his own pragmatist view in 1907, we would arrive at an eloquent defense of the Gould approach, one that would suggest the pianist's larger aesthetic view, the open-endedness of his interpretations, his disinterest in authenticist performance practice, and even the distinctive sound he made at the keyboard. In James's words, the pragmatist "turns away from abstraction and insufficiency, from verbal solutions, from bad *a priori* reasons, from fixed principles, closed systems, and pretended absolutes and origins. He turns towards concreteness and adequacy, towards facts, towards action and towards power."[12] A rationalist musician like Schnabel subscribes to a top-down ontology with the possibility of music that is "better than it can be performed," with works presenting "problems of interpretation" and requiring a "pure enough" interpretive approach.[13] By contrast, a Jamesian pragmatist like Gould deploys an instrumental or bottom-up theory of truth, where resolutions are not predicated upon preexisting belief or Platonic absolutes, but instantiated through everyday experience. Likewise, the rationalist Schnabel subscribed to an overarching manner of musical-aesthetic morality where instances are judged by a transcendental standard, while pragmatist Gouldian aesthetics were organized around a system of ethics and a method of evaluation that was performative and local.

More importantly for the purposes of the present book, pragmatist thought helps us understand recordings as full counterparts to the printed music—as vehicles of truth. Thinkers have long pondered the ontological role of printed musical texts. By contrast, the recording can seem a peripheral, commercialist, and aesthetically ungrounded thing. I choose to focus on James and Rorty, writers who help us talk about recordings not in traditional text-critical terms of musicality and authenticity, but as instrumentalist vehicles of truth—quick conduits to what James admiringly called "this real world of sweat and dirt."[14] They provide a tangible, immediate, and readily available solution to the increasing alienation of printed scores and classical-music performance from everyday life. Helpfully free in some ways and provocatively rigid in others, recordings can help musicians share in the ambition of Rorty, who, in Charles Guignon and David R. Hiley's paraphrase, proposed "reeducat[ing] ourselves so that we will see the aim of inquiry not as correctly representing reality, but as increasing human freedom and expanding our possibilities of interpretation and self-understanding."[15]

James was convinced that human thought is more usefully pointed to creative and tangible ends than, as per Platonist metaphysics and its copy theory of knowledge, to imitation. In James's view, the rationalist notion of truth involves copying as closely as possible a fixed reality that is "complete and ready-made from all eternity." James speaks instead of an instrumental theory of truth, where ideas become true only "in so far as they help us to get into satisfactory relations with other parts of our experience."[16] He ends the essay "Pragmatism's Conception of Truth" by showing his bewilderment over Platonist tautologies: "The notion of a reality calling on us to 'agree' with it, and that for no reasons, but simply because its claim is 'unconditional' or 'transcendent,' is one that I can make neither head nor tail of."

Just what the rationalist musician is "called on" to copy is not entirely clear. *Werktreu* culture demands an "authentic" realization from the interpreter—authenticity entailing correspondence with an authoritative model. ("Of undisputed origin, genuine" is one of the definitions the *Oxford English Dictionary* gives for the word *authentic*.) Implicit in this idea of authentic interpretation is the notion that a single, best rendition lies in wait, influencing all performance choices but never appearing in itself. In Lydia Goehr's description, music scholars increasingly reject such notions of authenticity insofar as they suggest the "positivistic, alienated and abstracted discourse of formalism." She says recent thinking has moved "[away] from principles and ideals of unity, sameness and singularity towards plurality, difference and diversity, from the ideal of correct (*werktreu*) or authentic interpretation towards that of multiple and diverse interpretations."[17] In his book on Schnabel's ideas of interpretation—a volume written largely with that pianist's cooperation—Konrad Wolff says it is not the composer's state of mind at the point of writing that the performer must try to recover, but the permanent and real aspect of the musical creation:

> The term 're-creation' has often given rise to the misunderstanding that the interpreter can attempt a revival of the personality of the composer at the moment of creation. The futility of such attitudes is generally acknowledged. We know that all interpretive re-creation depends on the awareness of the structure and objective character of a composition.[18]

A Jamesian pragmatist would categorically resist these invocations of futility, calling them defeatist. The circular thinking that James saw in idealist rationalism of his time would also seem to underlie ineffectual—and Schnabelian—notions of "music greater than it can be played." James saw rationalists just as musicians might see avatars of absolute music like Schnabel: as standing ready to "extract a quality from the muddy particulars of experience, and find it so pure when extracted that they contrast it with each and all its muddy instances as an opposite and higher nature."[19]

TEXTS AND PERFORMANCES

Schnabel developed something like an *Urtext* manner of objectivity, wiping the textual slate clean like a good Cartesian skeptic well before it was fashionable for musicians to do so. He hypothesized and valued faithfulness to the composer's intentions and was intent on separating a central performing text from interpretive convention. Here he could be contrasted with Ignacy Paderewski, who was quoted as saying that "a musical composition, printed or written, is, after all, a form, a mould; the performer infuses life into it."[20] Refusing to separate the musical work from its performance, Paderewski was the antithesis of an "intellectual" Platonist of Schnabelian stripe. David Dubal describes Schnabel as a kind of corrective, pointing out that "what he did was to wipe away a great deal of emotional and literary nonsense concerning Beethoven. He played without what he called 'inside dynamics,' which 'were used as substitutes for genuine expression.'"[21] Schnabel also stressed centrality and rationalism when he produced his print edition of the Beethoven sonatas, and his editing was quite novel at the time for involving conscientious consultation of Beethoven's manuscripts. In this respect, Alfred Brendel—who never granted authority to sources purely on account of "authenticity," either as a pianist or as a scholar—declared Schnabel almost too beholden to Beethoven's manuscripts and early editions. As Brendel would have it, Schnabel didn't quite wipe his textual slate clean enough:

> Bülow is the first editor to be credited with the attempt to retrace mentally Beethoven's compositional processes; unfortunately, his intellectual method was not equal to his purpose, and he did not pay sufficient attention to the original material. Schnabel, whom I respect as one of the great pianists of his time, was in many ways anti-Bülow: he removed the latter's autocratic 'corrections', but accepted a number of obvious mistakes in the original texts with a kind of pedantic deference.[22]

A rationalist editor must presume a rationalist composer, in some sense: when considering great music, Schnabel understood all compositional decisions to be logical ones. In his Beethoven sonatas edition Schnabel became especially concerned with the opening of the finale to op. 110, a passage he explained in extraordinary fashion:

> With the lavish abundance of interpretation-signs, seventeen in number (not counting the pedal-signs) all in sharp contrast one to the other,

and extending only over the few notes from the 'Recitativo' to the 'Adagio ma non troppo' Beethoven wished to impart an exhaustive, forcible description of his conception of unrestrained expression. Owing to the inequality of the bar-lengths, the complete freedom of plastic form becomes apparent as well.[23]

Here Schnabel imputes a single compositional resolution to a wide-ranging musical span, a passage so diverse as to exhibit "complete freedom of plastic form." And by imputing such creative uniformity to a passage of such "unrestrained expression," he enlists Beethoven into his own form of rationalism. Schnabel was a Platonist who understood scores and autographs to be compromised approximations of the noumenal work, but the closest phenomenal manifestation we have of the composer's thoughts. The performer's job, then, is to observe the phenomenal in light of the noumenal. Wolff explained this as follows:

The true meaning of notation is not apparent until the spirit of the work is apprehended, for what is written down is only comprehensible in connection with what cannot adequately be expressed by the symbols of musical notation. The interpreter has two tasks which are inseparable. He must absorb the score as it is, and he must try to perceive the composer's *idea* behind it.[24]

And Wolff continued: "Almost always the interpreter will make important discoveries in reading 'with renewed curiosity.' If at all possible the original text should be read. It is the surest way of stimulating the impulse to reproduction in the interpreter."[25] Accordingly, Schnabel undertook his analyses "from the inside out" as he described them. Wolff recalled an exchange he had with his teacher over the mediant key of the second subject of the "Waldstein" Sonata, first movement. The student gave historical-structural reasons for thinking the key unusual for a sonata movement in a major key, but Schnabel countered by saying the key counted as a surprise because of its acoustic distance from the tonic, and that no reference to theory or contrasting sonata examples was called for. In short, he saw nothing contextual in the use of the mediant.[26] There might be a parallel here with one of Schnabel's mannerisms as a pianist, namely his hurrying of sequenced and transitional passages, a kind of structural averting of the eyes. Wolff said Schnabel was averse to playing transitional sections "expressively rather than 'structurally,'" and spoke of his interest in "the relative expressive weight of the various sections of a composition"—with emphasis surely on the qualifier "relative" rather than on "expressive."[27] Might this have been Schnabel's way of responding to the nongeneric aspect of transitions, or perhaps—conversely?—to their relative lack of compositional ideas?

Schnabel's Beethoven stood out in the 1930s and 1940s for its sense of organicism. By several accounts, including that of his student William Glock, his performances of larger works were unusual in the way they integrated detail into a larger whole. According to Glock's recollection, Schnabel heard Beethoven's harmony in textural and polyphonic terms: "It was precisely his articulation of scale passages, accompaniments, and figurations of every kind, as well as his power of individualizing every strand of the texture, that helped to make his playing unique. It was not the melody that suffered, but the other elements which took on an unheard-of vitality."[28] Another way to describe this act of textural enlivening is to say that Schnabel heard Beethoven through the prisms of Bach and Schoenberg rather than, say, as a *terminus post quem* before Schubert and Wagner.

In contrast to Schnabel, Gould took no interest in autograph sources, and in his writing and criticism the composer's texts and even compositional style rarely got a look-in. When Bruno Monsaingeon asked him to comment on specific Mozart performances, Gould praised Robert Casadesus for "beauty," Eileen Joyce for "real devotion," and Alfred Brendel for "zest and affection."[29] This vague, even naïve method of description is typical of Gould. Why the disinterest in paper-borne authority, and indeed in any insinuation of the *intentio auctoris*, which would have helped him ground his observations and—as was his ambition, let it be recognized—come across as literate and intelligent? Because Gould saw a composition's textual aspect as a complicated and messy business, and as a true pragmatist thought the performer duty-bound to acknowledge that state of real-life disarray. Gould's two recordings of Mozart's Sonata in C, K. 330, are a case in point, the 1958 recording being almost five minutes longer than the 1970 version; several of the fugues from the *Well-Tempered Clavier* are even more extreme, with BWV 878, for example, clocking in at 4:17 in Gould's 1957 performance and at 1:46 in 1969. These disparities show an imaginative mind taking an example of common-practice music and teasing out its textual possibilities to extremes, risking incursions into the bizarre and the arbitrary, and testing the various prospects for coherent musical wholes that may or may not have anything to do with the composer's thinking. With these disparities, Gould typically emphasizes the variety of possibilities that could be subsumed within the work itself.

A direct comparison of Schnabel and Gould in a specific Beethoven passage will help contrast the former's music-textual centrism with the latter's belief in the innate decenteredness of texts. The movement in question is the brief *prestissimo* Scherzo of the Sonata in E Major, op. 109. Here Schnabel invests primary sources with such literal authority for purposes of his own 1935 printed edition that he dissuades the modern player from filling out the bass octaves in mm. 68–69 and m. 161 because Beethoven's manuscript does not.[30] By way of contrast, Gould blatantly ignores most of Beethoven's performance indications in his 1956 recording, most conspicuously flattening out contrasts of *fortissimo* and *piano* into an unvaried *mezzo forte*. Gould did this because he believed that a text, as opposed to the work that such a text might aim to communicate, was unavoidably trammeled by historical vicissitude—by the incidental trends, fashions, and exigencies of the era.[31] As if in compensation for such uncertainty, he tended while performing to simplify musical structures to the verge of primitiveness.[32] His slighting of the varied dynamics in Beethoven's Scherzo, his making the composer's rough places plain, does serve to simplify the movement's structure: he emphasizes the recapitulation by finally pulling back at the retransition (mm. 97–104), thereby making it unmistakably clear that the movement is in sonata form.

Given all these differences of view, how and why did Gould find common ground with Schnabel? The answer might sound facile, but I believe their aesthetic camaraderie boils down to a shared sense of wonder—the awe and promise of transcendence that the culture of absolute music inspired in both pianists. The two musicians perceived a significant excess, a too-much-ness, in the music at hand, but—and here we approach their differences of opinion regarding textuality and authorship—they had very different understandings of that excess and what the performer should "do" with it in performance. Both believed that this surplus minimized the significance of any one performer and any one performance, but Schnabel and Gould's aesthetic parallels stop there. As Schnabel understood it, the musical piece had an excess of quality or value; while it had a more quantitative excess in Gould's eye, meaning the piece of music is always more than can be contained in any single performance—it demands the multiplicity of different takes.

SCHNABEL'S BEETHOVEN AND THE INDIVIDUAL

Schnabel was the first to fix a cycle of the Beethoven sonatas and concertos for permanency on records, though at the time he did not think of the project as any kind of aural *Gesamtausgabe* but more tentatively called it an "experiment."[33] The records introduced this music to a wider public, though one can still wonder whether Schnabel catered to or helped invent a demographic of music-lovers with neither a piano nor access to "live" performance. By way of their popularity with both *Kenner* and *Liebhaber*, these records proved instrumental in reconciling what Charles Rosen calls "the double nature—private and public" of Beethoven's piano sonatas.[34] An eminent teacher with students of various nationalities, editor of a celebrated print volume of the Beethoven sonatas, and the first to inscribe all the sonatas as an aural text, Schnabel would seem to epitomize Rosen's professional. He was unsurpassed as a Beethoven authority in those very decades when recordings became a standard accoutrement of middle-class American and European homes.

In terms of performance, Rosen says recordings indirectly caused the Beethoven sonatas to become a culture of the few rather than the many: vinyl made them both accessible and abstruse. At the same time, as I mentioned in my discussion of readerly texts in chapter 1, recordings introduced these same works to new sets of listeners. Schnabel believed absolute music to be a music for the very few, and so found himself opposed in principle to this mass mediation. For him, absolute music originated as a private metaphysics:

> By the art of music I understand here the comparatively very young art of *absolute* music, and never applied or auxiliary music. This absolute, autonomous, independent music has developed into what is perhaps the most exclusive medium for the spiritual exaltation of the active individual in an intimate, private sphere of personal experience. Music is one of the performing arts with which, in exercise, one can be alone, entirely alone. Theatrical art is not comparable with music because the actor always reproduces or represents what is in everybody's orbit of experience. He uses language, the means of communication of all men. He can hardly act alone in his home. He needs an ensemble, and he is a part of visible human acts.[35]

Schnabel recognized a hierarchy of more- and less-faithful renditions of compositions, in a top-down aesthetic where loyalty to one originative intent—namely the composer's—necessarily limits the number of listeners the music can connect with. Performers are duty-bound to uphold the vision of the one in the interests of the few. Even the symphonic repertoire was a minority interest before recordings, its listenership "very limited, comprising at most a few thousand people."[36] Writing in 1945, when the American publicity for Toscanini was really taking off, Schnabel declared himself suspicious of the record industry's attempts to put absolute music into "mass circulation." By the same reasoning, Schnabel expressed reservations about performing some Beethoven piano works in public, but especially the Bach keyboard compositions that epitomized his idea of musical intimacy. Schnabel believed that absolute music's "spiritual exaltation of the active individual" required individuality in listening and reception as well as individuality in performance, even if that meant mediocre music-making. This is why he lamented the death of amateur performance at the hands of "mechanical reproduction" and its perpetuation of professional standards—or as he put it, "the machine's" furtherance of "the conception of the 'better' being the enemy of the 'good.'" Though a strong believer in the authority of the *Urtext,* he did not believe cultures of music-making to be hierarchical and authoritative in the same way: "When audiences are superior to performers it is by no means harmful to art. On the other hand the cry for 'first class' services only may contain some dangers for it."[37]

A Schnabel paradox is often commented upon: that he professed to despise recordings, especially for their musical fixity. "The variety [of absolute music] seems inexhaustible," Schnabel remarked. "It corresponds to the uncountable differences in combinations of qualities among men." Yet he appreciated the usefulness of recordings for the individual listener and committed examples of such musical variety to the invariable permanency of shellac. Perhaps he did this to demonstrate the very next sentence of his statement, that "what men have in common is much more than what separates them."[38] The inconsistency here between variety and fixity does not lie specifically with Schnabel but is innate to the recording process itself and to Schnabel's realization that it represented the way of the future. To use his own terms, recording exacerbates tension between the performer's love of "spontaneity, directness, multiformity" and the way the recording gives listeners "a choice of what to play. They can repeat it, and are in more intimate contact with it."[39] For logistical and commercial reasons, reaching the listening multitude in this way required textual fixity: there was no way, at least before the Internet and streaming audio, of transmitting different "live" performances of a composition to different homes. The result was, perhaps paradoxically, wider access to a narrower range of performance styles, as well as an increasingly institutionalized performance culture for art music, which has in turn encouraged a new uniformity of interpretation. Before the text could become accessible to the many, it needed to be closed off and stabilized.

Schnabel believed in individualism rather than collectivism and thought recording an instrument of the second. He liked to repeat Goethe's questions: "What is the universal? The single case! What is the particular? Millions of cases!"[40] The undisputed aspects of a culture, in other words, originated from the individual and not the consensus. According to Wolff, Schnabel "managed to preserve that full direct contact with music as a listener which distinguishes the music-lover, and liked to refer to himself as an 'amateur' in that sense."[41] We might even conclude that the only thing he liked about recording was its capacity to isolate and enhance what he called "intimate contact" with the moment. In Wolff's description, this translated for Schnabel into organizing melodies metrically, loosening monometric rhythms with discreet rubato, and drawing crescendos through off-beat notes.[42]

BEYOND ORIGINALITY

Said declared Gould an entirely new kind of musician: in describing the Canadian pianist he does away with the reductionist idea of composer-performer-listener rendition and invokes "a unique and plastic aesthetic space" where a performance becomes a multidirectional dynamic and an area that the listener inhabits rather than connects with. He denies the usual sequential notion—that the listener attends to Gould who has in his turn attended to Bach.[43] Said's notion of space allows for interpretive judgments that have no clear origin in the compositional text or its performance-practice accoutrements. (A more obviously text-based, non-Gouldian form of execution would count as "authentic" in Nelson Goodman's sense, in that it sets up acceptable concordances between the written music and the performance.)[44] In invoking "aesthetic space," Said might also have acknowledged that we don't hear Gould—or any other pianist—in a vacuum. In vernacular musical practice, the listener can't help but observe Gouldian characteristics that have nothing to do with Bach (the pianist's nervy bohemianism as emphasized in his album photos, for example, and films of him playing the piano much as one drives a car), and possibly also properties of Bach that have no connection with Gould (the composer's fervent Protestantism).

We're approaching a prime Gouldian paradox here, namely the coexistence of his compositional and textual agnosticisms with his almost puritanical belief in music's absolute-ness. Gould's "purity," "freedom," and "plasticity" hinge in large part upon his absolute-music ideals. Gould often went so far, whether intentionally or incidentally, as to marginalize the practical-historical aspects of Bach's dance suites by playing the pieces impractically fast or slow. But that is not to say he shared Schnabel's belief in "music that is better than it can be performed." To the contrary, Gould lived by the possibility that another version of the work, at least as viable as the one enshrined in a printed *Urtext,* might be out there for the playing. In this sense Gould approached the Schoenberg circle's philosophical precepts, by which a work could be enhanced through performance and transcription. Schoenberg's arrangement of a concerto grosso by Handel, a composer he berated, offered him a forum for explicitly "improving upon" the composition in his own Concerto for String Quartet and Orchestra (1933).

For Gould, performance offered a kind of platform that wouldn't perhaps enable him to improve a work in the Schoenbergian sense so much as give opportunities for testing new and sometimes impudent views of its musical structure. Gould became Walter Benjamin's surgeon-cameraman: hyperreal, invasive, deeply penetrating of the "web" that is reality, practitioner of a kind of montage.[45] In Bruno Monsaingeon's mini-documentary preceding the video production of the 1981 *Goldberg Variations,* we hear Gould refer to the tenth take of Variation 12—with a smile, but perhaps only half in jest—as having "sort of a Dixieland" feel. In Myers's view, Gould's process of "pulling apart" and "reconstructing" a composition permits the listener "a deeper and more complete understanding" of the music by offering an opportunity to reevaluate her "attitude" toward it and "to 'rethink' the entire piece, if necessary."[46] The pianist suggested such possibilities with his reaction to one take of the Italian Concerto last movement, as captured in the 1959 film spot *On the Record:* "Although it lacks some of the contrast, it is quite good. It certainly has a great deal of spirit, and it holds together." Here Gould invoked, yet again, structural abstractions obeisant to a hypothesized notion of the work.

In short, Gould's conceptions were work-driven rather than composer-driven. Here his verbal discussions of music are entirely at one with his performances. In the Beethoven Sonata op. 10, no. 2, Gould slowed his tempo for the first-movement recapitulation and unexpected appearance of the submediant key (D major instead of the tonic F major). In defending this decision, he professed interest in the *intentio operis* as opposed to the score instructions: "Now, nothing of that sort is indicated in the score," Gould confessed with regard to his tempo change, "but that kind of harmonic drama is something that no one can ignore, surely."[47] On those occasions where he did mention score details, he avoided the intentionalist sleight of hand of imputing musical events to the composer. Traditionally, discussions of absolute music avoid any division between what Umberto Eco calls the empirical author and the model author: the analysis becomes immanent within the act of composition whenever the analyst makes a statement like "Beethoven creates a sense of expectation by delaying arrival on the dominant." This is just the kind of metatheoretical semantics that Gould habitually avoids. Or he opts instead to attribute some kind of agency to the work itself, as when he anthropomorphizes musical structure in Beethoven's Sonata op. 109:

> The first movement of Op.109, a veritable précis of a sonata-allegro, omits the presentation of a subsidiary thematic group, substituting an arpeggio sequence of secondary dominants. This sequence, although entirely without motivic connection with the preceding sentence, relieves the harmonic anxiety of the precipitous opening bars by confirming the impression of a dominant modulation. However, when the corresponding moment in the recapitulation arrives, this episode is not satisfied with a literal transposition of itself, not content to assuage the ardor of the principal theme, but breaks away to build an artful variation upon itself, a variation which, for the first and only time in the movement, aspires beyond the diatonic circuit of E major.[48]

For someone who empowers music with the ability to compose itself, as it were, it is no surprise that Gould chose recorded takes not by their fidelity to the printed text, but by their success in piecing together a larger whole that should be understood in compositional rather than stylistic or historical terms. And he did indeed produce a lot of takes. Myers recalls of Gould's *Well-Tempered Clavier* sessions: "We recorded ten or even fifteen different versions of some of the preludes and fugues." Yet these takes were not attempts—executed with different degrees of success—to realize Platonic, idealized visions of Bach's compositions. "Nearly every one was perfect, note for note, yet still completely different," Myers adds. "It was an amazing experience to see how each version became something completely new in Gould's hands."[49] To judge from the video and audio footage that survives of Gould's recording sessions, he selected takes not by their fidelity to the printed music or freedom from mistakes, but according to what one might call an "imagined integrity" that they presented for the composition as a whole—according to the *intentio operis*. For instance, he defended his playing of the fifth variation of the first movement of Mozart's Sonata in A Major, K. 331, as an allegro rather than the specified adagio:

> As the penultimate variation, it's second in velocity only to the finale of the movement, according to the scheme I employed. . . . The idea behind that performance was that, since the first movement is a nocturne-cum-minuet rather than a slow movement, and since the package is rounded off by that curious bit of seragliolike exotica, one is dealing with an unusual structure, and virtually all of the sonata-allegro conventions can be set aside.[50]

In short, Gould differed from Schnabel in his pragmatist belief that there are no principles for the performer to follow beyond those that might be subsumed within a considered, sounding rendition of the musical work it-self. This is not the same kind of individual text-invention as a single player using performance experience or considerations of musicality to decide, for instance, that a phrase mark must be an editor's mistake or a metronome marking a misprint. Gould invoked a more "everyday" notion of the musi-cal text than the one implied by such common, authorship-induced perfor-mance decisions. He presumed written scores to be intrinsically underdeter-mined, and in departing therefrom seemed to ask if we don't use vague, circular notions of musicality and style to preclude the dirty details and puz-zling surprises of the true world of experience—in short, if we might not be constructing a false rationality for our own assurance. Gould's controversial account of Mozart's structure in K. 331, presented whimsically above in ac-cord with an acknowledged *intentio operis*, certainly doesn't fall into the hermeneuticist trap of believing that details of the text can tell us much be-yond what we are already intent on knowing before we see it.[51] In his liner note for his early—and, as already mentioned, scandalous—record of the last three Beethoven sonatas, Gould points out such textual deception at the same time that he disallows the music any a priori otherworldliness:

> These sonatas are a brief but an idyllic stopover in the itinerary of an intrepid voyageur. Perhaps they do not yield the apocalyptic disclo-sures that have been so graphically ascribed to them. Music is a mal-leable art, acquiescent and philosophically flexible, and it is no great task to mold it to one's want—but when, as in the works before us now, it transports us to a realm of such beatific felicity, it is the happier diversion not to try.[52]

A pragmatist, bottom-up theory of truth clearly emerges in this liner note, where Gould argues with prolix, echt-Gouldian iconoclasm that late Beethoven is marked by resignation and stoicism rather than transcendence. Gould's essay is the work of a twenty-four-year-old individualist, but there are points of resonance with his later writings, and the anti-idealism is too meticulous to be only a posture:

> Marliave's mention of "the intimate and contemplative appeal to the ear" illustrates an approach to these works based upon philosophical conjecture rather than musical analysis. Beethoven, according to this hypothesis, has spiritually soared beyond the earth's orbit and, being delivered of earthly dimension, reveals to us a vision of paradisiacal en-chantment. A more recent and more alarming view shows Beethoven not as an indomitable spirit which has o'erleapt the world but as a man bowed and broken by the tyrannous constraint of life on earth, yet

meeting all tribulation with a noble resignation to the inevitable. Thus Beethoven, mystic visionary, becomes Beethoven, realist, and these last works are shown as calcified, impersonal constructions of a soul impervious to the desires and torments of existence.[53]

We could summarize Gould's pragmatist approach by saying that he traded the Schnabelian rationalist's externalized, unilinear, and limitless goal of "doing it right" for a kind of informed marketplace of meaning.[54] He read the first movement of Mozart's K. 331 sonata as "a nocturne-cum-minuet" and the finale as a "curious bit of seragliolike exotica." These specific and monadic qualities, understood as factors of the work per se and not of the composer's intention, serve paradoxically to increase rather than limit interpretive possibilities: they allow the reader, as Gould says, to set aside "virtually all of the sonata-allegro conventions." These are amusical or even neologistic qualities, and they lead the Gould-style reader not to interpret in a specific way but to *exclude* certain mainstream ways of interpreting. In this way, Gould's reading methods were the perfect inverse of, say, Leonard Bernstein's. Paul Myers, who produced recordings for both musicians, put the comparison this way: "[Gould] was really quite modest. He regarded himself as eccentric in what he chose to play, and hoped people would enjoy it. Bernstein was more inclined to say: 'I'm playing it because God told me this is how it should be.'"[55] Another producer for Bernstein, John McClure, remembered the conductor reading scores in the same dogmatic terms:

> Then there were the almost cabalistic rationalizations that loomed invisibly behind even minor musical decisions but that would suddenly emerge if you questioned a tempo [Bernstein] had chosen. Not only would he be unreceptive to your input, but it would be made abundantly clear to you that Mother Nature, God, and the Baal Shem Tov had established this tempo long before the composer had even conceived the work, and that if he changed this tempo, you would have to change all the tempi in the work, and possibly the tempi of all of Western music since 1800.[56]

Gould and Bernstein read the musical text in completely different ways, then—the former using it as an avenue of possibility, and the latter as a means of prohibition. It's no surprise, therefore, that they eventually clashed so spectacularly: according to the pianist's biographers, it was Bernstein's infamous disclaimer before their confrontational 1962 Carnegie Hall performance of the Brahms D minor concerto that sealed Gould's decision to retire from concert-giving.[57]

GOULDIAN PRAGMATISM

If Schnabel's rationalism was oriented to the individual, to the composer and the single listener, Gould's diffusion of textual authority—away from the singularity of an *Urtext* and toward the multiplicity of recordings— suggests an eminently pragmatist strategy by reason of its electronic-media orientation. Pragmatist textual criticism from Rorty, Richard Poirier, and Jeffrey Stout has encouraged us to draw no distinction between interpreting texts and using texts. Tortuous hermeneutic systems are traded for living, sleeping, crying, fighting, bleeding, and emoting with, over, and on the text. Rorty gives us a thumbnail sketch of the particular labors involved: "Reading texts is a matter of reading them in the light of other texts, people, obsessions, bits of information, or what have you, *and then seeing what happens*."[58] In a banal sense, the recording simply gives the interpretive idea the wide circulation it needs in order to be heard "in the light of other texts, people, obsessions, bits of information, or what have you."

Rorty would have appreciated the usefulness of calling Gould a pragmatist. For one, it helps us understand why people have criticized Gould the way they have. This pianist faced the same kinds of criticisms aimed at pragmatist philosophy: accusations of naïveté, reductiveness, evasiveness, indulgence, revisionism, inconsistency, lack of principles—even incompetence.[59] Some of these allegations were automatic responses to a renegade presence, for Gould really fit no categories of style or thought. Modernist? Classicist? Neo-Romantic? New objectivist? Rearguard? His was an interstitial muse, everywhere yet nowhere. No doctrine, with no result foreseen. The Gould style is historically anomalous in any context or aesthetic, censured by one critic for being sensuous and condemned by another for severity. But if Gouldian pragmatism is not deconstruction, neither is it synonymous with relativism and pluralism. On the one hand, he—as James criticized the rationalists of his time—might well have accused *Urtext*-minded musicians of falling in love with their own self-enclosed and self-serving aesthetic and stylistic systems, of trying to suppress music's innate and indeed precious "malleability" under the cover of rational certainty.[60] He did replace the rationalist goal of correctly representing reality with the project of finding new interpretive possibilities, and this might sound and look on the surface like textual play à la Roland Barthes. But Gould shied away from talking about composers or their scores and hated any notion of competitive reading, which is what deconstruction often seems to be about.

Accusations of easy relativism have often been levied at pragmatism, the most frequent answer—Rorty's for example—being that the pragmatist thinker must, on the contrary, undertake the difficult task of creating her own internally consistent system of inquiry. (In music performance, we can take inquiry to mean the whole system of interpretation and sound production, since inquiry would refer to the performer's relationship with the printed text—a relationship that could connect to most, if not all, characteristics of a performance.) Comparisons between performers are especially odious, but by way of example one might contrast Gould's Bach with Ivo Pogorelich's Chopin. Neither performance style could exist without recordings: both assume a wide stylistic acquaintance on the part of the player as well as the listener. That's not to say that either is necessarily eclectic, only that they assume the possibility of escaping, bridging, or digressing from musical traditions in a way that would have mystified listeners a century ago. But does the implication of bricolage suggest the alienation of these recording-born fragments of performance style? Openness to being imitated is one sign of inner consistency: Gould's Bach is so imitable that many pianists copy it without knowing the origin of the clockwork rhythm and naked sound; it would be harder to tell Pogorelich's Chopin from Michelangeli's or Argerich's or to describe it in individualized, concrete terms. More important, the persistent question arises of how different aspects of a Pogorelich performance fit together or fail to do so, while it proves more difficult to imagine a selective hearing of Gould: there's no separating the Canadian pianist's dry tone from his metronomic rhythm, for example, or the broken chords from the in-your-face miking. Critics tend, by contrast, to point to the fracturedness of Pogorelich's interpretations: "The effect is of a series of fantastic vignettes," wrote Tim Parry of a Chopin disc, "each as magnificent as the last, but only loosely bound together—episodic rather than cumulative. The whole should be more than the sum of its parts, but here it is less."[61]

Pragmatism, best described as an antiphilosophy, became the antipode to logical positivism and to the analytic tradition of Bertrand Russell, Ludwig Wittgenstein, and—much more recently—Daniel Dennett. Pragmatists went beyond such questions of "schools" and became the gadflies of twentieth-century institutionalized philosophy, taking pleasure in their peripheral status: James leaned as much toward psychology as philosophy, conventionally defined, and took as his antecedents not only Darwin but the uncategorizable perspectivism of Nietzsche. As a kindred spirit, Gould practiced a kind of anti-pianism and indeed—as some might have it—an ad hoc musicality. He was the opposite of the Schnabelian professional: a peripheral musician in terms of schooling and location, he graduated from the Toronto Conservatory at fourteen but was linked neither with one of the European musical epicenters nor with an internationally known studio. Within Alberto Guerrero's piano class, Gould asserted his independence already as an adolescent. He burst onto the international scene as if from nowhere early in 1956, entering Columbia's studios at that very special time in the mid-1950s when the prosperous baby-boomer markets were beginning to open, there was an appetite for novelty, television was starting to revolutionize public sensibilities, and it seemed as if anything could happen in North American culture. Gould made his premiere recording of the Goldberg Variations, his first wide-distribution release, at Columbia's New York 30th Street studios in early June 1955. A similar musical vernacular had been discovered eleven months earlier in a Memphis recording studio by a nineteen-year-old truck driver named Elvis Presley.

It doesn't belittle Elvis's or Gould's skills and importance to say that in both cases mass mediation transformed into an international cultural yardstick what would have been little more than a musical-cultural quirk only a decade or two earlier. Elvis's sensational appropriation of African-American musicianship seems inevitable in hindsight, given the gradual falling-away of musical-aesthetic divisions between black and white Americans across the first half of the century. But the Gould singularity was all the more startling for developing from centuries-old absolute-music traditions that were still firmly entrenched in the 1950s. Like Elvis's early fans, Gould's admirers and detractors came up speechless when confronted by his anomalous, mix-and-match musicality. Israeli-Canadian pianist Peter Elyakim Taussig remembers his first Gould hearing: "Suddenly you get a sound that no one has ever heard before. . . . We've never [heard] anything like this. It's like, 'Where did this guy come from?'"[62] Támas Vásary called Gould "a genius who is able to see things in a work which I never thought existed."[63] And just what does such astonishment mean in musically specific terms? Just what is the effect of Gouldian instrumental truth in current, pragmatist, everyday terms? When I asked Sergey Schepkin, Gould enthusiast and devoted Bach pianist in his own right, if Gould's monadic "eccentricity" didn't prove intimidating, causing a closing-off rather than an opening-up of truth and meaning, he strongly disagreed. Schepkin also gave some examples of Gouldian truths, using his pianist's perspective to specify their "cash-value in experiential terms" as James might have described it:[64]

> With the exception of his *Well-Tempered Clavier,* I don't really consider Gould's oddities to be oddities: he didn't really want to shock, or *épater les bourgeois.* His was an incredibly pure and free spirit, and it's

that quality which was so incredible—something childlike, completely pure and unspoiled. And angelic. He can communicate with the infinite without any airs. [The work performed] becomes a game, and he has an awful lot of fun playing it. For me this purity, and the freedom of Gould's spirit, this is extremely stimulating. That's why it's not intimidating to listen to him, in fact it's liberating: I think he opens up the mind, the soul, the sound, and of course he can help develop one's technique immensely.[65]

As an added benefit, the perspective of classical pragmatist philosophers helps us understand certain key aspects of Gould's personality. Pragmatists argue against the goal of aligning one's self correctly with something nonhuman—whether that be the deity, as philosopher John Dewey described one contrary mind-set; ideas of the absolute as discussed by James; or *werktreu* conceptions of the musical composition. Pragmatist thinkers also resist discussing competing claims on truth and tend to look more to the future than to historicist justification. "First are those," writes Rorty in contrasting the nonpragmatist with the pragmatist outlook, "whose highest hopes are for union with something beyond the human—something which is the source of one's superego, and which has the authority to free one of guilt and shame. The second are those whose highest hopes are for a better human future, to be attained by more fraternal cooperation between human beings."[66] The second of Rorty's categories, the pragmatist view, fits Gould's hatred of music-making as a public blood sport, and his willingness to trade *werktreu* thinking for the listener's cooperative presence in the musical experience.

REIDENTIFYING GOULD

Nelson Goodman speaks of "reidentification" of a work. A work is open to reidentification if adherents recognize it as an aesthetic object, acknowledge this aspect on more than one occasion, and feel compelled to imitate it or model other aesthetic objects on it.[67] The idea might seem close to Kivy's "repeatability," but it is in fact rather different in that it is not an aspect of the original so much as a property that others impute to it.

Ironically enough, the young Gould "reidentified" Schnabel's 1942 recording of the Beethoven Fourth Concerto, taking it in verbatim and *en bloc* in a painstaking act of "Schnabel impersonation," as he called it. What the thirteen year old prepared was less an interpretation of Beethoven than a full-scale reproduction of Schnabel's take on Beethoven. Even beyond that, the replication became a kind of meta-reidentification. He took a pragmatist view of a rationalist performance, cheerfully attaching textual importance even to the mechanical details of its reproduction:

> I faithfully traced every inflective nuance of the Schnabelian rhetoric, surged dramatically ahead whenever he thought it wise—that is to say, in most reiteratively inclined and/or motivically awkward situations—and glided to a graceful cadential halt every four minutes and twenty-five seconds or so while the automatic changer went to work on the turntable.[68]

The anecdote would seem to epitomize Kivy's assertion about performances as artworks: that a sounding rendition can, like a compositional opus, create its own systems of signification and identity and thereby take on properties of endurance and repeatability. Especially since what Gould repeated was very much a mediated version of Schnabel's performance, the story would make it even clearer that Kivy's "repeatability" notion must presume some idea of mechanical reproduction. But Gould's story has more than a touch of the apocryphal to it and likely tells us more about his own aesthetic than his predecessor's. The most Gould's recollection can tell us about Schnabel's performance of Beethoven's Fourth Concerto is what James might call its "cash-value" for everyday reality. If the tale seems to exemplify Kivy's assertion about performances as artworks, it would also make it clear that Kivy should have applied his ideas to a theory of performance reception rather than to a theory of performance per se. Gould's "Schnabel moment" doesn't necessarily call for a model of the intrinsic endurance and repeatability of the German pianist's interpretation—such an idea seems strangely causal, and Schnabel would have been appalled at exerting so specific an influence. Rather, it places endurance and repeatability in the eye of the beholder.

A more plausible performance reidentification—a Gould moment, perhaps—occurred when Dmitry Sitkovetsky made his popular transcription of the Goldberg Variations (for string trio of violin, viola, and cello) under the influence of Gould's 1981 recording. Gould's CD became, as Sitkovetsky himself says, "the starting point and direct influence" for his transcription. "I tried as much as possible to follow his way of reading [the composition]," he acknowledges. "One reason I dedicated it to his memory is because it is a testament to his interpretation." Even the use of three instruments on three solo lines was predicated on Gould's clarified manner of performance: "I did the transcription in three parts because Gould gave each voice its own personality," Sitkovetsky explains. "It's so clearly defined, unlike any other pianist. So that clarity was the call for me to do something I'd never done: I'd never made a transcription before but from then on I've actually made quite a few."[69] While this edition cannot be considered a transcription of Gould's Bach, it does confer paper-and-ink, textual legitimacy on some of the Canadian pianist's more individual ornaments, tempos, and articulation choices. Specifically, we could say Sitkovetsky's edition simply put some aspects of an aural tradition into writing: it recognized and codified the textuality of a performance that had gained enormous aural currency by means of a best-selling record. Specifically, we could mention Gould's characteristic *portato* articulation in secondary voices as one of his reidentifiable traits, transcribed by Sitkovetsky as pizzicato rather than bowed notes in the viola line of Variation 19 (see ex. 2; Sitkovetsky acknowledges the influence of Gould's articulation here).

Another example of reidentifying Gould—of showing how one of his more famous recordings has been "used" as well as listened to—was provided in 2006 by Zenph Studios, which digitally extracted performance information from his 1955 *Goldberg Variations* recording and then rerecorded the "Gouldbergs" on a Yamaha Disklavier piano. Predictably, Zenph's attempt at precise reidentification has caused some critical handwringing. To Toronto music critic Colin Eatock, Zenph's efforts smack of cultural pathology: "The past should be respected and remembered, but a culture that becomes so completely fixated on the past and reproducing the past is, I think, in trouble."[70] Eatock, doubtless gripped by a certain implicit technophobia, sees qualitative difference in what are really quantitative degrees of reidentification. Sitkovetsky "reproduces" Gould only a bit more freely than Zenph, though a good deal less technologically, and no one accuses him of fixation. In any event, Sitkovetsky's arrangement and Zenph's "re-performance"—as they call it—are only the tip of the reidentification iceberg: pianists have found the Canadian pianist's Bach so enlivening and also so imposing that they have been engaging in Gouldian reidentification and nearly mechanical reproduction for half a century now. Indeed, Gould's art can seem designed to inspire fixation, or can seem to presume its own powers of fascination. Even those who claim independence from his example as a Bach performer sound like they are modeling the "revisionary ratios" discussed by Harold Bloom in *The Anxiety of Influence*.[71] Isn't the current fashion of playing Bach on the piano with little pedal, to cite only one instance, due largely to Gould's influence? "Nothing quite appeals like Gould's Bach," writes critic Philip Kennicott in a state of obvious conflictedness, simultaneously acknowledging and rejecting this pianist's widespread impact:

EXAMPLE 2.   J. S. Bach, Goldberg Variations, var. 19, arranged
for string trio by Dmitry Sitkovetsky. Courtesy Doblinger
Verlag; copyright 1985, all rights reserved.

Nothing has been quite the same since. . . . Gould was monumental,
but the world didn't stop rotating on its axis when Gould left Bach to
the next generation. To everyone who lives with Gould and only with
Gould, brooking no new insights or stylistic innovations in the performance of Bach on the piano, I want to ask: What's wrong? Don't you
like warmth? Don't you like tone colour? Don't you like your Bach to
dance with a real sense of joy?[72]

These efforts at reidentifying Gould—in which Kennicott hears a re-
pressive near monopoly—are based in recording and its possibility for exactitude and the widest possible, that is vernacular, dissemination. However, one could ask if print media hadn't encouraged similar kinds of
imitation cultures much earlier. There is a certain nineteenth-century quality to the Bach-Gould-Sitkovetsky edition, which recalls an era when less
distinct lines of division were drawn between work and performance than
now. Such fluid conceptions of performer-transformed works were in fact

the rule rather than the exception before the twentieth century. Jim Samson describes a culture of "work-as-performance" in nineteenth-century Europe, an aesthetic that was particularly vibrant outside central Austro-German traditions. "A polarity between the work-as-text and the work-as-performance became increasingly marked during the nineteenth century," Samson notes, "notably in the reception histories of early-nineteenth-century repertories: consider the reception of Beethoven, as against that of Rossini or Paganini."[73]

As Samson indicates, this culture of work-as-performance expanded because the early nineteenth century saw intertwined changes in concepts of composer, performer, work, and text. It continued on into such publications as Alfred Cortot's famous "instructive edition" (*édition de travail*) of Chopin's works, where that master pedagogue interspersed the compositions with preparatory exercises of his own design. Some of these preparatory exercises and interpretive advisements are so lengthy as to become lessons covering more pages than the pieces they apply to. It is doubtful that Cortot's alternate fingerings do much to subjectify Chopin's music. But there's no such neutrality to advice like the following for the Étude in C-sharp Minor, op. 25, no. 7, where Cortot uses the high Romantic device of musical explanation through programmatic exegesis:

> A truly musical interpretation of this admirable piece demands that,
> above the poignant lament of the bass, fraught with passion and regret,
> devoured—it would seem—by a dramatic and unconsolable love,
> should soar aloft, far away but penetrating and perfectly distinct, the
> wounded treble, sad and tender of the right hand.

Cortot states in his foreword that he has assembled a text "unimpaired by doubtful traditions and misprints which have been too often superstitiously respected in previous editions." Note, however, that he describes this not as an original rendering but as "a final text"; any lingering suspicion that it might represent some kind of *Urtext* disappears when one finds him writing, with respect to op. 25, no. 7, that "the rare pedal-marks indicated by Chopin are obviously unsufficient for an expressive rendering of this Study. We advise using the pedal almost constantly."[74] Do all these additions reidentify and perpetuate Cortot in the same sort of way that Sitkovetsky and Zenph reidentified Gould? Given Cortot's wealth of evocative anthropomorphisms, quotations about composers and works, metronome and pedal markings, and even precise timings for each piece, these *éditions de travail* do indeed codify a specific way of playing Chopin. The question then becomes, Do they show printed editions functioning more "pragmatistically" than recordings? The answer must be no: the recording, more than notes printed on the page, is the ideal "cash-value" medium for "reading . . . and then seeing what happens," as Rorty puts it.

THE PRAGMATIST RECORDING

By definition, recordings resound with "the noise of facts"—to borrow James's admiring description of Herbert Spencer's writing.[75] Recordings thereby qualify as the pragmatist medium par excellence: it is redundant to speak of a *Gebrauchsaufnahme,* or a "utilitarian recording," because the recording is as much an object as a text, something that elicits use-as-reading and reading-as-use. The recording makes its way into film and TV soundtracks, advertisements, phone ringtones, Web sites, Facebook postings, shopping mall PA systems, and electronic games.[76] In the process, its very factuality becomes discursive: the online critic might hate Gould's 1981 *Goldberg Variations* for musicological-stylistic reasons, the lawyer down the street might love it for its sheer energy, and your boyfriend could be pointedly indifferent. A weird urban myth about synchronisms between it and the *Wizard of Oz* movie might surface in Poughkeepsie. No final or ultimate reading would emerge from any of this, contrary to the Platonist's desires and expectations: each evaluation "simply gives you one more context in which you can place the text," as Rorty describes the process, "one more grid you can place on top of it or one more paradigm to which to juxtapose it."[77]

The recording has pragmatic potential because, unlike the edited score, it is does not aim to preclude other versions; or if it ends up doing so, does so only by force of its example. It is, in fact, exactly this kind of open·and democratic validity of meaning that defines pragmatist "living with" the text: the pragmatist music-lover would seem to have a large CD collection and no critical editions or *éditions de travail* on her shelves. It is of course the recording that supplies a picture of a playing style: it is like the photograph of a face, as opposed to a verbal description of the same. A pianist playing Chopin with careful attention to Cortot's directions will always sound less like Cortot than Cortot himself. Truth be told, though, the Zenph-ed Gould sometimes sounds less like that pianist than someone painstakingly playing the Goldberg Variations according to Gould's written directions, reminding us that digital information is information, after all, and in the wrong context sounds more like verbal description than intuitive musicality.

There is a culture where musical interpretations are discussed according to rationalist merits of musicality, authenticity, and so forth and a culture where such interpretations are left to compete in a marketplace, with the most meaningful performances—whatever that might mean in broader terms—rising to top currency. The first describes the world before recordings, at a time before one could speak of competing interpretations. In early nineteenth-century Paris, say—a hotbed of rival pianism—people spoke more of competing performance styles than of competing performances per se. Performance competition did occur in the form of the concert face-offs between, say, Liszt and fellow virtuoso Sigismund Thalberg. But those were rare events, nothing like the current scenario where a listener can almost instantaneously compare sixteen different renderings of the second theme in the first movement of the "New World" Symphony, including two or three different performances by the same conductor and orchestra. An online streaming resource like the Naxos Music Library counts as the ultimate musical-pragmatist tool in that it positively invites such cash-value comparisons. The pragmatist finds none of the marketplace interpretations off-limits, though some will inevitably be discarded as boring, confusing, clumsy, weird, or otherwise nonuseful. Meaning comes about not through deciphering of coded textual significance, but through a quasi-Darwinian process where interpretations vie for public use and attention; the pragmatist looks not for scriptural exegesis, but for a joy ride.[78]

Instead of a market, Rorty invokes another kind of forum: conversation. He says the only constraints on inquiry are conversational—or more specifically, "those retail constraints provided by the remarks of our fellow-inquirers."[79] Because it has come to involve instantly accessible, permanent, and indeed tangible performances, the aesthetics of musical interpretation has through recordings become a pragmatist phenomenon, pragmatist in the sense that it now involves, as Rorty describes pragmatist inquiry in general, "deliberation concerning the relative attractions of various concrete alternatives."[80] As a pragmatist, Rorty didn't oppose rationality per se. What he railed against was the notion of a rule-driven and rule-constrained rationality, the idea that reason can be separated from desire. To the pragmatist, any campaigns in the name of truth and knowledge are necessarily messy and endless. Rorty would have approved of Glenn Gould's comparison of Mozart performances, as described above, according to open-ended and desirous—as opposed to rationalist—criteria like beauty, affection, and zest. Gould's status as musical pragmatist—post-Platonic, post-Kantian—is nowhere more obvious than here. Others might wish to declare one Mozart interpretation more viable than another based on tempo, lack of ornamentation, or other such absolute criteria. For example, a rationalist might hear Daniel Barenboim's finale for the Mozart Piano Concerto in C Major, K. 467, and entirely rule it out for being impossibly slow, no matter what other virtues it might have.

Following Rorty, we might ask, Exactly what does it mean to use a musical text? We can say that using a text is not interpreting one, an activity that in itself proves eminently useless. Citing E. D. Hirsch's differentiation between textual meaning and significance, Rorty equates use with the second category, which he calls a process of "relating the text to something else" as opposed to "getting inside the text itself."[81] So how exactly have Gould's recordings proved relate-able to other things? Usefulness largely follows upon pervasiveness, in the pragmatist's view. Yes, plenty of useless things can exist, provided—as a Darwinian might say—there are no selective pressures acting against them. But an inverse correlative nonetheless holds true: that something is unlikely to prove useful in any real sense if it is rare or of low-visibility. Gould enjoyed an entirely different order of sales than Schnabel, and his best-seller status shows that a large public—not only a "deep" listenership but also a wide demographic—has found at least some Gould performances to be relevant. Not only have his recordings been reidentified by Sitkovetsky and Zenph Studios; they have been used as movie soundtracks (including Gould's own partly improvised soundtrack for the 1972 film version of Kurt Vonnegut's *Slaughterhouse Five*), sent into interstellar space on the Voyager spacecraft, and even provided the rationale for an art film about Gould himself (François Girard's *Thirty-Two Short Films about Glenn Gould*, 1993).

In broader terms, Rorty's form of pragmatism could be described as a vernacular practice, insofar as both pragmatism and vernacularism oppose orthodoxy, academic approaches, and preordained principles. Gould had spectacular success in founding just such a vernacular practice in Bach. He proved useful in that he allowed himself new forms of Bachian meaning, redefinitions that are populist rather than institutional. His recordings appeal to listeners in inverse proportion to their number of presuppositions. As Said realized, Gould is difficult to summarize within standard musical-aesthetic terminology. This puts one in mind of James's essay "What Pragmatism Means," where that author tells us how the pragmatist resists "some illuminating or power-bringing word or name," and gives as examples absolute terms—like "God," "Matter," "Reason," or "The Absolute"—that tend to shut down reasoning and argument. James exhorts us instead to "bring out of each word its practical cash-value, set it at work within the stream of [our] experience." As he points out, "[Pragmatism] appears less as a solution, then, than as a program for more work, and more particularly as an indication of the ways in which existing realities may be *changed*."[82] What this means in musical terms is that new and sometimes unusual interpretive ideas can permanently change our understanding of the compositions themselves, but the performance in question then takes on heuristic value, and the interpretive project begins rather than ends at that moment. While the printed scholarly edition and the rationalist performance retain some kind of external standard to guide them—or at least pretend to do so—the pragmatist recording runs the danger of deflecting performance traditions or, as a rationalist like Alfred Brendel might put it, subjecting the piece to interpretive "eccentricity."

A pragmatist would say that meaning is defined by practice, not by precept. If Gould hated competition, musical and otherwise, he still showed an unusual willingness to compete with himself: neither of Gould's two recordings of Bach's BWV 878 fugue has yet trounced the other nor were they meant to, though a Rortian might find the fast, earlier version too slippery and idiosyncratic to be especially "useful." The pragmatist recording of an "absolute"-musical work thereby introduces a kind of textual tension: Gould's recordings have gained an audience large enough and created enough textual noise of their own to threaten the referential nature of the composer's own texts. Cornelis de Waal summarizes C. S. Peirce on this point of renegade interpretation:

> The ultimate belief, or as Peirce also phrases it, the final opinion, is a permanently settled belief. The phrase 'permanently settled belief' refers in this context to a belief that no future inquiry can undermine; that is, no future inquiry can show it to be false or cast any doubt on it. The locution 'by an indefinite community of inquirers' is further added to filter out any distorting elements that may result from the peculiarities which individual inquirers may bring with them, such as a propensity for conspiracy theories, a general distrust of mathematics, or a desire to interpret everything as part of the overall plan of an all-powerful and benevolent God.[83]

Such peculiarities do exist in the world of art music performance: Lazar Berman recorded a *Gaspard de la nuit* with even sextuplets at the opening of "Ondine," Otto Klemperer released a Mahler Seventh Symphony that lasted over 100 minutes while something closer to 78 is the norm, and Leopold Stokowski gave Tchaikovsky's *Romeo and Juliet* a quiet coda of his own devising. These digressions haven't gained many adherents, if any, and haven't changed ideas of interpretation, in part because they don't jibe with the composer's texts, but also because such anomalies shut these performances out of wider interpretive discourse: they disallow "an indefinite community of inquirers" from integrating them into a comparative grid of louder, quieter, slower, faster, more monometric, more flexible, and so on.

RECORDING AND AUTHORITY

The pragmatist view allows us to understand how the authority of the printed text has for the most part yielded to the influence of the recording, and yet how a world held under the sway of the recording has not become an unprincipled slag heap of arbitrary meanings. In such a world, pragmatist thinking shows how fears over the possibility of "distorting peculiarities" from "individual inquirers" are unfounded.

Both Schnabel and Gould saw records as occasioning a "birth of the reader," though to different effect. For both, absolute music represented the highest form of the art not by reason of any universality, by being everything to everyone, but because it was particularly meaningful to the individual creator and listener. In Schnabel's view, absolute music represented "the emancipation, individualization, specialization of art." He noted that "such a transmutation into absolute music occurs when a gifted person, charged by the forces of individualism and dualism, can no longer sympathize sincerely with the established institutions for the satisfaction of spiritual desires."[84] For Schnabel, who looked ahead with fear to "the day . . . when everything will be for everybody," recording represented just one aspect of a general "attempt to move an 'Ivory Tower' to a widening market." In his view, then, the advent of the reader did indeed necessitate—as Barthes would later describe it—the death of the author, or perhaps the death of the work in the poietic sense, since the fate of compositions worried Schnabel more than the future of composers.[85]

Recordings, in all their latter-day proliferation, have helped erode the Western humanist faith in originality. At the same time, there can be little doubt that Gould's streamlined version of the Scherzo to Beethoven's op. 109, as described above—a reading he might be the first to admit would have no place in a nonelectronic, unmediated world—is deeply original in that it downplays Beethoven's own originality. Given Gould's reasoning, the reading no doubt intends to be faithful to Beethoven's work by being unfaithful to its letter. The imperfect textual representation of Beethoven's music is expanded to include all manuscript sources, even the composer's intentions that those sources are supposed to represent. And the work, the entity to which the interpreter remains faithful, is found to lie deeper—or higher or further out—than anyone had suspected.

When Gould spoke of technology as a moral force in the modern world, he clarified by saying that it had a streamlining effect, enabling humans to cast aside some of their more mundane foibles: "I believe in 'the intrusion' of technology because, essentially, that intrusion imposes upon art a notion of morality which transcends the idea of art itself."[86] Among these human weaknesses Gould counted virtuosity and competition, two characteristics that his streamlined reading of Beethoven's Scherzo deemphasizes: gone are the abrupt dynamic juxtapositions, soft-pedaled are the sudden cadential eruptions. As embodied on a recording, these Gouldian decisions—he recognized no distinction between the musical-interpretive and the technological—no doubt count among his examples of technology as "charitable enterprise": a means "to remove people from the very things—the self-conscious things, the competitive things—that are detrimental to society."[87]

There's no indication that Gould ever read James or any other pragmatist philosopher that I mention. According to his friend Peter Ostwald, however, in the late 1950s he was obsessed with George Santayana—specifically with Santayana's novel *The Last Puritan*, which Gould talked about "incessantly." Santayana had specific points of disagreement with James but was his student for a time and sympathized significantly with Jamesian radical empiricism. According to H. T. Kirby-Smith, these two thinkers shared the belief that

> we have no right to take for granted that anything exists outside our
> own consciousness. This is the undeniable argument of the transcenden-
> tal philosopher; this is the inevitable 'solipsism of the present moment,'
> as Santayana called it. James would have us proceed by willing into exis-
> tence what we need; he would have us make our ideas into realities.[88]

Of Gould's particular fixation with the Santayana book, Ostwald recalled that it "reflected much of the spirit of his own aestheticism and Glenn almost seemed to be thinking of himself as 'the last puritan.'"[89] The novel offers a rare glimpse into Gould's ethical sense, helping us understand how his almost Emersonian individualism might or might not have related to his belief in technology and strong feeling for morality. The "last puritan" with whom Gould empathized so strongly was Santayana's protagonist, Oliver Alden, a pure-minded, East Coast man who bears the lifelong weight of an inborn idealism and sense of duty. In the prologue to his novel, Santayana describes Oliver as having no "timidity or fanaticism or calculated hardness." He experienced "hatred of all shams, scorn of all mummeries, a bitter merciless pleasure in the hard facts. And that passion for reality was beautiful in him."[90] Yet Oliver is tragically destroyed by his own idealism, misplaced in a world offering no hope of transcendence. He falls victim to an irreparable division between nature and the spirit: in Irving Singer's description, this protagonist lives out Santayana's own conviction "that tragedy arises from any division within a person's being that prevents him from living in accordance with his own vocation."[91]

If this serves as a good description of Glenn Gould—and it does fit his poignant loneliness and indeed otherworldliness—then it is tempting to think of recording as his very own instrumental method of truth, an enterprise he considered both charitable and profoundly liberating of his own pained individuality. It was a practice that Gould remade in his own image and that became his lifelong method of forestalling disillusionment by "making ideas into realities." In a way that no one had ever really imagined, let alone attempted, he made it his own personal way of transforming internal dialogues into the very grandest "noise of facts."

was made, they extended the span of known musical sounds—previously set by an Edison cylinder of Handel recorded in 1888—by 28 years.[1] With realization of this murky but still quite audible recording, we know how one French woman sang midway through Napoleon III's reign, seven months before the election of Abraham Lincoln, and seventeen years before Edison patented his phonograph. Digital technology, or more specifically the numerical algorithm that has brought about centralized audio storage and retrieval, has performed the miracle of extending aural history itself.

WATER MUSIC

Music will become like water: fluid and without borders, omnipresent, filling all voids, necessary but communal, owned by no one but shared by everyone, a service rather than a product, and for all intents and purposes accessible at no cost. This was David Bowie's prediction for a not-too-distant future of information sharing and digital connectedness, a prophecy developed by David Kusek and Gerd Leonhard in *The Future of Music: Manifesto for the Digital Music Revolution*.[2] It is an attractive vision, but will the litigious bloodlust of the RIAA (Recording Industry Association of America) be deflected so easily? Examples of art music are only infrequently attended by issues of litigation, cash flow, and cornered markets, and so the question arises of just how "classical" musicianship might fit into these digital aquaria of the future. Or will the digital flood completely sweep away absolute-music aesthetics, making Beethoven just another iTunes entry between the Beastie Boys and Bix Beiderbecke? I think the answer must be no. Elsewhere in this book, I describe some of the ways that recording culture has actually served to uphold absolute-music aesthetics into the twenty-first century. I have also offered examples of the influence that absolute music exercises on the reception of pop, but especially on the tellingly named genre of classic rock. Clearly, we will continue to see the kinds of cultural cachet traditionally associated with symphonies and sonatas, and these will continue well into "the digital music revolution."

But that says nothing specifically about the place of instrumental art music in a digital world—a more difficult question. Absolute music in Western classical traditions might seem resolutely "waterproof" in the face of rising digital tides, since it is defined by authorship, genre, and construction—identified according to principles of exclusion rather than inclusion.

Absolute music has long been held up as music oriented to content and nothing else, as "music for music's sake," to quote the common art music definition. Heinrich Schenker, a primary author of the absolute-music aesthetic, emphasized musical content enough to call sound superfluous, or even foreign, to the composition:

> Basically, a composition does not require a performance in order to exist. Just as an imagined sound appears real in the mind, the reading of a score is sufficient to prove the existence of the composition. The mechanical realization of the work of art can thus be considered superfluous. Once a performance does take place, one must realize that thereby new elements are added to a complete work of art: the nature of the instrument that is being played; properties of the hall, the room, the audience; the mood of the performer, technique, et cetera. Now if the composition is to be inviolate, kept as it was prior to the performance, it must not be compromised by these elements (which after all are entirely foreign to it).[3]

Schenker understands the composition, which he describes as an authored and inviolate entity, to be a form of intellectual property. Yes, he was reacting to extreme interpretive liberties that would never pass muster today. Arthur Rubinstein, for example, recalled some early public performances where he would—with no very great concern—finish playing a different composition than he began. An extreme case of violating authorship! But acknowledging the context for Schenker's anger can't change the importance his ideas of compositional authorship have had for the bold and ambitious expansion of music copyright at the end of the twentieth century. And this is perhaps absolute music's most lasting legacy for the present age—the concept of the inviolable work that must be owned and respected. Intellectual property is the logical outcome, the ideal realization, of absolute-music aesthetics. Schenker's stressing of the composition's made-ness over its performability turns musical works into, if we can ignore some of the commercial overtones of the word, products—or, as Nicholas Cook describes musical works in late capitalism, "autonomous musical texts, intellectual properties that are to be delivered from composer to performer."[4] Contrast this with the view of Kusek and Leonhard, who insist again and again that musicians won't fully enter the "digital era" until they jettison old-fashioned notions of music as intellectual content and as a manufactured good:

> Let's define a product as something that is made or created by a person or machine, especially something that is offered for sale. Is that what music is all about? Is music a product? Is it only something that you

can "make a substantial profit on?" We think not. Music is a combination of entertainment, communication, and passion, an ephemeral occurrence, something intangible, and something that is experienced in everyday life. Music today is proliferating and expanding at an unprecedented rate.[5]

Kusek and Leonhard claim that digital platforms are transforming our ideas of what it means to own such products. They predict that digital connectivity will change material access and ownership—in both its lowercase-*o* and uppercase-*o* senses—and will thus continue to push a shift of emphasis from musical product to musical experience. "The increasing multitude of choices," they forecast, "will outpace the single-minded purveyors of intellectual property that have sold us 'culture' as a solid good for the past one hundred years." While Kusek and Leonhard foresee a future of informational liquidity, John Seely Brown and Paul Duguid speak of perennial fixity and deny any predictions that fluidity will triumph over fixity, or vice versa. Authorship stands more of a chance in Brown and Duguid's picture than it does in Kusek and Leonhard's, as does classical music, a form oriented to the cultural fixities of composers and works. Brown and Duguid speak of "information fetishism" and aim to expose utopianist predictions that the information age will eliminate the basic fixities of printing on paper, stabilized knowledge, institutional organization, and human consolidations of power. As they point out, paper is still very much with us, even though its demise has been prophesied again and again for at least half a century. Paper represents a perennial and perhaps even necessary mode of fixity, in part because its particular manner of fixity doesn't preclude portability. They conclude that "paper and ink established a useful balance—light enough to be portable, but fixed enough to be immutable." In its turn and in its own rather different way, computer information straddles fixity and fluidity without eliminating one or the other: "The digital world, too, pulls against immutability, while simultaneously adding a layer of confusion."[6]

Brown and Duguid would be hard-pressed to find comparable agents of permanence and authorial fixity in music's case, since the number of music listeners has long since exceeded the number of people who read printed music. With people spending more and more time with music, but fewer and fewer actively engaging with it in printed form, listening is relying on paper less and less. In this sense, literature and music are enacting different destinies in the information age, since the Kindle is unlikely to triumph over paper the way the Walkman and iPod have.[7] And then there is the question, neglected by Brown and Duguid, of how fixity grows ever more expensive, while fluidity has become synonymous with economy.

The question arises, Which cultural forms are likely to hold onto their "fixed" manifestations in this ever-greater push toward a bigger and faster return on money and smaller footprints of storage space? Tolstoy novels and art books about Fabergé eggs will probably remain household items in fixed printed form; Tchaikovsky symphonies, not likely. Within twenty years we will probably be able to say the same thing of library collections.

Paper, and cultural fixity more generally, are clearly emblematic of larger cultural priorities. Classical instrumental music—increasingly "unfixed" in its currency—has gone from being a definitive cultural form, serving as a point of reference for musical styles across the spectrum even when it didn't get very wide currency, to a style among the others. It has gone from being capital-*m* music to another cultural form (*just* another cultural form?), and an exponential broadening of the record market is largely responsible for these breakdowns of hierarchy. Cultural cachet ultimately sits with a specific coordination between access and perceived ownership. Here increases in broadband technology and the high-speed duplication of "perfect" digital files will continue to influence ideas of meaning and cultural worth. Kusek and Leonhard are convinced that "access and ownership will ultimately converge," by which they mean possession of music in the digital era will both hinge upon and entail access to that music, that access will *replace* ownership in a sense.[8] If a Beethoven symphony or a Beck song can be called up at any time, say, through streaming audio, there's no need to own it on a CD or as a computer file. Kusek and Leonhard even refer to the physical CD as simply a means of " 'tagging' the music that we like in order to be able to listen to it later."[9]

A technological idealist of Kusekian and Leonhardian stripe would say digital techniques of recording and distribution have already had a democratizing effect. In book publishing, video, librarianship, and of course music—indeed, in most aspects of contemporary living—digital platforms and the Internet have certainly antagonized corporate copyright-holders and given the pink slip to many commercial administrators and arbiters of cultural meaning. Only twenty years ago, a music-lover had to connect directly and indirectly with multiple mediators simply to gain access to music, and the musician herself had to do much the same to connect with listeners. The list of these middlemen could go on for pages: record company executives, musicologists or music appreciation instructors, A & R people, agents, managers, copyright lawyers, musicians union officials, record store buyers (those deciding which music titles a brick-and-mortar retailer would stock), radio program directors, concert promoters, accountants, piano tuners, all of them and many others had various degrees of influence on what music was heard when, how, and by whom. In "the digital age," the music-lover is likely to connect more directly with the musician, without the dozens of layers of subjectivity and moneymaking that once came between them. Cultural intermediaries will regroup rather than disappear, however. Potential listeners still need help finding the music; advertising will continue to play a large role to that end, as will artist management and the more influential online search engines.

Kusek and Leonhard, inspired by Lawrence Lessig's arguments against current interpretations of copyright law, say that watchdogs like the RIAA deal in obsolete and oligarchical notions of intellectual property. Again, they accuse the record industry of being hooked on the idea of selling content, and content in the material form of physical objects at that, when it actually sells services. And this obsession is one reason for the big record labels' zero-tolerance policy toward file sharing, a policy that Kusek and Leonhard say is out of step with the statistical nature of ownership that software makers have already more or less accepted. The software industry is living reasonably well with the fact that some 57 percent of its users don't pay for the programs they use, a proportion that could well be a fact of life for all electronic merchandise. As a type of product-obsessed corporate honcho *avant la lettre*, Schenker would have been unhappy with such figures. He certainly preached zero tolerance when it came to the prospect of the composer surrendering control of any kind over her work, and disallowed the performer any kind of creative contribution, saying "each work of art has only *one* true rendition." Schenker maintained this one-way philosophy to the extent that he saw the composer, be she slogger or virtuoso, as necessarily the best interpreter of her own music:

> It is the great masters of composition who must be considered the best performers! We may be sure that Chopin's renditions were better than Tausig's, and Beethoven's than Bülow's. . . . Because what ought to be known in order to perform a sonata by Beethoven is not known, the musical world found it easy to assign a role to reproduction in music that is in appalling contrast to its real origins.[10]

Kusek and Leonhard are diametrically opposed to a Schenkerian world of composer domination and ownership, but they present us with an equally remarkable scenario: a world of re-creation without creation. They look forward to a universalist musical current with neither boundaries nor barriers, one involving no division between composing and interpreting. All creativity and effort becomes performative within their digital river. They say nothing about originality, perhaps because it is part and parcel of the RIAA's opus-oriented mind-set: in the future they foresee, bricolage and influence will replace composition and creation. This is not a world without novelty, greatness, or "progress," but such things are seen as incremental processes and not the grand, author-driven narrative of revolutions and paradigm shifts:

> After all, neither culture nor art are made in a vacuum. Rather, they are always a blend of many influences, some of which are utterly new, some very ancient. Should we not be able to take the pieces we need, give credit where it's due, and move on to creating something new? Where will a system lead that restricts a pyramid of innovation, inch by inch, year after year?[11]

"Access and ownership will ultimately converge." The thought has many ramifications and can be interpreted to mean that the person who provides access to the work—namely the performer—is becoming the de facto composer of that work. This means, in effect, that when Itzhak Perlman is heard playing a Bach partita or Bruno Walter leading a Haydn symphony the entire musical experience becomes the violinist's or the conductor's doing.[12] Performance is becoming reified and culturally constructed in much the same way composition once was, and so principles of digital access will inevitably lead to a situation, which would dismay Artur Schnabel as well as Schenker, where there is simply no such thing as a great work without a great performance.

THE MANY GOULDBERGS

The convergence of access and ownership means that musical performance faces scrutiny, analysis, and aesthetic discussions that it didn't encounter even two decades ago. Digital technology has rendered our relationship with the musical past more complex, giving vertical color, depth, and variety to a musical history that we've long scrutinized and labored over—but still misunderstood—in the linear, horizontal dimension. Many of the classic blues records, for instance by Bessie Smith and Robert Johnson, have been subject in the past to blunt, overambitious, and even historicist noise-filtering techniques that made it difficult to hear the singer's words, let alone the timbral fluctuations and "sit" of the voice. More recent technology cocktails, for instance the flexible toolkit developed by Andrew Rose of Pristine Classical, have exacted such "vertical" revelations that they have in essence helped expand the aural context "horizontally."[13] One reason the technological revelations can prove so dramatic with popular and folk music is that there is no score to help the listener imagine she is hearing details in the recording that she actually is not. A previously unheard aspirate in Johnson's "Sweet Home Chicago" would be a major revelation, a discovery comparable to unearthing an unknown eight-bar passage in Beethoven's "Eroica" Symphony.

With classical music, however, the sheer number of recorded versions and possibilities results in ontological complications. Exactly who can be said to have authored—who "owns"—the Goldberg Variations when Glenn Gould's is the only recording of that opus available in a huge chain of discount stores? Doesn't that make the music almost as much Gould's as Bach's? It was the pianist himself who first referred to "the Gouldberg Variations," and his jesting title has become more apropos than he could ever know.[14] What we see now is an oligarchy of iconic retailers joining forces with iconic performers. Before the arrival of music purchasing on the Internet, the buyers at Walmart exercised more control over Americans' musical tastes than any music director, government figure, or educator could ever hope to wield. Gould's especially distinctive manner of access to Bach has in effect bolstered such musical actions by replicating itself: an Amazon.com music search for "gould bach goldberg" turns up no fewer than fifty hits, including the recording from 1955 (fig. 5) and the second performance from 1981, each circulating in various remasterings and repackagings. Even if the potential purchaser were to log onto the Web and take a shot in the dark, there's still a strong chance Gould would be her guide to Bach's composition. More to the point, while someone wanting to buy a Goldberg Variations recording is faced with only one Bach-related decision—to purchase or not to purchase this Bach composition—she has at least ten options to choose from if she decides to go Gould. The following eleven formats are quite easy to find: the 1955 version is available on (1) a heavyweight 150-gram LP imported from Japan, (2) a CD in its original 16-bit length, (3) a 20-bit CD, (4) a DSD-mastered CD, and (5) a $65 gold-plated Japanese CD; while Gould's 1981 performance is available in the same five formats (6–9) as well as (10) on the simultaneous 1981 analog master first released in 2002 and (11) as remastered with DSD technology for Super Audio CD in 1999.

Without digital technology, these possibilities for rehearing, dissecting, rebalancing, and even "reperforming" earlier renderings could never have been entertained. "Back in the 1970s," remembers Ward Marston, "when we were working entirely in the analogue domain, we never imagined these techniques would be available to us, at least not in our lifetime."[15] Before PCM, the only real option was to reissue Gould's 1955 recording with a new equalization curve. For twenty-eight years after its initial

FIGURE 5.   Gould's 1955 recording of Bach's Goldberg Variations. Columbia, 1955; courtesy of Sony Music, all rights reserved.

release, if we disregard Columbia's 1968 "re-channeling for stereo," there was one way to hear this iconic performance—truly and only one, since the pianist himself retired from concert-giving in 1964. Tim Page recalls that the 1955 LP, which stayed in the catalogue basically unchanged for almost three decades, became a talismanic presence for early baby boomers. It was something to share: young and aspiring suburban intellectuals saw Bergman films, read Sartre and Camus, knew the "cool jazz" of Miles Davis and Lennie Tristano, and turned each other onto the Bach album covered with thirty candid snapshots of the gesticulating pianist.[16] One rising young star in the musical firmament, a composer-conductor by the name of Leonard Bernstein, picked up the LP when his wife was carrying their second child, and the two listened to it repeatedly as a source of comfort during the difficult pregnancy. "It became 'our song,'" he remembered.[17] But after compact disc and PCM masters hit the market in 1983, the remasterings began to increase almost exponentially, and the performance became less iconic than ever present—less "our song" than "everyone's song."

At the same time, remaster producers became freer and freer in interpreting the original 1955 Columbia "text," the increasing resolution of Sony's CD reissues allowing them to work with more ping, transparency, and brighter overtones to Gould's trademark piano voicing. PCM technology not only allowed new ways to update, clarify, and nuance the original 1955 tape; it also brought about the unintended democratization of allowing anyone and everyone to copy and manipulate the recording in their own fashion. Before CDs hit the market, Columbia/CBS held the master tapes, and the best any potential remaster producer could do was work from the commercial LPs—noisy pressings in the United States with quieter records coming out of Japan. Professional digital recorders were expensive and rare enough in the early 1980s that CBS had to shunt a single Sony machine from studio to studio and arrange sessions around its availability. Once digitally mastered compact discs came out, though, anyone buying a copy held something comparable to a master tape. And when home computers developed audio capabilities and increasingly cheap software became available, just about anyone with a PC and a sensitive pair of ears could do as fine a remastering job as CBS or Sony itself. Perhaps a better one: producer Mark Obert-Thorn decided to alter the CBS-Sony sound in a fundamental way in his 2005 remastering of the 1955 Gouldbergs for Naxos. "From my perspective," Obert-Thorn writes in the liner notes for the Naxos disc, "it seemed as though Sony's engineers filtered the highs in order to cut the tape hiss for their CD. I found that by playing back the LPs using the proper EQ, there were more highs, more openness and therefore more impact to the recording, even compared to Sony's latest efforts."[18]

Of course, such interpretive rethinks and re-rethinks of "classic" albums aren't the exclusive domain of classical music. Rethinks are a main ingredient of most pop studio productions from day one, because a basically unstable *mise-en-son* has been endemic to popular music since the arrival of multitracking and the general use of the mixing board to supplant physical acoustics—all standard pop studio practice since the mid-1960s. One striking parallel to the Gouldbergs comes with the 2009 rerelease of the Beatles' *Rubber Soul*, the first since the original 1987 CD. This 1965 album, widely recognized as the first to define the band's own style, and indeed the first of their LPs to contain all original material, has seen a splintering of opinion and interpretation not unlike that surrounding the Gouldbergs. Fans found producer George Martin's remix for the first 1987 compact disc controversial from the start, and the album's reception was fragmented even further by the presence of an original mono LP—the mixdown attended to most carefully by the band members—along with the 1965 stereo mix, and by the different song lineups for the original U.K. and U.S. releases. The only solution in 2009 to this multiple *Rubber Soul* partisanship was to re-release all three versions, though some fans were left desiring the even greater interpretive digital invasiveness of a surround-sound edition.[19]

All this said, it seems various factors are likely to keep the Gouldbergs interpretation franchise going well after the *Rubber Soul* reissues have slowed or stopped. First, the absolute-music aspect of Bach's composition—even if a derelict, reified remnant of such—can maintain a teasing semblance of inscrutability. The margin of this difference is of course narrowing, as dictated in large part by the simple passage of time: *Rubber Soul* is itself taking on absolute-music qualities and in fifty years could well surpass Bach's piece in terms of imputed depth, timelessness, and cultural cachet. Second, as if to enhance the mysterious wordlessness and antiquity of Bach's composition, Gould will always be a greater puzzle than the Fab Four, a musical-intellectual-personal blank space that cries out for resolution or filling as opposed to disclosure; posthumous diagnoses of Asperger's syndrome are less revealing of the pianist himself than useful as a measure of our interrogative, perhaps aggressive interest in the musician.[20] Third, the absence of a stereo master for the 1955 Gouldbergs will—a bit like some eroded Egyptian hieroglyphs or an iffy section of the Dead Sea Scrolls—always inspire a certain hermeneutic necessity and a craving for renewed currency and recontextualization. The rise in number of Gouldbergs can't be attributed to recording technologies alone, to be sure. In addition to the Gouldian enigmas—mysteries of personality intertwined inseparably with disquieting and uncategorizable displays of musicianship—one also has to mention an increasingly fragmented listening market, and an international megacorporation's increasing pressure for return on a musical style with diminishing market share. It would be more difficult to imagine such contexts surrounding the Beatles and *Rubber Soul*.

A remarkable Sony offering certainly raised the Gouldbergs stakes in 2007, a year after the original recording entered public domain in Europe (a lapse that Obert-Thorn's remaster was the first to take advantage of). For this most recent version of the Gouldbergs, Zenph Studios used cutting-edge software to extract performance data from the acoustic information on Columbia's original tape and then replayed the extracted data on a Yamaha Disklavier Pro piano. Zenph's software documents more parameters and an exponentially larger number of gradations thereof than the Duo-Art process preserving early twentieth-century piano performances on paper rolls.[21] Zenph's stated purpose was to liberate Gould's performance from the technological limitations of its time. Sony Classical recorded the Zenph playback at the Glenn Gould Studio in Toronto and, to bring Gould's half-century-old mono version completely up-to-date, released it in surround-sound stereo on a DSD-recorded hybrid Super Audio CD (see fig. 6). It says a great deal about the iconic nature of Gould's 1955 recording, not to mention its enviable sales figures, that Zenph chose it for their first "re-performance." In essence the audio software engineers become art restorers, lavishing Gould's 1955 tape with the kind of curatorial effort once reserved for Michelangelo's *Last Judgment*. As with those restorations, however, a certain controversy attends the inevitable guesswork. Until the secretive Zenph engineers go public with their process, we can only wonder how they extracted measurements for the two basic factors in piano performance data: (1) the actuation time for each note, which is inherently ambiguous with any acoustic as opposed to MIDI instrument; and (2) the force with which the note is hit, the question here being how a degree of key velocity, an absolute measurement, can be ascertained from volume, which is a relative measure.[22] They must have been even less certain in answering such questions as when the pianist lifted his fingers from keys and how he might have used the pedals.

These questions ensure that there are yet no ontological terms to describe Zenph's wholesale retextualization; they label it a "re-performance," a performance of a performance. Whatever we choose to call it, the CD represents a new stage in reformulation of classic recordings. This latest hybrid disc seems designed to be everything to everyone—targeting audiophiles, surround-sound home-theater folks, Gould fans, and headphone users, in addition to any old-fashioned music-lovers who might still be in the market. The final analysis could be that new technological transformations have served to bring the 1955 Gouldbergs more in line with both the written and oral aspects of early twenty-first-century musical practice. The various transformations from Obert-Thorn, Zenph, and Sony itself have helped the record find new markets, or the series of reformulations would surely stop, and that increase can only help perpetuate Gould's performance as a musical text and as a renewed influence on younger musicians. Perhaps the only clientele left out in the cold are the long-term fans of the original recording,

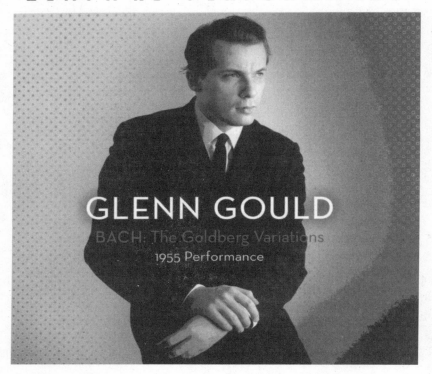

FIGURE 6.   Zenph "re-performance" of Gould's 1955 *Goldberg Variations*. Sony Classical, 2006; courtesy of Sony Music, all rights reserved.

who tend to find the Zenph rendition less like a renewal of first love than meeting a high-school crush after plastic surgery.

Kusek and Leonhard say the music industry is becoming oriented more to service than to content in "the digital age," even if the larger companies are still trying to fight off that inevitability. The Gouldbergs phenomenon helps us see how true their assertion is with regard to classical recordings. Looking only at market dynamics, one could say the availability of eleven different versions of one performer's take on a piece of music either shows a strong market value for that interpretation—making it a content-driven situation—or, conversely, that the many versions betray diminishing cultural value—putting the Gouldbergs in a kind of service market where the discs disappear as discs and become different points of access to the performance. The sheer ubiquitousness of the Gouldbergs places it close to an accessory franchise, what with the 1955 and 1981 versions, various packages with both versions in tandem (*A State of Wonder* is the title of a three-disc set with a fifty-minute Gould interview and 1955 studio outtakes), and Bruno Monsaingeon's film of the 1981 sessions (given the same cover as the 1981 audio recording, confusingly enough). One important point that needs mentioning here is the tendency for industry conglomerates to buy masses of cultural "content," such as music recordings or photo images, to leverage sales of more immediately profitable products like hardware and software.[23] Sony stands out here as an electronics giant, one that added music to its holdings when it bought CBS Records in 1988. (That conglomerate became larger yet in 2004 when the Sony music group merged with Bertelsmann, Sony afterward buying out BMG's ownership of RCA to give it 100-percent ownership of all Columbia, CBS, RCA, and of course Sony masters.) Such a move reveals as simplistic some of the notions that Kusek and Leonhard develop, for musical content is not always used as "content-ually" as they seem to assume: Sony likely uses the Gouldbergs as content to help sell computers, Blu-ray Disc players, cameras, shower radios, headphones, and MP3 players, but in such a way that it is not, strictly speaking, "musical content." We need to talk about digital platforms facilitating an array of content types and putting them to use in a service economy.

TRUTH AND AUTHENTICITY

Recording techniques are powerfully subjective avenues for information, but in the case of classical music they pretend to transparency. Truth became a prize commodity for the home and a significant, omnipresent trope when digital (PCM) techniques entered the domestic audio market in the late 1970s and early 1980s. These tropes had surfaced earlier with Dolby noise reduction, but the intellectual purity of binary code ensured their omnipresence when digital techniques arrived in the living room. Marshall McLuhan had been equating recorded music with the printed word for some two decades, describing them both as practices of "information retrieval, part of the 'technological expansion of consciousness.'"[24] Advertisements for the first CD players adopted a rather different tone in promising "the purest, cleanest sound, absolutely faithful to the original recording" and "the full beauty of Mahler or the Moody Blues as never before."[25] "Quite purely and simply," a 1983 Philips ad informs the reader, "a Philips Compact Disc player reproduces music precisely as the performer intended.

Giving you pure, perfect sound that will last for ever. (We mean eternity.)"
(see fig. 7). When digital remastering first appeared in ad copy in the mid-
1980s, truth and authenticity became tropes for the music-lover's relationship with the past. PolyGram Classics and Jazz began to assure CD buyers
that it provided an utterly clear and impartial perspective:

> Digitally Remastered means that what you hear is the quality of the
> original recording, because it has been newly mastered with the use of
> digital technology and the master tape is now a digital tape. Every pre-
> vious mastering using analogue technology produced only a copy of
> the original recording, and every copy contained more background
> noise and distortion than the original.[26]

This presents the accretions of time ("every copy contained more background noise") as a form of ideological spin, with white noise and distortion invoked as metaphors for misinformation. Or data corruption could
take on more physical connotations: to Telarc's declaration that "during the
recording of the digital masters and the subsequent transfer to disc, the
signal was not passed through any processing device (i.e., compression,
limiting or equalization)," one critic responded: "Sounds like a social dis-
ease!"

Truth is a difficult matter because it is eternally lashed to falsity, its dialectical other. A strong enough falsehood can give the impression of
veracity—consider the adage, attributed to Hitler among others, that people would rather believe a large lie than a small truth.[27] Forceful truths can
end up encouraging some people to prefer deception, especially if they come
after a period lacking in truthfulness. Elements of Gestalt psychology
further complicate understandings of aural veracity. Even the seemingly
straightforward matter of reducing tape hiss and 78 surface swish can alter
the sound of the music and introduce a new subjectivity by changing the
background from which it emanates—for how can the musical sound itself
be truthful if the very lack of it smacks of inauthenticity? Here the separation of musical sound from recording medium began in earnest with Dolby
noise reduction in the late 1960s. Michel Chion, the scholar of film sound,
gives some idea of how Dolby NR changed the sounds by changing the
silence that surrounds them:

> Paradoxically, Dolby and other current sound techniques increase the
> feeling of a silence surrounding the voice, in creating around it a differ-
> ent frame. Before modern sound, every sound and every silence in a
> film was embedded in a continuous background tone that provided a sort
> of sonic continuum. Since Dolby increases dynamic contrast, it makes
> silence deeper, and from these silences the voice emerges differently.[28]

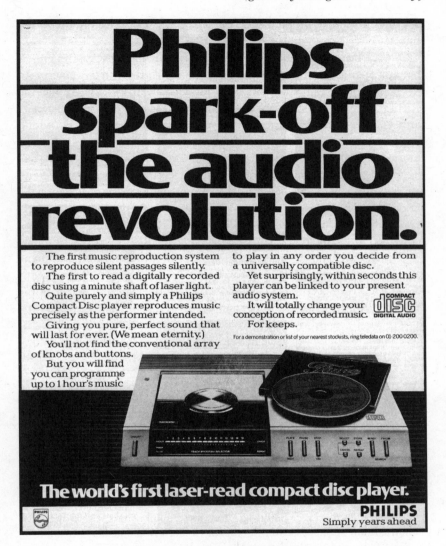

FIGURE 7. Ad for first Philips CD player, 1983. Courtesy of Philips Electronics, Eindhoven; all rights reserved.

Speaking in 1985, Isaac Stern took a neologistic approach—devising terms like "un-noise" and "real silence"—to describe his distrust of the transformative capacities of digital silence: "At the moment, it's the silence which I find a problem. Often it isn't a real silence at all, but a vacuum of 'un-noise.' There's very little ambient feeling, no sense of listeners tensing and concentrating. And that's as vital a part of musical experience as the sound itself."[29]

One reason we might be more willing to trust white noise than silence is that humans seem to place more confidence—find greater truthfulness—in excess information, in aural plenitude rather than in scarcity. And so the lack of information in musical silences sounded suspicious to some listeners until PCM recording became transparent enough to offer compensating detail in the musical sound itself. There was also the sense that PCM transparency could display the new wealth of timbral variety offered by authentic instruments and historically informed performance practice, and thereby also act as a kind of high-density ventriloquism for their rationalizations and principles, providing an example of two symbiotically developed, hand-in-hand truths. Asked in 1981 to comment on future music reproduction technologies, Christopher Hogwood chose to describe new possibilities of "historical appropriateness" and "true museum documentation." He didn't specifically connect digital recording and playback with this music-historical project, but—at least with the explosion in the number of recordings across the 1980s and 1990s—PCM did help bring about a market where record companies could engage in the far-reaching, accessible, and contextually sensitive manner of publishing that Hogwood associated with the book industry:

> A number of other recent developments encourage me to look forward to an increasing use of recordings as a means of establishing a sense of historical appropriateness in the ears of a worldwide public. . . . Now it is possible to see true museum documentation being undertaken; recordings of historic, sometimes unique, instruments under conditions that could rarely be achieved in a live concert; the assembling of specialist teams of players from many countries, recorded in controlled acoustics selected to match the repertory and instrumentation. . . . This all seems to suggest an attitude in classical recording comparable to that of the standard literary publishers and the scrupulousness with which a new edition of Shakespeare, Goethe, or Goldoni would be done. Byrd, Beethoven, and Vivaldi deserve the same.[30]

The simultaneous arrival of digital mastering and period-instrument performance in the mass market stands as a prime example of the intertwining of musical aesthetics and recording technologies in the later twentieth century. Both were developed and sold to a wide buyership in the late 1970s and 1980s under the banner of authenticity, just as music-making more generally took on new intimations of purity, clarity, and truth. One 1983 U.K. ad announced completion of Hogwood's "unique recordings of

Mozart symphonies, performed on authentic instruments" and abetted by "superlative digital sound"—a feat of dual purifications. Realism had been on offer since the advent of high fidelity in the late 1940s, but the audio industry promised something more specific with digital recording and the CD: specifically, a kind of aural-musical *Urtext*. As Stanley Sadie described the comparison in 1981,

> The term ['Early Music'] now represents less a statement about the music's date than about the performers' approach to it. . . . It nowadays means to most people a way of playing that, to parody a once-famous hi-fi advertisement, seeks for "the closest possible approach to the original sound" ("original" meaning as played at the time, not as played in the studio).[31]

Recording technologies in the 1980s were certainly of their time. If "authenticity" was offered by both the dominant recording method and the ascendant performance style, permanence was also. It was promised that CDs would never wear out, "giving you pure, perfect sound that will last for ever. (We mean eternity.)" Authenticist performance would likewise transcend the vagaries and subjectivities of time. "Almost more than any other portion of the musical repertoire," wrote Hogwood in 1986, at the time he started taping his Beethoven symphonies cycle, "Beethoven's symphonies are the victims of received opinion; as the epitome of a 'classic' they suffer a double prejudgment, both of intention and effect." By studying the specific makeup of ensembles at Beethoven's premieres and knowing how those orchestras changed from one symphony to another, Hogwood said, the performer can circumvent such modern misconceptions and "make our starting point what the work *is*, not what we would, with hindsight, design or expect it to be."[32] While making no such extreme claims of ontological objectivity, Andrew Parrott hoped that, in making "the attempt to recapture historically accurate performing styles," musicians essaying Bach could avoid "that general-purpose (late-romantic?) style which used to be applied indiscriminately to all music. With Bach this has generally involved mindless legato, insensitive tuning, a sanctimonious manner, senile tempos and dull, opaque textures."[33] Hogwood and Parrott described historically informed performance as the historically situated approach, and "received opinion" and the "general-purpose" style as both ahistorical and rooted in a particular time—the late twentieth century in Hogwood's case, the late nineteenth according to Parrott. These are presumptuous and extravagant claims, as was soon pointed out by Richard Taruskin, who insisted, after finessing away the more obvious straw-man aspects of Parrott's "general-purpose" style, that it is in fact the authenticist styles that are contemporary and subjective.[34]

I would link new audio techniques of the time with these same beliefs; it can't be simple coincidence that both authenticist performance practices and commercially viable digital recording overran the markets at about the same time as the vulgar Hegelianism in Francis Fukuyama's epochal book *The End of History and the Last Man.* All three historicist pursuits hinged upon the notion that the present could transcend earlier dialectics through the sublation of Hegelian *Aufhebung,* the simultaneous changing and upholding of what has already occurred. For Fukuyama that end point was capitalist constitutional democracy, which in his own description

> may constitute the "end point of mankind's ideological evolution" and the "final form of human government," and as such constituted the "end of history." That is, while earlier forms of government were characterised by grave defects and irrationalities that led to their eventual collapse, liberal [constitutional] democracy was arguably free from such fundamental internal contradictions. This was not to say that today's stable democracies, like the United States, France, or Switzerland, were not without injustice or serious social problems. But these problems were ones of incomplete implementation of the twin principles of liberty and equality on which modern democracy is founded, rather than of flaws in the principles themselves.[35]

For a musician oriented to authentic performance practice, the particular end of "history understood as a single, coherent, evolutionary process" was—as Hogwood described it—an understanding of "what the work *is,* not what we would, with hindsight, design or expect it to be." For the audiophile, the end of history arrived with a reasonably priced and unbreakable disc that was equal to "the quality of the original recording" and sounded "precisely as the performer intended." Both authenticist performance practices and digital audio techniques aspired to be nonstyles, styles "without a style," that were—like Fukuyama's neo-Hegelian views—paradoxically born from a fear of history and a wish to deny it.

All three of these shining, endist truths of the 1980s—the necessity of constitutional democracy, the nonarbitrary nature of authenticist performance styles, and avoidance of distortion through digital audio—hit the hard wall of reality in the 1990s. At the risk of trivializing human suffering, we could find similar collapses of rationalist idealism in the Yugoslav wars of 1991–2001, realization of the historically untenable aspects of authentic performance practice, and identification of jitter (or clock timing error) as an audible degradation of the audio signal in CD players. This last was identified in 1990 as an inconsistency in spacing successive samples, a timing discrepancy introduced into the audio signal between the master clock—usually contained with the disc transport—and the digital-analog converter.[36] Analog distortion had been eliminated, but—notwithstanding earlier promises of "absolutely faithful" and "pure, perfect sound"—a new, digital form of noise had simply taken its place.

With the help of technology, we have involved ourselves in a kind of Zeno's paradox with the musical past. That past might once have resembled a material and stable entity, enshrined in paper and shellac and vinyl, but now it seems to shift and evade us the more intensively we scrutinize it. Consider, for example, Soundmirror's stunning DSD remasterings of Charles Munch's and Fritz Reiner's mid-1950s tapes for RCA's *Living Stereo* hybrid Super Audio CD reissues. The disparity between these remasterings and the earlier Red Book CD incarnations, not to mention the tinny and distorted 1970s LPs, can only make one wonder just where and what "the original recordings" are. And how we can continue to exact more and more "fidelity to the original source" when it seems what we are really hearing—or at least paying for—is not technology-assisted documentations of the past but recent technology per se. Perhaps the situation offers literal exemplification of McLuhan's famous assertion that "the medium is the message." Current technology does allow us to extract more information from the original media now than the original engineers were able to hear even on their best equipment. As an example, Obert-Thorn mentions recently arranged playback of the optical-film Selenophon recordings of Toscanini's 1937 Salzburg opera performances, which reveal a wider frequency range than was previously thought possible with that medium. Some recent transfers of acoustic recordings also exhibit a much wider frequency range than was considered possible to record at the time.

We can't really speak of the three 1980s truths being disproved. From an early twenty-first-century perspective, however, we can say they have become neither lies nor active truths, but brittle, highly contingent truths inextricable from a landscape of changed and changing principles. For example, any "end of history" has not in fact materialized with constitutional democracy as commonly defined, but with a complete, immanent, and technical stifling of differences through rationalized and obligatory bureaucracies. Aden Evens feels digital audio technology is innately limited by a pure and rigid equivalence to "form" rather than individuality. From this perspective, digital audio sounds perfectly fitting to the Western democracies that had been dehumanized by the cold war, 9/11, and six years of Republican Party oligarchy in the United States:

The digital captures the general, the representable, the repeatable, but leaves out the singular, the unique, the immediate: whatever is not formal. Actuality always exceeds its form, for it moves along lines that connect singularities; the actual is not a neat sequence of frozen or static moments but an irreducible complex process that cannot be cleanly articulated in time or space. By contrast with the actual, the formal includes only stasis, what remains fixed long enough to be measured, determined, specified. . . . The digital is nothing but form, and form can always be perfectly reproduced with the right *formula*, anytime, anywhere. A digital world has no uniqueness or immediacy, for it is inherently generic, treating every place as an abstract space represented by reproducible numbers, every object as a type defined by precise values. To live in such a world is to have reproducible and generic experience.[37]

As an account of how digital recordings sound to the ear, Evens's version is questionable. But as a description of early twenty-first-century aesthetics and politics, and how information has become equivalent to power, it is uncanny. We have been made to sacrifice individualities for expediency and civil liberties for the sake of national security—giving up uniqueness for safety in numbers, in various senses of that word. But that is only one example of how we are constantly measured, monitored, protected, and "protected" by data that are invisible and nonnegotiable. To use Evens's terms, the formal has vanquished the singular by offering it safeguards. "The digital" is a manifestation of the zero-tolerance, nuclear-option, clamping-down policies of recent political bureaucracy: courtesy of their discreteness, exactness, purity, and pure formality, data strings by definition involve "arbitrary and selective" operations that prove "vastly powerful." Whatever the benefits of new technology, one can now on an hourly basis be denied entry onto an airplane or into a building, service in a restaurant, or a business transaction on account of nonnegotiable data from an unknown source. The technology of zeroes and ones and off-on subjects actuality to a system of thresholds, to absolute distinctions that can involve no compromise: "The digital, by virtue of its discreteness, establishes an absolute standard of sameness and difference, distinct thresholds that are either crossed or not."[38]

(RE)MASTERING THE PAST

Digital remastering techniques started bringing up similar questions of authenticity and "truth" with regard to old recorded performances at just about the same time contemporary performance practice began specifically to oppose late Romantic traditions (as Parrott did in his statement above). Like historically informed performance practice, the new software-based remastering techniques promised to clear away the encrustations of time for a pristine view of the "original" article. These advances in sonic clarity have allowed previously unheard nuances to be brought out in beloved old records, often changing analysis and judgment of the performances themselves. Remarkable improvements in bandwidth, signal-to-noise ratio, and resolution have been made possible by various audio-technological developments (see the list below). When directed at predigital artifacts, these digital techniques are commonly described in terms of recovery, clarification, and renewal; they are considered transformative and progressive, creating a version of the recording that is not simply different, but up-to-date and indeed superior to the old. The 2006 guidebook *Go Digital: Keep the Past Alive!* informs the reader: "We all have a lifetime of memories from before the digital age. . . . Discover how to breathe new life into material you thought was frozen in time forever."[39] A different interpretation comes from Michelle Henning who, in discussing the aesthetic implications of digital photography from a Hegelian perspective, tells us that digital technology is not a vector pointing to the future but yet another case where "the moment of the arrival of the new is simultaneously a reinvention of the old, yet in reinventing it also transforms." She explains the paradox:

> We experience new media and technologies in old and familiar contexts and not necessarily in a 'pure' form. It would be possible to gather together enough instances of this intermingling to demonstrate that what we have is not so much a digital culture, in the sense of new media overtaking and displacing old ones, as the increasing digitalization of older media. If a new technology cannot be conceived of in isolation, but only in relation to the means it displaces, and the media it affects, then the idea that it might be the determining factor in social changes and changes in consciousness becomes difficult to maintain. In addition . . . newness and oldness are bound together, in terms of the formal aspects of the image, and in terms of what it represents.[40]

This is the old question of how new media enfold earlier ones. In McLuhan's view, old media simply become content for new media.[41] Henning goes a step further to explain, in aesthetic terms, why new technologies would ever in fact be turned on earlier images—or earlier sounds, in our case—instead of being used exclusively to create new ones. In his book *Bauen in Frankreich* (1928), Siegfried Giedion went back to Marx's conclusion that new building techniques tended in his own time to appear cloaked in past practices—iron and glass imitating stonework for instance.

For his fragmentary *Arcades Project*, Walter Benjamin consulted Giedion in preparing his own discussion of return: he described one form of retrospection that involved denaturalizing the present and connecting with the past and its still-open promises, and another that stressed continuity between past and present.[42]

Digital recording, to judge from advertising copy of the 1980s, falls into the first of Benjamin's two categories. In a 1984 Sony ad promoting home CD technology, we read that "for decades, the goal of the recording industry and audio manufacturers has been to recreate as perfectly as possible the sound of a live performance—the sound of the concert hall. Until now that goal has been elusive."[43] This presents the technology not as a dramatic new arrival, but as the culmination—success at last!—to a long-term quest. Such a culmination follows its own end-of-history narrative and is good marketing because it suggests a wise investment and no possibility of obsolescence. Home audio histories are full of sudden discoveries that turned out to be flashes in the pan—especially with analog equipment, where various makeshift devices promised dramatic improvements—and in the early 1980s the industry was still smarting from the market failure of quadrophony. By presenting PCM not as something new but as a "reinvention of the old"—as the culmination of a long technological search, and a means of reviving already-familiar and beloved recordings—customers were assured their trust would be rewarded. The following list gives some context for PCM and later digital audio technologies by showing in approximate chronological order how they fit in with and instigated various advances in home audio mastering, new channel mixing, high-end signal encoding, and file transfer:

Dolby noise reduction (Dolby A introduced to the professional market in 1966, followed by Dolby B and Dolby C for the home market)

PCM recording and playback (Denon eight-channel PCM recorder introduced in 1972)

Soundstream four-channel digital recorder with 16-bit converters running at 50 kHz (introduced 1977)

Sony 501ES adaptor, allowing semiprofessional PCM recording on videotape at 16-bit word length and a 44.1.kHz sampling rate (introduced 1984)

Commercial noise shaping and reduction systems, including Sonic Solutions' NoNOISE software (launched 1986) and CEDAR (Computer Enhanced Digital Audio Restoration, introduced 1988)

Various downsampling techniques (such as Sony's Super Bit Mapping, launched in 1993 as one-step system of dithering and noise shaping down to CD-compatible 16-bit word length; and JVC's K2 24-bit analog-to-digital converter, introduced in 2002)

Five-channel surround sound (five plus the Low-Frequency Effects or subwoofer channel, thus the standard surround format of "5.1 channels")

Direct Stream Digital (DSD) designed for commercial use (1-bit process simplifying digital-to-analog conversion, introduced to home audio by Sony in 1999)

Super Audio CD (SACD) systems, with DSD 1-bit encoding and playback at 2822.4 kHz (supplying four times the data stream rate of regular CDs; launched 1999)

DVD-Audio, allowing stereo playback at up to 24-bit length and 192 kHz (launched 2000)

Studio masters (recorded with DSD; or at 24 bits and 172 kHz or higher) downloaded to hard drive or otherwise formatted for nonoptical media (24-bit and 176.4 kHz recordings introduced to the market by Reference Recordings in 2008, as their HRx system)

This list gives an idea of how digital techniques could present new possibilities for musical democratization—by giving entry to any number of opinions on how an important performance of the past should be heard, and allowing various options for experiencing its particular cultural significance in the present. Do you think, for instance, that Carlo Maria Giulini's approach to the *Andante marziale* from Tchaikovsky's Second Symphony would be the be-all and end-all of Tchaikovsky interpretation if only it were a hair faster? Cheap digital editing techniques have made it easy for you to knock the tempo up without changing pitch. More generally, said techniques allow any performed musical work to be separated from the aspect that Jacques Attali said it was inseparable from—namely, its own "incompressible lapse of time."[44] In the first movement of Bach's Italian Concerto, an extension of the one-beat rest at the end of bar 4 disfigures an otherwise beautiful rendering by the young Russian pianist Youri Egorov (once available on both the Pavane and Astoria labels). Removing this presumptive fermata took me only two minutes with some free Audacity editing software, and now the reading stands as one of my favorite Bach performances. Such nips and tucks can become an addictive game, a type of cosmetic surgery or, better said, a sort of genetic engineering: the possibilities are many, and Pandora's box opens with such subjective and selective ventures after truth and finality.

The various digital remastering methods, in addition to allowing revision of a performed composition's "incompressible lapse of time," permit changes in an aspect commonly couched in visual terms—namely, resolution. Increased resolution means greater detail and sharpness in the sonic image—in a phrase, a higher degree of aural truthfulness. But changes in resolution, offering a difference of degree and not of kind, might seem relative and relatively unimportant. They have certainly been marginalized by traditional histories of science with their misleading, scientistic emphasis on qualitative revelation—the notion that discovery represents a qualitative rather than quantitative change in awareness. Some of the problem must stem from the fact that resolution is as much a psychological aspect—a subjectivity, an awareness, a kind of circumscription—as it is a function of optics or technology. A listener cannot really imagine any need for higher resolution until she actually experiences such a change—moving from a 16-bit Red Book CD to a 24-bit signal downsampled to CD, say, or a Super Audio CD recorded with DSD technology—and then at a stroke the earlier, lower resolution appears deficient and difficult to go back to. The level of detail instigates an addictive, even necessary, form of awareness.

We can draw useful comparisons between the use of computers for remastering recordings and their use in the technology of adaptive optics—for example in correcting for atmospheric distortion with telescopes. Adaptive optics have allowed astronomers to make stronger claims in classifying distant galactic structures and deciding what lies at the center of nebulas—in short, to make qualitative as well as quantitative distinctions.[45] These powers of adaptive optics increased exponentially with the advent of computers. But those corrective adaptations are easy enough to make because all astronomical phenomena will suffer the same kind of distortion if viewed at the same time and from the same place. (Chronological) distance is accompanied by a different sense of arbitrariness in the case of remastering recordings. Here the variables preventing an "objective" or clear hearing of the original performance will vary not only according to the recording circumstances themselves, and of course the playback system, but also by the kind of wax, shellac, tape, vinyl, or sampling rate used to store and transmit the recording.

The more distant in time the performance becomes, and the more technological developments between the old performance and ourselves, the more questionable any idea of an original or "true" sound becomes. From their first transfers to vinyl in the 1950s until the 1990s, there was only one "version" of Artur Schnabel's Beethoven cycle, the original EMI LPs or CDs—take them or leave them. A new remastering of Schnabel's Beethoven cycle could simply transform notions of his pianism in the same way critic Richard Osborne heard Marston's remaster of Claudio Arrau's pre–World War II records changing standard accounts of that pianist's development: "In the past, I have seen it suggested that the playing of the young Arrau as evidenced by the early Polydor recordings was brilliant but a trifle chilly— the famous depth and 'carry' of the sound not yet fully developed. The present transfers rather undermine that theory."[46] Jed Distler encountered similar "digital revisionism" with Leon Fleisher, finding that a CD reissue changed his impression of the tone that pianist cultivated in the 1950s: "The earlier recordings show Fleisher to be less of a colorist per se, yet the flinty tone I took as gospel via the original LPs acquires noticeable round- ness and depth on CD."[47] In both Osborne's and Distler's hearings of past keyboard greats, digital technology became a tool for seeking out—or at least getting closer to—historical and musical truths.

TERMS FOR REHEARING

With old recordings of deceased musicians, the medium is a dark glass but our only perspective. This innate relativity is not always acknowledged. In discussing his work on the 1982 vocal retrospective *A Record of Singers,* Keith Hardwick invoked a specific sonic-musical verity: in remastering a series of muted Pathé 78s, he deemed it necessary "to *increase* the surface noise so as to get a truer sound."[48] But where would such articles of truth lie? Just what kind of sound did Charles Panzèra himself make that a re- master should be truthful to? He is no longer around, and not many re- main of those who heard him "live" at his peak. Because tonal quality is such an important element in musical interpretation, the difficult question now arises of how much of his tone—indeed how much of his perfor- mances themselves—are owed to the performer, and how much to the reis- sue engineers.

The terminology varies from moderately specific terms like "depth," "carry," "brilliance," "flintiness," and "roundedness" to more subjective descriptions. To cite just one example of the latter, critic Allan Kozinn compared an early CD of Mozart's "Jupiter" Symphony with its LP equiv- alent and "not only found the CD version *sonically* better, but felt it gave the performance itself a more captivating edge."[49] A bolder claim came from critic Alan Blyth, who, comparing the CD of Herbert von Karajan's second recording of the Verdi Requiem with the equivalent LP, greeted the digital-playback version thus: "Anyone possessing the new medium will be in for an impressive experience, for the added immediacy and truth of the recording seem actually to add stature to the interpretation."[50] What does it mean, exactly, when a new technology can seem to alter a recorded performance materially and exact a qualitative change in its musicality?

If digital information represents an all-subsuming and all-connecting river, then those who speak of digital audio techniques in such objective terms might learn from the digital video (DV) theorists who have pondered the specific visual feel of DV. The best summary of DV might be to say that while film—still the standard for cinema chains as well as most art-film houses—stakes out a normative visual middle, digital is commonly used to explore marginal areas of high definition and low definition. At either extreme, DV can give the feel of intimacy as well as coolness, a lack of authorial presence, an anonymity, and basically an unmediated and charged impression having the character of pure you-are-there information. DV offers the voyeuristic view of the surveillance camera, the reality show, and the unedited home video, and it can be manipulated to create noisy, eerie, grungy effects (as in the death-hastening video featured in Hideo Nakata's 1998 horror film *Ring*). Filmmaker Matt Hanson, having interviewed several directors experienced in both emulsion film and digital video production, offers an array of adjectives that go some way toward summarizing the visual aesthetic: terms that arise include "authentic," "immediate," "ordinary," "discomfiting," and "truthful."[51] Given these digital differences in the video world, one can only wonder how much we truly understand the aesthetic qualities of digital audio, qualities that vary of course depending on sampling rate, bit length, and other factors. Or have the commercial and purely reportive aspects of home audio discouraged us from speaking of it as anything but transparent, entirely inaudible?

A rare opportunity for comparison is offered by a reissue of Glenn Gould's 1981 recording of the Goldberg Variations. The CBS engineers originally recorded these sessions with an early Sony digital machine, using an analog tape recorder at the same time as a backup. When Sony prepared a remastering in 2001, the reissue producers found themselves going back to and preferring the analog tape. As a result the remastering was painstakingly prepared in accordance with the original editing notes, and the 1981 Gouldbergs were then reissued from the analog master. Producer Louise de la Fuente used some revealing terminology when she described the differences: "Digital technology delivered a very clean, quiet sound—free of tape hiss and LP surface noise—but it was also brittle, compressed, and not quite 'musical' to many listeners' ears." In her comparison, she surprisingly declares that "with properly aligned machines and perfectly calibrated Dolby units, analogues' fidelity was far superior to anything digital had to offer."[52] The adjectives are interesting, including statements of quality and realism but also aesthetic distinctions. "Clean," "quiet," "brittle"—these descriptive terms aren't far from the terminology surrounding DV; and the affective qualities, no matter what generation of digital equipment they apply to, threaten to expose the aural myths of digital transparency. They also suggest that invocations of invisibility and truth seeking are simply a mythical addendum to histories of digital audio.

Remastering has become an interpretive art form unto itself over the past twenty-five years, thanks to the various improvements mentioned above that have been brought about by introducing music to computer languages. "I have become much more self-critical," says Marston. "That's one of the things about this new technology—there's so much that *can* be done, and you reach a point where you realize you could put in another 100 hours and that the gain would be so small you doubt anyone would notice."[53] Remastering producers like Marston, Obert-Thorn, and Michael J. Dutton are musical interpreters for a new age and have more interesting ideas about the music than do many present-day musicians. They have their own fans, listeners who appreciate their individual approaches to shellac 78s. Those approaches range from the noninterventionism of labels like Opus Kura, Symposium, and Pearl to the more liberal software applications characteristic of Testament, Pristine Audio, and Dutton (see fig. 8). With these methods arranged as a continuum, we can see, for instance, the kinds and degrees of intervention that CEDAR techniques have made possible. Such software developments aren't responsible for the extremes in this spectrum of intervention, since record producers have been dampening treble response and simulating stereo for decades. What software *has* brought about is the subtle gradations of approach between the extremes, the possibility for personalized variegations of sound. Marston has remarked: "It's hard to say what distinguishes my transfer work from that of Seth [Winner] or Mark [Obert-Thorn] or from Bryan Crimp or Roger Beardsley in England. We each have our own platonic ideal of what a transfer should sound like."[54] An opportunity for comparison is provided by Artur Schnabel's cycle of Beethoven piano sonatas, which became available in several competing remasterings after entering the public domain. While few listeners now prefer the filtered approach of the 1991 EMI set, no clear consensus

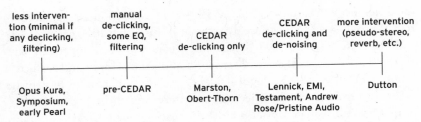

FIGURE 8.   "The spectrum of intervention" in audio remastering (examples not exhaustive, provided for comparison only). Courtesy of Mark Obert-Thorn.

has chosen between the bright and noisy, curatorial laissez-faire of the Pearl engineers or the smoother yet also more dynamic sound of Obert-Thorn's method on Naxos.

It's no doubt because of such complexities that some remastering engineers describe themselves in terms resembling positions in professional philosophy debates: Obert-Thorn describes himself in Naxos promotional material as "a 'moderate interventionist' rather than a 'purist' or 're-processor,' unlike those who apply significant additions and make major changes to the acoustical qualities of old recordings." He goes into more useful detail on his brand of "moderate interventionism" when he describes his transfers of the Schnabel Beethoven cycle. It's worth quoting Obert-Thorn at some length on his philosophy:

> The problem of how to deal with the higher-than-average level of surface crackle inherent in HMV shellac has led previous transfer engineers down one of two paths. One way has been to use heavy computerized processing to keep the noise at a minimum. While this made for a relatively quiet result, many critics felt that the piano's tonal qualities had been sacrificed to an unacceptable degree. Another approach went to the opposite extreme, filtering minimally and even apparently boosting the upper mid-range frequencies in an attempt to add a percussive brilliance to the piano tone. Although this produced a clearer result than the first method, many listeners were put off by the relentless onslaught of surface noise that this approach to filtering and equalisation exacerbated.
>
> For the current transfers, I have tried to strike a balance between these two positions. In order to start with the quietest available source material, multiple copies of British, French and American pressings have been assembled, and I have chosen the best sides from each. Computerised declicking (although not denoising) has been employed not only to remove clicks and pops, but also to reduce surface crackle to a minimum without harming the upper frequencies. My approach to

filtering has been to stop at the point at which more than just surface hiss was being affected; and my equalisation has aimed for a warm, full piano tone which I believe is more representative of the original recordings.[55]

The operative word here is "believe": while Marston invokes individual Platonic ideals and Hardwick speaks of truth, Obert-Thorn talks about a restorative process of stripping away. His mind-set would seem to lie more with the goals of art restoration, and one imagines he'd agree with the printed manifesto of the BBC Legends remaster series: "Renovating a historical sound recording, like restoring a painting, is a highly delicate process." The BBC writer continues in a vein of studied impracticality: "The recording must be digitalized and tonally refurbished to conform to today's audio standards, preserving its original character and the performing artists' intentions without any distortion." In both Obert-Thorn's and the BBC philosophies, the challenge is said to lie with balance and the sound of the performance as it might be freed from the period restrictions of the medium that contains it. Digital editing techniques—as opposed to razor blades—have allowed increasingly precise algorithms for pinpointing and removing ticks, pops, and even speed irregularities.[56]

Some of this is restorative, an attempt to counteract the decay of tape and shellac. But in the end the simile of art restoration doesn't wash, for the record remastering venture is closer to Proustian subjectivity than to archeological objectivity. Making the original musical *son* even more *perdu* is the ever-increasing number of subjectivities that get involved with digital remastering. One of the most contested of these is the technique of rechanneling recordings for surround-sound systems. How to pull five or six surround-sound channels out of a stereo recording of a solo piano or violin? Are the rear channels given over the ambient reverb, or something more active?

Digital technologies have made remastering more of a subjective process, then, but it need not be a presumptive one. As an example, I offer a treasured performance that has been subject to different approaches—different incursions in search of meaning. One of the most widely cherished recordings of Bach's *Well-Tempered Clavier* is that by the Swiss pianist Edwin Fischer, cut on 78 rpm shellac between 1933 and 1936 by British Columbia, on a Bach Society subscription. Now that they have entered the public domain, Fischer's performances are available in several competing remasters from different companies. These labels have contrasting philosophies on sound, piano tone, 78 rpm surface noise, and—by extension—just how these great performances are to be heard and understood in the twenty-first century. In 2007, former copyright-holder EMI released a straightforward high-definition remaster—probably from the original metalwork, dubbed at 96 kHz and a 24-bit length and "noise-shaped via the Prism SNS system for optimum sound quality"—on 16-bit Red Book compact discs. The piano sound is more distinct and transparent than on EMI's previous CD set, and certainly clearer and more bell-like than on engineer Stuart A. Rosenthal's muffled remaster for the Naxos label. Both of these are examples of a moderate interventionist approach, though Rosenthal applied too much filtering and ended up with a dull sound.

The third and more dramatic option involves equalizing the old recording to bring it in line with some kind of ideal or "correct" frequency curve. The Pristine Classical label has done precisely this with Fischer's Bach as well as other public-domain titles. Their remasterings do pull more life and vibrancy from the old shellacs, air checks, and (especially) early mono LPs than one might have thought possible. But Pristine's engineers make hefty presumptions in the process, presumptions so considerable one wonders if the original musicians and producers would have accepted the results. Again, it is recent digital software that has allowed—perhaps encouraged—these presumptive incursions into the musical past and coaxed the remastering engineers into such historicist expeditions. Pristine's Web site gives more detail of the historic and acoustic rationales behind this process, which they call XR remastering:

> Many people have become used to hearing old recordings with that "vintage" sound we associate with them and perhaps think that's how they really sounded, or should sound. But the fact that an orchestra was recorded 70 years ago doesn't mean that the overall sound of an orchestra has really changed much in 70 years, and if you were to go back in time and listen to that orchestra in the flesh, you'd find it sounded very different to a recording of it made at the time. The fundamental relationship between root frequencies and their harmonics which gives an instrument its characteristic sound is well defined, and a 1930's clarinet should follow the same laws of physics as a 21st century clarinet in this respect. . . . How, though, can we define what the flaws in the recording chain were, without recreating the exact recording with the same equipment? XR addresses this by working backwards from a tonal ideal, to produce a very precise equalisation curve that brings the tonal characteristics of the older recording towards that ideal.[57]

A fine example of technology used as a means of "inventing the old"! This is a presumptive aural historicism akin to the authenticist thinking of Christopher Hogwood, described earlier. Can we presume to separate a clarinet so easily from its resonance in a hall, especially if we have no idea where the microphones were or how many people were in attendance to absorb the sound? The Pristine engineers answer so strongly in the affirmative that they also offer a line of "Ambient Stereo" remasterings where—using software apparently developed as recently as 2007—they extract the frequencies of room ambience from a mono original and then spread these across a full stereo spectrum while leaving "the direct signal (i.e. the original mono sound of the musicians) . . . preserved and tonally unchanged." Pristine describes the result of their present-to-past induction as a revelation, indeed a genuine and genuinely paradoxical "invention of the old": "What appears to the listener is a whole new sense of place, and a degree of 'air' around the performers which is entirely believable and consistent with the recording."[58]

So audio technology is becoming more and more a matter of "inventing the old," remastering techniques and even digital-production artifacts are taking on aesthetic qualities, and the vehicles for Fischer's *Well-Tempered Clavier* and Gould's *Goldberg Variations* seem to multiply almost overnight. In this brave new, postdigital, world, remasterings are more and more performance-like in that, given their subjective and myriad differences, they complement rather than replace each other. When Fischer's Bach was first released on LP in 1960, the new edition clearly offered sonic and performative information that had lain hidden under 78 rpm swish, and the old shellacs could be tossed out. Now, however, the collector could well hold onto three editions for different listening moods (the reticent Naxos version for rainy days, maybe, and the more lively EMI version for sunny and outgoing frames of mind?), different playback equipment (the hazier Pristine CDs for the unforgiving fluorescent noncoloration of solid-state amplifiers?), and of course contrasting musical styles (the greater clarity of the EMI techniques suiting the thicker five-part fugues, the relative body of the Pristine remastering appropriate to the virtuoso preludes in Italian style?). And then there is the growing market for audiophile LP pressings of classical as well as popular music, offered at premium price to those listeners preferring analog coloration to digital clarity. Some collectors still prefer their old forty-year-old LPs or their twenty-year-old CDs, particularly if recent digital remastering leaves too bright and busy of a high end to the sound. In short, given the greater variability of sound made possible by digital mastering techniques, the differences between multiple CD versions have become qualitative rather than quantitative— a matter of taste, of musicality as much as technicality.

THE DUSTBIN OF ANALOG HISTORY

Wishful discussants of digital democratization fail to realize that any format or technological change entails jettisoning material, and digital is no exception. Kusek and Leonhard shortsightedly assume that the connectivity and openness of digital platforms will mean equal and fair access to just about everything—that the digital waters somehow connect the Pacific Ocean to all tide pools, culverts, and forgotten backwoods creeks. In truth, while digital has entailed a certain democratization of content, at the same time it has allowed corporations and other large institutions new and newly stringent nondemocratic modes of controlling access to that content. There is far more music buried in history than Web archivists and LP-to-MP3 converters will ever care to pick up, even if they were allowed to, and even if a massive music digitizing project like Google Books were somehow devised. Much music and music-making will be left behind to decay with the cylinders, discs, and tapes on which they are inscribed. Even if Kusek and Leonhard did acknowledge these mass consignments to the dustbin of history, would they take the next logical step and agree that ideologies lie behind such severances—what we might call technological ideologies?

Historians have been speaking for several decades of an increasing disparity between history and memory. Digital platforms have become the dominant vehicles of history within that divergence—culling and streamlining culture while nondigital forms attend distractedly to memory as a "sacral, innocent, and immediate" impulse, to borrow art historian Daniel Abramson's description. In Abramson's estimation, memory drives the pandemic if scattershot practices of memoir writing, memorial building, and historic preservation. "It works freely by evocation, similarity, metaphor. Memory dreams in fragments, gaps, and dissipation." Against all odds, especially the institutionalized sense of past that resides in history, memory struggles to see and hear what has been left behind:

> Against the apparent biases of history, memory stirs. Memory privi-
> leges the private and the emotional, the subjective and the bodily.
> Against history's rationality, the reveries of memory rebel. Against
> history's officialism, memory recalls hidden pasts, the lived and the lo-
> cal, the ordinary and the everyday. Against history's totality, mem-
> ory's pluralism blooms.[59]

When technological regimes change, items of memory aren't randomly excluded from history but are discarded in line with certain strictures and requirements—in other words, in accordance with reigning historicist ideologies. Specific performance types are jettisoned whenever one recording-technological paradigm overtakes another. When the mandate for authenticity had a market impact more or less simultaneously in historically informed performance and in recording technology, the changeover to compact disc meant that anything of suspect "authenticity" was largely dropped and forgotten. While collecting 78s and old LPs over the years, I have found the search for orchestral arrangements a fascinating enterprise. Among the anachronistic goodies I've come across on shellac and vinyl are Felix Mottl's arrangements of Lully and Gluck, Felix Weingartner's orchestration of the "Hammerklavier" Sonata, Constant Lambert's instrumentations of Grétry, Morton Gould's and Andre Kostelanetz's "operas for orchestra," and other such nonauthenticist horrors. Even Ravel's consummate orchestration of Schumann's *Carnaval* and orchestral excerpts from Handel operas—fashioned into delightful suites by Thomas Beecham and Charles Groves—seem to have disappeared from view. While in the days of mono LP it seemed one out of every three Chopin records consisted of orchestrations, some of them ingenious and fascinating, now the only such items left are the few standard Glazunov versions and the Roy Douglas arrangements from *Les Sylphides.*

To understand all the jettisoning, we have to interpret inauthenticity in a broader sense. Some great musicians were set to one side when the world went stereophonic: Dmitri Mitropoulos, Artur Rodzinski, and Sergey Koussevitzky are three of the conductors who had dozens of records in circulation in the mono period but died before or shortly into the stereo era and are now represented by only a fraction of their output. Their recordings were largely dropped from the catalogue in the 1980s. Some staples of these conductors' catalogues have been reissued on CD: Mitropoulos's premiere recording of the Mahler First from Minneapolis, Rodzinski's complete stereo *Nutcracker* with the Royal Philharmonic, Koussevitzky's Sibelius Second Symphony from Boston. So the large-scale disappearance of their work would seem to indicate a rather nefarious cooperation between technological change, shifts in musical aesthetics, and political inclinations: the motion to jettison probably began with changes in musical attitude and styles and was finally carried out through the technological change, or perhaps using the technical aspect as a premise. Much of Mitropoulos's work on record, in particular, is intensely exciting but also rhythmically wayward and lacking in the poised phrasing, centered tone, and executive polish that seem de rigeur these days. The mono reproduction must have became a convenient fact that helped serve such musical-aesthetic distinctions.

One voice for musical pluralism who has been almost entirely denied a voice in corporate-controlled digitalia is the American pianist Oscar Levant (1906–72). For a time George Gershwin's friend and pianistic right-hand man, and later a celebrity on film and radio, Levant made a few dozen records between the 1940s and 1960s ranging from 78 rpm to stereo LPs. One, at most two, of these recordings is available today on CD. I think the reason for Levant's current neglect lies with the individuality, perhaps the nonschooledness, of his style—some might now call his playing unnuanced or perhaps even unmusical. In the words of one critic, "[Levant's] *Rhapsody in Blue* is played with vehemence, and he moves from one section to the next like a cat batting a hapless mouse. *Second Rhapsody* and *Variations on 'I Got Rhythm'* are hammered out with the violence of urban warfare . . . it's very nearly brutal."[60] Had he been in a better mood, our assessor might have couched his verdict in terms closer to Levant's own eulogy for Gershwin's pianism: "I had never heard such fresh, brisk, unstudied, completely free and inventive playing." Ottie Swope arrived at a similar description for Levant's pianism: "[Oscar] played so ecstatically and so brilliantly, it was wonderful."[61]

The almost single-minded lack of nuance in Levant's playing is paradoxically its most striking aspect: from a current perspective, it is notably non-notable. And nuance is the very quality that so much of the conservatory-professionalization of musicianship over the past century has, at least in the United States, worked overtime to instill. Musicality is the word that would now be used to describe this kind of standardization, a kind of institutionalized performers' humanism. Levant's playing sounds remarkable now for its utter lack of the elastic, breath-oriented phrasing, the granting of ample space for inhalation and exhalation, that makes up the affecting but quite formulaic musicality of today. This, and his at-best sporadic attention to a singing tone, mean that Levant's Chopin recordings make for ear-opening listening. The exclusion of his pianistic style from the catalogue, like the expunging of Gordon Jacob's orchestrations of Couperin, mark a conscription into musical alterity—a process of removal that transpired in the 1980s right at the time of changeover from LP to CD. The digital expurgation of Levant and Jacob, the banishment of their subjective and indeed "ecstatic" contrariness in a time of truth-seeking self-denial, counts as a prime example of Tzvetan Todorov's maxim that "knowledge of self passes through that of the other."[62]

With said knowledge passed, the musical self duly affirmed, the contrary other is now to be forgotten. The historian Edward L. Ayers has commented on the practical disappearance of nondigital historical resources:

"Material that is not digitized risks being neglected as it would not have been in the past, virtually lost to the great majority of potential users."[63] Katie Hafner, a writer for the *New York Times*, goes further: "As more museums and archives become digital domains, and as electronic resources become the main tool for gathering information, items left behind in nondigital form, scholars and archivists say, are in danger of disappearing from the collective cultural memory, potentially leaving our historical fabric riddled with holes."[64] In the world of print, the rush is on to digitize materials from about 1870 to about 1950, a period when many publishers used high-acid paper. In the world of recorded sound, many magnetic tapes from the third quarter of the twentieth century are losing their emulsions. While many archival sources themselves are deteriorating faster than they can be maintained, the increase in cultural production is putting an added strain on archives' and libraries' ability to digitize materials. Add to this potent mixture recent government and university administration budget cuts and intense pressures to streamline library collections and floor space, and a bleak future—bleak immediate prospects, even—seems in store for all institutional paper, vinyl, and optical media. The period from about 1960 to about 1990 is threatening to disappear entirely from cultural memory, since it falls between the stools of historic preservation and immediate present-day relevance. In short, panic is setting in over the likelihood that our collective cultural memory is a diminishing digital domain, with evidence seen every time paper, shellac, vinyl, and even polycarbonate CDs are shunted into distant depositories or just into the dumpster.

If recording technologies can act as henchmen for changes in musical-interpretive taste, they also serve as functionaries of corporate control. While the Internet offers unprecedented access to unprecedented numbers of styles and performances, increasing corporate agglomeration in the music industry, along with stiffening enforcement of copyright, means that more and more recordings are owned and policed by fewer and fewer people. Levant originally recorded for Columbia, which was bought out by Sony Corporation, so his recordings fly below the radar of corporate profits, but the company's copyright policies won't allow marginal fandoms to put the music online. According to Tim Brooks, a historian of television and electronic media, "Sony . . . has asserted ownership to the earliest products of its predecessor companies" all the way back to Berliner discs of the 1890s.[65] To complement such chronological acquisitiveness, the centralized Internet basis of MP3s and other digital formats allows music industry behemoths unprecedented and theoretically limitless legal control, including forms of cyberpatrolling, which it would not have enjoyed in the analog era. Brown and Duguid see a disquieting element inherent in software code itself, which "now makes it possible to decide in fine degrees of detail not only who can or cannot use a certain digital text, but also how it can be used. . . . [It can] prevent the public from getting ultimate access to a copyrighted object forever. The 'public domain' and all the public goods connected to it have no part in the new encoded balance."[66] Major players in the recording industry have instituted just such a protective system: the encoding and enforcement of so-called Digital Rights Management, a centralized plan that may or may not be on the way out now because of growing public anger and decreasing revenues. Given the dual influences on recordings of material decay and virtual control, it comes as no surprise that a 2005 study by the Library of Congress and the Council on Library and Information Resources found that 84 percent of the sound recordings made in the United States from 1890 to 1964 have become aurally, physically, and legally inaccessible. "Copyright is a very blunt instrument," Brooks has commented. "Once you have copyright, you have total control; there's very little room in the copyright law even for preservation, much less reissuing material."[67]

U.S. copyright protection is more stringent than in any other country, but the rest of the world is catching up. In the United States, a 95-year copyright term begins with recordings published in 1972, meaning they will be delivered into public domain on January 1, 2068. Records made before that date, however, have even longer legal protection: since there was no federal law protecting musical renditions made prior to 1972, the clock started ticking on those recordings in that year rather than when they were first published. Thus an 1890 cylinder recording made by the John Philip Sousa Band will remain under copyright for 178 years. European Union laws have kept recordings under copyright for 50 years, but American styles of control are proving internationally contagious, and pending E.U. legislation would lengthen the span to 95 years. And U.S. legislators are expected to extend the copyright period even further: the Supreme Court has gone on record as allowing Congress to extend copyright protection as many times as it wishes, so long as it is not ad infinitum. Obert-Thorn's rendition of the 1955 Gouldbergs for Naxos is not available in the United States, Australia, and Singapore "due to possible copyright restrictions." Since the new E.U. rules are likely to allow grandfathering of previous remasterings, the disc will probably remain in the European catalogue. But no more third-party Gouldberg renditions would be legally possible, in any country.[68]

Why should we care about diminishing access to two deceased pianist-eccentrics, each obscure in his own way? Because it behooves us to look after memory just as urgently as we must criticize history. As with the disappearance of Levant's highly individual take on Chopin, the barring of further takes on Glenn Gould will leave our options diminished by more than a factor of one. In their most basic estimation, digital techniques have allowed classical music the distinctive art form that we might call interpretation of interpretations. But aural digital democratizations are now likely to cease with the copyright extension, and that art form will come to an end. The question then arises: In a world where pianists imitate Glenn Gould so closely that they might as well be recordings themselves, why shouldn't fans and record producers also be allowed to interpret and contextualize Gould's Bach—and other referential performances—in and for their own time? The day may arrive when licenses to reinterpret past interpretations will be requested and granted by record companies more often than publishers pass along permissions to perform compositions—a point in time when it will become more difficult to differentiate between works and performances, and perhaps the need for such differentiations will be irrelevant. The Zenph "re-performance" description could, in short, turn out to be a prescient one—a thumbnail rendering of the major endeavor in twenty-first-century classical music, indeed its dominant and most significant avenue of creativity.

5. Beethoven and the iPod Nation

The long-playing record, popularly known as the LP, appeared shortly after World War II. Columbia Records introduced it to the American market
as a medium for classical music, under the assumption that longer discs
had greater commercial potential with Beethoven than they might with
Bing Crosby: the company's first LP ads promised "a truly new experience
in listening pleasure—complete symphonies on a single record." The
medium initially offered five times the side length of 78 rpm shellacs, allowing listening sessions to be measured in hours rather than minutes.
And a single LP was able to encompass most every work from the Austro-
German symphonic tradition before Bruckner's Eighth and Mahler's Second. Those first vinyl discs held about seventeen minutes of music per
side, and side lengths increased to roughly thirty minutes within several
years.[1] So the LP defined a range of possibility when it arrived in 1948. But
the compact disc, when it arrived thirty-five years later, set a firm terminus ad quem, imposing a more-or-less rigid seventy-minute limit on a
classical market accustomed to the gigantism of Wagner operas and Mahler
symphonies. The CD did serve musical continuity with its lack of side
changes, allowing listeners a new form of uninterrupted "listening pleasure" that encompassed the linear compositional spans of complete symphonies.

Though the LP presented a more flexible time-heuristic than the CD,
both formats became commercial measures of aesthetic experience as well
as containers for sound—they represented new bottles for old wines, potential time spans to be filled up with music. When MP3 files and players
like the iPod arrived in force some twenty years after the CD, the new
technology contrasted with the LP and CD in that it was significantly
non-bottlelike. In its main difference, MP3 made durational possibilities of

media largely irrelevant: an MP3 file is "nonclassical" in orientation in that it is not time-specific, stretching to three seconds, three hours, or any length in between. The MP3 thereby shifted musical phenomenologies away from the durational parameters typical of art music, at a time when the public appeal of classical music was already in significant decline, at least in North America. While the 78 rpm disc, the LP, and the CD all served to define and limit stretches of musical information—that was their function—the MP3 removed such limits, or more accurately it moved the argument away from those discussions. In fact, to mention MP3 in the same breath as the older technologies is to risk comparing apples and oranges: it is neither a medium nor a recording method. It is a form of data compression and decompression, a lossy codec that cuts corners to reduce file size and expedite transmission and storage. It cuts those corners strategically, in such a way as to psychoacoustically minimize undesirable artifacts. MP3 can be described even more narrowly as a container technology—a format "designed to execute a process on its contents," as Jonathan Sterne puts it.[2]

Lossy codecs like the MP3 have made sound files more mobile in a time of limited bandwidths, able to zip from Toronto to Tokyo in seconds. They have thereby ushered music into the information age, wreaking profound musical and cultural changes with their mutability and speed of transmission. From the broader cultural perspective, the MP3 could be described as an "intellectual technology"—social anthropologist Jack Goody's term for a tool, like print or video media, that instigates a new "cognitive potentiality for human beings." Conrad Shayo and Ruth Guthrie, authorities in information science, point to the specific market shifts heralded—or brought on—by lossy codecs. They call MP3 a "disruptive technology," their word for a technology that "offer[s] a different value proposition to the market and tend[s] to appeal to new categories of customers who have different perceptions of product value."[3] These issues are all the more pressing because lossy codecs such as MP3 promise to become the dominant format within less than ten years. Since art music has become just as technology-dependent as pop, but has long since ceased to dictate format or market decisions, we need to ask three important questions: how art music itself represents a type of information—in other words, just how amenable to art music MP3 is, how MP3 technology influences consumption of art music, and how lossy codecs might affect its future.

One important thing to say right off is that MP3, as a form of computer information that is involved with no optical medium, has rendered music largely immaterial and invisible, free from physical parameters or limits.

Marshall McLuhan might have said that MP3 suggests a changeover from "the eye" to "the ear," and thereby contrasted it with the first music transmission technologies in Western culture—the notation systems that European monastic scribes devised for teaching and collecting plainchant, in other words to serve the eye more directly than the ear.[4] Since those origins over a thousand years ago, technologies of music dissemination have generally helped speed up the geographical and cultural dissemination of music: while it could take a medieval scriptorium days to enter a chant into the pages of an illuminated *liber gradualis,* lossy codecs like MP3 allow a four-minute pop song to be compressed, transmitted, and then decompressed almost instantaneously.

Since bandwidth is increasing over time while dimensions of musical utterances are not, one might wonder if MP3 is in fact a temporary audio encoding standard—a kind of stopgap measure that will become obsolete before this book reaches the end of its own shelf life. There are, however, suggestions to the contrary, along with clear evidence that our age has consistently chosen connectedness and speed over any pretense to high fidelity—not to forget that popular music has long since spawned a committed "low fi" culture all its own, as fuzzboxes and the recent craze for vintage analog equipment bear witness. Indeed, when we see MIDI outlive the CD, as it surely must, a low-density format will outlast one with higher concentrations of information. For years now, media authorities and music-lovers alike have been calling the compact disc moribund even while the MP3—a technology offering only about a tenth of the information flow of a regular CD—only increases in popularity. Not only does it remain popular, MP3 has also been a stable technology for years, and the increasing popularity of lower bit-rate downloads, even while far higher resolution technologies like Super Audio CD (SACD) are struggling for market share, would suggest that MP3 is going to be around for quite awhile—whatever means of exchange and storage may arise to change the way we connect with it.

Corporate sales statistics bode well for the MP3, even though they represent at most a partial picture of music's dissemination, both legal and officially illegal, through digital files. According to a 2008 report from the International Federation of the Phonographic Industry, "legal" downloads—that is, online corporate music sales—rose 40 percent worldwide between 2006 and 2007 and grew from 11 percent of the total music market to 15 percent. Over the previous year, from 2005 to 2006, digital sales rose 65 percent and expanded from 5 percent of the total market to 11 percent.[5] Although these figures show the CD still dominating the global market, they must represent only a relatively small part of music downloads. The future of the CD seems particularly gloomy when we look at specific countries, especially prime digital-enthusiast nations like the United States and South Korea. Digital files accounted for almost 30 percent of the total corporate music market in 2007 in the United States, while in South Korea—one of the world's most-connected societies—digital downloads comprised 60 percent of corporate music sales. The sheer number of downloads is also imposing at the global level: according to Nielsen SoundScan figures, more than a billion digital full tracks were sold in 2008, up 28 percent over 2007. Increases in digital sales are of course led by the youth market: a 2003 survey backed up the apparent importance of MP3 for the under-twenty-four crowd, and especially for adolescent music-lovers, with specific numbers.[6]

It is, in part, this youth-market aesthetic that leads me to invoke an "iPod nation" in this chapter's title. Specifically, the neologism intimates the germane relationships between digital files, the devices they're played on, and the musics heard. A nation is a political entity, and portable music players now define a more stable, tightly knit, and immediately visible community than the musical styles and file formats themselves. Musical tastes have splintered while hardware affiliations have consolidated around the MP3 player and the cell phone.[7] This trend becomes most obvious when we compare brick-and-mortar stores and online sellers: thirty years ago it would have been easier to find a retailer selling only country music records and tapes than it would have been to find a store selling only radios or Discmans; but today even Walmart and Best Buy sell Górecki alongside Garth Brooks, while the popularity of MP3 players has led to suppliers that offer nothing but hardware and attendant paraphernalia.[8] For several reasons, hardware now has a monopoly on techno-cultural chic, or possibly on chic of any kind. The iPod question now seems in fact primary, outpacing type of music as well as software and file type. And this is as true of art music as it is of pop: long gone are the late 1970s and the possibility of making a classical LP a best seller either by recording Leonard Bernstein or emblazoning the words "digital recording" across the cover.

People love their music players and are happy to let them shape their musical tastes, while at the same time many recent listeners cultivate a "format agnosticism." Format agnosticism—so-called—is the belief that no single format type is superior to any other, a situation that has followed increasing awareness of ownership-power issues. An analogous movement can be found in the trend toward open-platform software, where we see large numbers of people refusing to commit to one developer and the controls instituted by that developer. With media file types, a person practicing format agnosticism would find no inherent superiority to .avi or .mpg presentation of the same film (seen as video content), and likewise no reason to prefer one bitrate over another, or whether they see the movie on the silver screen or on the TV. A prime example of my hardware-over-format assertion is the otherwise quite inconceivable habit of watching epic widescreen films like *Ben Hur* on the 3.5 inch screen of an iPod Touch. Much the same might be said of listening to Mahler's Third on an iPod, as imported at 112 kbps. In summary: just as musical tastes are extending and atomizing laterally, liable to encompass various styles while embracing none in particular, younger people are developing a new disinterest in media types. Only the hardware, the mobile-and-connected aspect, the iPod in the broader sense, remains as a constant.[9]

MUSIC, INFORMATION, ORIGINALITY

What is the significance of encoding Beethoven, Brahms, Berg, and Birtwistle as numerical data? In the words of Richard Mansfield, the arrival of digital audio means music has been "fractured into millions of pieces. Or, as the professors like to say, music has been massively deconstructed. It's now in bits—meaning that computers (and you) can manipulate it in pretty much any fashion you wish."[10] Through this fracturing, MP3 and its fellow codecs have swept music up into the mammoth waves of cultural change and exchange unleashed by ever-smaller, ever-stronger, and ever-cheaper hard drives. So the Nobel-winning physicists who discovered what is now known as giant magnetoresistance, an effect that allowed construction of flash drives and other consumer-market forms of nanotechnology, should by rights have chapters devoted to them in music history books. Peter Grünberg and Albert Fert have had a far more profound impact on music writ large than many of the middling composers who appear in such texts: Grünberg and Fert helped turn music into information, and a partner to digital methods of creativity, Internet exchange, and the high-speed global marketplace. The thought of reducing music to digital information might be thought heretical by cultural anthropologists and musicologists alike, but heresy is the last idea that would come to mind in the corporate boardrooms, Webmaster offices, and Music Genome Project studios that now control so much of the marketplace.

Some clarification of the term "information" is necessary here, as well as an explanation of how music has changed over the years as an information commodity.[11] Given the rise of publishing and ticket-selling in the nineteenth century, the emphasis on music as product is not inappropriate to absolute-music discussions. Four related, and sometimes overlapping, terms should first be explained. (1) *Information* is a selected and concentrated form of data, usually contrasted with data representing raw facts in large quantity.[12] The most basic informational content of music resides in the pitches, rhythm, dynamics, and articulation as indicated in the score; specific performances of specific repertoire, for instance Arthur Grumiaux and Clara Haskil performing the Beethoven "Kreutzer" Sonata, could be represented at their most basic by sound waveforms.[13] (2) *Information goods* are information that is bought and sold; information goods with an appreciable shelf life are often inseparable from their means of storage and transfer, as seen with books, magazines, and maps; or more time-sensitive information goods would likely be transmitted as electronic data.[14] As an information good, the Beethoven "Kreutzer" Sonata would most likely reach the market in the form of a printed score; the Grumiaux-Haskil performance would reach the market on a CD or MP3 file. (3) *Experience goods* are commodities that must be experienced in order to be valued; most information goods are experience goods, since the buyer isn't likely to know if the latest best-selling novel, the newest news magazine, or the latest band's most recent album is worthwhile until she reads or hears some of it. To get around this difficulty, many Web-based businesses rely on branding and samples.[15] So-called common-practice examples of classical music tend to differ from recent popular examples in that their prime determinants are deceased and they are less obviously an experience good. In an information goods market, Grumiaux's and Beethoven's names function as a kind of branding for manners of musical experience that have been in circulation longer and more consistently—and perhaps more predictably—than Björk's or Beyoncé's.

The present chapter approaches musical information in terms of one recent method of information control and storage. In that sense, I focus most directly here on the subject of (4) *information technology*, the system and infrastructure that organize and provide access to information. Examples include software, the Internet, e-mail, radio stations, high-speed wireless, memory chips, disk drives, and VCRs. Information goods often comprise systems technology: music scores and CDs do, incorporating writing systems that interact respectively with the musician's score-reading ability and the disc player's laser tracking mechanism and DA converter; in describing MP3 specifically as a "container technology," Sterne points out its dual capacity for restricting and packaging information. The importance of MP3 as a "disruptive technology" can be gauged by the fact that various parties have held it responsible either for the impending death of recorded music or for its resurrection. Larger record companies have held both positions. As such big labels were astonishingly slow to understand, codecs like MP3 are a boon to music sales in that they impose dramatically lower reproduction and distribution expenses than CDs, whether sold through brick-and-mortar retail stores or online merchants.[16] MP3 takes those reductions even further than the CD, which offered lower reproduction costs than the LP, but not much lower distribution costs. Summarizing its special market importance, Sterne describes MP3 as "a form designed for massive exchange, casual listening and massive accumulation."[17]

Music involved various information systems long before the invention of computers and data processing. Musical style is itself an information technology system, as Milton Babbitt pointed out in 1958 when he separated "the public's own music" from a new modernist category marked by a "high degree of contextuality and autonomy," and more precisely by an increased variety of pitch relationships made possible by a more "efficient" tonal vocabulary. Babbitt summarizes the style thus: "This increase in efficiency necessarily reduces the 'redundancy' of the language, and as a result the intelligible communication of the work demands increased accuracy from the transmitter (the performer) and activity from the receiver (the listener)." With this description, Babbitt proudly emphasizes the status of his works as experience goods, describes their elegance as information systems, and tells us that they have a highly developed information technology and demand the same of their listeners.[18] But he doubtless overstates the differences between his "contextual" music and, say, Beethoven's *Grosse Fuge* or the late piano works of Liszt and Brahms. In fact, Babbitt's description could apply to many nineteenth-century examples of "absolute music." The originality cult of the Romantic period is by definition a culture of "contextual" thinking, and the lack of redundancy that Babbitt found in the new music of 1958 also marks the three composers mentioned above, particularly in their late period: listeners will notice that examples of absolute music, if compared generally to popular music, dance music, or illustrative program music of the same period, tend to repeat less, make fewer full stops, invite less consistent bodily response, and avoid some musical-affective topoi common to the Romantic period.

Described in Babbitt's terms, absolute music becomes an aesthetic of information deprivation. But then as early as 1810, E. T. A. Hoffmann praised Beethoven's trading of mundane detail for spiritual wealth in his instrumental works, his emphasis on the unknowable over the knowable.

In short, Hoffmann's Beethoven exegesis sounds rather like Babbitt's description of the late 1950s "specialist composers" (including Babbitt himself, presumably). As Hoffmann understands it, Beethoven's art serves as an example by virtue of its exclusion and abstraction:

> Instrumental music must avoid all senseless joking and triviality, especially where it is intended to be taken as absolute music and not to serve some definite dramatic purpose. It explores the depths of the soul for the presentiments of a joy which, nobler and more beautiful than anything experienced in this narrow world, comes to us from the unknown land; it inflames in our breasts an inner, rapturous life, a more intense expression than is possible through words, which are appropriate only to our limited earthly feelings.[19]

Such a culture of absolute music involves two paradoxes. It manifests itself in the careful delimitation and meting out of musical-structural information that characterizes the Viennese symphonic tradition before Mahler. This could be described as an abstract discourse, insofar as it follows schematic, rhetorical, or overtly teleological designs rather than more obviously natural "disintegrated" forms modeled on poetic content.[20] And yet the symphony—insofar as it might be said to begin with Haydn's "London" Symphonies and Beethoven's "Eroica"—was also written for an enlightened public rather than an aristocracy. Charles Burney once made the declaration that a listener needs to involve herself in the right imaginative processes if she is to understand the composer's designs, as indeed she must. As if in agreement, Haydn chose sonata form as a way of writing intelligibly within an instrumental idiom—and the sonata designs of his later symphonies do tend to be more straightforward than those in his piano sonatas, for example.[21] As its second paradox, such a self-important but delimited and informationally self-conscious culture of music might have worked as public discourse two centuries ago but now seems like a carefully constrained rivulet buried deep within the information tsunami unleashed by the mass media. Or, to borrow Babbitt's own metaphor for twelve-tone music, the music once defined as "absolute" could appeal for the same reasons a quiet cul-de-sac might: "There are those of us," he professes, "who prefer the relative quiet and solace of the dead-end street to the distractions and annoyances of the crowded thorough-fare."[22]

The composer who makes structure an explicit aspect of expression—examples would include Haydn and Anton Bruckner, Babbitt and Sofia Gubaidulina—has mastered the information technology that we call musical form. But similar kinds of algorithmic mastery go into the contexts surrounding musical performance and dissemination, not least among them the design of the instruments on which sonatas are played and the concert halls where symphonies are heard. The same can be said of the mechanical reproduction devices that record music and play it back. "Aesthetic production today," Fredric Jameson observes, "has become integrated into commodity production generally: the frantic economic urgency of producing fresh waves of ever more novel-seeming goods (from clothing to airplanes), at ever greater rates of turnover, now assigns an increasingly essential structural function and position to aesthetic innovation and experimentation."[23] It is difficult not to conclude, at least from an art music perspective, that recording and industrial design initiatives have largely usurped compositional technology. Is it coincidence that Schoenberg announced his twelve-tone method only several years before electrical recording and the ensuing exponential rise in recording innovations, for instance with the microphone? As several scholars have noted, modernist composers began writing complex music that demanded and presumed multiple hearings at the same time that recording technology enabled such detail to be heard in repeat auditions.[24] One could also be forgiven the suspicion that any present-day reincarnation of Beethoven's or Ellington's genius is not to be found in the music downloaded onto an iPod, but with the designer at Apple—specifically, Jonathan Ive—who has given the device its special feel and distinctive physical profile. The iPod, in short, is more original than any of the music now stored on it.

With his idea of "the ecstasy of communication," Jean Baudrillard diagnosed a postindustrial "obscene delirium" of instantaneous "readability," "fluidity," and "availability." He identified a state of informational saturation and said it had caused a collapse of traditional dualities of near-far, subject-object, representation-communication, and private-public into one cool surface of immanent and immediate experience. In such a state of all-permeating information—what computer-science types now commonly call a condition of "connectivity"—instrumental hierarchies and instruments of cultural cachet break down to the point where Bartók merges with Jonathan Ive and Debussy becomes indistinguishable from Freenet. The iPod, or whichever MP3 player one chooses, is styled, crafted, and built for all-day listening. It indulges a calm but irrefusable passion for unbroken informational exchange and has thereby made manifest the ecstasy of communication—a state that Baudrillard described as "too great a proximity of everything, the unclean promiscuity of everything which touches, invests and penetrates without resistance."[25]

LITERACIES

Literacy is a recipe for human connection with an information system, and a person who is said to be literate has assimilated a particular information technology. Literacy therefore isn't simply the ability to read and write a language but has a wider acculturative meaning: someone can qualify as "computer literate," "unix literate," or "algebra literate," for instance. Literacy ultimately becomes a social attribute: it is a system of signification and social values that a population can gather around. (McLuhan included "separateness of the individual" and "uniformity of codes" among his characteristics of "literate societies.")[26] While literacies allow people to come together into communities, they also entail division between cultures and what might be called noncultures. Certainly the word "illiterate" implies class distinctions, at least as it comes up in everyday U.S. parlance. And in the final analysis, the cognitive aspect of individual signification is inseparable from this social aspect. Jeanne M. De Temple and Catherine E. Snow differentiate between literacy "in the individual, psycholinguistic sense" and literacy deriving "from access to literate cultures, in the social, constructivist sense." But they describe these "psycholinguistic" and "social" definitions as "two sides of the same coin."[27]

Absolute-music cultures largely served as the basis for mainstream Western conceptions of musical literacy. To be considered musically literate, someone must—at the basic conservatory level—be able to sight-read, be fluent in solfege, and aurally find their way around a musical form of some length and complexity. Musical literacy in this sense is synonymous with the musicianship skills taught in music schools. And yet the absolute-music cultures that served as their basis and rationale are in retreat, as are cultures of art music generally, and we are now in the midst of a wholesale revision of musical literacy (though whether conservatories will ever make or even notice the change remains to be seen). Over the past half century, assimilation of a musical culture—as Babbitt's discussion of "contextual" music might suggest—has become less a matter of familiarity with its notation and more a matter of understanding its particular deployment and configuration of information. In this sense, MP3 and the iPod are—with their increasingly small and ever-more capacious hard drives and flash drives—instruments of mass familiarization. Accordingly, new conceptions of musical literacy will doubtless define music in the larger social and acculturative sense described above, as measured by familiarity and acquaintance with music of many different kinds. In short, musical literacy is becoming a matter of extending familiarity laterally rather than vertically, to varieties of musical style and expression rather than to finer and finer aspects of individual works.

In Steve Jones's view, music information systems say a great deal about cultural topographies as well as musical communities: "Network technologies used for music distribution are technologies of geography and of audiences. They have consequences for how people get to music and for how music gets to people."[28] We have to wonder, then, what kind of role Beethoven symphonies would be allowed in a world of MP3 systems. Loading the Seventh Symphony, say, onto an iPod would seem to strike up a geopolitical confrontation between Austro-German music-structural thinking and Silicon Valley notions of connectedness, portability, and lifestyle accessorization. As a kind of information technology, literacy is a geographical process, a kind of voyage, and the role that Steve Jones sees technology playing in "getting to" music has become equally important in "connecting with" music aesthetically, musically, and spiritually. A market dominated by MP3 would be oriented toward circularity and randomness, and in such a market the model of integral linear thinking could possibly, and ironically, become a kind of minority vernacular practice. Art music cultures would then, as David Barton describes such a situation in terms of general literacy, appropriate and subvert the dominant paradigm. Vienna would have to work overtime to personalize the Apple logo:

> Vernacular practices can be responses to imposed literacies. Some vernacular responses to official literacy demands disrupt the intentions of those demands, either functionally or creatively, to serve people's own purposes, sometimes they are intentionally oppositional to and subversive of dominant practices. Writing graffiti and defacing notices would be an example of this, especially where it is used to challenge official public messages. What is interesting here is how people make literacies their own, turning dominant literacies to their own use, by constant incorporation and transformation of dominant practices.[29]

Writing in the 1960s and after, McLuhan spoke of media "literacies," proposing that media shape *us* in a more profound sense than we shape *them*. "Media," he wrote, "bring about new perceptual habits." McLuhan spoke for instance of typographic conditioning and film literacy—humans developing new ways of focusing the eyes and understanding sensory experience to the degree that they were influenced by typography, and ways of intuiting narrative continuity between images as they were influenced by film. In this sense, McLuhan understood media to be modernized forms of language. And we can describe compressible digital sound files in terms similar to those he uses to describe language: "Language does for intelligence," McLuhan explained, "what the wheel does for the feet and the body. It enables [intelligence and body] to move from thing to thing with greater ease and speed and ever less involvement."[30] Substitute "MP3" for "wheel" and "ear" for "feet" in that sentence, and we arrive at an astute summary of the MP3's importance.

This relationship between person and "medium," which we could rephrase as the connection between the music-lover and an information technology, is a fascinating dynamic that McLuhan elsewhere called a servomechanism:

> By continuously embracing technologies, we relate ourselves to them as servomechanisms. That is why we must, to use them at all, serve these objects, these extensions of ourselves, as gods or minor religions. · An Indian is the servo-mechanism of his canoe, as the cowboy of his horse or the executive of his clock. . . . Man becomes, as it were, the sex organs of the machine world, as the bee of the plant world, enabling it to fecundate and to evolve ever new forms.[31]

Such a collapse of the subject-object duality is an informational matter, as Baudrillard pointed out in describing his own "ecstasy of communication." More specifically, it represents a perfectly transparent "tactic of potentialities linked to usage" where a wealth and instantaneity of feedback encourages car and driver, user and machine, to become one. In Baudrillard's words, instead of "expenditure, consumption, performance," the new technology manifests "regulation, well-tempered functionality, solidarity among all elements of the same system, control and global management of an ensemble."[32] The *Oxford English Dictionary* includes the informational feedback idea when it defines a servomechanism as "a powered mechanism in which a controlled motion is produced at a high energy or power level in response to an input motion at a lower energy level; esp. one in which feedback is employed to make the control automatic." A bicycle would be a prime example of the servomechanism in this sense—as a technology and as a device, it blurs any division between the driver and the drived, between the user and the thing used. I believe Baudrillard's ecstasy and McLuhan's servomechanism describe the MP3 and iPod more elegantly than Jonathan Sterne's description of the lossy codec as "a psychoacoustic technology that literally plays its listeners." Sterne refers here to the "lossy" aspect of the format, but he could just as well have been referring to the easy portability of MP3: the increasingly small digital sound file formats are bringing music so close and conveniently to listeners for so many hours of the day, making for an increasingly intimate system of self-regulating feedback, that an onlooker might well ask—as she would upon seeing someone ride a bicycle—just who is playing whom.

As music-lovers have moved from cylinders and gramophone horns to iPods, operating sound reproduction devices has become less and less like playing musical instruments. While getting the desired sound out of a gramophone (or even a turntable) could involve delicate and often quite personal adjustments—physical efforts that seemed aesthetic, nuanced, jerry-rigged, vaguely musical—an iPod Nano has no moving parts and is almost entirely noninteractive. Clearly, there is more to operating an MP3 player than the on-off switch: the flywheel demands a certain delicacy of touch more suited to a sensitive clavichord than to a power generator, but then such delicacy is largely owed to the miniaturization of the device as a whole. In any event, there is nothing "fuzzy" about the digital rationality of the MP3 player: any ergonomic subtlety is beholden to the binary, yes-no logic of its circuits, while the priceless aesthetic of a Bechstein piano or Guarneri viola sits with its particular and largely inscrutable form of "maybe."

And then there is the new way that the iPod connects with our anatomy. McLuhan declared media technologies to be strategic extensions of the human body: "The wheel is an extension of the foot," he observed in 1967, "the book is an extension of the eye, clothing an extension of the skin, electric circuitry an extension of the central nervous system."[33] If he had lived to experience the iPod, he probably would have seen it as a kind of servomechanistic implantation of musical literacy. The trademark iPod earbuds would be symbolic here: actually penetrating into the ear canal, they reduce to less than zero the distance between reproduction and ear. Never has an information technology been worn so closely to—indeed, so far *into*—the body. And, with the recent trend toward iPod-wired jackets, shoes, sunglasses, and even underwear, the technology is indeed worn in all possible meanings of the word.

In the grand ecstasy of communication, then, the MP3 and iPod have made the servomechanism of musical pleasure run tighter and more efficiently than ever before. (The transistor radio introduced a new measure of portability and musical individualism when it broke into the American market in the early 1960s, but today's MP3 players are something else altogether—not least because they allow the user to choose precisely what music she wants to hear when.) Technological determinist as he was, McLuhan read a certain servility into the word "servomechanism," such that the mechanism obeys the force producing the input motion or energy.

This would help explain the popularity of the iPod's shuffle option, a feature that would take over and lend its name to the cheapest of its players, namely the iPod shuffle. Shuffle-play makes it all the more difficult to answer the question of whether a human plays the MP3 player or vice versa. According to Apple's ads, putting their MP3 player on shuffle gives a listener "the ultimate exercise in uncertainty." Elsewhere, Apple's literature asks, "Does it have a mind of its own?" In his book on the iPod, Steven Levy summarizes many owners' suspicions that "the iPod, despite being the inanimate object that it was, would *decide* which artist it was in the mood for."[34] The iPod owners Levy has spoken with have become servomechanisms, indeed.

"The iPod is the first music carrier," Dylan Jones points out, "and digital music technology the first delivery system, to affect the music industry in the same way as music itself."[35] I take this audacious statement to mean that MP3 represents a musical revolution more than a media development. Jones is equating the iPod with Beethoven's second-period, heroic style or Elvis's electrifying Sun sides rather than with the invention of the long-playing record. In his view, MP3 is the first information technology to have the direct kind of impact, ontological as well as aesthetic, delivered inside to the listening mind itself, that was previously the province of music and musicians. I outlined above some reasons for this power, among them MP3's potential removal of all interruptions, time limits, and problems of access. For composers and songwriters, this change could have an impact not only on the length of musical utterance, but also on the internal organization of those utterances: for instance on phrasing, use of silence, or the amount of musical material. MP3 represents such a new way of arranging and transmitting musical information that we can speak of new kinds of literacy, ways of accessing "the music" as well as connecting with the information technology itself—in other words, accessing the mode of access. Morton Feldman realized the new kinds of literacy demanded by long forms when he observed: "The longer the piece, the less material you start with."[36] He could just as well have been referring to the long and unbroken musical stretches offered by the iPod.

INDIVIDUAL AND GROUP

Absolute music was built upon an isolationist aesthetic. In this conception, central to Western art music as a cultural construct, the listener experiences the work alone, as an isolated individual. And yet the work, as discussed, exercises its particular power by inspiring empathy or feelings that aspire to universality. In Tolstoy's novella *The Kreutzer Sonata*, a piece of absolute music precipitates an individual mind-set akin to madness: Beethoven's composition helps send the jealous husband Pozdnuishef into a hypnotic, almost crazed, and eventually murderous state. Pozdnuishef finds the condition bearable when the music has a "purpose," but when it doesn't, it delivers him into a condition of nervous, treacherous excitement. The absolute-ness, the music's condition of universality, merges with its power of individuality and inspires in him a state of dangerous and empowering delusion:

> How am I to express myself? Music makes me forget my true situation. It transports me into a condition not my own. Under the influence of music I seem to feel what I do not feel, to understand what I do not understand, to be able to do what I am not capable of doing. Music seems to me to act like yawning or laughter. I am not sleepy, but I yawn when I see others yawn, as, without any motive for laughter, I laugh when others laugh.[37]

In Pozdnuishef's thinking, music proves so powerful in all its forceful intimacy—"It has a terrible effect," he says—that society should avert its eyes. But that is symptomatic of this character's pathology. More commonly, absolute music asks all humanity to bear witness to its universal meaning: "Be embraced, ye millions, This kiss is for all the world!" (Seid umschlungen, Millionen, Diesen Kuß der ganzen Welt!), insist the basses in Beethoven's setting of Schiller for the Ninth Symphony.

But the piece of absolute music—whether a symphony or string quartet—is still to be contemplated in isolation, no matter how universal its message. In chapter 5 of E. M. Forster's *Howard's End*, Helen is so overwhelmed by Beethoven's message in the finale to his Fifth Symphony that she suddenly feels the need to be alone and, abandoning her companions, quits the concert hall:

> Beethoven chose to make all right in the end. He built the ramparts up. He blew with his mouth for the second time, and again the goblins were scattered. He brought back the gusts of splendour, the heroism, the youth, the magnificence of life and of death, and, amid vast roarings of a superhuman joy, he led his Fifth Symphony to its conclusion. But the goblins were there. They could return. He had said so bravely, and that is why one can trust Beethoven when he says other things.
> Helen pushed her way out during the applause. She desired to be alone.[38]

Forster treads a fine line in this knowing passage between universality and individual relevance, between public and personal, and in so doing plumbs the absolute-music aesthetic better than many a learned musicological tract. In the section of Helen's interpretation that precedes this passage, we watch as she drifts away from other interpretations of the music and into her own—a perspective that has no time for structural detail, like the transitional passage on the drum that her brother Tibby "implored the company generally to look out for." Helen's approach to the movement takes on an us-versus-them quality. Beethoven is on her side, encouraging the grand emotional purview that sets her apart from her companions, and having the courage to speak the truth: when it comes to the reassuring but too facile belief that the goblins could be easily banished as mere "phantoms of cowardice and unbelief," the composer shows how he "knew better" than "men like the Wilcoxes, or President Roosevelt." The reader presumes Helen knows better, too, than those upper-class people of wealth and power.[39]

The relation between the individual and universal in Beethoven's music also surfaces in Thomas Mann's *Doctor Faustus,* in a conversation between composer Adrian Leverkühn and his friend Serenus Zeitblom. Here, though, the individual impulse is said to have usurped musical organization, or at least remade structure in its own image. Any division between the personal and the collective is not played out in the emotional narrative of the music, as Helen Schlegel heard in the Fifth Symphony, but instead disappears into the musical-structural fabric of a composition. (Leverkühn and Zeitblom discuss Beethoven's music generally, not the Fifth specifically.) Once consigned to particular points in the sonata form, individualistic development spills over and becomes the main rationale of Beethoven's structure:

> 'The musical conventions being destroyed today have not always been so very objective, so fixed from without. They were consolidations of living experience and as such fulfilled a task of vital importance for a long time: the task of organization. Organization is everything. Nothing exists without it, and art least of all. But aesthetic subjectivity now took over that same task; it set about to organize the work of art out of itself, and in freedom.'
> 'You're thinking of Beethoven.'
> 'Of him and the technical principle by which imperious subjectivity took control of musical organization—that is, by development of a theme.'[40]

The individual element dominates here in two ways. As in *Howard's End,* the author casts his explanation of Beethoven the composer of absolute music as a monologue—undertaken here by Leverkühn, with Zeitblom acting as prompter. ("I don't quite understand," Zeitblom exclaims a bit further in. "Music grows old." Leverkühn responds to him in turn, and then goes into a discourse on the historical dynamic between musical elements.)[41] Forster and Mann, speaking through Helen Schlegel and Adrian Leverkühn in such fashion, give the impression that Beethoven's music is a matter for individual rather than communal reflection. Second, in both books individual subjectivity is seen to win out over a historic and perhaps oppressive objectivity—not necessarily the culture of musical "absoluteness" per se— and that is what makes Beethoven's music so great and meaningful. Forster, Mann, and some other fiction writers are adept at conveying the full dialectic of Beethoven as a composer of instrumental music. He was the apex of the Viennese symphonic tradition and the definitive figure in absolute music, but at the same time—because of the intensely subjective and ultimately triumphant quality of his narratives as "histories of a theme"—he represented the beginning of the end for musical abstraction.[42]

As it aspires to universal meaning and is based in group culture and yet is meant to be contemplated alone and without discussion, absolute music is modeled upon Judeo-Christian religious experience. Carl Dahlhaus points to a 1797 novella passage by Wilhelm Heinrich Wackenroder as an example of aesthetic contemplation taking on the character of religious devotion: "Whereas music, in the form of church music, used to partake of religion as revealed in the 'Word,'" remarks Dahlhaus, "it now, as autonomous music capable of conveying the 'inexpressible,' has become religion itself."[43] The absolute-music aesthetic is also indebted to cultures of silent reading, insofar as they can be separated from religious tradition: in the late Middle Ages more and more European laity took up the monasterial practice of silent reading and were thereby, in the words of Henri-Jean Martin, able "to internalize and individualize their dialogue with God."[44] As described by Steven Roger Fischer, this developing practice made intellectual discourse more diversified and less dogmatic even before the arrival of Gutenberg and printing from movable type:

> That essence of 'medieval reading,' passive listening-*and*-reading, was diminishing. Active silent reading now prevailed, which demanded engagement. Hereby a reader became a doer, insofar as an author was now merely a guide who showed her or his silent and invisible audience a variety of paths. If early medieval listener-readers had almost always heard one chorus of voices singing Christian litany in harmonized unison, 'humanist' scholars of the late Middle Ages were silently reading an entire world of voices, each singing a different song and in many tongues. And with increased literacy the laity no longer required

the Church's intercession, for through personal and silent reading the divine dialogue had become by and large private and solitary.[45]

Apart from a very general trend from community toward increasing isolation, there isn't a consistent relation between reading-aloud practices and music-listening conventions across the years. A relatively small culture of reading aloud did arise at about the same time public concerts became widespread, and in the same countries. Jane Austen remembered in 1808 that her family read to each other throughout much of the day. Dickens arranged highly popular tours where he would recite from his own novels. Fischer reminds us that when authors undertook such practices these often initiated feedback on developing texts and served as aids to revision. Whitman's constantly evolving *Leaves of Grass* is a prime example, honed through the author's many readings, and reaching print in various editions between 1855 and 1891. Across the nineteenth century as a whole, however, Richard Leppert, Jonathan Sterne, and Lydia Goehr have remarked upon an increasingly stringent encroachment of silence on the music concert experience as *werktreu* cultures took hold.[46] "Even public spaces became more and more private," remarks Sterne, in order to allow individual contemplation of "the music that [audiences] had enshrined as autonomous art." Remember the Schlegels' experience listening to Beethoven's Fifth in the concert hall, where it is Helen—silent, "enwrapped," and least banal because most imaginative among the group in her interpretation of the music—who comes away with the deepest emotional experience.

Just as a lot of concert music from the nineteenth through the mid-twentieth century aspired to the status and prestige of absolute music, so "serious music" listening at home—as modeled on the concert experience—was largely a communal activity. At least at first, this probably had as much to do with the influence of precisely scheduled "live" concert radio broadcasts as it did the domestic use of recordings per se. One also shouldn't forget the simple economic reasons for communal listening: records and sound reproduction devices were more expensive than now, and not many families could afford them. But once they became mass-market commodities, victrolas, gramophones, and stereo systems were advertised and sold as social aids and vehicles for communal functions. Open-speaker portable systems were a social tool—from the Close 'N Plays at school dances to boom boxes and the setup carted around in the 1970s by DJ Kool Herc to stir up block parties in the Bronx. Some of these promotions—"The invitation included the Decca," reads a 1927 British portable gramophone ad showing a happy socialite bounding out the door—presented the sound reproduction machines as accessories sure to facilitate fun and popularity. Others—a familial 1961 Reader's Digest advertisement of the Beethoven symphonies under René Leibowitz's direction as "a unique and wonderful listening experience!"—portray the nuclear suburban family's absolute-music encounter as a confluence of socialization, individual appreciation, and modern convenience.

But the social implications of the absolute-music experience are by no means definite. Is listening to Beethoven an individual or a communal encounter? It is an intensely private experience for Helen Schlegel, yet the conclusions she draws—"Life could have no other meaning"—are universal and axiomatic, and drawn at the expense of those people who don't "know better." For Pozdnuishef, the Beethovenian experience is so deeply private and particularized as to divide or even imperil society. Beethoven's Sonata for Violin and Piano in A Major, op. 47 proves frightening enough to make him envy cultural practices in China, where "music is regulated by government, and this is as it should be." The listening culture of the iPod is likewise ambiguous, which might in fact represent its prime suitability to Beethoven and Brahms. The iPod invites an isolationist listening experience as a musical vehicle and servomechanism—to return to McLuhan's analogy, the Amerindian didn't share his canoe! It certainly brings the music in close, almost implanting it into the brain. And this isolationist implantation of technology would seem a natural match for music that Babbitt—in describing his own extension of the absolute-musical aesthetic—termed "contextual" rather than "public." Babbitt sounds like a card-carrying iPod listener when he asks to be left alone in his musical isolation: "After all, the public has its own music."[47]

But the question remains as to how much of this isolation is truly individual, and how much is commercial construction. With his concept of "the 'We'" as instituted by the music market, Theodor W. Adorno traced out some of this ambiguity and deception: "The din and to-do of entertainment music feigns exceptional gala states; the 'We' that is set in all polyphonous music as the a priori of its meaning, the collective objectivity of the thing itself, turns into customer bait." As Adorno describes it, "the 'We'" is the culture industry's way of creating a public (with singular indefinite article), as well as the individual music-lover's sense of belonging to, and participating in, it:

> By circling them, by enveloping them as inherent in the musical phenomenon—and turning them as listeners into participants, it contributes ideologically to the integration which modern society never tires of achieving in reality. It leaves no room for conceptual reflection

between itself and the subject, and so it creates an illusion of immediacy in a totally mediated world, of proximity between strangers, the warmth of those who come to feel a chill of unmitigated struggle of all against all.[48]

Not only is Adorno's concept of "the 'We'" highly dialectical, but there remains some question as to whether the iPod and Walkman listeners stand apart from or constitute an integral part of it. (Though he did live to see the transistor radio, Adorno didn't deign to theorize it specifically. Would he have seen a transistor radio–user indulge more of a "regression of listening" than the 1930s radio listeners he discussed?)[49] Michael Bull takes the Walkman to be the definitive instrument of "the 'We,'" a means of entering into the fabricated community Adorno describes.[50] But I disagree and say the iPod listener constitutes a public of one. Contrary to Bull, I understand Adorno's "the 'We'" to be an aspect of live concert culture, one that the personal stereo—with its isolationist scenario—works to subvert. At the same time, I read "the 'We'" as a partial travesty of absolute-music culture, a cynical appropriation of its universalist aesthetic: Adorno's "proximity between strangers" sounds like a caricature of Schiller and Beethoven's "All men become brothers, Under the sway of thy gentle wings" (All Menschen werden Brüder, Wo dein sanfter Flügel weilt).

I have omitted another aspect of Adorno's "the 'We'" as Bull discusses it, and that is its creation of a sense of immediacy by forestalling "conceptual reflection between itself and the subject." In short, the listener is kept too busy and sated to notice the work or even the moment-to-moment presence of music itself—an element of the equation that could only defuse immediacy. She is so urgently and intently familiarized that she doesn't realize if there is or isn't anything to be familiarized *with*. (Adorno puts this slightly differently in his essay "On the Fetish-Character in Music and the Regression of Listening": "The delight in the moment and the gay façade becomes an excuse for absolving the listener from the thought of the whole.")[51] But here again I would disagree with Bull and ask if the tight servomechanism of MP3 and iPod really allows the listening experience to be as empty—and, in the final analysis, as heavily mediated—as all that. Cultural-technological naysayers like to show the iPod inducing an insularity in its listeners, and then berate it for turning music into aural wallpaper. Sterne presents Adorno as author of a simplistic, and therefore inaccurate and indeed non-Adornian, regression of listening: "The ideal listener implied by the mp3's psychoacoustic coding is Theodor Adorno's nightmare: the 'distracted' consumer of mass culture. In a media-saturated environment, portability and ease of acquisition trumps monomaniacal attention. . . . At the psychoacoustic level as well as the industrial level, the MP3 is designed for promiscuity."[52]

iPod users themselves often bring up a particularly active aspect of listening that the theorists rarely mention: they say it's not the music that is consumed in a state of distraction, but rather the *non*musical side of the experience that is structured *around the music.* "When I'm listening to the Walkman I'm not just tuning out," said one personal stereo user in 1989. "I'm also tuning in a soundtrack for the scenery around me."[53] The technology simply supplies so much music so continuously—hardly a bad thing when stated in those terms—that it forces the rest of the everyday world to become its accompaniment, or better yet forces the listener to imaginatively reconfigure the phenomenal world in a way that enhances the music or otherwise helps bring out its meanings. Speaking for myself, whenever I'm connected to my iPod and listening to Brahms or Stravinsky, or James Brown for that matter, I'm much less interested than usual in my visual environment. I tend to find the not-music falling into place around the music, in a way that recalls Nietzsche's words about *Tristan und Isolde,* that "the listener *forgets* the drama and wakes up again for it only after the Dionysian spell [of the music] is broken."[54] Nietzsche sounds like yet another iPod user here, and his experience with Wagner is, not coincidentally, "absolute" at its essence: astonished by this music's power to transfix the listener and supplant everything else in the listener's purview, including the words being sung, he calls *Tristan* "the greatest symphony written."

CANONS FROM SHUFFLES

If a piece of music represents information configured in a certain way, canons of favorite and important musical works represent what could be called metatechnologies of musical-aesthetic information. Developments in media and technology are causing canons to change, both in content and in structure. One reason for this is that media-related change tends to radically expand, or sometimes diminish, the number of choices available to consumers. And all consensuses, no matter how socially significant or durable across time, are to some degree created and supported by a limitation of options. (The assertion goes against a capitalist myth that choices are made from an open field of equal options, and that consumer choice is a kind of metonymy for the democratic process—in short, that buying is like voting.) As the common-practice music repertory came together in the nineteenth century, there were limited opportunities for publication, given the cost of engraved plates, and so publication was really only possible at the exclusion of other composers. Conducted by Brahms between 1859 and 1861, members of the Hamburger Frauenchor tried to boost his sales by repeatedly asking for his music in Hamburg shops.[55] The idea of Brahms's music being hard to access seems all the stranger now because we are accustomed to the less-restricted, less-concentrically conceived, dissemination that is now possible through MP3s and the Internet more generally.

MP3 has an inherent "mission," Sterne believes, a need to follow certain self-propounded exhortations: "Travel great distances frequently and with little effort! Accumulate on the hard drives of the middle class! Address a distracted listening subject!"[56] Stated in these terms, the MP3 undertaking sounds like a mission to increase literacy, a cultural phenomenon that presupposes an abundance of texts made available at affordable prices. In this sense, MP3 servers come to resemble the lending libraries that Carl Shapiro and Hal R. Varian believe helped raise literacy rates in early nineteenth-century England: "The availability of low-cost entertainment motivated many to learn to read. . . . The publishers who served the new mass market for books thrived, while those who sold only to the elite disappeared. As the market grew, people started to buy rather than rent their books."[57]

Regarding the conversion from what Fischer calls "passive listening-*and*-reading" to a more active, diverse, and personalized form of reading, technological "determinists" of a McLuhanesque stripe might summarize that change as a shift in media—from one publication technique to another. And a large-scale media change can occur only if it enlarges the market substantially, as Shayo and Guthrie suggested with their idea of a "disruptive technology." "The MP3 is designed for promiscuity," Sterne notes—which is true, but one generation's promiscuity becomes another generation's canon-making process, and we should remember that the same sort of comments once greeted comic books and the popular novel. The sudden increase in readership and texts in early nineteenth-century England caused many to predict a tragic end to literature, and this kind of prophecy has recurred many times since: "I dare not compliment their pass-time or rather kill-time with the name of reading," Samuel Coleridge wrote of the new readers among the laity. "Call it rather a sort of beggarly day-dreaming, during which the mind of the dreamer furnishes for itself nothing but laziness and a little mawkish sensibility."[58] His rant resembles the accusation, aired frequently over the past twenty years, that personal stereos turn music into aural wallpaper. But an entirely new canon, a reading vernacular, originated from the crisis that Coleridge lamented—namely the genre of the popular novel.

If limitations of access help define or at least perpetuate a canon, proliferation of authors and texts begets a fragmented market. Over the past five decades or so, the gradual lowering of record prices—and, naturally, of prices for the electronics to play them on—has in itself contributed to the dismantling of absolute music as a kind of aesthetic consensus. A 1945 Columbia advertisement lists 78 rpm sets of staples like Brahms's First Symphony and Dvořák's Ninth at the Office of Price Administration ceiling price of $4.85—or $41.50 in year 2000 dollars, as calculated by changes in the consumer price index. (Popular music was priced slightly lower than classical.) Available at cheaper and cheaper prices, recordings and recording technology helped bring about the broadest dissemination of art music, a glut of Beethoven symphony interpretations, and eventually by the 1990s a market so fragmented that it could hardly support an art music canon. Now the wide availability of music on the Internet has shifted this fragmentation process into overdrive. Could absolute music have ever become such a far-reaching cultural construct if nineteenth-century music-lovers had had access to a near-infinite number of disposable 99¢ music downloads and the almost immediate turnover of taste and aesthetic that they encourage? The music-loving public, if they were given that avenue of quick-and-easy musical acquisition, might have latched permanently and all the more strongly onto Domenico Cimarosa's operas and forgotten the sometimes obscure Mozart entirely.

The very size of the iPod gives it an almost infinite variety of musical, or musical-structural, possibilities: one model has 160GB and can hold 40,000 songs, or more than 110 days of continuous music. (It's only a matter of time before a visionary composer or musician tailors a single and continuous "work" to the thousand hours of an iPod's memory and leaves far behind Morton Feldman's previous record of five or six hours for his String Quartet No. 2 of 1983. With Karlheinz Stockhausen's passing, Brian Eno would seem the logical candidate.) If you felt so inclined, you could load your 160GB player up with Wagner's *Parsifal* and be the first person in history to hear the opera with no pauses or interruptions, except cursory nods to the composer's between-act breaks. (Formatting the work as one single and continuous five-hour digital file would take some finagling but is certainly doable with the help of sound file editing software.) After challenging your aural fortitude by hearing *Parsifal* straight through end to end, you would find your 160GB iPod big enough that you could give Wagner's

Bühnenweihfestspiel some context by going right on to the entire *Ring* as well as a thousand other MP3-encoded operas, and thereby more than exhaust the entire repertory of mid- to late nineteenth-century music dramas that represented Wagner's competition on the European continent. For example, a quick cut over to Meyerbeer's *Les Huguenots* or *Robert le Diable* might shed some light on the Bayreuth master's pretense of dislike for *grand opéra*, Meyerbeer's work in particular.

The iPod can extend a person's musical, stylistic, aesthetic, and historical reach in an entirely new way. In Dylan Jones's estimation, a library of instantly accessible digital music files represents "an endless multiplicity of truths, a string of infinite possibilities."[59] Those infinite possibilities could include, of course, shuffling *Parsifal* with Japanese Gagaku, Esquivel, grindcore, and Cistercian chant. I can only believe that instructive and constructive situations will result from the information-technological "anomalies" of playing a Beethoven symphony (mentioned here as metonymy for absolute music and linear thinking) on an iPod. As an unusually flexible information system, MP3 promises the possibility of exit from "the new segregations of taste and audience" that Will Straw lamented in 1997:

> Magazines, radio formats and the broader logics of social differentiation have circumscribed tastes and buying patterns within predictable clusters. What has been lost, arguably, are those (politically ambiguous) moments of crossover or convergence which regularly undermined music's usual tendency to reinforce social and racial insularity. Stumbling around the record superstore, 'lost, driven crazy,' the paths we follow are likely, nevertheless, to map the stubborn lines of social division.[60]

But it would be just as feasible to go the opposite direction with the iPod, and take the traditional composer-, genre-, and chronology-driven option of listening to Brahms symphonies or Mozart piano concertos all the way through. An iPod can be turned into the ultimate canon demonstrator: a listener could witness composers' formal "progress" and their intricate and subtle experiments in generic thinking by assembling Beethoven's string quartets in immediate chronological order, for example, or all the Haydn symphonies or the complete Scarlatti keyboard sonatas. Try doing *that* with a CD or record player! Such massive, canonic assemblages become a double-edged sword, however. Compacting the Great Quartets or Great Symphonies listening experience so tightly, in a way that wasn't possible before the iPod, clarifies and perhaps justifies the canon, but it can also bring out in a new way the negative aspect of canons and canonic thinking. In short, the iPod's massive storage capacity—and, for the user, the daunting

prospect of formulating a kind of *Gesamtausgabe*—invites musical reex-
amination and stock-taking. Dylan Jones's wincingly titled little book *iPod,
Therefore I Am* takes shape around a mission to fill his new 40GB iPod with
all the music that has informed his life—classical, popular, world beat,
ripped from CDs, LPs, and tapes. The project opens his eyes to the fact that
all canons must shift and change over the years, and he also comes face-to-
face with their definition. In short, he finds his wireless, portable, and startlingly capacious iPod becoming a kind of externalized musical-aesthetic
conscience:

> The big thing about the iPod, I thought, was the way in which it forces
> you to listen to your life in a new way. . . . And as for the canon, well,
> it just wasn't going to work. There are many so-called classic albums
> that I have never particularly seen the point of, and when I started fill-
> ing my iPod I realized I had been too lenient with them. . . . My iPod
> didn't care a fig for the canon, and it wasn't going to start liking records
> just because it ought to, just because *Rolling Stone* and *Q* and *Mojo*
> said it ought to.[61]

In pondering musical staples, Jones also looks into the perennial differentiation of official from vernacular canons—the list of works one should
know, as opposed to the list of works one would like to hear. He brings up
the desert-island-disc question, and then asks: "What would be the point
of bringing your eight favorite records with you? Wouldn't it be better to
take eight things you didn't know, eight records you could grow to love
just by dint of listening to them ad infinitum?"[62] Here the tightly wound
servomechanism of the iPod—with its impatient, faster than immediate
feedback loop between musical pleasure and track-change switch—has
merely brought to a head an issue that has become important in several
music cultures. The kind of choice Jones refers to has even become an urgent one with concert art music, as shown by the fact that the fifth edition of the time-honored *Norton Anthology of Western Music* has traded
once-canonic scores by Elliott Carter and Gunther Schuller for perennials
by Rachmaninov, Gershwin, and Samuel Barber. If iPods had dealt with
the same kind of repertory, MP3 listeners would probably have dropped
American experimentalism and third-stream music some thirty years ago:
the cultural selection process is of course far slower in print than in digital
music media, and even slower when administered by academics.[63]

In short, an iPod brings home the fact that canons were never meant
for end-to-end listening. The Great Symphonies? The Great Piano Trios?
All fifteen Shostakovich string quartets? In the MP3 culture of nonstop
enjoyment, so very different from the old concert culture or even from

the practice of marathon concerts, such axiomatic categories prove coun-terproductive. If a listener hears all Beethoven symphonies in a row, the composer's various ways of "playing" with the sonata form ideal-type could blur together into mere idiosyncrasy. Without non-Beethovenian exemplars for comparison, the restless individualities crowd out the para-digmatic structural and stylistic normalities that—functioning as con-trasting, negative examples—give those distinctions meaning. For another matter, such canonic-generic trawls tend to produce progressive exhaustion or distraction and thereby run counter to the compositional-developmental presumption that composers develop more important, or at least new, things to say as they move through time and experience. To give just one example: hearing Mahler's symphonies end to end would negate the great leave-taking in the finale of the Ninth. This wouldn't be an issue of too-easy access or of overexposure. Rather, an iPod listener experiencing a Bau-drillardian state of "ecstatic communication" and the subject-object collapse that comes with it would find the whole idea of leave-taking unintelligible: seeing no difference between public and private, explicit and intimate, she could only wonder what manner of extinction the music seems concerned with, from whom and by whom, and why it might be relevant.

PLAYLISTS, OR RUFFLED CANONS

So if musical canons are largely incompatible with MP3, what might take their place? How is absolute music to be organized and heard on a 2,640-hour iPod? The answer is playlists: anti-intellectual, miniaturized, tailored to the individual listener and momentary whim, canon replacements for the twenty-first century. Indeed, anyone searching for today's most re-vealing criticism of canonic thinking will find it in the expanding popular literature on playlists. The term has been around for some decades, origi-nally referring to the preset record-spinning schedules at radio stations. But now, in the time of iTunes and the breakdown of albums into individual songs, the playlist has taken on the more personal meaning of individual track assemblages that are arranged around specific, and often whimsical, themes. "You can do anything with a playlist," observes Mark Ellingham. "Historic overviews of artists, retrospectives of a micro-genre that passed everyone else by, lists of the greatest soul songs ever, classic hip-hop, or prog rock that stands the test of time. Or something more flip, like the weirdest covers ever recorded, or songs about the moon, or rain, or stars, or chickens and insects, or jelly, or getting drunk."[64] In Dylan Jones's view, playlists fill a void left by the demise of the album and fuel the acquisitive urge that comes with owning an iPod: "If songs really are little houses in which our hearts once lived, then surely it's our duty to build gargantuan pleasure palaces where they all can live. After all, the iPod is nothing if not a memory box."[65]

The *Rough Guide Book of Playlists* offers 500 such playlists to organize personal MP3 listening, arranged in four categories:

Artists: Marvin Gaye to Nick Cave, Björk to Manu Chao, Rufus Wainwright to Thelonious Monk, Frank Sinatra to Franz Ferdinand

Genres: Britpop to Krautrock, dub to Motown, bebop to bhangra, punk to drum 'n' bass, fado to gangsta rap

Themes: Broken hearts, motoring music, protest songs, covers that beat the originals, the Summer of Love . . .

Quirks & Silliness: Singing drummers, aliens, chickens and insects, drinking songs, and even music raved about in Murakami novels . . .[66]

To substantiate the personal element, the book also presents a number of playlists written up by individual musicians. Two examples will illustrate that type: Keith Richards's list includes Delta blues, Little Richard's "Good Golly, Miss Molly," and Hank Williams's "You Win Again"; the list by Kronos Quartet violinist David Harrington encompasses tracks by Schubert, Dvořák, Bach, and Pärt as well as work of Bessie Smith, Jimi Hendrix, Ravi Shankar, Howard Zinn, and the Aka Pygmies.

Playlists can be quasi-canonic and quasi-generic. They represent miniaturized, individualized, and finessed versions of earlier canonic formulations, though they are much more listening heuristics than aesthetic constructs. It should come as no surprise that such overarching aesthetic conceptions are rooted in information systems of the listener's own time. While earlier notions of canon were book-based conceptions—organized into composers and works, and sometimes involving quasi-bibliographic labels like "library"—the playlist is rooted in the menu and search functions found in computerized devices. All one has to do is scroll through an iPod to understand how playlists are organized, and why they are structured the way they are. They usually aren't hierarchical or internested, as traditional canons often are, but lateral—in the sense that Jones describes today's form of "lateral listening," where one is "just as likely to buy a Bob Dylan compilation or a repackaged Oasis album as . . . the new CD from Kelis or Coldplay."[67] Another way of describing the lateral aspect of playlists is to say they can connect any point to any other and every other. Described in media terms, the playlist sounds like a form of individual rebellion against the print-published literary culture of "closed" texts and public monologues as portrayed by Steven Fischer:

> Different now is that public reading is a monologue: it is no longer a dialogue that might yield a better work. Society has become too large for this, and the book industry's accountants have first say. Much of today's radio and TV announcing and programming involves reading, but to a faceless audience, with little or no human response. Texts in general are no longer plastic, but stone: the printed word is final.[68]

Of course, the ultimate if paradoxical expression of computerized playback is the iPod's shuffle-play option. As already suggested, there is some debate as to just how liberating and challenging shuffle playback is. Not surprisingly, Apple's publicity has taken a proclamatory approach: "Random is the New Order" reads their oxymoronic advertising copy. "Welcome to a life less orderly. As official soundtrack to the random revolution, the iPod shuffle songs setting takes you on a unique journey through your music collection—you never know what's around the next tune." Steven Levy takes a similar perspective, calling shuffle-play "the *techna franca* of the digital era." He sees it as a kind of Barthesian empowering of the reader over the previous tyrannies of authorship:

> [It is] not just a feature on a gadget but an entire way of viewing the world, representing the power that comes from aggregating content from a variety of sources and playing it back in an order that renders irrelevant the intended ordering by those who produced or first distributed the content. Google shuffles the Web, and iPod shuffles the music.[69]

Niall Lucy took a more skeptical view of shuffle-play, at least as found on CD players: "The shuffle function on CD-players builds in this capacity to 're-arrange' musical texts, though the capacity is extremely minimal and no great cause for thinking that consumers have been 'liberated' or that they are naturally 'creative' or 'transgressive' in their interactions with the textual products of corporate culture."[70] Apple's perspective has since won this debate, by leavening the randomness with the playlists phenomenon. Since Lucy made his comment, shuffle-play has become an aspect of playlists—such that the iTunes shufflings are usually not really random, but taken from playlists that the user has at some point compiled for herself. In short, some randomnesses are more random than others. (Apple has also introduced a more stringent shuffle option, accessible through the "autofill" function in iTunes.)

It is difficult to trace the source of this "random revolution"—culturally, ontologically, and more strictly speaking, musically. "The linear experience is gone," notes rock musician John Mayer. "There's a new digital etiquette. The iPod scroll bar has changed the chemistry of listening, and we're now a skip-forward generation."[71] In the view of critic Kelefa Sanneh, an iPod shuffle "will let you hear your favorite music in a totally different context. Narrow obsession has come to seem less appealing than broad familiarity [of the] scrupulously eclectic world of . . . iPod shuffle owners, all of them finding ways to make chaos part of their listening experience."[72] An unbeliever would attribute shuffling to laziness or attention deficit disorder before she would be able to see any aesthetic purpose to it, but then there is a long tradition—at least in art music—of seeing indolence in discontinuity and emphasis on the moment. The iPod's very possibilities of access, intercession, interruption, and repetition would seem to run counter to the basic philosophical, ontological, and formal rationales of Beethoven symphonies. Whenever they engage in this iPod-induced abandonment of "the linear experience," music listeners of today fly in the face of the structural ideas developed by music theorist and Brahms acolyte Heinrich Schenker. They open themselves up to the same accusations of wanton discontinuity and indolent shortsightedness that Schenker aimed at certain performers: in 1925 he complained of players who "plod along from one passage to the next with the laziest of ears and without the slightest musical imagination." Some time later, he specifically criticized Mozart performances as "unimaginative, stiff, humdrum, constantly oriented to the next line of tones."[73]

Schenker made room within his analytic method for the concept of formal "interruption" (*Unterbrechung*), if only to reconcile his linear paradigm with that most tonal yet least directional of musical forms: the ternary, or ABA. In the case of a ternary or sonata-allegro form, the fundamental *Ursatz* could be divided through *Unterbrechung*, but only between the dominant-supported arrival on scale-degree 2 and the cadential arrival on degree 1 in the fundamental line. In short, Schenker viewed instrumental form—and his structural perspective has proved definitive and fundamental to any history of absolute music—as an integral unit, with any possibilities of "interruption" highly formalized. A form must continue and finish once it begins, or it will cease to be a valid tonal form—and in Schenker's judgment the only authentic forms are tonal forms. Such a formal theory is not open to use of the pause, back-track, and forward-track buttons on an iPod—at least if one still wishes to call what she's hearing a "performance" of Bach, Beethoven, Brahms, Chopin, or whichever composer she is hearing. (Schenker did not recognize Mahler, Debussy, or Stravinsky as composers worthy of comparison to anyone in the Austro-German canon and would therefore probably have said that shuffling their works does them little if any harm.)

Thus the Schenkerian perspective. But a number of important examples expose as something of a myth the assumption that shuffling movements by Beethoven, Mahler, or Brahms would ipso facto contravene and violate those composers' structural thinking. In reality, there are some instances of symphonic-compositional "shuffling" from the composers themselves, though of course these don't exceed certain music-structural limits. (No music that sounds genuinely "shuffled" came along until Ives, Cage, Berio, and Schnittke—composers who considered the absolute-music aesthetic only one allusive possibility among many.) Mahler, for instance, had trouble deciding on the order of movements in his Sixth Symphony: his first edition of the score has the Scherzo second and the Andante third, but he performed and republished the work with those inner movements in the opposite order. The 1963 Mahler Society edition returned to the original sequence, and most conductors do likewise, but the revision has its advocates—Simon Rattle and Claudio Abbado among them. This example doesn't present an isolated case but should encourage us to ask whether other composers had similar "crises of ordering" and were just more intent than Mahler on denying or covering them up. When he conducted his First Symphony, Mendelssohn was in the practice of substituting the Scherzo from his string octet for the original third movement. Bruckner had some traumatic vacillations regarding large-scale form and orderings of symphonic material, and even supplied entirely different slow movements for the two versions of his Fourth Symphony. Schubert often left symphonies and piano sonatas unfinished, and some sonata autographs survive with movements in indeterminate order, and so players are forced to make hard decisions about what constitutes a Schubertian work and an idiomatic sequence. Sviatoslav Richter, for one, was in the practice of playing the unfinished E Minor Piano Sonata, D. 566, with its sonata-form Allegretto placed not second as found in most printed editions, but third and last, which he thought brought the work to a more appropriate conclusion.[74] And then there is the issue of encored repetitions in concert performance. Contrary to today's *werktreu* practices, nineteenth-century performers would not infrequently reprise a movement if it particularly pleased the audience: starting with the symphony's premiere in 1813, the Allegretto second movement of Beethoven's Seventh proved so popular that conductors were often forced to repeat it at least once before they could go on to the Scherzo. Isn't this equivalent to pushing the "repeat" button on an iPod or Discman? Today, concert audiences aren't even allowed any avenue of approval between movements, so there is no possibility of "repeats" by popular demand.

This similarity isn't our only hint that MP3 and iPods give the lie to the supposedly inviolate orderedness of absolute music, and that they will indeed return some art music practices to aesthetics that held sway before the construction of absolute-music ideals. The iPod and MP3 are already wreaking such great change on musical markets, ontologies, and literacies that it's difficult to imagine that any music anywhere will escape its impact—at least within the so-called developed countries, where "culture" is increasingly hard to separate from corporate capital. Current MP3 users certainly share some literacies, aesthetic interests, and social habits with the European concert cultures that surfaced during the Industrial Revolution—for example in London in the 1790s and in Vienna in the first decades of the nineteenth century. Among these we could count interest in the kinds of performance cultures that disappeared with developing *werktreu* convictions, general musical novelty, mixing of genres and individual movements, willingness to impose on the concert program or the musical subject itself, and general disinterest in what would later be called concert protocol. The museum culture of the late nineteenth-century concert—what Lydia Goehr calls "the imaginary museum of musical works"—had not yet formed, and a lack of standardization meant concert-giving took a variety of forms. These included the Viennese *Akademien* that often went on for hours and could comprise individual arias alongside entire symphonies.

An art-as-religion aesthetic formed a prime aspect of the museum of musical works, and this is lost in the corporate iconicity of Apple's iPod. How much of a look-in can the musical work get when played on a device that, to meet Steve Jobs's demand, was designed "to look so good you'd want to lick it"?[75] In his 1936 essay "The Work of Art in the Age of Mechanical Reproduction," Walter Benjamin described modern commodity culture and its destruction of the aura that once surrounded objects of veneration. From a Benjaminian perspective, MP3 would represent an extreme stage in the mechanical reproduction of music inasmuch as this technology expedites, or even encourages, duplication: "Digital copies," Shapiro and Varian remind us, "are perfect copies of the original. For digital content, production is reproduction."[76] One Benjamin declaration would have to wait until MP3 before becoming true in most senses, at least with regard to music: "For the first time in world history, mechanical reproduction eman-cipates the work of art from its parasitical dependence on ritual."[77] MP3 certainly goes some way toward eliminating concert-hall rituals, conven-tions that have been especially dominant (some would say oppressive) in the world of absolute music. It has done the same for the once-endemic practices of turning the record over, cleaning the LP, changing the CD, and other such home-listening routines—rituals that were as celebratory and incantatory in their way as church practices. The iPod has become some-thing of a religious icon in itself, however: technology has made it possible for the mechanical rituals of recorded music playback to become rituals of corporate chic.

6. Photo/phono/porno

Susan Sontag called photography an "ethics of seeing," and by analogy recording could be termed an "ethics of hearing."[1] Photography's traditional truth-telling powers stem from its long association with photojournalism. Recording owes such truth implications to the absolute-music heritage, the work concept, and to the art-religion idea originating with Friedrich Schleiermacher and Ludwig Tieck—legacies by which music recording becomes a form of scripture, a means of faithful transmission for timeless edicts.[2] Ethics is largely inseparable from politics, whether instituted in photography, recording, or any other endeavor. The microphone and the camera, as part of their peculiarly implicit form of ethics-politics, feign impartiality when in truth they remake reality in their own image: their power lies in the ostensible transparency of purpose under which they point the onlooker to *this* image in *this* way and at *this* time. The picture-taking process reformulates or entirely supplants any reality residing in the scene photographed, even in photos that pretend to be impromptu and candid. Or reality is *especially* supplanted in such photos, as epitomized by fashion shots. Seeing a heavily posed, made-up, coiffed, Photoshopped, and yet studiously informal *Cosmopolitan* cover, one might easily recall Walter Benjamin's observation about movies that "the equipment-free aspect of reality here has become the height of artifice."[3]

Photography has long been torn between objective reportage and creative artifice. In Sontag's account, it has historically represented "the struggle between two different imperatives: beautification, which comes from the fine arts, and truth-telling, which is measured not only by a notion of value-free truth, a legacy from the sciences, but by a moralized ideal of truth-telling."[4] Photography was long thought parasitic to painting because of the way it pursued and propounded beauty, and it took decades for the discipline to achieve the resourcefulness and critical respect that eventually qualified it as an art form. But Walter Benjamin turned this common historical analysis upside-down, saying the mechanical reproduction aspect of the photo made it transformative rather than accessory—not a matter of modified artistry so much as a question of wholesale ontological change. "Much futile thought had been devoted to the question of whether photography is an art," Benjamin averred. "The primary question—whether the very invention of photography had not transformed the entire nature of art—was not raised."[5]

Michael Chanan felt compelled to ask the follow-up question: "Could the same not be said of recording—that it has transformed the very nature of music?"[6] Apparently no such transformations had yet taken place by the late 1950s, when Decca record producer John Culshaw heard some musicians describe recording as a matter of "transcribing the notes."[7] But even going that far back, at least with a studio auteur like Culshaw, recording could not represent direct and transparent transcription for the same reason performance can never be like decryption: it is too creative and musical an act in itself. If recording were a straightforward form of transcription, different musical styles should be amenable to the same manner of recording. But songs on the Beach Boys' *Pet Sounds* album are inextricable from the recording process that preserved them, while the apparent aesthetic unity of Beethoven's Piano Sonata op. 110 usually incites a purist approach with few edits and few microphones.[8] To a listener familiar with *Pet Sounds* and with op. 110 as recorded by Artur Schnabel or Claudio Arrau, any attempt to reverse these scenarios—catching an unedited, one-off performance of "Wouldn't It Be Nice" on two-track tape, say, or improvising a piecemeal and multitracked studio account of the Beethoven—would sound quaint at best, and aesthetically defective at worst.[9]

With their recording culture differences, Beethoven and the Beach Boys show us how recording, as the final public and commercial realization of projects in an increasing number of compositional styles, can in and of itself represent a reply to writing music—though musical creation then answers in turn. While popular styles are rooted in diachrony and process, so-called classical music embodies a synchronic aesthetic. The aesthetic-cultural construct of "inspiration," integral to the mythologies surrounding Western art music, requires instantaneity from its creators as well as unanimity, purity, single-mindedness, and compliance from its performers and record producers—or at least demands that they profess commitment to such.

Perhaps paradoxically, these ethics and objectivity discussions also raise issues of identity. As soon as the photographer turns her lens on a human action, the question arises of just who is being objectified. Controversy soon surrounded Joe Rosenthal's famous 1945 war photo "Raising the Flag on Iwo Jima," specifically the questions of who the six U.S. servicemen in the photo were, whether this was the first such flag-raising on the captured island, and indeed whether the whole thing was posed for the camera. When the subject of the photo is itself an artwork, it is the photographer's identity that becomes entangled in questions of value and vice versa. If Robert Mapplethorpe had taken a shot of Picasso's *Les Demoiselles d'Avignon* or Frida Kahlo's *Roots*, would the resulting image represent a work in itself, and, if so, should that work be described as a Picasso-Mapplethorpe or a Kahlo-Mapplethorpe? And would our answers be different if the photographer were my next-door neighbor instead of the celebrated Soho imagist? When it comes to the question of who and what a recording represents, we could follow photography theory and say that technologies of depiction have brought about a fragmentation rather than a consolidation of the musical self. The independent photographic image of the self certainly marked a complication of identity, indeed an epochal event in human history. As Roland Barthes noted, photography revolutionized the human image by separating it from its referent for the first time, differentiating the two in terms of time and space: "I want a History of Looking. For the Photograph is the advent of myself as other: a cunning dissociation of consciousness from identity."[10] Recording clearly did the same when it divided human sounds from their referents, the player from her sound, the singer from her song, and the composer from her melody.

THE INSTANTANEOUS WORK

Figures of speech often reveal political agendas, and the persistent photographic similes for recording point to its specific cultural import as an "ethics of hearing." People have compared recordings to photographs almost since Thomas Edison and Emil Berliner produced the first commercially viable sound reproduction machines in the 1880s. Fred Gaisberg (1873–1951), the first person to fit the modern description of a record producer, and the man who first entrusted Enrico Caruso, Joseph Joachim, Ignacy Paderewski, and Arthur Rubinstein to wax, declared it his purpose to take "sound photographs" of performances.[11] The comparison was widespread until the mid-twentieth century; over the period the gramophone was busier recording pieces of music than devising the explicit and process-based studio creations that arose in the 1960s with expert editing techniques and multitracking. But the photograph simile is still popular and active today. I give several examples chosen more or less randomly from James Badal's book of conductor interviews: Simon Rattle describes a record as "a recording of an event in a moment of time," while Antal Doráti says "it is like a photograph which catches a person in a moment," and Christopher Hogwood explains it as "a type of photograph of an event." Pierre Boulez understands a recording to be "just a picture of the score taken by somebody."[12] The fact that so many have for so many years compared recordings with photos rather than with films, for instance, says a great deal about the function of recordings as well as about ontologies of the musical work.

The contrast with producers of popular music records, who invoke photography much less frequently, is instructive. George Martin brought up the idea of musical acts rather than documentations of such when he spoke of his early studio work with the Beatles, before the explicitly artistic studio projects that helped transform popular music: "I was out to get *performances*," he recalled, "the excitement of the actual live action."[13] Two things that differentiate a recording of classical music from one of popular music are their conceptions of the composition (or song) being documented, and their attitudes toward recording as it might relate to writing music. Here we could recall some hit-makers who both wrote music and produced records. According to Brian Wilson, "To make a great record, it definitely helps to start with a great song, but as I saw and heard at those Gold Star sessions [with Phil Spector], a record has to be a total sound experience for the listener. So the idea became, for me at least, to try to make the listener feel the way I did when I first wrote the song."[14] A number of pop producers have described such a confluence of studio production with performance and composition in a synthesis that is basically alien to classical music recordings. Lamont Dozier recalls a synchretic moment when "Where Did Our Love Go" clicked into place at the same time that Diana Ross's singing style did. The song was originally written for the Marvelettes, and it took Ross into new, low parts of her range. Fleshing out the vocal arrangement in the studio, Dozier asked at the spur of the moment for a rapid-tempo "baby-baby," and so it happened that "the only way Diana could do it was to sing 'baybeh, baybeh' in that low and sultry way. All of a sudden that was her sound, whereas previously she had been up in the air."[15] Alan Parsons remarks on the convergence of the studio engineer's job with that of the popular musician: "They are both expected to have the skills of one another, and there are not many musicians around who don't know every last detail about recording techniques."[16]

In short, producers and musicians have over the years habitually described the classical recording as (1) a photolike documentation of an object or event (not a process, performance, or communication) and as (2) a point (not a span) in time. Both aspects clearly arise from the heavy work-orientation of classical recording—its obsession with the kind of aesthetic object that, according to tradition, finds its purest form in examples of absolute music. By way of contrast, musical processes were documented by the studio efforts of many popular musicians; and that culture of change and adaptation continues, of course, in the practice of cover versions, remixes, samples, and mashups. To locate a single aesthetic object within this array of practices surrounding James Brown's "Sex Machine," say, would be like hitting a moving target.

With recordings of much instrumental concert art music, however, the aesthetic object—that is, the work—is not only singular, but instantaneous. As discussed by a variety of influential Austro-German aesthetes across the nineteenth and twentieth centuries, the musical work was in fact an antiprocess—regardless of Beethoven's protracted sketching, say, or Arnold Schoenberg's favored practice of "developing variation." According to Hegel, the authentic artwork was required to "produce itself spontaneously in strict coherence and in a single outpouring."[17] As Heinrich Schenker understood them, the great composers "experienced even their most extended works not as a sum total of measures or pages, but as entities which could be heard and perceived as a whole."[18] As Schoenberg described it in his essay "Brahms the Progressive," the kind of musical organization informed by perfect structural foresight—namely by genius—stems from "the state of mind . . . which conceives an entire work in one single creative moment and acts accordingly." To explain the paradoxes of this working-from-inspiration, instantaneity-within-sketching scenario, Schoenberg reached for further paradoxes: "*Inspiration* is a lightning-like [*blitzartig*] appearance of extraordinary duration, which dissipates slowly and ends only a long time after it has fulfilled its purpose."[19]

Schoenberg included this observation in a prose fragment titled simply "Inspiration," and the German *Einfall* reveals through its etymology the momentary and sudden—the "*blitzartig*"—aspect of *das Idee* in German intellectual history. *Fall* is equivalent to the English "fall" or "drop," though it can also carry the related meaning of "case" or "situation." The prefix *ein-* points the fall inward. Thus in the Germanic view, inspiration is something that occurs suddenly and unwittingly, dropping in on the mind as if by accident. The word stops just short of invoking the touch of God's hand or a quick brush with the Muses as the force behind the fall, divinity acting as the source of inspiration. (The main hall of the Musikverein in Vienna, perhaps the world's central temple to absolute music, has the nine Muses painted on its ceiling as if testifying to the inspirational, and therefore *blitzartig*, aspect of great music. An artist doesn't mingle or cohabitate with a muse, but is touched instantaneously by one.) Great works are additionally instantaneous in the sense that they propitiate a historicist culture and also get caught up in it: one could divide the history of the symphony into two parts, for example, the first encompassing those works written before the "Eroica," and the second containing those written after it; standing at the juncture between these two epochal halves, the time Beethoven spent on actual composition of the "Eroica" becomes infinitesimal.

If the masterpiece of absolute music embodies an instantaneous conception for the aesthetician and cultural historian, it should likewise represent a mere instant in the mind of the interpreter. When an interviewer asked Herbert von Karajan how he was able to impart a sense of "overall stability, a kind of musical wholeness" in performing a Bruckner symphony, the conductor answered in visual and tactile terms: "This comes, too, from an overall knowledge of the work. If you can feel and see the whole work laid out before you as you begin, then this will be achieved."[20] Pierre Boulez, a formalistically inclined conductor of a different stripe, has made much the same statement. He describes the recording as a fixed instant-within-an-instant, a snapshot of an object that the performer pins down to a single moment: "A recording, you know, is a picture," Boulez points out. "You take a picture of a work at a certain time."[21] Clearly, in Boulez's view a classical composition is something to be "taken" or "snapped" rather than "shot," as one does a movie. In discussing elsewhere the conductor's job in the recording studio, Boulez specifically introduces the idea of the musical object: "As far as instrumental music is concerned, one is responsible for the musical object, and the recording engineer is responsible for transmitting that object as faithfully as possible within limits that are naturally scaled down." And he adds, a bit later in the same interview: "You try to reconstruct in the studio what you did during the concert, rather as if you were galloping after an image. You really have to concentrate on the work and what it means, at that point."[22] Boulez understands recordings as a form of musical documentation. With his highly pragmatic or even denigrating view of records vis-à-vis musical compositions, he might well agree with Artur Schnabel's Platonic estimation of great music as "better than it can be performed"—or, one feels compelled to add, recorded.

Boulez has usefully trod, at least after his early years as modernist *enfant terrible*, a midway path between idealism and realism, between the theoretical and the practical. His 1977 essay "Invention/Recherche," in which he attempts a timely reevaluation of compositional invention in an electronic age, offers a prime example. Boulez wrote the article the year he left conducting the New York Philharmonic to take up directorship of IRCAM (the Institut de Recherche et Coordination Acoustique/Musique, Paris), and it reads like a preparatory stock-taking. He opens with the statement that "invention is today faced with a number of problems particularly concerned with the relation between the conception, we might even say the vision, of the composer and the realization in sound of his ideas."[23] The changing, though in some cases stubbornly fixed, ideas of technology that Boulez cites are not only electronic but also concern manufacture of acoustic instruments. However manifested, technological invention has far outrun compositional invention, perhaps even rendering it irrelevant:

> Techniques of recording, backing, transmission, reproduction— microphones, loudspeakers, amplifying equipment, magnetic tape— have been developed to the point where they have betrayed their primary objective, which was faithful reproduction. More and more the so-called techniques of reproduction are acquiring an irrepressible tendency to become autonomous and to impress their own image of existing music, and less and less concerned to reproduce as faithfully as possible the conditions of direct audition; it is easy to justify the refusal to be faithful to an unrecorded reality by arguing that *trompe-l'oeil* reproduction, as it were, has little meaning given that the conditions of listening and its objectives are of a different order, that consequently they demand different criteria of perception. This, transposed into musical terms, is the familiar controversy about books and films on art: why give a false notion of a painting in relation to the original by paying exaggerated attention to detail, by controlling the lighting in an unusual way, or by introducing movement into a static world?[24]

In Boulez's view, technology has caused a music-textual dilemma: it has encouraged the recording to become something of a text unto itself, but at the same time it has caused a love of sound for sound's sake to crowd out the composer's presence; recording has, in short, exacerbated a rift that Boulez's senior colleague Ernest Ansermet described as a split between "the musical presence" and "the concrete or sonorous presence." The technologically determined scenario that Boulez sees the composer facing, though he doesn't quite describe it in these terms, is in fact one driven by popular music and the pop market. He doesn't wish to see "the composer" face a world where, as Theodore Gracyk describes rock and roll, music has become "essentially dependent on recording technology for its inception and dissemination."[25] There is more than a little prophylaxis to Boulez's stewardship of IRCAM and his interest in real-time digital interfaces—these are attempts to bring technology to bear upon what he calls the "real object" rather than its assembly, dissemination, and sale. "What the microphone picks up has to be real, because if you start manipulating the microphones in an exaggerated way, the reality you convey is not a very good one. . . . In variety shows [pop recordings?], the sound-takes are entirely different because there is no real object."[26] Certainly, Boulez's "Invention/Recherche" essay diametrically opposes rock and roll–record culture as Albin Zak describes it:

> While the verb 'to record' can have a passive sense to it, meaning something like 'to register,' 'to archive,' or 'to document'—all implying the preservation of something that already exists—rock and roll records do not simply capture and make portable an image of a performance. Presenting a transparent representation of some natural acoustic reality was never the point. Records were meant to be distinctive worlds of musical sound with the power to make their way into the consciousness of a mass audience, and the record-making process was a matter of building those worlds.[27]

When Boulez advocated a documentary role for the recording (rather than its function as a kind of composer-sanctioned text, the transmission purpose that Stravinsky advocated), he anticipated the claim that recordings are like photos in art books—and therefore cannot help but give "a false notion of a painting in relation to the original." Here one can see T. W. Adorno's influence on Boulez's thinking: he embraces the idea of an auratic and originary text but like Adorno rejects Benjamin's notion that the aura surrounding the original has "decayed" out of social necessity—because of "the increasing significance of the masses in contemporary life" or, more specifically, "the desire of the contemporary masses to brings things 'closer' spatially and humanly."[28]

RECORDING THE SELF

Stravinsky, in contrast to Boulez, described the recording as a function of his published compositional text—first and last a documentation of the composer's intentions. He resisted the very notion of interpretation, thereby discounting the contribution of performers and the subjectivities of the recording process itself.[29] In his view, the recording is essentially coincident with the work without in any way displacing or replacing it: one imagines if Stravinsky were in charge of preparing an art history book, he would leave little if any white space around the images of the artworks so the viewer might differentiate between the reproducer's frame and the painter's. An editor with a Stravinskyan aesthetic of reproduction might even take the image of the artwork to the very edge of the page, implying that it has a life and a presence beyond the reproduction that the printed image can allude to only dimly. Certainly one could imagine how the role of art book editor, trained to transmit an "original" literally and painstakingly, would behoove a Stravinskyan formalist. Stravinsky let no opportunity go by for equating interpretation with distortion and he considered the records of his music conducted by Leopold Stokowski, a musician he abhorred, to be misrepresentations—in much the same sense as a lithographer could falsify Vermeer's *Lady Reading at the Window* by changing its colors or throwing it out of focus.

Riffing on these various photographic roles for recordings, one could describe Stravinsky's records as instructional-classificational, rather like J. J. Audubon's book *Birds of America* or an artist's *catalogue raisonné.* Like such books of images, Stravinsky's recordings were meant to be considered together rather than as individual statements: he categorically declared them "indispensable supplements to the printed music." David Hamilton takes this assertion not to mean "that future performances ought slavishly to imitate Stravinsky's recordings—but to proceed in ignorance of them could be likened to using a corrupt edition of a classic work."[30] The *catalogue raisonné* represents a summary bringing-together of an artist's work (or a particular phase of her work) as annotated and presented by a central authority on the subject (one meaning of *raisonné* is "carefully studied"). The purpose is more to bring together an oeuvre than to present individual works in the best possible light—*catalogue raisonné* images can often be small or in black and white, just as an individual Stravinsky-led recording can be a disappointing muddle when heard in isolation; their import and influence are cumulative. As Hamilton understands them, Stravinsky's records were largely intended "to propagate his music." This composer's stubborn resistance to musical ideal-types, except in the case of paradoxical one-off essays in genre like the Violin Concerto, made his originality all the more challenging for listeners. And for performers: in Hamilton's estimation, the recordings were an attempt to introduce compositions embodying "factors antithetical to the foundations of our notational system, and therefore also antithetical to the earliest-formed and most confirmed habits of many performers."[31]

Stravinsky's and Boulez's recordings represent premeditated cultural reportage and for better or for worse carry the ethical overtones of high-art documentation. While Stravinsky said that his recordings served a textual or prescriptive function, Boulez's work in the studio performs a *con*textual function for his own music. He has documented for the microphones not only his own major works, which are markedly few in number, but also more importantly those particular repertories that influenced and inspired his compositional efforts. Among his many releases were the first recordings of other composers' masterworks to attain a high standard and enjoy international distribution: Boulez's recordings of *Wozzeck, Lulu, Die Jakobsleiter, Die glückliche Hand,* Ligeti's Violin and Piano Concertos, and the entire Webern oeuvre with opus numbers all became influential touchstones in appreciation of those composers. But his recordings really did not initiate performance traditions. Boulez's recording catalogue represents an act of advocacy, but—contrary to Stravinsky's—does so as an assembly and description of particulars rather than as substantiation of any one body of music. (As a perhaps incidental detail, Columbia/Sony have never to my knowledge packaged Boulez's complete recordings as a set, while they have done so with Stravinsky's recordings several times.) Some evidence of this can be found in the range of Boulez's recorded output, which is both startlingly far-reaching and unusually narrow. On the one hand, Boulez has consistently performed Wagner, Mahler, Ravel, and Roussel and done so in a way that accentuates originalities in their specific scores. On the other hand, he is notoriously selective when it comes to works by Stravinsky and Messiaen, and that selectivity betrays the particularly oedipal relationship he has had with those composers.

One imagines Boulez would agree with a 1953 essay on photography by William M. Ivins, curator of the prints collection at the Metropolitan Museum, New York, from 1916 until 1946. Specifically, Ivins's main assertion about photography—that it came to serve as "a basis for connoisseurship of the modern type, that is for the study of objects as particulars and not as undifferentiated members of classes"[32]—would elegantly describe the role recordings have played in Boulez's larger musical project. In the book *Prints and Visual Communication,* Ivins claims that "the greater a work of art is, the more it is a bundle, not of similarities to other things, but of differences from them." But he finds irony in the conviction that words are for the most part only able to describe similarities. Differences between artworks are of the essence and are only "clearly communicable in non-verbal ways. While the photograph is far from being a perfect report, it can and does in practice tell a great many more things than any of the old graphic processes was able to."[33] Boulez's recordings of Bartók, for instance, tend to downplay qualities that this composer shares with quite a few others: his folkloric elements (which can sound like exoticism), taste for rousing conclusions (which can be attributed to lingering industrial-age romanticism), and neotonal foundations (personalized through dominant substitutions). How else to help the public warm, then, to Bartók's more individual taste for percussion instruments, cluster chords, and forceful mixed meters than to make sure these elements find prominent if balanced voice within the controlled and repeatable context of a recording, a format that encourages study as well as pleasure?

Boulez has recorded widely as if to demonstrate Benjamin's statement that "mechanical reproduction of art changes the reaction of the masses toward art."[34] More than anyone, certainly more than anyone in American academe, Boulez has created a cachet for twentieth-century music and almost single-handedly made it commercially viable on records. This could be called a documentary project. But the word fails to describe the particular way Boulez's recordings have helped—in much the same way Ivins describes the influence of photographic reproduction in his own field—to finesse, break apart, and individuate many monolithic or even paranoiac conceptions of "the modern." His recordings have helped transport many modernist works from the new music ghetto to the international marketplace and, more important, put a musical face to many iconic and even feared composers. Boulez himself is certainly among these, and his larger recording project ultimately becomes indistinguishable from his compositional course—not in the Stravinskyan fashion of the recording transmitting and substantiating the composition, but the two engaging and merging in a kind of conversation. When Boulez released Mahler symphonies almost simultaneously in the mid-1990s with his own *Répons* and other hefty recent completions, he presented us with a kind of Mobius strip where interpretive stance and compositional influence converge and facilitate each other.

So both Stravinsky and Boulez thought of their own recordings as attestations of truth and believed them to be confirmations—either direct or indirect—of artistic identity. Stravinsky understood recordings of his music to be a kind of looking glass and said that records should mirror his own compositional likeness. Now, after Jacques Lacan and after Barthes, we might find naïveté in his expectation of such truths vis-à-vis the self. As Barthes describes the phenomenon of seeing a likeness of the self, a split between the photographic self-image and its referent necessarily complicates the very ideas of resemblance and recognition:

> Who is like what? Resemblance is a conformity, but to what? To an identity. Now this identity is imprecise, even imaginary, to the point where I can continue to speak of 'likeness' without ever having seen the model. . . . Finding myself an uncertain, amythic subject, how could I find myself 'like'? All I look *like* is other photographs of myself, and this to infinity: no one is ever anything but the copy of a copy, real or mental.[35]

A recording splits "consciousness from identity" most clearly in the performer's case. Without recordings, singers and most instrumentalists could never know their sound as others hear it: we all know the shock, even disgust, of hearing our own voice as recorded, since it sounds so different from what we hear resonating through our own skulls. The discrepancy becomes an identity issue. For the violinist, with instrument propped firmly under chin, it is only slightly less startling to hear her own playing on record. For the musician who plays in public, the ensuing question of whether to attend to the sound heard in the head or that heard on record is usually answered in a kind of plebiscite: everyone but the singer or violinist hears the latter, so it is of primary importance. For the performing musician, then, the advent of recording radically transformed playing or singing into a strange kind of deaf person's ventriloquism—the self, as heard outside of and separate from the self, is to be attended to by the self. Certainly musicians had always asked colleagues to step away and give feedback after listening vicariously to them and also "for" them, but that process was and is qualitatively different from hearing oneself play. When the musician encounters a recording of herself and thereby becomes an object of the gaze, there ensues a contest between her sound as self—the original and intimately known sound, heard as both sender and receiver—and her sound as other, emanating from outside the body and therefore more difficult to control.[36] The effect of a heavier bow-stroke, for instance, can be understood immediately when the player performs and listens in real life; while the same change in sound might be more puzzling, more difficult to size up and connect with its cause, when the player hears it on a recording. That puzzling disjunction would result, in part, from separating in time the specific muscle contractions of the bowing arm from the specific sounds that reach the ear as a result of the bowing.

Much the same can be said of the composer and the elements borne of her will and intention. While the recording's "dissociation of consciousness from identity" prompts questions about tone from the player, for the composer the contradiction between what is heard and what is recognized can be felt in the irreconcilability, for example, of an inner-ear tempo with an actual-performance tempo. We could follow Barthes here and ask a question along the lines of the following: "A tempo is a conformity, but to what?" Aaron Copland seemed on the verge of asking this question, even after decades of conducting in the studio and the concert hall, when he said: "I hope my recordings of my own works won't inhibit other people's performances. The brutal fact is that one doesn't always get the exact tempo one wants, although one improves with experience."[37] Copland didn't address conducting per se in this statement, or how difficult it is more generally to actualize a compositional tempo. Rather, he acknowledged the problems in recognizing as one and the same a thought when it is still unsounded and part of one's thinking and control, and that thought when it has sounded, been severed from one's consciousness, and then fixed in space and time on a record. Just as the violinist might find it difficult to recognize her tone after it has been separated from the bowing-arm sensations that produced it, the composer often has difficulty identifying aspects of a compositional thought after she no longer has control over that thought.

PHOTOGRAPHIC TRUTH

As a way of closing in on the veristic possibilities enshrined in records, a believer in the photographic aspect of records might first ask, What kinds of truths are documented by photographs? Photography was considered a technological marvel for its first half century, and with a certain lazy causality people believed its truth to be inextricable from its modernness: the images from a camera were truthful because they were modern, and modern because they were truthful. But those early and rather glib notions of modernity and truth are not ones we can easily understand in the twenty-first century. The hybrid term "art-science"—used in 1870s Britain to describe photography of the time—is one that might puzzle us today, even if it has a certain resonance with current computer graphics. A British photographer of the mid-nineteenth century, the renowned Henry Peach Robinson (1830–1901), championed the practice of combining five or more images into a single photograph, which resulted in a detailed, highly theatrical, and deep- and uniform-focus image that looks like a modern-day diorama. Other artist-scientists of the time blurred divisions between photography and painting with elaborate poses and retouchings.

The new century brought the American fin-de-siècle Photo-Secession movement which mandated that, in the words of its leader, Alfred Stieglitz (1864–1946), "photographs [should] look like photographs." The writer Marius de Zayas, one of the more modernist voices associated with the Photo-Secessionists, nevertheless grappled with basic definitions of photography, art, and truth on into the 1920s: "Art is the expression of the conception of an idea," wrote de Zayas in 1913. "Photography is the plastic verification of a fact. The difference between Art and photography is the essential difference which exists between the Idea and Nature."[38] By the 1970s, photography had enough of a history that Susan Sontag could declare the past to be its central subject, its "truth" and its "fact." In her view, the photograph is at least as much "about" the time that has passed since the shutter snapped as it is "about" the people or things pictured. She called photographs "incitements to reverie" and noted: "What renders a photograph surreal is its irrefutable pathos as a message from time past, and the concreteness of its intimations about social class."[39] Sontag demonstrated her photo nostalgia even more pointedly in a discussion of movies, which she said "resurrect the beautiful dead; present, intact, vanished or ruined environments; [and] embody without irony styles and fashions that seem funny today."[40]

Are recordings of instrumental art music similarly nostalgic? I would answer no, and say they refer more definitively to (pseudo-instantaneous) musical works than to specific performing musicians, playing styles, or points in time, and in that special sense are not time-sensitive. (Again, I would point to this particular disparity between recordings and photographs as evidence of the continued "presence" of absolute music—perhaps its main presence today.) Photographs are not equivalent to the work, as asserted earlier, unless the images in question happen to be photos from an art history text. As if to contradict Sontag, Roland Barthes made the statement in his book *Camera Lucida* that there is no Proustian pathos when one point in time reaches toward another for fulfillment or substantiation of its meaning and importance (what Barthes calls "protensity," literally the quality or act of extending). As Barthes describes it, the photograph does not "call up the past" but more blankly attests "that what I see has indeed existed." The particular melancholy of the photographic image, according to Barthes, is the fact that "it is *without future* (this is its pathos, its melancholy); in it, no protensity, whereas the cinema is protensive, hence in no way melancholic (what is it, then? It is, then, simply 'normal,' like life)."[41]

If a recording of concert art music indeed "attests" that something heard "has indeed existed," that thing is the composition rather than the performance. A CD of Heifetz playing the Siciliana from Bach's First Sonata for solo violin would map more completely onto a music-lover's memory of this composition than onto his or her conception of Heifetz's playing. Complicating and indeed fragmenting any impressions of the Heifetz-ness of the record would be the fact that the Vilnius-born violinist recorded this music twice, in 1935 and again in 1952. In short, an audible rendering of Bach's Siciliana presents more performance-interpretation variables than it does compositional-textual variables: and this is one reason why there are two Heifetz-Siciliana documents out there muddying the musical waters, but only one Bach Siciliana.[42]

I argue, in short, that the classical recording is taken to represent a work more often than it signifies a performance. This might or might not answer the question of why more classical musicians and recordists didn't follow the lead of pop practice and develop more obviously creative production techniques—develop them with the aims of transmuting the work into recorded sound, as it were, and constructing an entirely new experience from it. The primary answer to this question must lie again in what Lydia Goehr, borrowing a term from Immanuel Kant, calls the work's influence as a "regulative concept." She differentiates between constitutive and regulative notions, the former representing the "rules" of procedure and the latter the reason for following said rules.[43] It becomes clear that across the history of Western instrumental art music, the work has been endowed with a good deal more regulative significance than has any notion of performance—indeed, one speaks of a system of ethics surrounding works rather than their performance. The exceptions are those strange cases where performances are reified as if they were works and, with compositional ethics thrust upon them, become objects of restorative rather than creative ingenuity. As an example we could take Wayne Stahnke's software-assisted method of "recreating" Rachmaninov's piano roll performances, which Daniel Pollock describes as an act of "resurrecting" and compares with fine-art restoration, saying that "both involve the meticulous and time-consuming excavation of an original work by removal of overlaying accretions and corruptions."[44]

Sight tends to dominate over sound in human conceptions of reality.[45] The gaze is a sensibility that structures our visual field and by extension our subjectivity, while there is no equivalent for voice or hearing. Indeed, sound is both everywhere and nowhere at once. "The ear favors no particular 'point of view,'" observes Marshall McLuhan. "We are *enveloped* by sound. We say, 'Music shall fill the air.' We never say, 'Music shall fill a *particular* segment of the air.' . . . We simply are not equipped with earlids.

Where a visual space is an organized continuum of a uniformed connected kind, the ear world is a world of simultaneous relationships."[46] Recording techniques and technologies have stepped into this aural breach, creating hyperreality through a particular expertise that redefines and ultimately supplants ideas of the purely "musical."

Photographs were able to revolutionize human conceptions of realism, at least those held by artists: photo images are no longer, as iconologist W. J. T. Mitchell puts it, "comfortably regarded as causally generated truthful reports about things in the real world."[47] But the "seeing is believing" axiom still tends to hold true, outside the photo lab and movie theater at least, and it remains fairly clear just what a realistic view through a camera lens would entail. With recordings, the question of realism—and, thereby, just what the whole purpose of recording is—remains more nebulous. High fidelity toward . . . what? Any answer to the question must involve discussions of time and technology, and here opinion is divided among those who think aural realism was an idea operative in the past, and those who think it will be actualized in the future. Writing in 1947, Adorno and Hanns Eisler found the human ear less successful than the eye at adapting to "the bourgeois rational and, ultimately, highly industrialized order." They thought the ordinary aural world entrenched in archaism, or even actively opposed to technological advancement. According to this perspective, any sense of aural realism would have to be regressive in its orientation:

> One might say that to react with the ear, which is fundamentally a passive organ in contrast to the swift, actively selective eye, is in a sense not in keeping with the present advanced industrial age and its cultural anthropology. For this reason acoustical perception preserves comparably more traits of long bygone, pre-individualistic collectivities than optical perception.[48]

EDITING AND REALISM

Glenn Gould held the opposing view that aural conceptions of fidelity and realism are relative and progressive. Extrapolating from Gould's thinking of the 1960s and early 1970s, Lydia Goehr decides that reproductive technology has transformed the very idea and desirability of "fidelity":

> When Glenn Gould wrote that 'for better or for worse, recording will forever alter our notions about what is appropriate to the performance of music,' he offered an argument comparable to that regarding photography's impact on painting. In both cases, the technology of recording or reproduction would make possible a new degree of fidelity,

representation or interpretative, formerly unrealizable. Unless the paint-brush could approximate to the condition of the camera, or the concert hall to that of the recording studio, painting and live performance would both have to reevaluate their traditional aesthetic (and for Gould their moral) purposes and possibilities.[49]

Paintbrushes and concert halls aren't the only institutions engaged by technology: the musical work is likewise challenged. The reality invoked by a recording is ostensibly a live performance of the music in question; but with recordings of instrumental concert music there is the additional reality that is the work, a reality for which there is no real equivalent in photography. Boulez says of the ontological conflation and more generally the idiosyncratic mode of representation endemic to audio playback, that "recordings . . . give the idea, especially for people who are not familiar with the score or are not too familiar with the score, that an interpretation is the score."

But then there is that commodified subset of truthfulness that we specifically call realism. Both photo and recording were presumed by their respective publishers to be realistic documents, representational stand-ins (of a sort) for the actual object. But we find it increasingly difficult to say just which reality the recorded musical document—in either pop or classical music—is supposed to be documenting. It is somehow easier to define the visual reality that Adobe Photoshop and other digital technologies have made it possible, or perhaps even tempting, to misrepresent.[50] Quite a bit has been written about digital audio techniques for surgically removing wrong notes, changing timbre and speed, and even improving intonation and giving musicians a stricter sense of rhythm. But those audio techniques are usually deployed with the aim of making the record more faithful to some determining paradigm, whether the printed music or conventional ideas of music-making. When Martha Argerich made her electrifying record of the Chopin Preludes in 1977, she decided to leave on the tape glaring blunders in Preludes No. 16 and No. 20. When digital editing came along and the notes were quietly corrected for a 1999 reissue in the *Great Pianists of the 20th Century* series, the adjustment contradicted annotator Bryce Morrison's implication that the clinkers verify Argerich's authenticity: "[Prelude No.] 16 numbers among Argerich's most savagely intense outbursts, a slip of the finger in bar 5 a mere spot, so to speak, on a blazing sun."[51] Clearly, the person who removed the wrong notes was intent on paying obeisance to the larger reality that is Chopin's op. 28. In that sense, the editorial cleanup tried to counteract the Chopin-Argerich hyphenation implied, from the first note, by this pianist's idiosyncratic and all-subsuming genius.

If pitches have become negotiable, recording has rendered notions of acoustic reality flexible as well. Recall producer Fred Gaisberg's remark about capturing "sound photographs" of musical performances. Gaisberg recorded musicians on shellac, of course, so there was no possibility of editing. By contrast, Walter Legge—Gaisberg's imperious successor at EMI—claimed for himself that he wished to document musicians' best capabilities for performance: "I wanted better results than are normally possible in public performance: I was determined to put onto disc the best that artists could do under the best possible conditions." Legge's "best possible" idealism justified editing, of course. But he also desired better acoustic results than were feasible in concert, saying he wanted "to make records which will sound in the public's home exactly like what they would hear in the best seat in an acoustically perfect hall."[52] Legge should have said "virtual" hall, since so many of his records were made at the Abbey Road Studios in London, not a "hall" at all—with his work of the 1950s and 1960s we see acoustic simulation arising as the synchronic equivalent to the diachronic artfulness that was editing.

Here we return to the important question of why classical musicians and composers understand the recording to be like a snapshot, while those in popular music seem to think it closer to a movie. The answer must lie not only with the ontological notion, already discussed, that what the classical recording frames is a single and instantaneous aesthetic object. There is also the more general notion that classical music is incompatible with the basic cinematic vocabulary of perspective changes and editing. A record documents a single and instantaneous aesthetic object, while film works to emphasize its own artifice through obvious changes in perspective and frequent editing. Christian Metz even speaks of the "cinematic fetish" of film technique.[53] The fetishism is only underlined when a filmmaker tries to cover up editing techniques—as Hitchcock did in *Rope* (1948), Orson Welles in the famous opening three minutes of *Touch of Evil* (1958), and Alexander Sokurov in his movie *Russian Ark* (2002), which was shot entirely with a Steadicam and ostensibly unedited throughout its entire ninety minutes.

Such feats of filmic continuity often cause a critical sensation. By contrast, most sound editors work as a matter of course to make classical recordings sound "real" and unedited—they would wish to be neither magicians nor surgeons. Classical performers, too, almost without exception, go on record advocating the need for long takes, even when tempos can be coordinated between takes, and splicing can be done inaudibly. Frequently contradicted by studio practice, this allegiance to "the long take" is an act of faith in the synchronic, organic, and unitary nature of the musical work— as well as in the performer's ability to comprehend that architecture, her ability to live up to Schenker's dictum that "the performance of a musical work of art can be based only upon a perception of that work's organic co-herence."[54] Conversely, classical editing tends to be described in cosmeti-cian's or perhaps embalmer's terms as "touching up"—what was living and organic is now presumed dead. These terms again originated with photog-raphy. Peter Henry Emerson, unsympathetic to the artfulness and consis-tent focus of photographers of his day, and thereby influential on later modernist photographers like Alfred Stieglitz, observed: "Retouching is the process by which a good, bad, or indifferent photograph is converted into a bad drawing or painting."[55] Stieglitz elaborated on Emerson's complaint and called retouching "unphotographic," a neologism that correlates with the supposed unmusicality of edited recordings.

In an interview, Christopher Hogwood has questioned these strange en-mities between film and audio recording. "I no more object to an edited record," Hogwood remarks realistically, "than I object to an edited film. No-body imagines they're going to the cinema to see a straight shoot."[56] Of course, one of the most incisive critics of the un-touched-up, long-take school is Glenn Gould—who retired from concert-giving in 1964 in order to devote himself entirely to making records. In his 1974 essay "Music and Technology," Gould chooses to disagree with a comment from Adrian Boult that splicing is detrimental to "the long line." The pianist points out in re-sponse: "He's wrong, of course—splicing doesn't damage lines. Good splices build good lines, and it shouldn't much matter if one uses a splice every two seconds or none for an hour so long as the result *appears* to be a coherent whole. After all, if one buys a new car, it doesn't really matter how many assembly-line hands are involved in its production."[57] In his 1966 essay "The Prospects of Recording," Gould brings up two related points: (1) the recording musician should not hold onto rigid ideas of musicality; and more practically, (2) it is hypocritical to shun and denounce editing when neither the performer nor the listener can usually tell from the final tape that editing has indeed taken place. Gould cites one example from his own recordings:

> It would be impossible for the listener to establish at which point the
> authority of the performer gave way to that of the producer and the
> tape editor, just as even the most observant cinema-goer cannot ever be

sure whether a particular sequence of shots derives from circumstances occasioned by the actor's performance, the exigencies of the cutting room, or the director's a priori scheme. That the judgment of the performer no longer solely determines the musical result is inevitable. It is, however, more than compensated by the overwhelming sense of power which editorial control makes available to him.[58]

The organic and unitary conception of the musical work inspired the long-take, long-line school of thought that Gould took exception to, so it is no surprise that the Canadian pianist cultivated a different aesthetic—one far removed from ideas of inspiration and instantaneity. "The purpose of art," Gould wrote in 1962, "is not the release of a momentary ejection of adrenaline but . . . the gradual, life-long construction of a state of wonder and serenity."[59] This describes an aesthetics of reception, yes, but then Gould understood reception to be a long and active process: as he would have it, there's as much creativity involved in what Jean Molino and Jean-Jacques Nattiez called the esthesic side of the musical transaction as there is in the compositional, or poietic, side. On at least one occasion, Gould encouraged listeners at home to interact with the recorded work and performance through repetition of favorite segments and creative use of the volume and tone controls.[60] In themselves, such beliefs and practices would diffuse any ontology of the work and prolong the entire musical "contract," while in the instantaneity model described above the entire experience is more or less finished as soon as the composer formulates her view of the piece—leaving the performance more or less irrelevant to the work itself.

FILM AND RECORDINGS

Why the double standard for visual recording and sound recording, namely the demands for artifice from the first and—Gould notwithstanding—the demands for realism, humanity, and transparency from the second? Part of the answer must lie in the origins of the two media. Film was devised to fulfill fantasy, while sound recording originated to fill utilitarian purposes. Partially deaf and no great music-lover himself, Edison initially conceived his cylinder recorder in 1877 not as an instrument of aesthetic pleasure, but as a device for documenting speech: in its first years, many referred to it in long form as the "talking phonograph." As a documentation of speech it wasn't initially considered useful as a recorder of Shakespeare or Keats recitations for repeated future enjoyment, but as a kind of Dictaphone purely for information purposes: the most sentimental role that Edison foresaw was preserving speech of the old and dying. In George Bernard Shaw's *Pygmalion* (1913), more widely known in musical form as Lerner and Loewe's musical *My Fair Lady*, Professor Henry Higgins uses a phonograph for yet another speech-related purpose: to help gentrify Eliza Doolittle by objectifying and removing her thick Cockney accent.

Despite the fact that music entered the recording process almost as an afterthought, it's tempting to think that the recording was designed expressly as a vehicle for musical works—to piggyback, as it were, on the individual musical opus, whether it was the song "Ta-Ra-Ra Boom-De-Ay," a Sousa march, or a Mozart sonata movement. Barthes talks about inextricability, describing how "a specific photograph, in effect, is never distinguished from its referent (from what it represents). . . . In short, the referent adheres."[61] But with a recording of instrumental art music, the musically absolute—or at least the memory or possibility thereof—interposes itself somewhere between the two, such that the recording does not become synonymous with its referent in quite the same way. The photograph was indeed originally devised as a kind of painting stand-in, as a substitute for the graphic artwork: it was invented through experiments with the *camera obscura* that was a popular artist's tool for perspectival work. And though the earliest writers talked about the photograph as a quintessentially modern invention, they mostly spoke of it as a picture, adapting ideas from the art world.

Film, in contrast to still photography, enjoyed no such parasitic relationship with a genre of artwork. In 1888, Edison described his moving-pictures project in simple terms as "an instrument which does for the eye what the phonograph does for the ear, which is the recording and reproduction of things in motion."[62] He opened his first Kinetoscope parlor in New York in 1894, where people paid a nickel to see a brief scene or a quarter to view five. He brought out his Vitascope projection system in 1896 and that year filmed a brief scene from a popular New York musical comedy, *The Widow Jones*. But this early cinema form was not based in drama or storytelling: among Edison's more popular early movies were a promotion of the Lehigh Valley Railroad and the documentary *Wreck of the Battleship 'Maine'*, which fueled American war sentiments against Spain. In 1894, Edison advertised one movie as an "illusionary spectacle of moveable figures." In short, the earliest films represented illusionary curiosities or documentations of life rather than artworks.

Like film, recording followed no model. But it differed from the Kinetoscope and Vitascope in being ostensibly transparent in the way that the telephone and telegraph were: its means were effaced in favor of the illusion that the artwork was somehow "there," at most framed by the technology rather than actually created by it. This was largely a lie, of course, not least because microphones are transducing devices rather than data transmitters. This pretense of transparency began to evaporate once electrical recording arrived and a variety of microphones of differing directivities was developed. With the appearance in the 1960s of 16-track and later 20-track mixing consoles, an array of techniques—not unlike the variety of possibilities that had been a common aspect of movies since D. W. Griffith—allowed producer-auteurs to create all new manners of sonic realities. Some recording producers aspired to the kind of auteurist reimaginings of musical compositions that screenplay writers and movie directors perform on original literary works as a matter of course. Examples would include John Culshaw, who spoke of a choice between "a literal transcription of musical notes onto a record" and "an imaginative approach to the same operation . . . with a view to presenting the music in a way that will especially appeal to the listener at home."[63] Culshaw became something of an exception in his profession, at least among classical producers, for choosing the second. The project he was most proud of was the Vienna rendition of Wagner's *Tristan und Isolde* with Georg Solti, Birgit Nilsson, and Fritz Uhl. It is surely the transcendent absolute-music qualities of *Tristan*, as first described by Nietzsche, that compelled Culshaw to take such risks with the work in the studio. "[*Tristan*] is the nearest thing I know to a musical drug," he confessed in Nietzsche-esque fashion. Aiming in his 1960 Decca production to rescue Wagner's masterpiece from being "just another opera," he used multitracking to realize "the intensity of Wagner's sound" in a way that proves impossible in the opera house— where "the acoustic is so 'dead' that Wagner's orchestra cannot produce the sound he had in mind." Technology allowed the orchestra to dominate those passages "where the literal meaning of the words is less important than the overall musical effect." And yet Culshaw said nothing specifically about the technological aspects of this project. He claimed that he took no liberties with the opera, saying that he and his associates were intent on "giving the score its head" instead of simply recording Wagner's work "in the ordinary way."[64]

Lydia Goehr neatly describes two opposing conceptions of audio-technological realism, and thereby helps us understand how "improvements" in technology have changed the mediated musical experience. With her contrasting binarism of "the perfect performance of music" and "the perfect musical performance," Goehr differentiates between music listening

situations according to "the presence or absence of visibly acting performers, or according, more abstractly, to the degree of humanness involved."[65]
The first conception of the pair is the Stravinskyan one, emphasizing what
Goehr calls "the vehicular and structured, 'Apollonian' ideal of a performance *qua* performance-of-a-work";[66] by contrast, the second conception
describes a performance situation where the listener sees the players sweat
and breathe and emote, watching them occasion a transcendent experience
of the work as performed. The perfect performance of music aims to disappear into the work while illuminating it, and the perfect musical performance emphasizes the momentary and unique experience of glimpsing the
composition through the interpreter.

Developments in audio recording and playback technology have served
both of these ideals, though not necessarily simultaneously. Thus recordings have become more "real" in both *werktreu* and performance terms.
Recordings have become higher in their fidelity to Goehr's first category
by making the mediated performance of the composition a more continuous experience. Continuity is a prime, definitive aspect of absolute-
musical culture: in addressing symphonic traditions, Adorno referred to
"the fiction that music is a pure tissue of deductions, in which everything
that happens follows with unambiguous necessity."[67] Recorded continuity
largely had to do with the increasing playing length of playback discs—
from the 4 minutes of the 78 rpm side to the uninterrupted 1,000 minutes
of 16-bit playback on DVD-Audio or the practically unlimited playing
time possible from servers and individual hard disks. But digital editing
also aided continuity by making splices less conspicuous. Developments in
audio technology have also come to serve Goehr's second category, the
category of humanness in music-making. Subtleties of the clarinetist's
breathing, the click of the pianist's nails as they hit the keys, the miniscule
differences of strength between the player's individual strokes in a
drumroll—such details were usually inaudible beneath 78 rpm swish, and
masked even by LP noise and tape hiss. It might come as a surprise that
when a panel of audio experts at *The Absolute Sound* were asked to define
audio realism, they spoke in terms of these informational subtleties rather
than of dynamic range or frequency range. In reporting their findings,
Jonathan Valin concluded:

> Musical thrills are tied to the delivery of low-level, performance-
> related information that other, lesser gear 'scrubs away' or buries be-
> neath its own noise floor and that tells us, for instance, how a singer is
> shepherding her breath when she sustains a note or a violinist is wiggle-
> waggling a string to add vibrato. I largely agree with this, though it

needs to be said that the addition of performance-related detail, low-level or high-, results in greater realism to the extent that it also subtracts from our sense that we're listening to an electro-mechanical reproduction.

Again, increased audio-technological realism comes back to the idea of adding visuality to the aural experience. Just as the growth of directional technology in the 1950s made microphones more like eyes, more capable of "seeing" sounds, and advanced speaker design allowed greater stereophonic (and, later, surround-sound) imaging, overall audio-technological subtleties seem to arouse the eyes as well as the ears. Valin continues: "Low-level details about performance and instrument . . . allow us to more completely visualize what we're also more completely hearing—not just what and who are making music but *how* it is being made."[68]

THE OBSCENE IMAGE

Whence the hunger for detail that has become known as high fidelity? Has increasing realism crossed the line from enhancement to excess? The photographic image is an innately aggressive artifact, a fact agreed upon by Sontag and Barthes. Sontag famously compared the lens to a gun, remarking: "There is an aggression implicit in every use of the camera." The assault is made all the more violent, in her view, by the medium's paradoxical pretense to shrugging ingenuousness: "Those occasions when the taking of photographs is relatively undiscriminating, promiscuous, or self-effacing do not lessen the didacticism of the whole enterprise. This very passivity—and ubiquity—of the photographic record is photography's 'message,' its aggression."[69] The photo's appearance of laxity is described differently by Barthes: "I can only sweep it with my glance, like a smooth surface. The Photograph is *flat*, platitudinous in the true sense of the word." For him, the aggressiveness lies in the photograph's intense preemption of the Gaze: the image supplies "no odor, no music, nothing but the *exorbitant thing*. The Photograph is violent: not because it shows violent things, but because on each occasion *it fills the sight by force*, and because in it nothing can be refused or transformed."[70]

The work as referential concept again separates recordings of concert art music from the movie and the still photo in that it does not allow for the central lack that defines those two photographic media. In Jean Baudrillard's view, the visual image exercises its particular power by enabling the viewer to grasp in [the subject] what is beyond their own grasp, to grasp the way they escape your grasp. . . . The trap is always the trap of resemblance, and what's interesting in the image, when it knows how to preserve its secrecy (and this also goes for cinema and painting), is that it defies all resemblance, that it seeks elsewhere what comes from elsewhere.[71]

Baudrillard calls this lack "the death at the heart of the image" and in describing it devises a paradoxical apposition of "this specificity of the image, this symbolic void which gives it its potency." This secrecy of the image is vanishing over time, much to Baudrillard's chagrin: he sees an increasing desire to compensate for or simply remove this "secret form of something's absence" by overloading images with information and explanatory verbiage: the image's symbolic void, in short, is not allowed to speak for itself.

When the image is utterly transparent and devoid of secrecy, it becomes "obscene" in Baudrillard's terms: exhibitionistic, direct, excessive, naked, overinformative. Baudrillard devised a duality between the seductive and the obscene, and Barthes wrote some years earlier about a similar dichotomy of "erotic" and "pornographic" imagery.[72] The factors on one side of Barthes and Baudrillard's duality (eroticism, seduction) withhold information, while those on the other (pornography, obscenity) go beyond surrendering themselves in a surfeit of detail. Indeed, Baudrillard defines obscenity as a form of exhibitionism. While the pornographic image is for Barthes utterly explicit, and therefore often boring, the erotic photograph does not focus on and fetishize the sex organs—indeed, it might not show them at all. In hiding the subject's primary sexual means, the erotic photo "takes the spectator outside its frame," Barthes notes, "and it is there that I animate this photograph and that it animates me."[73] Where the seductive-erotic image has the manifold meanings suggested by referents that are partly hidden (giving rise to a mad rampage of imagined, would-be signification), the obscene-pornographic representation collapses meaning into pure, immanent information. It doesn't create a set of interrelations where one term means something else, but instead short-circuits discourse: nothing is left behind for interpretation or discussion.

By this definition the detailed and nuanced recording is irredeemably obscene or pornographic—if anything, *too* real. As set down in the grooves of an LP, the microscopic pits of a CD, or the binary code of an MP3 file, recorded music counters the uncertainty by which Barthes defines art: "Art is . . . an ambiguity, it always contradicts, in a sense, its own message, and especially music, which is never, literally, either sad or gay."[74] Baudrillard causes no surprise at one point in *Seduction* when he turns to recorded playback as a simile for pornography: "Pornography is the quadrophonics of sex. It adds a third and fourth track to the sexual act. It is the hallucination of detail that rules. Science has already habituated us to this microscopics, this excess of the real in its microscopic detail, this voyeurism of exactitude."[75] I believe the first generation of musicians that felt compelled to compare "getting music from" scores with getting it from records operated from such a Baudrillardian view. Like reproduced music, the technologically mediated sexual experience is held in suspicion simply because it is too easy and leaves little or nothing to the imagination— because it embodies a dissolute combination of onanism and explicitness. Some classical musicians might even describe the recording in the same way Freud described the fetish: as a gratification-inducing emblem that is by itself inappropriate for the sexual (or, in our case, musical) function. Conductor Colin Davis, for one, finds "a different attitude altogether" between hearing music in the concert hall and on records; to the second experience he imputes "nothing at all except a desire to find pleasure."[76]

If the recording of concert art music is like a photo, what kind of photo does it most resemble? It resembles the pornographic shot in that it represents a single topic and subverts reading by presenting the topic with absolute unequivocation. By definition, the pornographic photo is entirely unambiguous, an acting-out of an emotional and psychic transaction that is intrinsically intimate, a flattening-out of a particular system of role-playing—it is, in short, something private made public, an improvisational act turned ritualistic and schematic. Barthes called such an explicit and unambiguous photograph *unary*, a category of strict reportage-images with pornographic shots as a subset. For him a pornographic photo could become erotic if it allowed the viewer distractions from the main subject or if it contained separate levels to be weighed and interpreted—in short, if it allowed itself to be read. "Nothing is more homogenous than a pornographic photograph," Barthes observes. "It is always a naïve photograph, without intention and without calculation. Like a shop window which shows only one illuminated piece of jewelry, it is completely constituted by the presentation of only one thing."[77]

Technology has made the obscene image all the more obscene by allowing higher levels of detail, and allowing such increases in resolution in an attempt to open new avenues of pleasure. One wonders why these questions are so recent: the oldest optic lens likely dates to ancient Assyria, while the abstract concept of resolution itself originated at least 10 years before Edison's phonograph experiment, and some 145 years before people started debating bitrates of audio files.[78] Undoubtedly some discussions of music and musical aesthetics have been replaced by discussions of aural resolution. But can the pleasure of, and in, the image be impeded by too many nuances? Has the day arrived when we actually see and hear more, and more clearly, than we wish? Some adult film actors, invoking pleasure in a more immediately physical sense, fear the increased resolution of HD video technology and believe it threatens their livelihood: "Imperfections are sexy, too," one star hopefully opined in a news story, while another added: "Maybe in a few years I might be worried."[79] Likewise, in the early 1980s, conductor Lorin Maazel predicted that digital playback would allow the public "to hear *everything*—perfectly" and also enable them "to distinguish between really first-class playing and second- or even third-rate performances."[80]

Perhaps this has happened: recording technology has certainly taken absolute music, which has throughout much of its history been notationally underdetermined by nature, and quite suddenly made it overdetermined— and unchanging. Given the importance of photographs for understanding phonography and pleasure more generally, it is appropriate that we still talk about the ear in terms of the eye and find that pleasure may yet decline under the aegis of optics. Perhaps the considerable number of listeners who found their senses "assaulted" by Culshaw's *Tristan*, who felt the recording subverting their need to keep Wagner's music "at arm's length," glimpsed and feared such a time—a time when technology will have helped usher music from seductiveness into the realm of the obscene.

7. Mahler as Imagist

Mahler's symphonies, though never truly neglected, didn't achieve wide popularity until the later decades of the twentieth century. Why they were so late finding broad appeal remains an absorbing question. Was it simply a matter of musical style? No, the wider public's late embrace isn't entirely consistent with the cliché of the ahead-of-his-time composer achieving belated recognition. Was it then an issue of cultural context and understanding? Writers do keep returning to the idea that Mahler represents some kind of nascent modernity or prescient postmodernity. In his celebrated essay "Mahler: His Time Has Come" (1967), Leonard Bernstein spoke not of listeners coming around finally to a difficult musical style, but of music-lovers being awakened to Mahlerian affect by the century's transfigurative horrors.[1] In trying to explain the Mahler phenomenon, others have looked not to technologically assisted warfare and genocide but to technological advances in middle-class leisure electronics—to the long-playing record as the first real means of reproducing this composer's long musical spans, or to high fidelity as a vehicle for his orchestral complexities.[2] But this explanation doesn't satisfy either: to leave Mahler's belated popularity at the doorstep of hi-fi is to oversimplify technology and people's ways of uncovering musical meaning.

Mahler's meanings have been largely facilitated by "mechanical" mediation, yes, but to understand this composer's reception we must bring together all three subjects: compositional awareness, listener understanding, and developments in audio technology. The three can be related through a notion of the imagistic sensibility. I borrow the term *imagism* from an early twentieth-century school of free verse that Ezra Pound described in terms of "luminous details" and "hard light, clear edges." Literary historian Theodore Maynard attributed to the imagist poets "a hunger for actuality,

for close contact. . . . Their hands must touch the wood of chairs, the skin of flowers—and reproduce in words the sensations of their curious fingers."[3] In attributing a similar sensibility to Mahler, I focus on his quasi-pictorial immediacy of images, his capitalization on—to borrow another Pound description of imagist poetry—"the intellectual and emotional complex in an instant of time."[4] The present day shares this image-oriented aesthetic with Mahler, but his contemporaries did not. His imagistic style of illustration, different in basic ways from the nineteenth-century modes of extramusicality that we now call program music, could not be widely grasped until later twentieth-century cultures of visuality and media-assisted convergence of the senses.

Mahler's music is promiscuously involved with images, just as our own time—a time when this composer dominates recording lists and symphony programs as never before—is deeply in thrall to the visual. In the view of iconologist W. J. T. Mitchell,

> it seems overwhelmingly obvious that the era of video and cybernetic technology, the age of electronic reproduction, has developed new forms of visual simulation and illusionism with unprecedented powers. . . .
> The fantasy of a pictorial turn, of a culture totally dominated by images, has now become a real technical possibility on a global scale. Marshall McLuhan's "global village" is now a fact and not an especially comforting one.[5]

Mitchell describes "postmodernism" as a broad reorientation from the logos to the image, from the syntactic to the iconic. As he presents it, however, this large-scale pictorial turn is attended and complicated by a deep-seated conflict: namely, a gut anxiety over the power of images. This imago-phobia dates as far back as condemnations of Christian idolatry and, we might add, as far forward as absolute-music partisans' condemnations of programmatic idolatries. Might not these two facts—of Mahler's importunate relevance and of our current visual urgency—be connected? And though Mahler is commonly called a prophet of postmodernism, might his professed loyalty to musical abstraction—to absolute music—demonstrate the age-old unease over imagery that Mitchell mentions?

Literary scholar Christopher Collins speaks of the need for "reading the written image" in certain bodies of literature; in similar fashion, Mahler asks his listeners to "hear the composed image." Consider a statement Mahler made to Bruno Walter when the latter was admiring the mountains near Mahler's composing retreat at Steinbach: "No need to look—I have already composed all that away" (Sie brauchen gar nicht mehr hinzusehen—Das habe ich schon alles wegkomponiert).[6] What a fascinating notion, one that Mahler couldn't have meant flippantly: that music can correspond so closely to a visual image that it conveys all its substantive and inherent qualities as thoroughly to the ears as the real thing does to the eyes. And that it can do so so completely as to supplant the physical image, literally emptying it of all meaning, the sign superseding the signified! Evidence of Mahler's imagism, if evidence were needed, can also be found in the visual inclination of his performance indications. An instrument becomes "suddenly prominent; never conspicuous until this point"; the orchestra divides such that an instrument or set of players finds itself "in isolated placement" from the ensemble; the composer instructs individual instruments or groups to sound "tenderly coming forward" (*zart hervortretend*), "wild" (*wild*, or *Mit grosser Wildheit*), "with humor" (*mit Humor*), "cocky" (*keck*), "crudely" (*roh!*), "gaudily" (*grell*), "gruffly" (*grob!*), "as if whipped" (*wie gepeitscht*), "like a breath" (*wie ein Hauch*), "like a whisper" (*wie ein Geflüster*), "calling" and "answering" (*rufend, antwortend*), or "as if eavesdropping on oneself" (*wie nachhorchend*).[7]

Mahler's picture-oriented performance instructions are of course implicated in his program-music skepticism. Almost resembling stage instructions in plays, and difficult if not impossible to translate into any particular manner of playing, they suggest a music that's been turned into a play of images. In this sense, they might sound like compensation for some lacuna in the music or the musical pretense—a kind of reverse, after-the-fact programmaticism. What Mahler's symphonies lack in detailed verbal premise, his performance indications would seem to make up for with visual suggestion—but a visuality that ultimately proves incompatible, untranslatable into musical-performance terms. What all this means is that these score instructions reveal an exceptional—and exceptionally wide—gap between words and music. In this final chapter, I explore this epistemic problem as it relates to Mahler's unique position vis-à-vis the absolute-programmatic duality. Mahler's work became so amenable to later twentieth-century media because of this disparity between words and music: he was late achieving wide recognition precisely because it was only in the later twentieth century, and with the approach of a "culture totally dominated by images" as Mitchell describes it, that listeners could hope to close the gap between his photographic sensibility and the realm of words. Paradoxically enough, Mahler's currency—his latter-day popularity, provocative "postmodernism," and burning relevance to the turn of the twenty-first century—originates with this cognitive disparity or, more accurately, with the need to bridge it. Photography, film, and the photographic aspects of recording hold out the promise of closing the gap, thereby clearing the way for Mahler's wide popularity in the later twenti-eth century. Historically speaking, Mahler now represents the end of symphonic absolute-music traditions—an aesthetic ideal and cultural con-struct killed off by the same media reproduction forms that his work seems to presume.

WHAT THE IMAGE TELLS ME

Mahler's Second Symphony began life as a symphonic poem—the one-movement, purely orchestral *Totenfeier*. After the premiere of the com-plete symphony, however, Mahler told several acquaintances of his dissat-isfaction with program music. In a passage of one such letter, "real" and "performance" become operative terms in his attempt to distinguish the genuine experience from musical imitation: "Because of the nature of mu-sic, I have imagined in certain passages something like the dramatic per-formance of a real event. The parallel between life and music is perhaps deeper and more extensive than can be drawn at present."[8] In his last sen-tence we can get some idea of why in 1901 Mahler made the fairly mo-mentous decision, as recounted by his friend Ludwig Schiedermair, to ex-punge his earlier symphonies of their titles and programs at the same time that he loudly announced "Death to programs!" and stopped giving extra-musical explanations to the public. When the composer made this state-ment, he was accusing programs (the conventional way of "drawing paral-lels at present") not of being too forceful in their meaning, but of being not meaningful enough: "If a composer himself has forced on his listeners the feelings which overwhelmed him, then he has achieved his object. The language of music has then approached that of the word, but has commu-nicated immeasurably more than the word is able to express."[9]

Though he outwardly became a musical absolutist, Mahler's symphonic style was so explicitly if also ambiguously evocative at all points in his ca-reer that listeners commonly describe it as cinematic and find the music sends them grappling after far-flung imagery. Just how are these musical images nonverbal, antithetical to words? The images "seen" in the music are different from, say, the narrations in Richard Strauss's tone poems in that they involve no proper nouns; they are vivid, explicit, and visual, but not specific. Mahler offers no musical renderings of Don Quixote, Raphael's *Sposalizio*, the Moldau River, or the Bells of Zlonice. And his imagism—in its nonverbal, nonliterary, nonspecific aspect—is largely in-compatible with the usual Romantic ideas of extramusical illustration, even when we consider the full spectrum of illustrative possibilities. Mahler's imagism is nonspecific, but neither is his sensibility, oriented to the musical equivalent of momentary retinal capture, consistent with the vaguer if still verbalizable Schumannesque notion of "poetic" music or with the invisible and impalpable inspirations of the quasi-autobiographical "inner program." Schumann differentiated between "poetic" musical characterization and "programmatic" storytelling.[10] Poetic music subsumed the generalized allusiveness of the character piece: the various barcaroles, spinning songs, *Liebesträume*, and *Blumenstücke* that displayed only vague extramusical influences. Similarly nonspecific is the idea—which Mahler himself discussed, probably under the influence of Wagner's writings on Beethoven—of an "internal" as opposed to illustratively "external" program. The "inner program" is a dramaturgical shape and color exemplified in the hero of Beethoven's "Eroica" Symphony, though it also took on a verbal aspect when Wagner ascribed a specific day-in-the-composer's-diary scenario to Beethoven's String Quartet op. 101. The closest Mahler came to this was the "hero" of his first two symphonies, who—as the composer himself described him—was carried to his grave in the "Resurrection" Symphony "and whose life I, from a higher vantage point, collect in a clean mirror."[11]

Interesting examples of Mahler's disjunctions of word from musical image are found in the headings that he gave the individual movements of his Third Symphony, but withdrew before publishing the score. These show us Mahler abandoning the merely extramusical for the metaphysical: after a long first movement detailing the arrival of summer, we hear six movements of a progressive Nietzschean hymn to nature, circling higher and higher in the grand scheme of creation and pure affirmation:

1. "Pan Awakes, Summer Marches In"

2. "What the Flowers in the Meadow Tell Me"

3. "What the Animals in the Forest Tell Me"

4. "What Man Tells Me"

5. "What the Angels Tell Me"

6. "What Love Tells Me"

7. "What the Child Tells Me" (movement relocated to the end of the Fourth Symphony)

What clearer indication could we have of this composer's imagistic powers than the relative pronoun "what," functioning six times here as pointer to an absent object? As examples of musical titling and description, the second through seventh headings are strange indeed: beginning with the relative pronoun "what," they are all clauses. Thus they contrast with more common manners of program music, which tend to affix as a section heading either a sentence ("Clouds rise up" is the title of one section of Strauss's *Alpine Symphony*) or simply a subject ("Night," "Sunrise," and "The Ascent," other section titles from the *Alpine Symphony*). If Mahler had conformed to such traditions he might have titled his second movement "The Flowers in the Meadow" or perhaps added an object to make it something like "The Flowers in the Meadow Tell Me about the Midday Sun." The verb he uses, *erzählen,* is commonly translated as "tell" but can also mean "narrate"—so these denizens of nature provide information in the form of tales, tell tales that pose as information, or offer simple fiction. With these titles, Mahler faults the word as music's inferior, its inarticulate relative, or he at least says that verbal and musical meanings differ in their essence.

Mahler's art aligns with Mitchell's notion of the pictorial in that it represents a sensory inundation and therefore operates alongside—rather than through—the quasi-linguistic meanings that arise from orderings of functional units. Instead of telling us specific stories like Till Eulenspiegel surrender to justice or the invalid's delirium in Sibelius's *Valse triste,* Mahler leaves us with dramatic instantaneities arranged in a not-obviously-logical order. He described as his own ideal a momentary situation where "the composition of a master becomes so vivid and alive that one involuntarily believes himself to experience in it an event, an occurrence."[12] This is not to say that Mahler's individual moments don't connect to other moments, only that their particular imagist worth—unlike the importance of individual lexemes within a narrative—doesn't necessarily reside in that connection. It follows from this that an imagist deals in things quite different from those parlayed in conventional narratives. Hammer blows, whippings, changes in physical placement, and nonsectarian resurrections are different conceptual entities than Don Juan, the Moldau River, the Swan of Tuonela, Putnam's Camp, or Arnold Böcklin's painting *The Isle of the Dead* (which became subjects of tone poems by Richard Strauss, Bedrich Smetana, Jean Sibelius, Charles Ives, and Sergei Rachmaninov, respectively). As Mahler frames and represents them, his images are the brilliant and anonymous kind we would see in *Life* magazine, captured in photos that send us running to their captions for explanation. By contrast, the second group sounds like well-known and well-worn images in the *Encyclopedia Britannica.*[13]

Mahler's images are not usually amenable to verbal discourse, and thereby differ from Richard Strauss's musical illustrations. The wind machine illustrating "The Ride through the Air" in Strauss's *Don Quixote* (Variation 7) counts as non-Mahlerian in being all iconic sound with no visual concert-hall aspect. This instrument, cranked by hand and "placed out of sight whenever possible," as per Strauss's instruction, makes little visual sense in a performance. But it more than compensates with the precise and unmistakable—not to mention commonplace—"windiness" of the sound it creates. If Mahler's instrumental images differ from Strauss's in their resistance to words, their distance from simple verbal inception and interpretation, they are close to the *Lied* composer's illustrative subtlety. When brooks babble, crows caw, or postilions blow in Schubert songs, any allusive obviousness from the piano would be counterproductive because the voice is already there to convey the scenario within the particular, supra-allusive realm of words. In "Gefror'ne Thränen" from *Winterreise,* for example, Schubert presents the image of teardrops—or, better said, the potential near image of them—in the form of accented offbeats in the piano alongside steady staccato quarter notes. In "Im Dorfe" from the same cycle, the barking of village dogs sits loosely within the piano's noisy and persistent neighbor-note figures—another ingenious manner of illustration that isn't descriptive so much as suggestive. When the listener understands the lyrics sung here ("Es bellen die Hunde, es rasseln die Ketten . . ."), the figuration can seem clearly illustrative; without the words, it could suggest ten different scenarios. In such passages, Schubert's accompaniments relate to words just as ambivalently as a Mahler symphony does: the extramusical image of dog or teardrop is central and omnipresent, but never obvious or all-subsuming.

MAHLER'S TREACHERY
OF IMAGES: *CECI EST UN MARTEAU*

One Mahler image stands out for its problems of musical translation: the hammer in the last movement of the Sixth Symphony. The word "hammer" simply appears in the score at the bottom of the percussion section, below the tam tam and *Rute,* and quarter-note strokes occur at two points in the finale with specification for "short, powerful, but dull-sounding strokes of a nonmetallic character." This "instrument," regardless of how an orchestra and conductor might interpret Mahler's indications, tends to contrast with Strauss's wind machine by leaving only a vague aural thumbprint in

228 / *Mahler as Imagist*

performance. Stemming from no known or specific musical agency, the sound image is usually not distinct enough to make the complete leap from musicality to visuality that the composer—or, more properly speaking, the work—apparently desired. So the composer's instructions are laconic and confusing, waxing specific only when they tell the player to avoid any tuned metallic sounds—meaning Mahler wanted to avoid any suggestion of the famous anvils in Wagner's *Das Rheingold*, scene 2. Percussionists are accustomed to working from strange instrument indications in scores. But Mahler's hammer indication is the inverse of, say, Rossini's puzzling request for *cinelli* in *Il barbiere di Siviglia* (where the usual orchestral "cymbals" would be stylistically out of place) or Sibelius's ambiguous request for *Glocken* in the finale of his Fourth Symphony (which could mean either tubular orchestral "bells" or Glockenspiel but is now usually taken to mean the latter). While Rossini and Sibelius use indistinct terms to cue more-or-less standard practices, meaning that their score difficulties boil down to problems of terminology and communication, Mahler uses clear words to specify something that is both idiosyncratic and foreign to musical custom.

Conductor and musicologist Norman Del Mar wrote of Mahler's hammer "this apparently simple term hides a multitude of possibilities," and he wondered at the ad hoc nature of each—"a matter of trial and error every time the symphony is performed." According to T. W. Adorno, writing in the 1960s, the hammer blows of the finale "have not been properly heard hitherto and no doubt await their electronic realization."[14] I have heard the work performed twice in concert, and each time a different hammer solution proved equally dissatisfying. In Chicago, the percussionist engineered a foot mechanism like a giant bass-drum pedal and jumped on it when the big moment came, causing the mallet head to strike the stage floor itself. A decade later, I saw a New York percussionist pick up what seemed to be a smallish solid steel plate, maybe three-fourths of an inch thick, and throw it down as hard as possible onto a podium about four feet square and two feet high. In addition to the stronger corporeal profile—involving more in the way of visible human "performance"—this second solution had more sonic impact, though it was of course even less hammerlike, visually speaking, than the Chicago mechanism. Mahler himself tried various "hammer" solutions in performance but failed to realize it to his own satisfaction. For the premiere, he had animal hide stretched across the top of an enormous wooden chest, but the contraption—to be "beaten with clubs," as Alma Mahler recalls—didn't perform to his expectations and was discarded.[15] These various attempts, past and present, each disappointing in its own way, show how Mahler's iconicism had gone so far as to outstrip musicality and, indeed, practical reality: his visual-imagistic demands had parted ways with his musical requirements.

The problem, the reason for the "trial and error" in performance, is that Mahler's "hammer" is more an image or theatrical-pictorial allegory than an orchestral instrument: a synchretic image suggesting a tool designed to fracture, drive, and reshape; an iconic implement suggesting hard labor and hinting at bodily injury and perhaps tragedy; a formidable weapon, in the manner of Thor's hammer in Norse mythology; a dramaturgical gesture, a peripeteia vehicle straight out of Greek tragedy; and, finally, a sounding instrument that can either visually resemble a hammer or make a big enough noise to be heard above Mahler's large orchestra, but not both. As for the hammer strokes themselves, much of their imagistic potential comes from their promise to redress an age-old "problem" of music semiotics—or indeed sidestep the question of music's expressive powers entirely. While several authorities have claimed that music cannot signify because it has no object to which a musical signifier can refer—it has neither semantics nor the ability to present any concrete aspect of the nonmusical world—with his hammer blows Mahler tries to insert just such an object in the most forceful and (apparently) unmistakable way. In other words, he attempts with his hammer strokes to redress the dilemma of musical signification as Naomi Cumming has encapsulated it: music "cannot do more than suggest 'possibilities,'" she writes in summary of earlier authors, insofar as it "presents 'iconic' signs, in which different kinds of indexical relations may be imbedded."[16] Mahler uses his hammer to change the rules and bypass this supposedly inherent limitation of music—the same limitation often cited by proponents of instrumental composition as an "absolute" art form. While the symphony as a genre involves historically substantiated practice, Mahler reveals a new timbre here and jumps to a different manner of discourse—from the musical as commonly conceived to the visual, and an event delivered by an iconic nonmusical object.

But certainly the words of the Sixth's program—of the composer's latently autobiographical "hero" metaphor—should enter at this point to help define and contextualize the hammer strokes. The programmatic description does add specificity but raises more questions than it answers. Our only source for the statement and program is Alma Mahler, an undependable source of information about her husband, and even if the statement and program were true, they were not intended for public consumption—so the "blows of fate" count as an incidental explanation at best.[17] Indeed, Mahler's hammer serves to show how he abandoned accepted avenues of programmaticism, to use the common music-historical term that applies so poorly. Like many of his performance instructions, the "hammer" of the Sixth opens up what Mitchell calls, in reference to René Magritte's metapictures, "the blank space between the text and the image." How, indeed, are images of hammering, whipping, and eavesdropping—so simple and vivid as words and as pictures—to be transmitted from composer to the printed page, and to the listener? There's no straightforward way to convey such qualities through words (in the score) to music (sounding in the concert hall) and then to relevant concepts (in the listener's mind). Roger Scruton speaks of some music incurring in the listener a situation of "hearing as"—of bringing about a certain metaperception that stands above and beyond the notes.[18] His example is the particular "hearing as" modality that causes the listener to *hear* a group of pitches *as* a melody and not as a constellation of pitches. The hammer blows in Mahler's Sixth occasion such a "hearing as" aspect and ask the listener to regard them as nonmusical, purely dramaturgical, or otherwise nonsyntactic events.

I emphasize again that the hammer doesn't count as Mahler's only instance of jumping directly from musical to imagistic discourse. We could also discuss the cowbells and the tied-together twigs against the side of the bass drum that he called the *Rute*, which he used less as musical instruments in any usual sense than as adjuncts to musical discourse, as metaphors for psychic and visual experience. Otto Neitzel, a critic who attended the Sixth's 1906 premiere, spoke of the *Rute* in explicitly imagistic if verbally clumsy terms, as "producing the impression of a sheeted ghost turning somersaults in one's bedroom" and reacted to the cowbells and celesta with the exclamation "Paradise on earth and Elysian fields above!"[19] In Mahler's own words, the cowbells represent "the last terrestrial sounds penetrating into the remote solitude of mountain peaks"—a description that manages to transform a sound into vivid pictorial terms that nevertheless have nothing to do with the sound's actual making. Mahler's imagism doesn't reside only in his choice of instruments. We could list various structural and textural aspects of his music that are conducive to the listener's visual impetus: trading in teleological (or perhaps absolute?) forms for multisectional structures, which encourage moment-to-moment listening; the recognizability of returning material even when that material has been changed in basic ways; the multitude of themes even when compositional processes are based on motives; the sense of perspective borne of general linear clarity, with a lyric sense imbuing even the most complex passages; and last, the extraordinary character if not necessarily beauty of tone-color and orchestration, providing a nearly anthropomorphic sense of instruments.

Art historian Victor Burgin has argued that the visual image is perpetually invaded by language: "Even the uncaptioned 'art' photograph is invaded by language in the very moment it is looked at: in memory, in association, snatches of words and images continually intermingle and exchange one for the other."[20] We could say the same of most program music and its iconic aspect—where meaning has rarely if ever been conveyed in strictly musical terms but is instead a cooperative venture between music and words. Could Strauss's *Don Quixote* ever hope to give an impression of Cervantes instead of Byron, say, if the composer hadn't paired the right music with the right words, as laid out in concert programs and the press? Michel Foucault could just as easily have been speaking of musical imagery as graphic imagery when, within a discussion Diego Velázquez's *Las Meninas* and its inclusion of Spanish royalty, he described a basic confrontation between the icon and the logos. If we substitute "music" for "painting," "musical" for "visual," and "hear" for "see" in the following, we arrive at an astute insight into the Mahlerian imagist problem:

> The relation of language to painting is an infinite relation. It is not that words are imperfect, or that, when confronted by the visible, they prove insuperably inadequate. Neither can be reduced to the others' terms: it is in vain that we say what we see; what we see never resides in what we say. And it is in vain that we attempt to show, by the use of images, metaphors, or similes, what we are saying; the space where they achieve their splendour is not that deployed by our eyes but that defined by the sequential elements of syntax. And the proper name, in this particular context, is merely an artifice: it gives us a finger to point with, in other words, to pass surreptitiously from the space where one speaks to the space where one looks; in other words, to fold one over the other as though they were equivalents. But if one wishes to keep the relation of language to vision open, if one wishes to treat their incompatibility as a starting-point for speech instead of as an obstacle to be avoided, so as to stay as close as possible to both, then one must erase those proper names and preserve the infinity of the task.[21]

With his own iconic imagism, Mahler does something very similar in exposing the fault lines in the discourse surrounding music and imagery. His work emphasizes the fact that images invoked in music, though heavily dependent on verbal discourse, resemble graphic images in that they are iconic and closed off to discourse—which is to say, perpetually encouraging of it. We could clarify Mahler's imagist problem by following in René

Magritte's footsteps and put on a canvas an image of a steel plate or a wooden chest with clubs and inscribe "Ceci est un marteau" (This is a hammer) at the bottom (see fig. 9). The painting *Ceci n'est pas un pipe* (This Is Not a Pipe) stems from Magritte's *La trahison des images* (Treachery of Images, 1928–1929) series. But Magritte's celebrated image is not a simple exercise in contradiction, according to Foucault, since image and words are mutually distinct languages and cannot gainsay each other. In his view, Magritte's real subjects are the act of naming and language's tendency to lapse into convention: "The drawn form of the pipe is so easily recognized that it excludes any explanatory or descriptive text. Its academic schematicism says very explicitly, 'You see me so clearly that it would be ridiculous for me to arrange myself so as to write: This is a pipe. To be sure, words would draw me less adequately than I represent myself.'"[22] Likewise with Mahler, who engaged in a naming game with his "hammer" indication and the problematic relation between it and the sound produced: Is it drum-like? Chest-covered-with-hide-like? Steel-plate-like? In any event, it is not metallic or anvil-like.

MAHLER AS PHOTOGRAPHER

So Mahler's profusion of images and his deployment of them seem to presume an age of mechanical reproduction. It remains to be said that the quality of the images themselves puts him in empathy with the later part of that history. Mahler wasn't an imagist in the manner of Dürer or Rembrandt or Delacroix, but in a more contemporary fashion—in a manner that both presumes and helps constitute "the age of mechanical reproduction." He had a specifically photographic sensibility: his music is as stymieing as it is evocative, in the same way that an image is ever more resistant to discourse the more realistically photographic it becomes. He presents few if any conventional mimetic references, the kind of explicit, objective, transient, and instantaneous imagery that theorists have associated with the photograph. Mahler's sense of photographic denotation means that his imagery is all but closed to description. A satisfying closing-off of Mahlerian meaning comes less often from prose than from making or finding the right visual image, from joining the sound to an image immanent in that sound and linking the one related image to the sound immanent within that image. Why immanent, exactly? Because his imagistic sensibility deals in "analogical plenitude," to use Roland Barthes's description of the photographic sign.[23]

ceci est un marteau

FIGURE 9. "Ceci est un marteau" (This is a hammer): an example of Mahler's treachery of images (with apologies to René Magritte).

In typical photographic manner, Mahler seems to present basic images that are iconic likenesses rather than coded representations, however fragmentary or obscured. If he avoids the programmatic subjects of other late Romantics like Dvořák, Tchaikovsky, Strauss, and Rachmaninov, he also tends to avoid their kinds of signs, figures, and topoi: no descending chromatic figures or ground basses to denote tragedy, for example. Strauss's "Das Grablied" from *Also sprach Zarathustra* is not very dirgelike, certainly in comparison with one of Mahler's funeral marches, but Strauss's drooping, chromatic descents suggest knowing satire, and someone noticing those alongside the title could easily hear this music both as a dirge and as a satirical lament. Mahler's compositional language, unlike Strauss's, does not presume the singularity and commonality necessary for such codes to function as if they were languages. His "message" is indeed consistently split against itself, paradoxical in much the way Barthes saw the photograph presenting two messages simultaneously,

> the one without a code (the photographic analogue), the other with a code (the 'art,' or the treatment, or the 'writing,' or the rhetoric, of the photograph); structurally, the paradox is clearly not the collusion of a denoted message and a connoted message (which is the—probably inevitable—status of all the forms of mass communication), it is that here the connoted (or coded) message develops on the basis of a message *without a code*.[24]

The photo, in other words, lies stripped of meaning by its very nature and definition—its uncodedness, its very pretense of objectivity. According to Barthes, a major aspect of the photo's uncodedness is its relative lack of the "supplementary message," the necessary "addition to the analogical content itself," that we commonly perceive as style. This is not to say that photographers have no style, only that they take stylistic absence as a premise when they formulate their own creative methods—the photographer's style presumes or at least assumes the impossibility thereof, in painterly terms. As Mitchell puts it, paraphrasing the Barthesian paradox, "One connotation always present in the photograph is that it is a pure denotation."[25]

Robert Morgan speaks of Mahlerian defamiliarization, a process where the familiar is continually recontextualized: "What initially sounds familiar always ends up sounding very different from what we actually expected. The paradox implicit in this conjunction supplies the crucial point: what seems strange and extraordinary on one level does so only because, on another, it is so familiar and ordinary."[26] This explains the most basic issue of Mahler's compositional language, which in his own lifetime was thought banal and ridiculously unoriginal. While style is commonly defined as the specific manner of choices an artist makes among her various options, this composer complicates such a definition by cultivating a symphonic universality that sounds like many styles or like none at all. Mahler's complex negotiation of the very possibility of style, discussed by Morgan in terms of defamiliarization, is introduced by Carl Dahlhaus as a form of musical realism:

> It is precisely by the act of forcing heterogeneous material to coexist, without glossing over the inconsistencies, that Mahler creates a panorama which truly fulfils the claim he made for the symphony: it stands as a metaphor in sound for a world which contains within itself high and low, the sophistication of fine art and artless vulgarity, with complete impartiality and with a sense of reality which is rooted in a sense of justice. In Mahler, the momentum of a deeply felt "universalism" effortlessly overrides the most extreme incompatibilities between the multifarious contents of the one work, very much as it does in the poetry of Walt Whitman.[27]

What Morgan understands as Mahlerian defamiliarization could also be seen as a specifically photographic perspective on memory, where something is so clear, recognizable, and even habitual as to become strange. (There are obvious parallels here with the uncontrolled symptom within the Freudian understanding of the subconscious.) It says something that Mahler becomes most lavishly "visual" and indeed extravagantly imagistic—if often banal—at those very points where he emphasizes the most familiar and transparent musical-structural codings—cadences, for example—over any obvious thematicism. The examples of such dazzlingly imaged cadences are too numerous to list here but would have to include, in the first movement of the Seventh Symphony, the luminous arrival on B major in preparation for the return to the tonic B minor and recapitulation twenty-one bars later. The harmonic arrival itself (see ex. 3) combines ecstatic harp arpeggios with trilling flutes and piccolos, and then an ascending, passionately long-breathed melody in octave-doubled violins—perhaps out of empathy with the harpist's moving fingers, the listener sees the moment in the mind's eye as a parting of some bejeweled curtain.[28] Such moments of retransition are traditionally moments of great tension and release in symphonic form, but here the arrival on B major, ostensibly just a preparation for B minor, threatens to upstage the actual point of thematic return three bars after rehearsal 42—a point where the orchestral

EXAMPLE 3.   Mahler, Symphony No. 7, first movement
(mm. 313–320).

colors retreat to darkness and opacity. A similar example can be found toward the end of the third movement of the Third Symphony, where rhythmic and melodic repetition quickly wrenches the music from the dominant
F major (the world of the nostalgic post-horn solo) to E-flat minor, which
then moves fairly rapidly back to the tonic C major sideways, as it were,

through the Neapolitan D-flat. Here structural convention requires, of course, that final arrival on the tonic be strongly emphasized in order to compensate for the harmonic detour. But the composer amasses quite an array of sonic resources in that project: tam-tam, cymbals, tambourine, triangle, and even a kind of written-out *stringendo* come together with tremendous purpose.

Mahlerian defamiliarization and repetition, as defined by Morgan, must represent forms of resistance against the incursion of discourse, against words and obligatory meaning. They are challenges to enforced convention, declarations of affinity with the icon rather than the logos. In photographic pretenses to objectivity, Barthes sees "an ethical paradox: when one wants to be 'neutral,' 'objective,' one strives to copy reality meticulously, as though the analogical were a factor of resistance against the investment of values (such at least is the definition of aesthetic 'realism')."[29] Mahler's reinforced, repeated, and spectacular cadential arrivals tend to take on just such an air of engorged convention. Perhaps the very grandest of them all is the recapitulatory return to the tonic key at the end of the first movement of the Eighth Symphony. Here the structural tension is released—appropriately enough, at the doxology "in saecula saeculorum" (for ever and ever)—through no fewer than seven identical dominant-tonic discharges, repeated immediately and verbatim as if to scorn convention and exorcise the music's own familiarity.

All this might suggest that Mahler was himself a modernist or even postmodernist before his time. Dahlhaus didn't attribute any particularly "new" sensibility to him, choosing instead in his discussion of realism to define a particular Mahlerian relationship with Romanticism and Romantic originality. But this composer's strange imagery-without-reference does seem to link him with the twentieth century rather than the nineteenth. His ineffable melancholy is the sadness of the contemporary photo image. If Mahler's imagery is realist and empty and exhaustive, it also carries the poignant flavor of evanescence and indeed passed-ness: to borrow Barthes's description of the photo, the Mahlerian image supplies an urgent sense that "what I see has been here . . . ; it has been absolutely, irrefutably present, and yet already deferred."[30] Like the intensity that Barthes saw emanating from a photo of his recently deceased mother, its brilliance is premised on the very death and irretrievability of its subject. Just such a sense is imparted by the close of the third movement of the Third Symphony as described above: repetitious and inflated but pointing to the final chord like an incendiary arrow, the urgent cadential passage is gone as quickly as it came. With its passing we witness the disappearance of a passage unique in this symphony and in this composer's output, if not in concert art music as a whole. There are plenty of other examples where Mahler pains us with the radiant transience of his imagery— presenting us with something that is at one moment gorgeously rendered and then at the next, to quote the specification for the long, long-awaited final chord of the first movement of the Third Symphony or that concluding the entire Second Symphony, "scharf abreissen" (abruptly torn off).

We can go further to say that Mahler's imagery is not only photographic, but recently photographic. His is not the photo image of William Fox Talbot and Nadar and Mathew Brady, but the photo of Eadweard Muybridge, Étienne-Jules Marey, Walter Benjamin, Edward Weston, Barthes, maybe even Andy Warhol and Chuck Close. Contrary to a drawing or painting or daguerreotype, the Mahlerian image seems to presume an unnamed subject, but one in a specific place and time. Unlike the subject who selectively takes in and relates the visions presented in Richard Strauss's *Till Eulenspiegel* and *Don Juan*—Strauss's music unfolds from a single narrator's perspective—Mahler's subject seems all-seeing but unknowable. Benjamin talks about the exhibition rather than ritual value of the modern photograph, in a description that could apply to Mahler's imagism. He points to Eugène Atget as a photographer of Paris streets circa 1900 without human objects, as if they were crime scenes rather than artistic subjects: his photos "demand a specific kind of approach; free-floating contemplation is not appropriate to them. They stir the viewer; he feels challenged by them in a new way."[31]

WHAT HAPPENS IN VENICE . . .

So Mahler possessed a mediated sensibility before his time. But how exactly have media returned the favor and tried to close the Mahlerian gap between music and words, thereby revolutionizing reception of this composer's music? For one, they have encouraged people to focus their eyes, ears, and general attention as a way of expediting meaningful connections between the ever-shifting sights and sounds in a Mahler symphony. Marshall McLuhan described such developments in *Understanding Media* as a form of media-cultural literacy, referring for instance in the post-Gutenberg era to typographical conditioning of the eyes and greater interest in a fixed visual point of view.[32] We can speak in McLuhanesque terms of specific twentieth-century, media-instilled manners of looking and seeing that help listeners in the "hearing as" and "seeing as" modes that Mahler's music demands. For example, he often requires his listeners to assume the kinds of prosthetic views and sensibilities that have become standard practice in film editing—the interlocking shots that suture the viewer into the film's subjectivity and narrative space, for example, and the crosscutting practices that put the viewer's eye in different places at the same time.[33] I speak specifically of prosthetic views of texture and ensemble: Mahler's is an art of the instantaneous moment, and his restless imagism conflicts with the traditional anchored-in-one-place position of the orchestra. He has a penchant for iconic events of different kinds within each work, indeed within each musical moment. For appropriate coordination of the aural with the visual, then, his shifting musical dramaturgy would seem to demand almost constant reseating of the ensemble. The hammer of the Sixth Symphony provides an example: for the best hope of aligning aural and visual aspects, the "instrument" itself should be up front and plainly visible, not at the back in the percussion section.[34]

Clearly, film has become the most influentially imagistic and most actively prosthetic of media. And so it comes as a surprise that Mahler's music has been used at length in only several films: Luchino Visconti's *Death in Venice* (1971), Ken Russell's *Mahler* (1974), and Mitsuo Yanagimachi's *Kamyu nante shiranai* (2005; released in the United States as *Who's Camus Anyway?*). It is surely significant that all three movies give Mahler's music the unusual function of accompanying on-screen acts of looking. Subjectwise, they focus on Mahler or the composer's incarnation in the form of Gustav von Aschenbach, the writer in Thomas Mann's *Death in Venice.* So in these three films, it is Mahler—or Mahler-Aschenbach—whom we see on-screen doing the gazing while we are hearing Mahler's music. Thus the Mahler passages that we hear are equated with the things viewed, the final implication being that the passages in question are, like points in nondiegetic scoring, created at and for those particular cinematic moments—and that it is Mahler himself who is conceiving the music thus in response to the things seen. By giving us Mahler's music and individual gaze at the same moment, these filmmakers ascribe the on-screen images directly to the symphony passages in question.

Certainly the three movies in question imply that Mahler's work facilitates or complements the gaze. The words "image" and "imagination" might share a common etymology, but what these Mahlers and Mahler stand-ins are seeing cannot be described as imaginary. If they were imaginary, Mahler's film music would function as film music traditionally does:

as inducement to fantasy through the act of gazing, or as incitement to fantasy more generally. Instead, these on-screen Mahler-accompanied gazers focus on what are—within the film diegesis—actual events. Two of the films show us the gaze as a channel of amorous desire, as accompanied by the Adagietto from the Fifth Symphony. Here, what Mahler-Aschenbach sees is the nonimaginary Tadzio—the object of his erotic love if not outright lust, in the sense of the original Greek *eros*. In Mann, Aschenbach is an aging writer who glimpses the beautiful boy Tadzio in Venice, where he has traveled in order to escape the drying-up of his inspiration—Mann's protagonist might be thought Mahlerian in that he has a conflicted and indeed dissolute sense of beauty. He is an incorrigible romantic thrown tragically upon the rocks of an antiromantic age, but Mann makes him a writer so that he might gaze through his eyes and connect vicariously with his desire. Visconti changes Aschenbach to a composer (back to a composer?), no doubt in order to introduce Mahler's music to the soundtrack as described above—as a direct aural aspect of the camera's gaze. But nowhere in the movie do we hear the Adagietto from the Fifth Symphony specifically as a creation of Aschenbach's, except within his own mind as he silently views objects of rare, transcendent, and dangerously calming beauty—Venice itself as he arrives in the city, and of course Tadzio.

The moviegoer is sutured most tightly into the subjective and narrative space of Visconti's film, interposed between the desirer and his desired, at the climactic moment of Aschenbach's death on the beach (see fig. 10a). So does the Mahler Adagietto function here as diegetic source music or as nondiegetic underscoring? Does the character Aschenbach really and specifically hear the Adagietto in his head at these critical moments where beauty lures him to his fate, or is this music provided for our sake as beholders of Visconti's and Aschenbach's art? The former is unlikely, since the music continues uninterrupted through the moment of Aschenbach's death and after, all the way through the final credits. We would do best to conclude that this scene shows us Visconti exploiting the Adagietto's imagistic power, which stands outside time, to the fullest. This last moment on the beach is where Tadzio, standing isolated and motionless for the first time in the movie and in Aschenbach's gaze, against the neutral or perhaps otherworldly backdrop of the sea, becomes most like his own likeness. The Adagietto overwhelms us with desirous beauty when it returns *fortissimo* to the tonic F major in second inversion (m. 30), and this moment coincides with the point in the final beach scene where Aschenbach and Tadzio reach spiritual intimacy. As if this imagistic point weren't clear enough, Visconti leaves a box camera on the beach, its lens pointing directly into the narrative

FIGURES 10A–B. The dying Aschenbach watches Tadzio in Visconti's *Death in Venice*, final scene. Warner Bros., 1971.

space as if a stand-in for Aschenbach's gaze. Tadzio, though now physically indistinct, fading with the late afternoon Mediterranean sun and Aschenbach's ebbing consciousness, "represents himself" to the fullest at this point: this, the moment of his beholder's death, is where the boy becomes his own image (see fig. 10b).

In his allusive and playful film *Kamyu nante shiranai*, Yanagimachi takes the Mahler-Mann-Visconti sequence of authorial intra-absorbments to the next level: the aging and desirous artist is here a former movie director who teaches film. Professor Nakajo is called "Old Venice" by his students because of his fascination with the Visconti film. True to his nickname, he develops a visual obsession with a student who resembles his late wife. He has multiple momentary encounters with the student, confrontations that Yanagimachi models on Aschenbach's glimpses of Tadzio *chez* Visconti: there is the semidistant glimpse in a crowd, the encounter in a restaurant with relatives, and the awkward mutual glance in passing. Overwhelmed by the woman's beauty and the failure of his filmmaking career, Nakajo finally locks himself in his office, dons a white suit and age-defying makeup, gets drunk on *sake,* and collapses in front of the TV as he watches *Death in Venice* and the moviegoer hears the climactic strains of Mahler's Adagietto. This refers to the Visconti scene—also accompanied by the Adagietto—where the white-clad and heavily made-up Aschenbach collapses in despair against a well after he has clumsily pursued Tadzio through the sooty and diseased streets of Venice. Two film students discover Nakajo lifeless on the floor and one, picking up the DVD box, announces that "Old Venice has turned into Aschenbach." Mahler's Adagietto wends its sensuous way through the entire scene of Nakajo's final degradation, as it does Aschenbach's. The music must be Yanagimachi's acknowledgment that the Mahler Adagietto has become, courtesy of Visconti, the ultimate soundtrack for the lovelorn gaze, for the simultaneous closeness and irretrievability of the desired image.

MAHLER AND FILM

As if the Mahler-Mann-Visconti line of reference wasn't allusive enough, we also have the train station scene from Ken Russell's film *Mahler* (1974) and its Mahler-Mann-Visconti-Mahler connection. In this particular scene of this dreamlike and sometimes hallucinatory film, we see the terminally ill Mahler waiting for his train to depart. He looks wanly out the compartment window toward the platform and notices Aschenbach, who in turn surreptitiously gazes at Tadzio, who is himself twirling thoughtlessly around pillars (again a direct reference to Visconti's film, to the first beach scene specifically). The composer's wife has left the compartment for some momentary errand, allowing this little scene to stand outside the movie's narrative and within the intertextual space of the film. There is a surreal aspect in seeing Mahler looking at Mann's, or should we say Mann and Visconti's, transformation of himself. This must be the composer Aschenbach rather than the writer Aschenbach. And why does Russell's Mahler smile so knowingly upon seeing Aschenbach with Tadzio? The composer has a gentle grin of recognition and complete understanding, but just what is it he is recognizing? It is as if Russell's minute-long *jeu d'esprit,* standing outside the filmic diegesis, also allows Mahler to stand outside time and survey the full reception history and influence of his oeuvre, past and future. His smile betokens full knowledge of the Visconti film and the influence it will have.

Russell's complex scene, occurring toward the start of his film, gives some idea of the manifold avenues of visual meaning that Mahler's imagism

FIGURE 11.   Alma becomes Gustav's shadow in Russell's *Mahler.* Mayfair Films / Visual Programme Systems Ltd., 1974.

has opened up in a picture-laden, postlinguistic world. As if in summary of earlier practice, it replays the Adagietto's adherence to postured schematics of bodies and beholders, to defined vectors of eyes and deflected gazes. But Russell, as a filmmaker less interested in biography than in "the union of the spirit and flesh, body and soul" of his subjects, takes Mahler's imagism a good deal further.[35] In his more fantastic exploration of Mahlerian imagism at other places in his film, he reverses the circumstances of the Sixth's hammer in orchestral performance. There we saw and heard percussionists working to exact an actual, "musical" realization of an ambiguous word supplied by the composer. Russell does the opposite when he searches for imagery in the less narrative-bound portions of his film: he proceeds from the sounding music toward concrete, real-life specifics and arrives at scenarios so resolute and visionary as to suggest single words without securing them. This kind of free music-toward-image association is the stock-in-trade of the music video. One such MTV-like scene in Russell's movie shows Alma trailing Gustav as his nameless shadow (see fig. 11). Even as her husband is fêted and celebrated, she remains anonymous and hidden behind a black veil, her existence as grim and banal as the solo trombone recitativo from the first movement of the Third Symphony that Russell uses to underscore the scene. This is phantasmagoric imagery, idiomatically "Mahlerian" in that it is both dreamlike and iconic-thematic: the moment could be inscribed with the descriptive-imagistic word "shadow," though such a term would fail to subsume or specify either the scene or the music itself.

Russell accompanies Mahler's music with dreamlike images, yet, in consistently linking those images with the composer's own on-screen gaze, he implicitly attributes them to Mahler himself. The "shadow" scenario focuses on Alma, but Gustav shares in its making by saying before it starts, "Don't say it, I know!"—attempting in vain to forestall his wife's exclamation of "I might as well be your shadow, from the notice anyone takes of me," which he has clearly heard many times. Likewise in the scene where the boy Mahler explores a nocturnal forest, the nature imagery is prefaced explicitly by the young composer's upward glance, meaning this is his imagery. The music accompanying—or better said, inciting—these nature images is a section of the development in the first movement of the Seventh Symphony, the harp-led "parting of a curtain" episode discussed above. Russell makes the sequence a bit comic by using stock footage of forest animals without matching camera angles and editing, resulting in a kind of montage caricature: the spider's web glistens, the owl looks for prey, the fox surveys its territory, the hedgehog forages, the jay nibbles on the branch, and the boy Mahler couldn't possibly be seeing all this without a field guide, a set of telephoto lenses, and days of patient waiting. But the sequence, shoving narrative continuity aside to make way for imagistic intensity, perfectly reflects the Mahlerian manner of preexisting and discrete schemata. This shows the heart of Mahler's style as a brilliant and unpredictable, if also nearly didactic and hairsplitting, manner of visual-photographic parable.

This scene in Russell's film, like the train platform scene, serves to substantiate previous associations between Mahlerian sounds and images. The director provides a moonlit scenario for that part of the development section of the Seventh Symphony, first movement, that commentators have over the years habitually—with no cueing from the literature or from Mahler himself—called "the moonlight episode." This is the G major section starting in m. 266, rehearsal number 32, introduced by triplets in the solo trumpet. Russell uses this music to accompany the boy Mahler's retreat to the forest at night: he sits beneath a tree, and the moon comes out from behind a cloud, allowing him to glimpse the surrounding fauna. I have found no source for the "moonlight" reference in the musicology literature and doubt in any event that Russell would be in touch with Mahler scholarship. In short, this sequence from Russell's film shows yet another listener interpreting a Mahler passage according to the same imagery, providing further evidence that there must indeed be something moonlight-ish in this evocative musical passage—some kind of imagistic encoding.

Given the evident "moonlight-ishness" of that passage of the Seventh, Mahler's imagery might not seem so impervious to the invasion of language after all. In the Sixth finale, his "hammer" inscription is the source of the music's imagistic meaning-potential, or at least the precipitating agent for it. Since Visconti, Russell, and Yanagimachi came to almost identical interpretations of the Adagietto, that movement would also seem—at some level, in some way—to carry an inscription of its own. What could it be? On the basis of documentary research and some circumstantial evidence, Gilbert Kaplan decided—decades after Visconti's and Russell's movies—that Mahler had penned the Adagietto as a valentine to his wife, Alma.[36] So the inscription the composer neglected to include above the Adagietto could be something as simple and as general, as poetic in the Schumannesque sense, as "Love." But the fact that these three film directors interpreted the movement in a more specific, and quite astonishingly similar, fashion leads one to believe that the unwritten inscription would have to be more definite and explicit, or perhaps cinematic. "Waiting for Fulfillment?" "Underage and Illicit Love"? "Hopeless Longing"? Such sobriquets could describe Aschenbach's and Nakajo's situations, as well as Mahler's own in the summer of 1910 when the still-youthful Alma was having an affair with Walter Gropius.

It is a significant comment on the strength of Mahler's imagism that these directors, in interpreting the same music, again managed to arrive at such similar *mise-en-scenes*. (Of course the films themselves have intertextual relations qua films, with Russell and Yanagimachi alluding to Visconti as much as to Mahler, but such filmic cross-references by themselves wouldn't be enough to carry the visual-musical connection if it hadn't functioned on its own and on another level from the beginning.) We could say, returning to the Mahlerian gap between musical imagery and words, that these three filmmakers agree more on the Adagietto's imagistic meaning, supposedly a subjective and interpretive matter, than conductors concur on the hammer part of the Sixth, which is actually written into the score.[37] Doesn't this difference of interpretation tell us something about musical meaning in absolute music? That it might be less delusional to search for truths and fixed ideas in our reactions to printed musical texts than in the texts themselves? We can at least conclude that the two

Mahlerian representations in question—the hammer-ishness of the Sixth's finale and the lovelorn bittersweetness of the Adagietto—are different in degree rather than in kind.

ENVOI: LISTENING IN THE AGE OF MECHANICAL REPRODUCTION

In all his imagistic brilliance, Mahler seems to pose a pair of questions that are deeply relevant to musical life in the age of mechanical reproduction and after "the pictorial turn." First, is the significance of concert art music really a function of its sound? And, second, even more basically, can one speak any longer of listening to music in any practical sense rather than watching-observing-listening to music?

There are too many examples of the latter activity, and attendant technologies, even to attempt a list. In this day of video and MP3 players, a time when music is astonishingly omnipresent and pervasive, watching the "musical" aspects of people's lives would mean simply observing everything they do: exercising, grocery shopping, museum going, working, even sleeping. At least one music label, Naxos, now offers DVDs with classical compositions accompanied by video footage of places known to the composers. While audiences have enjoyed intermittent musical accompaniment to movies for over a century, these discs provide complete performances of classical works accompanied by visual images; while MP3 players offer what some call the "soundtracks of our lives," these videos turn concertos and symphonies into something like "soundtracks of composers' lives." (Naxos's packaging for the Bach Violin Concertos does assure us that "these are the images that echo through Bach's music; an experience as evocative as the Brandenburg Concertos themselves.") Such music DVDs show people engaged more consistently by visual elements than by what they hear: play friends a Bruckner CD and some of them, including the musicians, will nod off; put on a DVD of Carlo Maria Giulini or Herbert von Karajan conducting the same work with the sound turned down, and their attention will be piqued. A similar lesson comes from YouTube, which an increasing number of people turn to as their first option when seeking out a specific piece of music. One would also have to mention visualizers, a feature of music software that supplements a song with spontaneous on-screen imagery, giving it a visual profile unique to every moment. In general, the domination of audio-visuality and increases in media convergence and e-connectedness mean that a person rarely experiences any kind of sound without a visual key or complement. Not long ago people "watched" TV, "listened to" the stereo, and "connected" on the telephone. Now all three happen simultaneously on a wireless 2 × 4 inch assemblage of integrated circuits that links, cues, merges, and supplements every activity by, with, and through the visual interface of its screen.

I repeat such techno-utopianist clichés not to promote commercial franchises, but only to show how present developments have decisively overturned absolute music's attempt to subjugate the visual to the aural. Over the last decades of the twentieth century, people grew ever more imagistic in their own epistemologies and conceptual thinking. Petra Stegmann and Peter C. Seel describe this general pictorial turn as follows:

> For some years now the concept of a *flood of images* is being evoked again and again in order to characterize the information age we are living in today. This fact led W. J. T. Mitchell to his concept of the 'pictorial turn' based on the assumption, that we live in a post-linguistic, post-semiotic culture dominated by pictures. Human experience—according to Nicholas Mirzoeff—is more visual than ever before, with new technologies leading to a situation where formerly non-visual phenomena—like satellite images or pictures from inner parts of the body—become part of the visual everyday life. The endless flow of the images that surround us every day—in mass cultural productions (newspapers, television, Internet, advertising, wrapping), in film and visual arts, as well as in mental images—has led to an exponential expansion of the cosmos of images, the exploration of which presents a new challenge to established scientific disciplines.[38]

The pictorial turn has of course had a profound effect on music—all music. Mahler, as incorrigible compositional imagist, is especially implicated in this "endless flow of images" and technologies of "mass cultural productions." Provocatively straddling styles and traditions, he helps us see program music as part of a broad, media-based playing out of dualities between within and without, logocentric and iconic. Program music displayed these dualistic qualities and this basis in media as early as December 1830, when printing enabled Berlioz to distribute his quasi-autobiographical program for the premiere performance of his *Symphonie fantastique.* Without such methods of reproduction and dissemination, Berlioz and no program music practitioner after him could have used words to precipitate images from music. Arguments against illustrative music, Eduard Hanslick's disputes with Wagner for example, often originate from the feeling that specific extramusical ideas force music from its natural avenues of expression.

But when Mahler rejected programs in 1901, as already mentioned, he was accusing them not of being too blatant, but of being too weak in meaning. If with the programs of his first four symphonies Mahler came to abandon the merely extramusical for the metaphysical, then his jettisoning of those programs need not count as admission of an absolute-music basis, so much as frustration with the very duality of absolute and programmatic.

In articulating various ways that images can relate to music and music to images, program music was part of a broader cultural trajectory from nineteenth-century cultures of absolute music and their subservience of the visual to the musical to later twentieth-century film-video cultures and their subservience of the musical to the visual. The Kantian hierarchy of musical and extramusical has been overturned—such that, as Michel Marie wrote, "cinema remains above all an art of the image, while its other elements (dialogue, written words, sound effects, and music) must accept its priority."[39] We must see local examples of program music against the broad, 150-year trajectory of the "purely musical" losing out to extramusical imagery. Indeed, absolute music could well be the only culture claiming direct connection to the logos, with no visual aspect whatsoever: even mathematics contains its own iconographic history, such that understanding the symbols necessarily involves some connection with their history. The duality between absolute music and program music is no longer useful or perhaps even understandable in the twenty-first century, either in description of twentieth-century scores or illustrative music from the nineteenth century, because media have forced a redrawing of the whole subject-object relation and an inversion of the traditional relationship between musical work and meaning. This inversion shows profound change in the relationship between public and private forms of the imagination. For young people now, the duality of music that purportedly "says" something and music that purportedly refuses to do so seems of less than little interest: music is music, and all music means *something*.

So perhaps Mahler's symphonies represent not a revolution so much as an inevitable development in the historical continuum of illustrative instrumental music. They help us draw aesthetic and historical connections between media of different epochs. But how exactly have later twentieth-century media promised to close the Mahlerian gap between musical images and words? For one, they have supplied us with exponentially larger imagistic-epistemological contexts. Film music, for example, has the basic function of clearing ground for the moviegoer's sense of fantasy and storytelling—in Claudia Gorbman's description, it "lessens defenses against the fantasy structures to which narrative provides access."[40] The movie theater and TV are everyman laboratories in everyday musical signification, and they are the main reason it is difficult to imagine today's listeners reacting to Mahler's onslaughts of eventfulness the way many did in his lifetime: with angry confusion, and complaints that his symphonies are unintelligible without programmatic assistance. But music's course has been affected by other manner of media involving integrated circuits and hard drives, and the "flood of images" has found its inevitable result in instrumental music's promiscuous, free-floating association. "Pure music," writes Nicholas Cook, "is an aesthetician's (and music theorist's) fiction; the real thing unites itself promiscuously with any other media that are available."[41]

Mahler's listeners have been liberated from the sensory deprivation of the concert hall by audio technology and by the movies, and their modes of awareness expanded and quickened through e-connectivity. Given the imagistic immediacy of this composer's music, they have a new and special mandate for wandering mentally and psychologically—not to mention physically in this age of portable media—in their search for meaning. Even in simple visual terms, the field of associative possibility has expanded exponentially. A listener trying to pin an explanatory image to Mahler's "hammer" today has far greater recourse than she would have had ten years ago, not to mention in Mahler's own time. A hundred years ago a hammer inquisitor might have gone to the library for a blacksmithing manual or a picture book on mythology. Some aristocratic attendees of Mahler's premiere, narrowly *gebildet* and knowing nothing of manual labor, might not even have had any idea what a hammer was. Today, however, a Google search yields 7.63 million "hammer" images almost instantaneously—and of an array that could encourage one to hear Mahler's percussive blows in terms of carpentry, civil engineering, wrestling, firearms, superheroes, horror films, Republican congressmen, hip-hop has-beens, cement-crushing machines, motorcycles, golf clubs, and vitamins. How can any music even pretend to remain "absolute" in an era that makes such connections? Who can prophesy the interpretive alchemies that might someday result from these musical-imagistic combinations?

The Internet has wrought profound change with its polysemic linkages and social redefinitions, but then we musicians hardly even understand older photographic developments and their ramifications for our art—that is, in terms of their effect on musical hearing, memory, and association. There's no question that photographic imagery came to supplant program music as a brilliant and especially fluid means of capturing and presenting images within the flux of time. In the broad, 150-year trajectory

of the "purely musical" losing out to the extramusical, with particular me-
dial points in Lisztian and Straussian brands of program music, Mahler
emerges as a prescient yet elusive figure: in his suggestion of photographic imagery, he counts as a precursor to the domination of image
over language and the "pictorial turn" instigated by mass reproduction.
People were awash in narratives a century and a half ago, while today we
are bombarded with images. On this basis, while program music may have
been supplanted by photography, it eventually came to be entirely replaced
by movies. We find early prognostication of this shift in formalist critic Eduard Hanslick's 1881 condemnation of the Liszt Piano Sonata. His piece of
criticism is both aesthetically conservative and astutely forward-looking.
Writing some five years before Mahler started his First Symphony and
Edison began the experiments that would lead him to the Kinetoscope,
Hanslick lambasted Liszt's most ambitious essay in absolute music as "an
ingenious steam engine that scarcely ever drives anything." Here Hanslick
went some way toward describing Liszt as a film composer *avant la lettre*,
explaining his masterpiece in terms of mechanism, virtuosity of means,
and inextricability from things extramusical, but also as a specifically
mechanistic conception that incorporated no imagery within itself.[42] Sound
film, that all-subsuming descendant of still photography, has indeed become the poststructuralist master trope in all the world's developed countries, and the imaginations of Mahler fans have taken all the more readily
and indeed promiscuously to its musical-imagistic playground. Visconti's
and Russell's striking and enduring interpretations of his music are proof
of this.

In the end, we must see and hear Mahler as an interstitial composer,
one that a multimedia age has taken to its heart. Profoundly imagistic, he
nevertheless wrote nonprogrammatic symphonies rather than music for
the nickelodeon and chose not to outpictorialize Richard Strauss in the
symphonic poem. In this sense, at least, his symphonies could in fact be
seen as a form of musical resistance to "the pictorial turn"—not the kind of
abstractionist balking seen in the Darmstadt composers after World War
II, a retreat into modernist abstraction, but perhaps a headstrong attempt
to recapture lost imagistic ground in musical terms. Which is not to say
Mahler tried to be more actively pictorial than Strauss and Smetana and
failed, but that he, exploiting the kind of brilliance seen in the mediated image, wrote music that forces its describers to devise new languages and new
locutions. Adorno came away from specific Mahler compositions speaking
of novel-symphonies and a "golden book of song [taken as] the book of
life."[43] The perpetual Mahler-Strauss comparisons could then lead us to a

realization: while Strauss wrote symphonic poems in rich description of existing literature—among them Cervantes's *Don Quixote* and Nietzsche's *Also sprach Zarathustra*—Mahler wrote symphonies of such imagistic wealth and depth that they urge listeners into imagining new and nonexistent, even oxymoronic, kinds of books. And this counts as yet another way this composer inverts nineteenth-century programmatic traditions: it is Mahler who supplies the imagery, while his listeners author the texts that conjoin them and give them meaning.

And what about technology per se? Whether the technology is photography, film, audio recording, or integrated circuits and flash drives, we can be sure it will never fully close the Mahlerian gap between music and discourse. The relation between any music and any form of discourse is of course an infinite relation, to extend Foucault's statement: music, whether it be from Beethoven or Björk, will always resist our wish to circumscribe and tame it. Even music theory and analysis operate through metaphorical language. But this doesn't mean technology is ineffectual or entirely accessory to the musical experience, or that the Mahlerian gap won't eternally tease listeners into long hermeneutic and technological campaigns. Mahler's gap, as I've described it above, almost begs for conclusion—and thereby drives performer and listener to kinds of extremes that aren't seen with other music. Will photography help us finally understand the object and purpose of the aching suspensions in the Adagietto? Or perhaps the perfect audio technology will allow us to comprehend them in the privacy of our ear canals and living rooms? Or surely sound film will answer all by finally providing the pertinent imagery? Might amplification and a detailed *Hammers through the Ages* PowerPoint help the listener make conclusive sense of the hammer in the Sixth? And so the campaign continues: Mahler's meanings can seem just as pressing yet just as distant as the receding horizon of technological fulfillment itself. In that sense, his symphonies not only stand as prime examples of absolute music "in the age of mechanical reproduction" but also serve to demonstrate another one of Benjamin's maxims. In hindsight, one could be forgiven for thinking the dictum was originally intended to describe this composer's art: for it was never truer than when said of a Mahler symphony, though not in any manner of interpretive closure, that "to an ever greater degree the work of art reproduced becomes the work of art designed for reproducibility."[44]

Notes

INTRODUCTION

1. Brian Massumi, "Translator's Foreword: Pleasures of Philosophy," introduction to *A Thousand Plateaus: Capitalism and Schizophrenia*, by Gilles Deleuze and Félix Guattari, trans. Brian Massumi (Minneapolis and London: University of Minnesota Press, 1987), xiii–xiv.

2. For an overview of philosophical perspectives, see Theodore Gracyk, "Listening to Music: Performances and Recordings," *Journal of Aesthetics and Art Criticism* 55.2 (1997): 139–50. Rattle interviewed by James Badal, *Recording the Classics: Maestros, Music, and Technology* (Kent, OH and London: Kent State University Press, 1996), 74; Roman Ingarden, *The Work of Music and the Problem of Its Identity*, trans. Adam Czerniawski (Berkeley: University of California Press, 1986), 27; Lewis Lockwood, "Film Biography as Travesty: *Immortal Beloved* and Beethoven," *Musical Quarterly* 81.2 (1997): 190–98.

3. In the United Kingdom, by contrast, there exists the AHRC Research Centre for the History and Analysis of Recorded Music, which aims to "promote the study of music as performance through a specific focus on recordings." A cooperative endeavor of Royal Holloway, University of London with King's College, London and the University of Sheffield, CHARM opened in 2004. It is scheduled to be succeeded in October 2009 by the AHRC Research Centre for Musical Performance as Creative Practice, which will shift focus to the interaction between performers and recordings.

4. Richard Taruskin, *Text and Act: Essays on Music and Performance* (New York and Oxford: Oxford University Press, 1995), 43.

5. Theodor Helm, *Beethovens Streichquartette* (Leipzig: Fritzsch, 1885), 168, quoted in Leon Botstein, "The Patrons and Publics of the Quartets: Music, Culture, and Society in Beethoven's Vienna," in *The Beethoven Quartet Companion*, ed. Robert Winter and Robert Martin (Berkeley, Los Angeles, and London: University of California Press, 1994), 107.

6. Paul du Gay, Stuart Hall, Linda Janes, Hugh Mackay, and Keith Negus, *Doing Cultural Studies: The Story of the Sony Walkman* (London: Sage, in association with The Open University, 1997), 23.

7. Robert Philip, *Early Recordings and Musical Style: Changing Tastes in Instrumental Performance, 1900–1950* (Cambridge: Cambridge University Press, 1992); Mark Katz, *Capturing Sound: How Technology Has Changed Music* (Berkeley, Los Angeles, and London: University of California Press, 2004); Timothy Taylor, *Strange Sounds: Music, Technology, and Culture* (New York and London: Routledge, 2001); Hans-Joachim Braun, *Music and Technology in the Twentieth Century* (Baltimore and London: Johns Hopkins University Press, 2002).

8. Du Gay et al., *Doing Cultural Studies*; Tia DeNora, *Music in Everyday Life* (Cambridge and New York: Cambridge University Press, 2000).

9. Colin Symes, *Setting the Record Straight: A Material History of Classical Recording* (Middletown, CT: Middletown University Press, 2004), 245. The most interesting part of the book is the chapter "The Best Seat in the House: The Domestication of the Concert Hall," in which Symes broaches the topics of sound spaces and listening locations.

10. Eric F. Clarke, *Ways of Listening: An Ecological Approach to the Perception of Musical Meaning* (Oxford and New York: Oxford University Press, 2005). The chapter that comes closest to my own concerns, which tend to be at once more materialist and work-oriented than Clarke's, is "Autonomy/Heteronomy and Perceptual Style," 126–55.

11. Philip Auslander, *Liveness: Performance in a Mediatized Culture* (London and New York: Routledge, 1999).

12. Evan Eisenberg, *The Recording Angel: Explorations in Phonography* (New York: McGraw-Hill, 1987); recently republished, with the addition of two brief afterwords, as *The Recording Angel: Music, Records, and Culture from Aristotle to Zappa*, 2nd ed. (New Haven, CT and London: Yale University Press, 2005).

13. Jonathan Goldman, "Éditorial: De la musique, de la contemporanéité et du plaisir," *Circuit—Musiques Contemporaines* 16.3 (August 2006), http://www.revuecircuit.ca/articles/16_3/01-editorial (accessed 4 September 2008); my translation.

14. E. T. A. Hoffmann, "Beethoven's Instrumental Music" (1810–13), in *Source Readings in Music History*, vol. 6, *The Nineteenth Century*, ed. Ruth A. Solie, rev. ed. (New York and London: W. W. Norton, 1998), 151.

15. A good place to begin regarding the question of absolute music as a cultural construct is Susan McClary's "Narrative Agendas in 'Absolute' Music: Identity and Difference in Brahms's Third Symphony," in *Musicology and Difference: Gender and Sexuality in Music Scholarship*, ed. Ruth A. Solie (Berkeley: University of California Press, 1993), 326–44.

16. Carl Dahlhaus, "Absolute Music as an Esthetic Paradigm," in *The Idea of Absolute Music*, trans. Roger Lustig (Chicago and London: University of Chicago Press, 1989), 1–17.

17. See also the rather different fan complaints that a David Bowie *Best Of* collection "desecrates" beloved songs by removing solo breaks: commentary as posted by "A Customer" at http://www.amazon.com/Best-1974–1979-David-Bowie/dp/B000009RNP/sr = 1–6/qid = 1171412867/ref = sr_1_6/002–6678616–4845608?ie = UTF8&s = music (accessed 11 November 2005).

18. Dahlhaus, *Idea of Absolute Music*, 7.

19. "The predominance of music without words, popularly called 'absolute music,' . . . is typical of music in capitalist society." Hanns Eisler, "Musik und Politik," in *Schriften 1924–1948* (Leipzig, 1973), 222, quoted in Dahlhaus, *Idea of Absolute Music*, 2.

20. Originally published in *Gramophone* in 1924, reprinted in Compton Mackenzie, *My Record of Music* (New York: G. P. Putnam's, 1956), 32.

21. Artur Schnabel, *My Life and Music* (New York: St. Martin's Press, 1963), 121.

22. Hoffmann, "Beethoven's Instrumental Music," 151.

23. One such list might begin with Simon Frith's *Sound Effects: Youth, Leisure, and the Politics of Rock 'n' Roll* (New York: Pantheon Books, 1981) and could end with Albin Zak's *The Poetics of Rock: Cutting Tracks, Making Records* (Berkeley: University of California Press, 2001).

24. Though she stops short of drawing contrasts between the social reach of popular music and the accessibility level of "absolute music," McClary does conclude her discussion of Schoenberg's, Babbitt's, and Boulez's abstractions with the following description of Earth, Wind and Fire's song "System of Survival": "The fact that this song reaches a wide audience, that it speaks in a comprehensible language of exuberant hope in the face of hardship is regarded not as evidence of selling out, but as a mark of success in an economy of prestige that rewards communication and political effectiveness. Earth, Wind and Fire cares if you listen." Susan McClary, "Terminal Prestige: The Case of Avant-Garde Music Composition," *Cultural Critique* 12 (1989): 81.

25. Walter Benjamin, "The Work of Art in the Age of Mechanical Reproduction" (1936), in *Illuminations: Essays and Reflections*, ed. Hannah Arendt and trans. Harry Zohn (New York: Schocken Books, 1968), 227; Gore Vidal, "The Top Ten Best Sellers according to the Sunday *New York Times* as of January 7, 1973," *New York Times*, January 7, 1973.

26. Lydia Goehr, *The Imaginary Museum of Musical Works: An Essay in the Philosophy of Music* (Oxford and New York: Oxford University Press, 1992).

27. Roger Scruton, "Absolute Music," *The New Grove Dictionary of Music and Musicians*, ed. Stanley Sadie and John Tyrrell, 2nd ed. (London and New York: Macmillan, 2001), 1: 36.

28. Walter Ong, *Orality and Literacy: The Technologizing of the Word* (London and New York: Routledge, 1982), 73–74.

29. "To say that ephemerality is a special quality of sound, rather than a quality endemic to any form of perceptible motion or event in time, is to engage in a very selective form of nominalism." Jonathan Sterne, *The Audible*

Past: Cultural Origins of Sound Production (Durham, NC and London: Duke University Press, 2003), 18.

30. Though he professed many times to hating recording, Artur Schnabel offered a startlingly practical vision where recordings could well replace both printed music and performance itself if it weren't for the human need to revisit and reinterpret musical works: "To become perceptible, music must each time be re-created from the memory. A gramophone record, the permanent reproduction of a temporary one, would have disposed of this necessity only if man would—and could—cease re-creating a composition after it had been mechanically preserved." Schnabel, *My Life and Music*, 230.

31. Robert Layton, "Karajan's Sibelius," *Gramophone*, October 1981, 523. Of course, locating the meaning of musical works in a specific—and often textually encoded—truth has its roots in theology and scriptural hermeneutics. In any event, I believe Layton invokes "truth" more metaphorically than specifically.

32. Nicholas Cook developed this idea of a musical work as a kind of shooting script, summarizing the comparison by telling his reader that "thinking of music as 'script' rather than 'text' implies a reorientation of the relationship between notation and performance." Nicholas Cook, "Music as Performance," in *The Cultural Study of Music: A Critical Introduction*, ed. Martin Clayton, Trevor Herbert, and Richard Middleton (New York and London: Routledge, 2003), 206.

33. Ingarden, *The Work of Music and the Problem of Its Identity*, 27; Michael Talbot, introduction to *The Musical Work: Reality or Invention?* ed. Michael Talbot (Liverpool: Liverpool University Press, 2000), 5; Michael Chanan, *Musica Practica: The Social Practice of Western Music from Gregorian Chant to Postmodernism* (London and New York: Verso, 1994). According to Nicholas Cook, however, the shift that Chanan describes—from music as social activity to music as individual and inactive consumption—has paradoxically helped entrench the idea of autonomous musical texts, intellectual properties that are to be delivered from composer to performer. Nicholas Cook, "Between Process and Product: Music and/as Performance," *Music Theory Online* 7.2 (April 2001).

34. Robert Heilbroner, "Technological Determinism Revisited," in *Does Technology Drive History?* ed. Merritt Roe Smith and Leo Marx (Cambridge, MA: MIT Press, 1994), 67–68.

35. Mitchell Morris, "Musical Virtues," in *Beyond Structural Listening? Postmodern Modes of Hearing*, ed. Andrew Dell'Antonio (Berkeley: University of California Press, 2004), 63. One wonders if Morris hears similarly infernal machines in the sampling of popular music of the 1990s, or if such examples of machine-based bricolage are intrinsically more human.

36. Sterne, *Audible Past*, 35.

37. Ibid., 95.

38. McLuhan does have the wider, if not necessarily deeper, historical view. For example, Sterne neglects the fact that Western European musicians had developed their own audile techniques at least as far back as the tenth

century. As examples of what he terms " 'indexical' images of sound," Sterné mentions Leon Scott's phonoautograph, Rudolph König's manometric flame, and Ernst Florens Friedrich Chladni's visualization of sound waves in sand (see "Machines to Hear for Them," in *Audible Past*, 31–85). But early medieval European music notation systems, which were more like simple pitch-time graphs than modern Western notation, offered " 'indexical' images of sound" some thousand years before Sterne's nineteenth-century examples.

39. Sterne, *Audible Past*, 21. One interesting view, striking a middle ground between these two extremes, is Simon Frith's understanding of recording technology as an analogy to musical instrument technology. Simon Frith, *Performing Rites: On the Value of Popular Music* (Cambridge, MA: Harvard University Press, 1996), 233.

40. Jonathan Sterne, "The MP3 as Cultural Artifact," *New Media & Society* 8 (2006): 839.

41. David Kusek and Gerd Leonhard, *The Future of Music: Manifesto for the Digital Music Revolution* (Boston: Berklee Press, 2005). Brown and Duguid describe such revolutionary visions as manifestations of "the replacement myth": what they call "the superficially plausible idea . . . that information and its technologies can unproblematically replace the nuanced relations between people." Their invocation of The Social here, specifically in opposition to what they call "information fetishism," betokens a rather more cogent perspective than Sterne's. John Seely Brown and Paul Duguid, *The Social Life of Information*, 2nd ed. (Boston: Harvard Business School Press, 2002), xvi–xvii.

42. Martin Heidegger, "The Question concerning Technology" (1954), in *Martin Heidegger: Basic Writings*, ed. David Farrell Krell, rev. ed. (San Francisco: HarperCollins, 1993), 312.

43. Robert K. Merton, "The Unanticipated Consequences of Social Action" (1936), in *On Social Structure and Science*, ed. Piotr Sztompka (Chicago and New York: University of Chicago Press, 1996), 173–82.

44. Heidegger, "Question concerning Technology," 319.

45. Ibid., 311–12.

46. Nelson Goodman, "Score, Sketch, and Script," in *Languages of Art: An Approach to a Theory of Symbols*, 2nd ed. (Indianapolis, IN: Hackett Publishing, 1976), 179–91.

47. "Because the essence of technology is nothing technological, essential reflection upon technology and decisive confrontation with it must happen in a realm that is, on the one hand, akin to the essence of technology and, on the other, fundamentally different from it. Such a realm is art." Heidegger, "Question concerning Technology," 340.

48. Heidegger, "Question concerning Technology," 320.

49. Marshall McLuhan, *Understanding Media: The Extensions of Man* (New York: McGraw-Hill, 1964), 12.

50. George Kateb, "Technology and Philosophy," in *Technology and the Rest of Culture*, ed. Arien Mack (Columbus: Ohio State University Press, 2001), 300, 299, 293.

51. Quoted in Cesar Saerchinger, *Artur Schnabel: A Biography* (New York: Dodd, Mead & Co., 1957), 224.

52. Michael Chanan, *Repeated Takes: A Short History of Recording and Its Effects on Music* (London and New York: Verso, 1995), 11.

53. Frith, "Technology and Authority," 244.

54. Robert Philip, *Performing Music in the Age of Recording* (New Haven, CT: Yale University Press, 2004).

55. The standard English version of Benjamin's essay has long been Hannah Arendt's edition of Harry Zohn's translation, as contained in Benjamin, *Illuminations*, 217–52. Benjamin's title, however, would be more accurately rendered as "The Work of Art in the Age of Its Technological Reproducibility," and the essay appears under that heading in the more recent translation in *The Work of Art in the Age of Its Technological Reproducibility, and Other Writings on Media*, ed. Michael W. Jennings, Brigid Doherty, and Thomas Y. Levin (Cambridge, MA: Belknap Press of Harvard University Press, 2008). There are of course significant conceptual and practical differences between "reproduction" and "reproducibility," but the earlier translation has been around for so long that to insist on changing the title now would doubtless cause more confusion than clarification. I have stayed with the earlier version for the title of my own book, for a similar reason: I wanted to declare an immediate connection not only with Benjamin's ideas, but also with the broad discourse on aesthetics and modernity that they unleashed.

56. Benjamin, "The Work of Art in the Age of Mechanical Reproduction," 221.

57. Scott Lash, "Critical Theory and Postmodernist Culture: The Eclipse of Aura," in *Sociology of Postmodernism* (London and New York: Routledge, 1990), 153–54.

58. Benjamin, "The Work of Art in the Age of Mechanical Reproduction"; T. W. Adorno, *Towards a Theory of Musical Reproduction: Notes, a Draft, and Two Schemata*, ed. Henri Lonitz and trans. Wieland Hoban (Cambridge and Malden, MA: Polity Press, 2006); McLuhan, *Understanding Media*; Friedrich A. Kittler, *Gramophone, Film, Typewriter*, trans. Geoffrey Winthrop-Young and Michael Wutz (Stanford, CA: Stanford University Press, 1999); Nicholas Cook, "Imagining Music," in *Music, Imagination, and Culture* (Oxford and New York: Oxford University Press, 1990), 71–121; id., "Words about Music, or Analysis versus Performance," in *Theory into Practice: Composition, Performance, and the Listening Experience* (Leuven, Belgium: Leuven University Press, 1999), 9–52; Jonathan Dunsby, *Performing Music: Shared Concerns* (Oxford and New York: Oxford University Press, 1995); Chanan, *Repeated Takes*; Peter Kivy, *Authenticities: Philosophical Reflections on Musical Performance* (Ithaca, NY: Cornell University Press, 1995).

59. Julian Johnson, *Who Needs Classical Music? Cultural Choice and Musical Value* (Oxford and New York: Oxford University Press, 2002); Lawrence Kramer, *Why Classical Music Still Matters* (Berkeley: University of California Press, 2007).

60. See T. W. Adorno, *Introduction to the Sociology of Music,* trans. E. B. Ashton (New York: Seabury Press, 1976).

61. McLuhan, *Understanding Media,* 64.

62. Among such books, each instructive in its way, are Timothy Day, *A Century of Recorded Music: Listening to Musical History* (New Haven, CT and London: Yale University Press, 2000); Sterne, *Audible Past;* and Symes, *Setting the Record Straight.*

63. Kramer, *Why Classical Music Still Matters,* 13.

64. Ibid., 16.

65. Ibid., 12.

66. Ibid., 28.

67. Quoted in James Huneker, *Chopin: The Man and His Music* (New York: Charles Scribner's Sons, 1900), 118.

1. THE RECORDED MUSICAL TEXT

1. Nicholas Cook, "Words about Music, or Analysis versus Performance," in *Theory into Practice: Composition, Performance, and the Listening Experience* (Leuven, Belgium: Leuven University Press, 1999), 10. Cook, Jonathan Dunsby, Peter Johnson, and Eric Clarke have led an institution of "musical performance studies," though Edward T. Cone paved the way with his books *Musical Form and Musical Performance* (1968) and *The Composer's Voice* (1974); see Jonathan Dunsby, "Musical Performance Studies as a 'Discipline,'" *Performing Music: Shared Concerns* (Oxford: Clarendon Press; New York: Oxford University Press, 1995), 17–28. For a valuable albeit provisional summary of performance within an ontology of the musical work, see Cook, "Words about Music," esp. 22–41; and id., "Analysing Performance and Performing Analysis," in *Rethinking Music,* ed. Nicholas Cook and Mark Everist (Oxford and New York: Oxford University Press, 1999), 239–61. See also José A. Bowen, "Finding the Music in Musicology: Performance History and Musical Works," in Cook and Everist, *Rethinking Music,* 424–51.

2. Peter Johnson, "Performance and the Listening Experience: Bach's 'Erbarme Dich,'" in *Theory into Practice,* 58.

3. Peter Kivy, "The Other Authenticity," in *Authenticities: Philosophical Reflections on Musical Performance* (Ithaca, NY: Cornell University Press, 1995), 108–42. For a more substantial discussion of performances and recordings according to Kivyesque ideas of "endurance," "repeatability," and "types with tokens," see chapter 2.

4. Eric F. Clarke, "Listening to Performance," in *Musical Performance: A Guide to Understanding,* ed. John Rink (Cambridge and New York: Cambridge University Press, 2002), 194.

5. Elsewhere in this book, I discuss ways that the textual aspects of absolute music have come to infiltrate popular music aesthetics; even there, definitiveness is a feature of connoisseurship and not of wide appeal. A wide public interest in musical rather than performance-texts may still arise as the first,

iconic examples of rock and roll recede farther into the past and become less directly intelligible.

6. We have reached a point where so many music-lovers—especially among young people—grow up with recordings as their main, or indeed only, form of listening, that the situation has reversed: for them it is the concert, not the recording, that comes to demand new literacies. See Michel Chion, *Audio-Vision: Sound on Screen*, trans. and ed. Claudia Gorbman (New York: Columbia University Press, 1994).

7. Alfred Brendel, "A Case for Live Recordings" (1984), in *Alfred Brendel on Music: Collected Essays*, rev. ed. (London: Robson Books, 2007), 345–51.

8. Michael Riffaterre, "Text Production," in *Semiotics of Poetry* (Indianapolis and New York: Indiana University Press, 1978), 47–80.

9. On the sales figures for *Chant*, how the album was exploited by EMI, and how it affected the Benedictine order who recorded it, see Norman Lebrecht, "Intimations of Sex and Incense," in *Who Killed Classical Music? Maestros, Managers, and Corporate Politics* (Secaucus, NJ: Carol Publishing, 1997), 284–92.

10. William M. Schniedewind, *How the Bible Became a Book: The Textualization of Ancient Israel* (Cambridge and New York: Cambridge University Press, 2004), 5.

11. Alfred Brendel defended his exclusion of Gould from a survey of Bach pianists as follows: "My intention was to separate serious performers from eccentrics. If belonging to the mainstream means the performer should bring to life the composer's intentions and make sense of a piece instead of obstructing it, as Glenn Gould almost always did, then I should be glad to belong to the mainstream and deplore those who don't." From an exchange between Brendel and Nicholas Spice, as cited by Ken Winters, "The Prodigal Son," *Great Pianists of the 20th Century: Glenn Gould* (Philips 456 808, 1999), 8.

12. Roland Barthes, "The Death of the Author," in *Image, Music, Text*, trans. and ed. Stephen Heath (New York: Hill and Wang, 1977), 147.

13. Schniedewind, *How the Bible Became a Book*, 1.

14. Ibid., 91, 85.

15. For a brief account of the textual aspects of Reformation history, see Patrick Collinson, "Words, Language, and Books," in *The Reformation: A History* (New York: Modern Library, 2003), 33–46.

16. For an influential description of Western art music in these terms, see Lydia Goehr, *The Imaginary Museum of Musical Works: An Essay in the Philosophy of Music* (Oxford and New York: Oxford University Press, 1992).

17. "Regulative concepts differ from constitutive ones: the latter constitute the fabric of a practice; they provide the rules of the game. New constitutive rules signal either a new game or a new version of an old game. Regulative concepts guide the practice externally by indicating the point of following the constitutive rules. In moral practices, certain constitutive rules are provided to indicate what one should and should not do. The point of following these rules is founded upon our grasp of concepts such as those of freedom, justice, and responsibility." Goehr, *Imaginary Museum of Musical Works*, 103.

18. Gunther Schuller, *The Compleat Conductor* (New York and Oxford: Oxford University Press, 1997), 21.

19. "Deliberately small tone in Mozart; delayed third beats in Schubert waltzes; unmotivated tempo changes in Schumann; senseless dryness of tone in Bach—all these and other mannerisms were rejected as such by Schnabel." Konrad Wolff, *Schnabel's Interpretation of Piano Music* (New York: W. W. Norton, 1972), 16.

20. Kivy, "Other Authenticity," 127. What is the ontological status of an event for Kivy, one feels compelled to ask? Certain branches of philosophy, such as Ingarden's, wouldn't allow events to "endure" because they are by definition temporally bounded. This would also make the repeatability of performance-events a problematic issue. Kivy likely borrows the idea of types and tokens from Nelson Goodman, as that author described the concept in "Seven Strictures on Similarity," in *Experience and Theory*, ed. Lawrence Foster and J. W. Swanson (Amherst: University of Massachusetts Press, 1970), 19–29.

21. Edward W. Said, "The Virtuoso as Intellectual," in *On Late Style: Music and Literature against the Grain* (New York: Pantheon Books, 2006), 119.

22. In the words of the book accompanying Sony-BMG's *Glenn Gould: The Original Jacket Collection*, "Sensation yields to scandal: Gould's feisty and headstrong treatment of the final triptych in Beethoven's pianistic 'New Testament' outraged critics no less than his sleeve notes." "Glenn Gould: The Complete Jacket Collection," *Glenn Gould: The Original Jacket Collection* (Sony-BMG 88697130942, 2007), 6.

23. Clarke, "Listening to Performance," 194.

24. Nicholas Cook, *Music: A Very Short Introduction* (Oxford and New York: Oxford University Press, 1998), 12.

25. Rosen, *Beethoven's Piano Sonatas: A Short Companion* (New Haven, CT and London: Yale University Press, 2002), 4, 7. One might argue against Rosen and his invocation of the amateur by saying that amateur performers have never taken to the "Hammerklavier," for example, just as they have steered clear of much of the "serious" piano music written after about 1800. Even Mozart, composing in the 1780s, drew a clear division between amateur and professional with his "Sonata facile" in C Major, K. 545. But I would rally behind Rosen's assertion by asking if there aren't in fact more levels and indeed layers of amateur performance than there are of professional musicianship. I well remember the carnage as I sloughed my own way through Beethoven's "Appassionata" Sonata as a twelve-year-old, and at best middling, keyboardist. I didn't play it well, and would not have dared play the music in front of anyone. But I certainly did enjoy the experience, and did consider the music part of my culture as an amateur pianist. After my father gave me Alfred Brendel's 1978 Philips box of the complete sonatas, however, I never again risked such a venture.

26. Barthes, "Death of the Author," 148.

27. "It will not, it seems to me, be very much longer before a more self-assertive streak is detected in the listener's participation, before, to give but

one example, 'do-it-yourself' tape editing is the prerogative of every reasonably conscientious consumer of recorded music (the *Hausmusik* activity of the future, perhaps!)." Gould, "Strauss and the Electronic Future" (1964), in *The Glenn Gould Reader*, ed. Tim Page (New York: Knopf, 1984), 93.

28. Gould, "Strauss and the Electronic Future" (1964), in Page, *Glenn Gould Reader*, 99.

29. Ibid.

30. Said, "Virtuoso as Intellectual," 132–33.

31. Greg adds in a footnote: "It will, no doubt, be objected that punctuation may very seriously 'affect' an author's meaning; still it remains properly a matter of presentation, as spelling does in spite of its use in distinguishing homonyms. The distinction I am trying to draw is practical, not philosophic." W. W. Greg, "The Rationale of Copy-Text," in *Collected Papers*, ed. J. C. Maxwell (Oxford: Clarendon Press, 1966), 376 and n. 4, quoted in D. F. McKenzie, "Typography and Meaning: The Case of William Congreve," in *Buch und Buchhandel in Europa im achtzehnten Jahrhundert*, ed. Giles Barber and Bernhard Fabian, Wolfenbütteler Schriften zur Geschichte des Buchwesens, vol. 4 (Hamburg: Hauswedell, 1981), 83.

32. Leonard Meyer, "Toward a Theory of Style," in *Style and Music: Theory, History, and Ideology* (Philadelphia: University of Pennsylvania Press, 1989), 3–37.

33. McKenzie, "Typography and Meaning," 82, 90–91.

34. Igor Stravinsky, *Poetics of Music in the Form of Six Lessons*, trans. Arthur Knodel and Ingolf Dahl (Cambridge, MA and London: Harvard University Press, 1947), 125.

35. D. F. McKenzie, *Bibliography and the Sociology of Texts* (Cambridge and New York: Cambridge University Press, 1999), 34.

36. McKenzie, "Typography and Meaning," 100.

37. John Culshaw, *Ring Resounding* (New York: Viking Press, 1967), 26.

38. Quoted in Joseph Horowitz, *Understanding Toscanini: A Social History of American Concert Life* (Berkeley and Los Angeles: University of California Press, 1994), 342n. Horowitz also paraphrases Samuel Antek's first-hand account of Toscanini's "indifference" at NBC Symphony recording sessions: "Listening to playbacks, he never commented on the beauty or texture of the sound, according to Antek; his attention focused on tempo, drive, and balance. Others, too, remember Toscanini listening to check the audibility of every instrument, yet indifferent to harsh or dull reproduction." Horowitz, *Understanding Toscanini*, 278. But RCA deserves part of the blame for the harsh sound quality of the final tapes: some question how well their commercial releases in fact represented Studio 8H, since the only "sweet spot" in the hall was just above and behind the conductor's head, and the recording crew was too frightened of the maestro to explore such acoustic issues thoroughly.

39. Quoted in Mortimer H. Frank, *Arturo Toscanini: The NBC Years* (Portland, OR: Amadeus Press, 2002), 34–35.

40. Ibid., 245.

41. McKenzie, *Bibliography and the Sociology of Texts*, 17.

42. For a summary of Stokowski's involvement with new sound technologies over the decades, see William Ander Smith, *The Mystery of Leopold Stokowski* (Cranbury, NJ and London: Associated University Presses, 1990), 144–45.

43. The two recordings have been rereleased in tandem on a single CD underwritten by the Leopold Stokowski Society (Cala CACD0541).

44. The photo is reproduced in Preben Opperby, *Leopold Stokowski* (New York: Hippocrene Books, 1982), 169.

45. Leopold Stokowski, "Recorded Music," in *Music for All of Us* (New York: Simon and Schuster, 1943), 229.

46. Stokowski, "Music and Motion Pictures," in *Music for All of Us*, 246–47. Stokowski refers specifically here to recording for movie soundtracks rather than to studio recording more generally, presumably because at that time (1943) recording onto film offered possibilities that wouldn't become possible with pure audio productions until the introduction of magnetic tape around 1950.

47. I use the phrase "heremeneutic circle" here as Umberto Eco does, as a description for interpretive tautology: "The text is an object that the interpretation builds up in the course of the circular effort of validating itself on the basis of what it makes up as its result. I am not ashamed to admit that I am so defining the old and still valid 'hermeneutic circle.'" Umberto Eco, "Overinterpreting Texts," in *Interpretation and Overinterpretation*, ed. Stefan Collini (Cambridge and New York: Cambridge University Press, 1992), 64. Stokowski's manipulation of dynamic range is an especially powerful aspect of the hermeneutic circle facilitated by technological advances. "Today we hear a true *crescendo* and *diminuendo* not possible in the early days of recording," Stokowski told an interviewer in 1953, "and only moderately successful in the first improved dynamic recordings made before and during the war, before a full frequency range was adopted." Leopold Stokowski, interview by Peter Hugh Reed, *American Record Guide* (1953), quoted in Oliver Daniel, *Stokowski: A Counterpoint of View* (New York: Dodd, Mead, and Company, 1982), 540.

48. Herbert von Karajan, "Technische Musikwiedergabe," in *Karajan: Eine Biographie* by Franz Endler (Hamburg: Hoffmann und Campe, 1992), 292; my translation; italics added.

49. Ibid., 290.

50. Stephen J. Pettit, *Philharmonia Orchestra: A Record of Achievement, 1945–1985* (London: Hale, 1985), 65, cited in Richard Osborne, *Herbert von Karajan: A Life in Music* (Boston: Northeastern University Press, 1998), 348.

51. Conversely, one imagines record producers proclaiming at sessions: "If we're going to take the trouble to dub in a major soloist on a cathedral-size organ, we might as well use them!" The only recording that comes to mind as respecting Saint-Saëns's single *forte* indication is Toscanini's 1952 version from Carnegie Hall with a little-known organist, performed for radio broadcast.

52. Richard Osborne, *Conversations with Karajan* (Oxford: Oxford University Press, 1989), 120.

53. In the words of Yehudi Menuhin, "Glenn's mind was so well organized that he didn't trust himself ever to be taken by surprise. He didn't like a situation where he wasn't in total control, of the music, of the people, of the voices." Peter Ostwald, *Glenn Gould: The Ecstasy and Tragedy of Genius* (New York and London: W. W. Norton, 1997), 228.

54. Gould, "The Prospects of Recording" (1966), in Page, *Glenn Gould Reader*, 333; Gould to Ronald Wilford, 21 December 1971, in *Glenn Gould: Selected Letters*, ed. John P. L. Roberts and Ghyslaine Guertin (Toronto: Oxford University Press, 1992), 172.

55. Gould, "Stokowski in Six Scenes," in Page, *Glenn Gould Reader*, 272. It is ironic that Gould said such things while collaborating, and collaborating so sympathetically, with Stokowski, who was in fact progenitor of the techniques of free bowing that I discuss above, techniques that in themselves represent artful and purposeful means toward "sweep and grandeur" and "approximation of ensemble."

56. Andrew Kazdin, liner note for CBS Masterworks 299002. For the fullest account of this "acoustic choreography" in Gould's recordings of Scriabin and Sibelius, see Kevin Bazzana, *Glenn Gould: The Performer in the Work; A Study in Performance Practice* (New York: Oxford University Press, 1997), 246–52. As Bazzana points out, there are connections with Gould's filmmaking interests and the techniques he developed in his radio documentaries. If we were to read Gould's statement about Rachmaninov's and Debussy's acoustic demands alongside his remark about Manhattan Center, we would have to conclude that in requiring a healthy acoustic Debussy and Rachmaninov betray their contrapuntal and intellectual deficiencies.

57. "In the future it will be possible to pick up and amplify any zone of frequency, and prolong it by reverberation. For example, if only the low frequencies are desired to be prolonged, this will be possible. . . . The length of this reverberation will be completely under control—it can be faded out with extreme slowness or almost immediately. Or one zone can be faded out slowly and the other two quickly—or any other combination of length of reverberation in any frequency zone that is desired." Stokowski, "Reflection and Absorption—Echo, Reverberation," in *Music for All of Us*, 98.

58. Karajan, "Technische Musikwiedergabe," 292–93. Compare Karajan's comments here with various Gould pronouncements, including that regarding "a doctrine that celebrates the existence of a mystical communication between concert performer and public audience (the composer being seldom mentioned)." Gould remarks: "There is a vaguely scientific pretension to this argument, and its proponents are given to pronouncements on 'natural' acoustics and related phenomena." Gould, "The Prospects of Recording," in Page, *Glenn Gould Reader*, 340. Karajan deeply admired Gould, beginning with their first collaboration in Berlin in 1957, in part because of their similar socioacoustic beliefs. On their first encounter and the long-standing mutual respect that followed, see Kevin Bazzana, *Wondrous Strange: The Life and Art of Glenn Gould* (Oxford and New York: Oxford University Press, 2004), 172–73.

59. Wolf-Dieter Karwatky, "Recording Grieg with Gilels," liner note for *Edvard Grieg: Lyric Pieces* (DG 449 721–2, 1996), 3.

60. Stokowski said in an interview: "Dick Mohr . . . informs me through the intercommunicating system of any variation in timing or any tonal imbalance which he knows to be *contrary to what we have planned.*" Leopold Stokowski, interview by Peter Hugh Reed, *American Record Guide* (1953), quoted in Daniel, *Stokowski*, 540; italics added. Reed goes on to say that "[Stokowski] has from the earliest association with reproduced music cooperated closely with technicians, and more often than not assisted them with musical advice in regard to the character and quality of reproduction"; quoted in Daniel, *Stokowski*, 540.

61. From a Deutsche Grammophon ad, quoted in Norman Lebrecht, *The Maestro Myth: Great Conductors in Search of Power* (New York: Citadel Press, 2001), 214.

62. Erich Leinsdorf, *Erich Leinsdorf on Music* (Portland, OR: Amadeus Press, 1997), 218.

63. See Schniedewind, "Josiah and the Text Revolution," in *How the Bible Became a Book*, 98.

64. See Michael Gray, "The Winged Champion: Mercury Records and the Birth of High Fidelity," *Absolute Sound* 60 (1989): 47–59; 61 (1989): 46–56.

2. RECORDING, REPETITION, AND MEMORY IN ABSOLUTE MUSIC

1. The description comes from Morton Feldman: "Decay . . . this departing landscape, *this* expresses where the sound exists in our hearing—leaving us rather than coming toward us." Morton Feldman, *Give My Regards to Eighth Street: Collected Writings of Morton Feldman*, ed. B. H. Friedman (Cambridge, MA: Exact Change, 2000), 25.

2. The important studies devoted wholly or in part to the importance of recordings in popular music would have to include Simon Frith, *Sound Effects: Youth, Leisure, and the Politics of Rock 'n' Roll* (New York: Pantheon Books, 1981); Theodore Gracyk, *Rhythm and Noise: An Aesthetics of Rock* (Durham, NC: Duke University Press, 1996); Allan F. Moore, *Rock, the Primary Text: Developing a Musicology of Rock* (Aldershot and Burlington: Ashgate, 2001); and Albin Zak, *The Poetics of Rock: Cutting Tracks, Making Records* (Berkeley: University of California Press, 2001).

3. Artur Schnabel, *My Life and Music* (New York: St. Martin's Press, 1963), 121.

4. Jacques Attali, *Noise*, trans. Brian Massumi (Minneapolis and London: University of Minnesota Press, 1985), 90, 110, 119–20.

5. Attali, *Noise*, 101.

6. Ibid.; italics in the original. Attali's analysis, and specifically its quasi-industrial notion of stockpiling, present us with an example of the post-Marxist image of the consumer as a type of worker, an active and vital force in

production. For one critique of this consumer representation, see Jean Baudrillard, "Towards a Theory of Consumption," in *The Consumer Society: Myths and Structures*, trans. Chris Turner (repr., London: Sage Publications, 1998), 69–86.

7. Attali, *Noise*, 100.

8. This kind of subscription service was pioneered by Walter Legge in the 1930s, with subscribers' prepayments assuring British Columbia that it would recoup costs for projects larger and more peripheral than it could otherwise undertake. Legge's first project of this type was the Lieder of Hugo Wolf; see Elizabeth Schwarzkopf, *On and Off the Record: A Memoir of Walter Legge* (New York: Charles Scribner's Sons, 1982), 215–17. The Book-of-the-Month Club gave this kind of subscription, one-shot project a characteristically American twist with its over-the-top marketing.

9. Attali, *Noise*, 100–101.

10. Scott Burnham, *Beethoven Hero* (Princeton, NJ: Princeton University Press, 1995), 62, 118.

11. We also entertain the tensions between that linearity and other temporal, cognitive paradigms in Austro-German intellectual history. Burnham notes: "For the entire age finds itself at a crossroads: preoccupations with consciousness, memory, and a sense of history are met by a renewed emphasis on the 'eternal return,' the mythic time of cyclical death and rebirth. These two temporal forces, linear time and cyclical time, create an equilibrium that results in the underlying temporal design of much of German romanticism." Burnham, *Beethoven Hero*, 123.

12. In this sense Bergson perfectly inverts the basic premise of Kant, which is significant considering the German philosopher's importance for absolute-music aesthetics. Bergson believes we conceptualize our inner world in relation to our formulations of the outer world—in rationalist-scientific terms, in other words—while Kant believed that we form our outward understanding according to structures of the mind itself. On the relationship between Bergson's thinking and Kant's, see Suzanne Guerlac, "Conclusion of the *Essai*," in *Thinking in Time: An Introduction to Henri Bergson* (Ithaca, NY and London: Cornell University Press, 2006), 93–105.

13. Henri Bergson, *Time and Free Will: An Essay on the Immediate Data of Consciousness*, trans. F. L. Pogson (New York: Harper, 1960), 154.

14. Ibid., 221.

15. Henri Bergson, *Creative Evolution*, trans. Arthur Mitchell (New York: Henry Holt, 1926), 305–6. See also Mary Ann Doane, "Zeno's Paradox: The Emergence of Cinematic Time," in *The Emergence of Cinematic Time: Modernity, Contingency, the Archive* (Cambridge, MA and London: Harvard University Press, 2002), 172–80.

16. Bergson, *Time and Free Will*, 154. Bergson's query is analogous to Karl Popper's questioning of the assumptions in inductive reasoning, particularly scientists' assuming an a priori principle of causality.

17. Quoted in Eva Badura-Skoda, et al. "Cadenza," *Grove Music Online, Oxford Music Online,* http://www.oxfordmusiconline.com (accessed 20 August 2008).

18. Harris Goldsmith, *High Fidelity,* July 1982, 52. Malcolm Macdonald, reviewing Kremer's recording of the Beethoven for *Gramophone,* concurred with Goldsmith and lambasted "the abrupt transitions of century," which he felt "totally disfigure an otherwise sound performance"; Malcolm Macdonald, *Gramophone,* June 1982, 27. The only concerto cadenzas that I have heard do the impossible in reconciling purpose with style, moment with context, and surprise with expectation, and do it in such a way that neither side of the equation disappears from view, are pianist Fazil Say's on his recording of Mozart's C Major Concerto, K. 467 (Naïve-Valois V4992). But critics have predictably censured Say along style lines, Stanley Sadie expressing perplexity over "the grotesque cadenzas, with hints of a Mozartian sugar-plum fairy"; Stanley Sadie, *Gramophone,* December 2004, 82.

19. Bernard Holland, *New York Times,* 11 November 1983.

20. Michael White, "Period Music Grow Up. Period," *New York Times,* 6 August 2006.

21. Christopher Hogwood, "Hogwood's Beethoven," *Gramophone,* March 1986, 1136. See chapter 4 for further commentary on Hogwood's remarkable statement as it pertains to late twentieth-century recording technologies.

22. Arnold Dolmetsch, *The Interpretation of the Music of the Seventeenth and Eighteenth Centuries,* corr. ed. (Seattle and London: University of Washington Press, 1946), 7, 14.

23. Henri Bergson, *Matter and Memory,* trans. Nancy Margaret Paul and W. Scott Palmer (New York: Macmillan, 1950), 104. See also Guerlac, "Matter and Memory: Essay on the Relation between Body and Mind," in *Thinking in Time,* 106–72.

24. Bergson, *Matter and Memory,* 153.

25. Ibid., 152.

26. See Richard Taruskin, *Text and Act: Essays on Music and Performance* (New York and Oxford: Oxford University Press, 1995), esp. "The Pastness of the Present and the Presence of the Past" (90–154) and "Resisting the Ninth" (235–61).

27. Susan McClary, "Sexual Politics in Classical Music," in *Feminine Endings: Music, Gender, and Sexuality* (Minneapolis: University of Minnesota Press, 1991), 71.

28. The Fourth Symphony was the first symphonic music to be electrically recorded when Landon Ronald led the Royal Albert Hall Orchestra for a 1925 HMV set that didn't enjoy wide international circulation. See Timothy Day, *A Century of Recorded Music: Listening to Musical History* (New Haven, CT and London: Yale University Press, 2000), 17. The Landon Ronald recording was never reissued, at least in the United States—evidence of the primacy of Stokowski's and Mengelberg's readings of the symphony.

29. Mengelberg's recording was last reissued in 1996 by both Dante Lys and GSE Clarement, while Stokowski's was available on a 1994 Pearl set.

30. John Warrack, *Tchaikovsky Symphonies and Concertos*, BBC Music Guides (Seattle: University of Washington Press, 1969), 25.

31. In McClary's defense, it should be mentioned that scholars of English and comparative literature have long allowed themselves similar presumptions: that Homer, Pindar, and Christopher Marlowe can be read directly from the page according to the cultures of silent reading that became common only after those authors had passed from the scene.

32. Alfred Brendel, "Notes on a Complete Recording of Beethoven's Piano Works" (1966), in *Alfred Brendel on Music: Collected Essays*, rev. ed. (London: Robson Books, 2007), 28; italics added.

33. Gunther Schuller, *The Compleat Conductor* (New York and Oxford: Oxford University Press, 1997), 21–22.

34. Christian Thielemann, "Feel Free to Imagine Whatever You Please!" liner note for *Bruckner: Symphonie Nr.5* (Deutsche Grammophon 477 5377, 2005), 4.

35. Roland Barthes, *The Pleasure of the Text*, trans. Richard Miller (New York: Hill and Wang, 1975), 3.

36. Eduard Hanslick, *The Beautiful in Music*, trans. Gustav Cohen (London: Novello, 1891), 43–44.

37. Nicholas Cook, "Between Process and Product: Music and/as Performance," *Music Theory Online* 7.2 (April 2001). See chapter 1 in this volume for another, more specifically textual discussion of Cook's important statement.

38. Carl Dahlhaus, *The Idea of Absolute Music*, trans. Roger Lustig (Chicago and London: University of Chicago Press, 1989), 7.

39. Gilles Deleuze, "Memory as Virtual Coexistence," in *Bergsonism*, trans. Hugh Tomlinson and Barbara Habberjam (New York: Zone Books, 1991), 59, 51–52.

40. Walter Benjamin, "On Some Motifs in Baudelaire," in *Illuminations: Essays and Reflections*, ed. Hannah Arendt and trans. Harry Zohn (New York: Harcourt, Brace, & World, 1968), 182, quoted in Michelle Henning, "Digital Encounters: Mythical Pasts and Electronic Presence," in *The Photographic Image in Digital Culture*, ed. Martin Lister (London and New York: Routledge, 1995), 231.

41. "Undoubtedly what is thus palpitating in the depths of my being must be the image, the visual memory which, being linked to that taste, has tried to follow it into my conscious mind. But its struggles are too far off, too much confused; scarcely can I perceive the colourless reflection in which are blended the uncapturable whirling medley of radiant hues, and I cannot distinguish its form, cannot invite it, as the one possible interpreter, to translate to me the evidence of its contemporary, its inseparable paramour, the taste of cake soaked in tea; cannot ask it to inform me what special circumstance is in question, of what period in my past life. Will it ultimately reach the clear surface of my

consciousness, this memory, this old, dead moment which the magnetism of an identical moment has travelled so far to importune, to disturb, to raise up out of the very depths of my being? . . .

"And suddenly the memory returns. The taste was that of the little crumb of madeleine which on Sunday mornings at Combray (because on those mornings I did not go out before church-time), when I went to say good day to her in her bedroom, my aunt Léonie used to give me, dipping it first in her own cup of real or of lime-flower tea. The sight of the little madeleine had recalled nothing to my mind before I tasted it; perhaps because I had so often seen such things in the interval, without tasting them, on the trays in pastry-cooks' windows, that their image had dissociated itself from those Combray days to take its place among others more recent; perhaps because of those memories, so long abandoned and put out of mind, nothing now survived, everything was scattered; the forms of things, including that of the little scallop-shell of pastry, so richly sensual under its severe, religious folds, were either obliterated or had been so long dormant as to have lost the power of expansion which would have allowed them to resume their place in my consciousness." Marcel Proust, "Overture," *Swann's Way*, trans. C. K. Scott-Moncrieff (New York: Henry Holt, 1922), 57–58.

3. SCHNABEL'S RATIONALISM, GOULD'S PRAGMATISM

1. John Duarte, review of the 1991 reissue of *Bach, "Italian" Concerto, D Major Partita, and E Minor Toccata*, by Glenn Gould, *Gramophone*, January 1991, http://www.gramophone.co.uk (accessed 24 May 2008).

2. Harris Goldsmith, "Schnabel's Beethoven," *ARSC Journal* 14.3 (1982): 87. Goldsmith pursues this text-or-execution duality further: "I don't know which are more objectionable—the mindless virtuosos, with unlimited technical resources and execrable artistic judgment, or the so-called 'serious' musicians, who proudly flaunt rhythmic sloppiness, overpedaling, and digital shortcomings like honorary badges."

3. See Alfred Brendel, "*Werktreue*—An Afterthought" (1976), in *Alfred Brendel on Music: Collected Essays*, rev. ed. (London: Robson Books, 2007), 30–41. For Brendel, who in his own description developed healthy suspicions as a child growing up in Nazi Austria, *Werktreue* became an almost propagandistic term. Lydia Goehr gives an idea of how faithfulness to the work became an encumbered form of faithfulness to the text: "The comparable duty of performers was to show allegiance to the works of the composers. To certify that their performances be of specific works, they had to comply as perfectly as possible with the scores composers provided. Thus the effective synonymity in the musical world of *Werktreue* and *Texttreue:* to be true to a work is to be true to its score." Lydia Goehr, *The Imaginary Museum of Musical Works: An Essay in the Philosophy of Music* (Oxford and New York: Oxford University Press, 1992), 231.

4. Umberto Eco, "Interpretation and History" and "Overinterpreting Texts," in *Interpretation and Overinterpretation*, ed. Stefan Collini (Cambridge

and New York: Cambridge University Press, 1992), 25, 64–65, and passim. It should be emphasized that Eco offers the *intentio auctoris* and *intentio operis* as aspects of different, and indeed mutually exclusive, readership systems. But that makes the terms all the more appropriate to a discussion of Schnabel and Gould, since these two musicians seemed to presume such different orders of meaning and interpretation.

5. Quoted in *Conversations about Bernstein*, ed. William Westbrook Burton (New York and Oxford: Oxford University Press, 1995), 65. I have been unable to track down the Gould interview that Myers refers to.

6. Artur Schnabel, *My Life and Music* (New York: St. Martin's Press, 1963), 229. In the 1961 version of the same book, Schnabel says the musician's ideal "is to materialize all he wants to materialize. He wants, of course, only as much as he at a given time *understands* of what music as a whole and music in a single example demands." Schnabel, *My Life and Music*, 132.

7. Edward Said, "The Virtuoso as Intellectual," in *On Late Style: Music and Literature against the Grain* (New York: Pantheon Books, 2006), 116–17.

8. Said, "Virtuoso as Intellectual," 117.

9. Edward Sackville-West and Desmond Shawe-Taylor, with Andrew Porter and William Mann, *The Record Guide*, rev. ed. (London: Collins, 1955), 98.

10. Taruskin writes: "Turning ideas into objects, and putting objects in place of people, is the essential modernist fallacy—the fallacy of reification, as it is called." Richard Taruskin, *Text and Act: Essays on Music and Performance* (New York and Oxford: Oxford University Press, 1995), 24.

11. This is the definition of rationalism formulated by Paul Oliver for the field broadly known as philosophy: Paul Oliver, "Rationalism," in *101 Key Ideas, Philosophy* (Lincolnwood, IL: NTC/Contemporary Publishers, 2000), 83.

12. William James, "What Pragmatism Means" (1907), in *Pragmatism, Old and New: Selected Writings*, ed. Susan Haack (Amherst, NY: Prometheus, 2006), 293.

13. Schnabel, *My Life and Music*, 121, 198, 140. Since Schnabel's three descriptions all originated within the same 1945 lecture series at the University of Chicago, it is not misleading to pull them together within one summary description of his philosophy.

14. James, "What Pragmatism Means," 303.

15. Charles Guignon and David R. Hiley, *Richard Rorty* (Cambridge and New York: Cambridge University Press, 2003), 30.

16. James, "What Pragmatism Means," 297. On the Jamesian notion of truth, see also Cornelis de Waal, *On Pragmatism* (Belmont, CA: Thomson Wadsworth, 2005), 42.

17. Lydia Goehr, "Philosophy of Music, §V Contemporary Challenges," *Grove Music Online, Oxford Music Online*, http://www.oxfordmusiconline.com (accessed 24 July 2008).

18. Konrad Wolff, *Schnabel's Interpretation of Piano Music* (New York: W. W. Norton, 1972), 15.

19. William James, "Pragmatism's Conception of Truth," in Haack, *Pragmatism, Old and New,* 325.

20. Ignace Jan Paderewski, "Paderewski on Tempo Rubato," in Henry Theophilus Finck, *Success in Music and How It Is Won* (New York: Scribner, 1909), 457.

21. David Dubal, *The Art of the Piano: Its Performers, Literature, and Recordings* (New York and London: Summit Books, 1989), 234.

22. Alfred Brendel, "Notes on a Complete Recording of Beethoven's Piano Works" (1966), in *Alfred Brendel on Music,* 23. Brendel is contradicted here by Stanley Boorman, who sees the significance of Schnabel's own markings in "the way they codify a performing view exemplified by the editor. Yet it is often difficult to determine exactly which annotations might have been in copies Beethoven authorized (in so far as that could imply specific approval), and which have been added by the later editor. At the other extreme are the so-called *Urtext* editions: here, the editor claims to have stripped away all later accretions to the musical text." Stanley Boorman, "The Musical Text," in *Rethinking Music,* ed. Nicholas Cook and Mark Everist (Oxford and New York: Oxford University Press, 1999), 403–4.

23. Artur Schnabel, ed., *Ludwig van Beethoven: 32 Sonatas for the Pianoforte* (New York: Simon and Schuster, 1935), 2: 807.

24. Wolff, *Schnabel's Interpretation of Piano Music,* 73.

25. Ibid. To this end, when a student approached a work for the first time Schnabel told her to avoid editions, even his own, and instead seek out the *Urtext* or autograph scores whenever possible.

26. Wolff, *Schnabel's Interpretation of Piano Music,* 120–21. There are instructive parallels here between Schnabel and his near contemporary Donald Tovey (1875–1940), who was one of the first music scholars of Germanic orientation to ridicule the prescriptive idea of sonata form as laid out by A. B. Marx (*Die Lehre von der musikalischen Komposition,* 1837–47) and Carl Czerny (*School of Practical Composition,* 1848–49). Particularly Schnabelian, perhaps, is Tovey's reference to a "sonata style" rather than a sonata form. D. F. Tovey, *Encyclopedia Britannica* (1911), s.v. "Sonata Forms"; reprinted in Tovey, *Musical Articles from the Encyclopedia Britannica* (London: Oxford University Press, 1944).

27. Wolff, *Schnabel's Interpretation of Piano Music,* 127.

28. William Glock and Stephen Plaistow, "Artur Schnabel," *Grove Music Online, Oxford Music Online,* http://www.oxfordmusiconline.com (accessed 18 August 2007).

29. "Of Mozart and Related Matters: Glenn Gould in Conversation with Bruno Monsaingeon" (1976), in *The Glenn Gould Reader,* ed. Tim Page (New York: Knopf, 1984), 33.

30. Schnabel, *Ludwig van Beethoven,* 2: 774. The composer states this motive entirely in octaves at other transpositions in the movement but in these two passages was clearly prevented from doing so by the lack of bass reach in

the piano he was then using. Both his 1817 Broadwood and his 1823 Graf extended three octaves below middle C.

31. Gould liked to quote the theologian Jean Le Moyne in saying that "the charity of the machine" has interposed itself between "the frailty of nature and the vision of the idealized accomplishment." Gould, "Music and Technology" (1974), in Page, *Glenn Gould Reader,* 354–55.

32. In the words of Kevin Bazzana, Gould wished "to impress [the] overall scheme onto the listener as a single controlling image, almost like an analytical graph. . . . In many Gould performances, the work appears to the listener as an immediately palpable shape—as a linear progression, arch, double arch, circle." Kevin Bazzana, "Performing the Work as *Gestalt,*" in *Glenn Gould: The Performer in the Work* (New York: Oxford University Press, 1997), 98–106; quotes from p. 101.

33. "Nevertheless, I eventually became convinced that in spite of all defects the value of recordings would still be great enough to justify them. Then I was very flattered at being asked—it was the first experiment along this line—to record all the works that Beethoven had written for the piano." Schnabel, *My Life and Music,* 97.

34. Charles Rosen, *Beethoven's Piano Sonatas: A Short Companion* (New Haven, CT and London: Yale University Press, 2002), 4, 7.

35. Schnabel, *My Life and Music,* 40.

36. Ibid., 5.

37. Ibid., 42.

38. Ibid., 146.

39. Ibid., 142, 184.

40. Artur Schnabel, *Music and the Line of Most Resistance* (Princeton, NJ: Princeton University Press, 1942), 58.

41. Wolff, *Schnabel's Interpretation of Piano Music,* 126.

42. Ibid., 169–70.

43. In Jean-Jacques Nattiez's analysis, what he calls "interpretation (performance)" connects with the musical score to create a "musical result"—the listener and the whole "esthesic process" of analysis and hermeneutics connect with this result, and not directly with the score or the performance. Jean-Jacques Nattiez, *Music and Discourse: Toward a Semiology of Music,* trans. Carolyn Abbate (Princeton, NJ: Princeton University Press, 1990), 73.

44. Nelson Goodman, *Languages of Art: An Approach to a Theory of Symbols,* 2nd ed. (Indianapolis, IN: Hackett, 1976), 113.

45. Walter Benjamin, "The Work of Art in the Age of Mechanical Reproduction" (1936), in *Illuminations: Essays and Reflections,* ed. Hannah Arendt and trans. Harry Zohn (New York: Schocken Books, 1968), 233–34.

46. "When he is in the studio, he likes to play as many as ten or fifteen interpretations of the same piece—each of them quite different, many of them valid—as though reexamining the music from every angle before deciding upon a final performance. . . . His provocative musical ideas, backed by complete

integrity of purpose and thorough academic understanding of the technical workings of a piece, make him either a musical devil's advocate or *enfant terrible*, depending on your point of view." Paul Myers, "Glenn Gould," *Gramophone*, February 1973, 478, quoted in Geoffrey Payzant, *Glenn Gould: Music and Mind*, rev. ed. (Toronto: Key Porter, 1984), 50.

47. Gould, "Of Mozart and Related Matters," 38.

48. Gould, "Beethoven's Last Three Piano Sonatas," in Page, *Glenn Gould Reader*, 56.

49. Myers, "Glenn Gould," 51.

50. Gould, "Of Mozart and Related Matters," 40.

51. See Richard Rorty, "The Pragmatist's Progress," in Collini, *Interpretation and Overinterpretation*, 103.

52. Gould, "Beethoven's Last Three Piano Sonatas," 57.

53. Ibid., 55.

54. For a similar description of Rorty's philosophical project, see Guignon and Hiley, *Richard Rorty*, 30.

55. Quoted in Burton, *Conversations about Bernstein*, 65.

56. John McClure, "Remembering Lenny," liner note for *Darius Milhaud / Albert Roussel / Arthur Honegger* (Sony MHK 62352, 1996), 5.

57. Otto Friedrich, *Glenn Gould: A Life and Variations* (New York: Random House, 1989), 101–8; Peter F. Ostwald, *Glenn Gould: The Ecstasy and Tragedy of Genius* (New York and London: W. W. Norton, 1997), 210–13.

58. Rorty, "Pragmatist's Progress," 105; italics added.

59. In Myers's summary, criticism of Gould involved accusations "of capriciousness, wilfulness, madness and a dozen artful musical devices." Myers, "Glenn Gould," 478. For an overview of criticisms aimed at Rorty, see Guignon and Hiley, *Richard Rorty*, 29–38.

60. William James, "On Pragmatism" (1907), in Haack, *Pragmatism, Old and New*, 112.

61. Tim Parry, review of *Chopin: 4 Scherzos* (DG 439 947–2GH), *Gramophone*, April 1999, http://www.gramophone.co.uk (accessed 12 July 2006).

62. Quoted in Random House *Read*, http://www.randomhouse.ca/readmag/volume3issue2/pdf/glenngould.pdf (accessed 14 March 2006).

63. Dean Elder, *Pianists at Play: Interviews, Master Lessons, and Technical Regimes* (Evanston, IL: The Instrumentalist, 1982), 137.

64. James, "Pragmatism's Conception of Truth," 311.

65. Sergey Schepkin, personal communication, 12 October 2006.

66. Richard Rorty, "Pragmatism as Anti-authoritarianism," in Haack, *Pragmatism, Old and New*, 667.

67. Goodman, *Languages of Art*, 52–56.

68. Glenn Gould, "A Desert Island Discography" (1970), in Page, *Glenn Gould Reader*, 439.

69. Dmitry Sitkovetsky, personal communication, 18 July 2007. Sitkovetsky's own recording of his arrangement, no doubt heard by most of those trios

that have recorded it since, has of course served to reidentify and perpetuate additional Gouldian aspects that Sitkovetsky chose not to put into print in his edition.

70. Quoted by National Public Radio, "New Technology Recaptures Pianists of the Past," http://www.npr.org/templates/story/story.php?storyId= 10439850 (accessed 9 June 2007).

71. Harold Bloom, *The Anxiety of Influence: A Theory of Poetry,* 2nd ed. (New York: Oxford University Press, 1997).

72. Philip Kennicott, "It's Time to Abandon False Idols," *Gramophone,* May 2001, A1.

73. Jim Samson, "The Practice of Early-Nineteenth-Century Pianism," in *The Musical Work: Reality or Invention?* ed. Michael Talbot (Liverpool: Liverpool University Press, 2000), 112.

74. Alfred Cortot, ed., *Frédéric Chopin: 12 Études Op. 25,* Édition de travail des oeuvres de Chopin [par] Alfred Cortot (Paris: Éditions Salabert, 1916), 48–49.

75. William James, "The Present Dilemma in Philosophy," in Haack, *Pragmatism, Old and New,* 286.

76. The Naxos Web site offers licensing of their recordings for use in films, TV productions, TV/radio commercials, Web sites, compilations, corporate promotional CDs, electronic games, ringtones, and educational projects; see http://www.naxos.com/licensing.asp.

77. Rorty, "Pragmatist's Progress," 105.

78. In this sense, recordings embody pragmatist principles by contravening the old-fashioned notion of final revelation as based in theism and, as Eco once observed, the myth that "secret knowledge" is equivalent to "deep knowledge." Eco, "Interpretation and History," 30.

79. Richard Rorty, "Pragmatism, Relativism, and Irrationalism," in Haack *Pragmatism, Old and New,* 642. There are of course parallels between my notion of a marketplace, Rorty's conversation, John Dewey's idea of democracy, and Habermas's conception of "communicative reason." They all suggest a world predicated upon everyday, instrumental, non-Platonist conceptions of truth.

80. Rorty, "Pragmatism, Relativism, and Irrationalism," 640.

81. Rorty, "Pragmatist's Progress," 93.

82. James, "What Pragmatism Means," 294.

83. De Waal, *On Pragmatism,* 25.

84. From Schnabel's 1933 lecture at Manchester University, reprinted in the 1970 edition of *My Life and Music* (New York: Dover, 1970), 236–37.

85. In 1945 he observed: "Some of the most delicate types of music are already conspicuously neglected. . . . Today, I would say, music has already suffered. I would, however, not say that public life has not been benefited." Schnabel, *My Life and Music,* 6.

86. Gould, "Music and Technology," 354–55. In thinking that is more bizarre and distant from current ethics, he also claimed that the instruments of

modern warfare are more moral than those of earlier periods: such weapons might kill more people, or so Gould reasoned, but the push button is less immediately animalistic and cutthroat than the bayonet.

87. Glenn Gould, "Rubinstein" (1971), in Page, *Glenn Gould Reader*, 290.

88. H. T. Kirby-Smith, *A Philosophical Novelist: George Santayana and the Last Puritan* (Carbondale: Southern Illinois University Press, 1997), 14.

89. Ostwald, *Glenn Gould*, 177. After discovering Gould's "Santayanism," Ostwald recommended he read a book of James's correspondence, but there's no sign Gould took up the suggestion.

90. George Santayana, *The Last Puritan: A Memoir in the Form of a Novel*, ed. William G. Holzberger (Cambridge, MA: MIT Press, 1994), 14.

91. Irving Singer, *George Santayana, Literary Philosopher* (New Haven, CT and London: Yale University Press, 2000), 53.

4. DIGITAL MYTHOLOGIES

1. Jody Rosen, "Researchers Play Tune Recorded before Edison," *New York Times*, 27 March 2008, http://www.nytimes.com/2008/03/27/arts/27soun .html (accessed 30 March 2008).

2. David Kusek and Gerd Leonhard, *The Future of Music: Manifesto for the Digital Music Revolution* (Boston: Berklee Press, 2005). Bowie's statement that "music itself is going to become like running water or electricity" appeared in the *New York Times* in June 2002 and is quoted in Kusek and Leonhard, *Future of Music*, 3. Of course, sixty-five years earlier Benjamin had quoted Paul Valéry's own prediction that "auditory images" would someday be provided "just as water, gas, and electricity are brought into our houses from far off to satisfy our needs in response to a minimal effort." Walter Benjamin, "The Work of Art in the Age of Mechanical Reproduction," in *Illuminations: Essays and Reflections*, ed. Hannah Arendt and trans. Harry Zohn (New York: Schocken Books, 1968), 219.

3. Heinrich Schenker, *The Art of Performance*, ed. Heribert Esser and trans. Irene Schreier Scott (Oxford and New York: Oxford University Press, 2000), 3.

4. Nicholas Cook, "Between Process and Product: Music and/as Performance," *Music Theory Online* 7.2 (April 2001).

5. Kusek and Leonhard, *Future of Music*, 37.

6. John Seely Brown and Paul Duguid, *The Social Life of Information*, 2nd ed. (Boston: Harvard Business School Press, 2002), 198.

7. Christoph von Dohnányi lamented music's increased fluidity twenty years ago, but his allegiance to paper now sounds so outdated as to be almost comic: "To be able to have a score," he predicted unhappily, "go for a walk, and read a string quartet! Very few people will do this because of all this Walkman business. They have their tapes." Quoted in James Badal, *Recording the Classics: Maestros, Music, and Technology* (Kent, OH and London: Kent State University Press, 1996), 67–68.

8. Kusek and Leonhard, *Future of Music*, 15, 27.

9. Ibid., 38. It should be mentioned here that media fixity and fluidity are themselves becoming fluid concepts. More and more vintage recordings are sold "on demand" as individually burned CD-Rs with uncertain shelf lives, while several recording firms are now issuing composers' complete-works editions on hard drives that might just survive longer because of their compactness and ease of use. Which of the two is the "fixed," and which the "fluid" format, or are these descriptions losing their meaning? And if optical media disappear entirely, as is often predicted, will we start seeing a variety of hard drives sold by cost and durability?

10. Schenker, *Art of Performance*, 77, 4.

11. Kusek and Leonhard, *Future of Music*, 44.

12. For another perspective on the increasingly important issue of hearing the work through, and synonymously with, the performance, see Eric F. Clarke, "Listening to Performance," in *Musical Performance: A Guide to Understanding*, ed. John Rink (Cambridge and New York: Cambridge University Press, 2002), 185–96.

13. For a list of Pristine Classical discs and downloads, see http://www.pristineclassical.com/index2.html.

14. See Peter Ostwald, *Glenn Gould: The Ecstasy and Tragedy of Genius* (New York: W. W. Norton, 1997), 116.

15. Quoted in "Ward Marston, Remastering 78s—The Meticulous Art of Cleaning Up Caruso and Other Classics for Today's Listeners," *Gramophone*, February 2003, 19.

16. Tim Page, "Glenn Gould," liner note for *The Original Jacket Collection: Glenn Gould Plays Bach* (Sony 64226, 1999), 5.

17. Leonard Bernstein, "The Truth About a Legend," in *Glenn Gould: By Himself and His Friends*, ed. John McGreevy (Toronto and Garden City, NY: Doubleday, 1983), 21.

18. Mark Obert-Thorn, liner note for *Bach: Goldberg Variations, BWV 988; Partita No. 5, BWV 829* (Naxos 8111247, 2007).

19. The 1987 George Martin stereo mix has been used as the basis for the 2009 single album re-release, while the original mono and stereo versions reappear in a new box set. Similar interpretive issues attend the other 2009 Beatles reissues, though not perhaps in quite the same tangled way as with *Rubber Soul*. See Allan Kozinn, "Original Beatles Albums to Be Reissued," *New York Times*, 7 April 2009, http://www.nytimes.com/2009/04/08/arts/music/08beat.html (accessed 7 April 2009). For a painstaking list of the moment-to-moment differences between the three *Rubber Soul* mixes, see the Norwegian fan club Web page: http://www.norwegianwood.org/beatles/disko/uklp/soul.htm.

20. See Timothy Maloney, "Glenn Gould, Autistic Savant," in *Sounding Off: Theorizing Disability in Music*, ed. Neil Lerner and Joseph Straus (New York: Routledge, 2006), 121–35.

21. There were numerous reports on Zenph's reprocessing of Gould's 1955 recording; one of the more revealing is Tim Page, "Ghostly Grand Piano: Technical Marvel Plays Like an Old Pro," *Washington Post*, 10 March 2007, www.washingtonpost.com (accessed 9 June 2007).

22. A particularly important ambiguity attends the second of these: without having measurements of Gould actually playing, one would have no way of knowing if the original Columbia engineers and producers compressed or expanded his sound for recording. The Zenph engineers then had to decide between using an even expansion (thereby assuming a linear relationship between acoustic values in the performance, which we can never truly know, and those on the original Columbia tape) or a parabolic one (where some kind of curve would try to mediate between the two sets of acoustic values). I thank Peter Tender for his extended conversation on the Zenph process, and his considerable help with describing and contextualizing the same.

23. "Sony's . . . purchase of CBS, complete with back catalogue, may point to a future in which hardware giants make wholesale copyright or purchases in order to head off legal restraints to an expanding market for their samplers and scanners. New technology needs content on an enormous scale." A. Cameron, "Digital Dialogues: An Introduction," *Ten-8* 2.2 (1991): 6, quoted in Celia Lury, "Movement and the Body of Photography," in *Prosthetic Culture: Photography, Memory, and Identity* (London and New York: Routledge, 1998), 177 n. 18.

24. Marshall McLuhan, *Understanding Media: The Extensions of Man* (New York: McGraw-Hill, 1964), 57.

25. From 1983 ad for the Hitachi DA-1000 and DA-800 CD players; 1983 ad for the Sony CDP-101 player.

26. As described on packaging for PolyGram and Universal Music Galleria reissue series and other digital CD remasters, 1987 through early 1990s.

27. Hitler averred in *Mein Kampf* that "in the big lie there is always a certain force of credibility."

28. Michel Chion, *The Voice in Cinema*, trans. and ed. Claudia Gorbman (New York: Columbia University Press, 1999), 167.

29. Quoted in Andrew Keener, "Stern and CBS," *Gramophone*, March 1986, 1118. Aden Evens came up with a similar account of how musical performance is misrepresented by digital audio's depiction of silence as a vacuum: "To play music expressively is to demonstrate a sensitivity to this background, not only to read the audience, to hear the space around the instrument, but also to contract the silence between, beside, or behind notes and to draw from this silence the appropriate contraction, just the right sounds." Aden Evens, *Sound Ideas: Music, Machines, and Experience* (Minneapolis: University of Minnesota Press, 2005), 17.

30. "The Next 30 Years: Twenty-Four Experts Speak Out on What's Coming in Audio, Video, Music, and Recordings," *High Fidelity*, April 1981, 61.

31. Stanley Sadie, "Early Music," *Gramophone*, December 1981, 861.

32. Christopher Hogwood, "Hogwood's Beethoven," *Gramophone*, March 1986, 1136.

33. Andrew Parrott, "Correspondence," *Gramophone*, May 1986, 1373.

34. See the essays on musical authenticity and contemporaneity that Taruskin wrote between 1981 and 1994, as anthologized in Richard Taruskin, *Text and Act: Essays on Music and Performance* (New York and Oxford: Oxford University Press, 1995).

35. Francis Fukuyama, *The End of History and the Last Man* (New York: Free Press, 1992), xi. The book had its beginnings in an essay titled "The End of History?" that Fukuyama published in 1989, the year the Berlin Wall fell.

36. For a detailed description of jitter within an account of one company's technology for reducing it, see www.wadia.com/technology/technicalpapers/ClockLink.pdf (accessed 10 March 2007).

37. Evens, *Sound Ideas*, 66–67.

38. Ibid., 70.

39. Colin Barrett, Steve Luck, Allen Zuk, and Keith Martin, *Go Digital: Keep the Past Alive!* (Cologne: Evergreen, 2006), back cover.

40. Michelle Henning, "Digital Encounters: Mythical Pasts and Electronic Presence," in *The Photographic Image in Digital Culture*, ed. Martin Lister (London and New York: Routledge, 1995), 221.

41. McLuhan, *Understanding Media*, 7–21.

42. "Just as Giedion teaches us to read off the basic features of today's architecture in the buildings erected around 1850, we, in turn, would recognize today's life, today's form, in the life and in the apparently secondary, lost forms of that epoch." Walter Benjamin, *The Arcades Project*, trans. Howard Eiland and Kevin McLaughlin (Cambridge, MA: Belknap Press of Harvard University Press, 1999), 458. Benjamin, like Sigfried Giedion, devotes much thought to the popularity of iron as a building material in the industrial era. He discusses how iron was first limited to transitory structures: before it became an eminently "formal and stable" material, it was initially distrusted as an "artificially prepared" substance. He then quotes A. G. Meyer on iron; Meyer's statement sounds much like Evens's thoughts on digital media: "[The] basic forms in which iron appears as a building material are . . . already themselves, as distinct snytheses, partly new . . . since such properties have been technically and scientifically developed and exploited precisely for *these* forms. . . . Between matter and material, in this case, there is a relationship quite different from that between stone and ashlar, clay and tile, timber and beam: with iron, building material and structural form are, as it were, more homogeneous." Benjamin, *Arcades Project*, 157–58. The books Benjamin refers to are Giedion's *Bauen in Frankreich* (Leipzig, 1928) and Meyer's *Eisenbauten* (Esslingen, 1907).

43. CBS CD advertisement, *Gramophone Compact Disc Guide and Catalogue* (Harrow, Middlesex: General Gramophone Publications, 1984), ad insert.

44. Jacques Attali, *Noise*, trans. Brian Massumi (Minneapolis and London: University of Minnesota Press, 1985), 101.

45. See Michael C. Roggemann and Byron Welsh, *Imaging through Turbulence* (Boca Raton, FL: CRC Press, 1996), "Introduction" and passim.

46. Richard Osborne, review of *Claudio Arrau: The Early Years* (Marston 52023–2), *Gramophone*, August 2000, 78.

47. Jed Distler, review of *The Essential Leon Fleisher* (Sony 88697 21581), ClassicsToday.com, http://www.classicstoday.com (accessed 20 February 2008).

48. Hardwick interviewed and quoted in Alan Blyth, "Here and There," *Gramophone*, November 1982, 540; italics in the original.

49. Allan Kozinn, "HF's Music Critics Take on the Compact Disc: The Digital Millenium Is (Finally) at Hand; But How Does It Sound?" *High Fidelity*, January 1983, 55; italics in the original.

50. Alan Blyth, review of *Verdi: Messa da Requiem* (DG 415 091), *Gramophone*, May 1985, 1375.

51. Matt Hanson, *The End of Celluloid: Film Futures in the Digital Age* (Mies, Switzerland, and Hove, UK: Rotovision, 2004), passim.

52. Louise de la Fuente, "From Digital to Analogue Technical Notes: On the 1981 Goldberg Recording," liner note for *Glenn Gould, A State of Wonder: The Complete Goldberg Variations 1955 and 1981* (Sony S3K87703, 2002), 22.

53. "Ward Marston, Remastering 78s," 19.

54. Barrymore Laurence Scherer, "Ward Marston: Audio Resurrectionist," *Wall Street Journal*, 25 August 2005, D8.

55. Mark Obert-Thorn, liner notes *for Beethoven: Piano Works Vol. 6* (Naxos 79882, 2004).

56. One of Marston's latest remasters removes a major obstacle to enjoying the musical attributes of flat disc recordings by Debussy, Grieg, Louis Diémer, and Raoul Pugno (Marston 52054). Marston has made these problematic records listenable with the help of digital techniques—specifically, software recently devised by Dimitri Antsos to correct the wide pitch-variation "wow" on the original sources. This is an excellent example of the defects that are fairly easy to work out with the help of computers, but more or less irresolvable without them.

57. http://www.pristineclassical.com/More/NaturalSound.html (accessed 1 September 2008).

58. http://www.pristineclassical.com/More/ambient-stereo.html (accessed 1 September 2008). According to the Pristine Classical Web site, the software they use for Ambient Stereo processing was devised by Algorithmix, using a process called K-Stereo that had in turn been produced by American audio engineer Bob Katz. The Algorithmix Web site calls K-Stereo "the world's first ambience recovery processor" and promises "a natural, diffuse ambient field which is extracted (derived) from the ambience in the source recording." http://www.algorithmix.com/en/kstereo.htm (accessed 1 September 2008). To judge from several remasters in Pristine Classical's catalogue, I would say their K-Stereo does offer the most dramatic improvement. (By comparison, their version of the Fischer *Well-Tempered Clavier* suffers from less-than-optimal

shellacs; EMI used the original stampers for their 2007 reissue, and benefited from their quieter surfaces and better definition.) One K-Stereo example is Pristine's version of Sibelius symphonies with Eugene Ormandy and the Philadelphia Orchestra, as recorded by Columbia in mono in 1954 (Pristine 177). The process does create a few metallic-sounding artifacts, but after comparing the remaster with good original LP pressings, I was quite astonished at how the Algorithmix process liberated the orchestral sound from the flat, inert, stuck-in-the-middle quality of the original mono production.

59. Daniel Abramson, "Make History, Not Memory: History's Critique of Memory," *Harvard Design Magazine* 9 (Fall 1999): 2.

60. Raymond S. Tuttle, "George Gershwin: Orchestral Music and Concertos," in *Classical Music: The Listener's Companion,* ed. Alexander J. Morin (San Francisco: Backbeat Books, 2002), 337.

61. Quoted in Sam Kashner and Nancy Schoenberger, *A Talent for Genius: The Life and Times of Oscar Levant* (New York: Villard Books, 1995), 16, 161. I should add that a number of other respected performances from midcentury tend to sound "very nearly brutal" when heard alongside today's self-conscious musicality, among them Bruno Walter's 1941–53 Beethoven symphonies cycle with the New York Philharmonic, many of Toscanini's interpretations, and Sviatoslav Richter's more imperious records from the 1950s.

62. Tzvetan Todorov, *La conquête de l'Amérique: La question de l'autre* (Paris: Seuil, 1982), 257–58, quoted in and translated by Michael Richardson, "Enough Said," in *Orientalism: A Reader,* ed. Alexander Lyon Macfie (New York: New York University Press, 2001), 215.

63. Quoted in Katie Hafner, "History, Digitized (and Abridged)," *New York Times,* 10 March 2007, http://www.nytimes.com/2007/03/10/business/yourmoney/11archive.html (accessed 30 January 2008).

64. Hafner, "History, Digitized (and Abridged)."

65. Tim Brooks, *Survey of Reissues of U.S. Recordings* (Washington, D.C.: Council on Library and Information Resources and the Library of Congress, 2005), 26, http://www.clir.org/pubs/abstract/pub133abst.html.

66. Brown and Duguid, *Social Life of Information,* 249.

67. Quoted in Hafner, "History, Digitized (and Abridged)."

68. I thank Mark Obert-Thorn for much of this copyright information, about which he has firsthand knowledge. I discovered an additional and telling detail while requesting rights and permissions for graphics in the present volume: it seems even Naxos's own cover art for the Gouldbergs, and other pre-stereo remasters, cannot be published or reprinted in the United States.

5. BEETHOVEN AND THE IPOD NATION

1. Almost from the start, LP side length was flexible. As CBS president Edward Wallerstein recalled, company engineers first brought him a disc of seven–eight minutes, and then one that was ten–twelve minutes long, but he declared neither "a long-playing record." Finally Wallerstein proposed seventeen minutes

per side, which "would enable ninety percent of all classical music to be cut on two sides of a record." Edward Wallerstein, "Celebrating the Fiftieth Anniversary of the LP: What Is a Long-Playing Record?" liner note for *Mahler: Symphony No. 1 in D Major "Titan"* (Sony MHK 63328, 1998), 32–34. By 1950, though, some of Columbia's LPs—Bruno Walter's record of Mahler's Fourth, and pairings of Mozart and Haydn symphonies—were approaching one hour in length. By the time CDs appeared, some Direct Metal Mastered LPs—on the EMI and Teldec labels for instance—were even exceeding CD duration.

2. Jonathan Sterne, "The MP3 as Cultural Artifact," *New Media & Society* 8 (2006): 839. For sake of convenience, I use the term "MP3" to refer not only to the twenty-five-year-old MP3 codec, but also to audio formats like MP4, AIFF, Apple's AAC, Apple Lossless, WAV, WMA, and Ogg Vorbis. Similarly, a certain lazy expediency has led me to refer habitually to Apple's iPod when I should also mention the Microsoft Zune, the Samsung T10, the ARCHOS Generation 5 players, and others—or, better yet, refer more generically to PMPs, or portable media players. I fully realize the commercial, sociological, and indeed political importance of these distinctions. In my defense, I would say I am simply falling in line with the old and characteristically American habit of allowing certain brand names—Kleenex, Coke, and Xerox among them—to substitute for all manufacturers of a commodity.

3. Jack Goody, *The Domestication of the Savage Mind* (Cambridge and New York: Cambridge University Press, 1977), 128; Conrad Shayo and Ruth Guthrie, "From Edison to MP3: A Struggle for the Future of the Music Recording Industry," *International Journal of Cases on Electronic Commerce* 1:2 (April–June 2005): 24.

4. McLuhan said of the phonetic alphabet that it gave users "an eye for an ear" and "translated tribal man into a visual world and invited him to undertake the visual organization of space." Marshall McLuhan, *Understanding Media: The Extensions of Man* (New York: McGraw-Hill, 1964), 84, 96.

5. http://www.ifpi.org/content/section_statistics/index.html (accessed 8 February 2009).

6. According to this survey, conducted in April 2003, digital music formats (including CD-Rs and digital MP3 files stored on a PC) account for 16 percent of American music collections, with this proportion jumping to 34 percent among teens aged twelve to seventeen and 30 percent among Americans aged eighteen to twenty-four. The survey also found that by April 2003, 80 million Americans had listened to digital music files that were stored on a PC, and 65 million had downloaded music or an MP3 file from the Internet. Study cited by Shayo and Guthrie, "From Edison to MP3," 14.

7. The cell phone is becoming more and more of a media convergence, a favorite do-everything device, and this might suggest hardware is becoming a nonissue. I would say the opposite, however: that such versatility only strengthens the consumer's love of hardware, and for the kinds of portability and convenience that define it, while music-lovers become more and more ambivalent about issues of recording format.

8. One of the first such companies was Digital Lifestyle Outfitters, founded in 2001. In 2005 the business sold $84 million worth of iPod cases, boom boxes, and dozens of other accessory types. See Jeff Grady with Patrick J. Sauer, "How I Did It: Jeff Grady, President, Digital Lifestyle Outfitters," Inc. The Daily Resource of Entrepeneurs, http://www.inc.com/magazine/20060901/hidi-grady.html (accessed 8 October 2008).

9. I am particularly thankful for Joseph Panzner's input with regard to this discussion of format agnosticism.

10. Richard Mansfield, *Savvy Guide to Digital Music* (Indianapolis, IN: Indy-tech Publishing, 2005), 13.

11. For a basic discussion of these terms, see Carl Shapiro and Hal R. Varian, "The Information Economy," in *Information Rules: A Strategic Guide to the Network Economy* (Cambridge, MA: Harvard Business School Press, 1998), 1–17.

12. *Oxford English Dictionary Online*, s.v. "information" 3.a, http://www.oed.com (accessed 18 February 2007).

13. As heard, the informational content of music and musical performances has been codified by (among other such systems) the Music Genome Project, which works to define "taste algorithms" of individual listeners by breaking songs into DNA-like strings according to "Background Horn Riffs," "Angry Lyrics," "Clarinet Solo," "Driving Swing Feel," "East Coast Rap Influences," and so on.

14. Shapiro and Varian, "Information Economy," 3–4.

15. Ibid., 5–6.

16. In Shapiro and Varian's summary, digital technology "is uniquely potent precisely because it sharply lowers both copying and distribution costs." Shapiro and Varian, *Information Rules*, 85. According to Shayo and Guthrie, with Internet technologies "the fixed costs required to set up press masters, packaging, and printing will be avoided. Also the costs of storage and transmission of the music is minimal." Shayo and Guthrie, "From Edison to MP3," 13.

17. Sterne, "MP3 as Cultural Artifact," 838.

18. Milton Babbitt, "The Composer as Specialist" (1958; "Who Cares if You Listen?"), in *Classic Essays on Twentieth-Century Music*, ed. Richard Kostelanetz and Joseph Darby (New York: Schirmer, 1996), 162–63. With his declaration that the new efficiency of the tonal language allows "a greatly increased number of pitch simultaneities, successions, and relationships," Babbitt also brings music in line with McLuhan's post-Euclidean analysis of sound as "essentially a unified field of instant relationships." McLuhan, *Understanding Media*, 275.

19. E. T. A. Hoffmann, "Beethoven's Instrumental Music" (1810–13), in *Source Readings in Music History*, vol. 6, *The Nineteenth Century*, ed. Ruth Solie, rev. ed. (New York and London: W. W. Norton, 1998), 151.

20. In describing Romanticism, Carl Dahlhaus invoked a duality between forms that were "either schematic (since form was incidental) or disintegrated (by adapting them to poetic content in the guise of a tangible subject)." Carl

Dahlhaus, *Nineteenth-Century Music*, trans. J. Bradford Robinson (Berkeley, Los Angeles, and London: University of California Press, 1989), 35.

21. "Sonata form, with both flexibility and formal possibilities, emerged as Haydn's chosen vehicle for the achievement of the new type of intelligibility which was possible in instrumental music." David P. Schroeder, "Symphonic Intelligibility and Sonata Form," in *Haydn and the Enlightenment: The Late Symphonies and Their Audience* (Oxford: Clarendon Press, 1990), 130–31.

22. Quoted in Fred Maus, "Sexual and Musical Categories," in *The Pleasure of Modernist Music*, ed. Arved Ashby (Rochester and London: University of Rochester Press, 2004), 169.

23. Frederic Jameson, *Postmodernism; or, The Cultural Logic of Late Capitalism* (Durham, NC: Duke University Press, 1991), 4–5.

24. "Is it only coincidence that over the same period as the introduction of the new technology of reproduction, the Western musical tradition experienced a revolution in its every aspect?" Michael Chanan, *Repeated Takes: A Short History of Recording and Its Effects on Music* (London and New York: Verso, 1995), 20.

25. Jean Baudrillard, "The Ecstasy of Communication" (1987), trans. John Johnston, in *The Anti-Aesthetic: Essays on Postmodern Culture*, ed. Hal Foster (New York: New Press, 1998), 153.

26. McLuhan, *Understanding Media*, 84.

27. Jeanne M. De Temple and Catherine E. Snow, "Conversations about Literacy: Social Mediation of Psycholinguistic Activity," in *Literacy and Motivation: Reading Engagement in Individuals and Groups*, ed. Ludo Verhoeven and Catherine E. Snow (Mahwah, NJ: Lawrence Erlbaum Associates, Inc., 2001), 55–56.

28. Steve Jones, "Music That Moves: Popular Music, Distribution, and Network Technologies," *Cultural Studies* 16.2 (2002): 229.

29. David Barton, "Literacy in Everyday Contexts," in Verhoeven and Snow, *Literacy and Motivation*, 26–27.

30. McLuhan, *Understanding Media*, 79.

31. Ibid., 46.

32. Baudrillard, "Ecstasy of Communication," 146–47.

33. Marshall McLuhan and Quentin Fiore, *The Medium Is the Massage* (New York: Random House, 1967), 31–40.

34. Steven Levy, *The Perfect Thing: How the iPod Shuffles Commerce, Culture, and Coolness* (New York: Simon & Schuster, 2006), 231.

35. Dylan Jones, *iPod, Therefore I am: Thinking inside the White Box* (New York and London: Bloomsbury, 2005), 192.

36. Quoted in Christian Wolff, "Feldman's String Quartet No.2," liner note for *Morton Feldman: String Quartet No.2* (Mode 112, 2002), 2.

37. Lev Nikolaievitch Tolstoy, *The Kreutzer Sonata*, trans. H. Sutherland Edwards (London: Remington and Co., 1890), 180.

38. E. M. Forster, *Howards End* (New York: Alfred A. Knopf, 1921), 41.

39. Ibid., 39–41.

40. Thomas Mann, *Doctor Faustus*, trans. John E. Woods (New York: Alfred A. Knopf, 1997), 203–4.

41. Ibid., 204-5.

42. "The persistent and profound influence of this one style on the history of musical thought, its status as the embodiment of Western art music, expressed through the imposing theories whose first principles are based on it, came to pass because a particularly compelling concept of self was animated by Beethoven's music and through it seems ever renewable." Scott Burnham, "Beethoven Hero," in *Beethoven Hero* (Princeton, NJ: Princeton University Press, 1995), 147.

43. Dahlhaus, *Nineteenth-Century Music*, 94. The novella is Wackenroder's *Herzensergießungen eines kunstliebenden Klosterbruders* (1797).

44. Henri-Jean Martin, *The History and Power of Writing*, trans. Lydia G. Cochrane (Chicago and London: University of Chicago Press, 1994), 509. It must be for similar reasons that so many recordings of classical music, not only of symphonic works but also piano music and opera, have been made in old churches. Often more isolated from traffic noise than concert halls, and generally possessing a more meditative and immediately pleasing ambience, they allow performers and listeners enough space and distance to "internalize their dialogue" with the music.

45. Steven Roger Fischer, *A History of Reading* (London: Reaktion Books, 2003), 202.

46. Richard Leppert, *The Sight of Sound: Music, Representation, and the History of the Body* (Berkeley and Los Angeles: University of California Press, 1993), 24–25; Jonathan Sterne, *The Audible Past: Cultural Origins of Sound Reproduction* (Durham, NC and London: Duke University Press, 2003), 160–61; Lydia Goehr, *The Imaginary Museum of Musical Works: An Essay in the Philosophy of Music* (Oxford and New York: Oxford University Press, 1992), 249–50.

47. Babbitt, "Composer as Specialist," 164.

48. T. W. Adorno, *Introduction to the Sociology of Music*, trans. E. B. Ashton (New York: Seabury Press, 1976), 45–46.

49. See T. W. Adorno, "On the Fetish-Character in Music and the Regression of Listening" (1938), in *Essays on Music*, ed. Richard Leppert, trans. Susan H. Gillespie (Berkeley and Los Angeles: University of California Press, 2002), 288–317.

50. Michael Bull, "The Dialectics of Walking: Walkman Use and the Reconstruction of the Site of Experience," in *Consuming Cultures: Power and Resistance*, ed. Jeff Hearn and Sasha Roseneil (London and New York: Macmillan, 1999), 203–4. Bull does open up some space for other interpretations when he speaks of an important dialectic "between technology as invasion and technology as resistance."

51. Adorno, "On the Fetish-Character in Music and the Regression of Listening," 291.

52. Sterne, "MP3 as Cultural Artifact," 836. I would say the question remains open of just how much, if anything, of the "distracted" mass consumer is predicated on MP3 technology. The facts that the technology predates the iPod and is indeed several decades old certainly complicate such an equation.

53. "Walkman (Listening to Music in NYC)," *The New Yorker*, 2 January 1989, 20; quoted in Paul du Gay et al., *Doing Cultural Studies: The Story of the Sony Walkman* (London and Thousand Oaks, CA: Sage, in association with The Open University, 1997), 93.

54. Friedrich Nietzsche, "On Music and Words" (1871?), reprinted in Carl Dahlhaus, *Between Romanticism and Modernism*, trans. Walter Kaufmann (Berkeley, Los Angeles, and London: University of California Press, 1980), 118; italics in the original.

55. A contemporary drawing of the sales campaign is reproduced in Imogen Fellinger, "Autographs, Published Editions and Arrangements," liner note for *Johannes Brahms: Chorwerke* (Deutsche Grammophon 449646, 1983), 88–89.

56. Sterne, "MP3 as Cultural Artifact," 839.

57. Shapiro and Varian, *Information Rules*, 95.

58. Quoted in Ian Watt, *The Rise of the Novel: Studies in Defoe, Richardson, and Fielding* (Berkeley: University of California Press, 1962), 200.

59. Dylan Jones, *iPod, Therefore I Am*, 149.

60. Will Straw, " 'Organized Disorder': The Changing Space of the Record Shop," in *The Clubcultures Reader: Readings in Popular Cultural Studies*, ed. Steve Redhead (Oxford and Malden, MA: Blackwell, 1997), 65, quoted in Steve Jones, "Music That Moves," 18.

61. Dylan Jones, *iPod, Therefore I Am*, 22–23.

62. Ibid., 158.

63. Of course, one could turn this around and say that MP3 technology is now much more amenable than records and tapes—and their brick-and-mortar purveyances—ever were to sustaining Carter and Schuller as market "fringe" tastes.

64. Mark Ellingham, introduction to *The Rough Guide Book of Playlists*, ed. Mark Ellingham (London: Rough Guides, 2005), ix.

65. Dylan Jones, *iPod, Therefore I Am*, 203.

66. Ellingham, *Rough Guide Book of Playlists*, back cover.

67. Dylan Jones, *iPod, Therefore I Am*, 140.

68. Fischer, *History of Reading*, 299.

69. Levy, *Perfect Thing*, 229.

70. Niall Lucy, *Postmodern Literary Theory: An Introduction* (Oxford and Malden, MA: Blackwell, 1997), 262 n. 7.

71. Quoted in Levy, *Perfect Thing*, 105–6.

72. Kelefa Sanneh, "Embracing the Random," *New York Times*, 3 May 2005, D1.

73. Heinrich Schenker, *Das Meisterwerk in der Musik: Ein Jahrbuch*. Vol. 1 (1925) (Cambridge and New York: Cambridge University Press, 1996), 325.

74. Richter performed the sonata in this configuration at the Aldeburgh Festival on 20 June 1964—as documented on his CD *Schubert—Chopin—Liszt* (BBC Legends BBCL4146-2, 2004).

75. Levy, *Perfect Thing*, 15.

76. Shapiro and Varian, *Information Rules*, 93.

77. Walter Benjamin, "The Work of Art in the Age of Mechanical Reproduction" (1936), in *Illuminations: Essays and Reflections*, ed. Hannah Arendt and trans. Harry Zohn (New York: Schocken Books, 1968), 224.

6. PHOTO/PHONO/PORNO

1. Susan Sontag, *On Photography* (New York: Farrar, Straus and Giroux, 1977), 1.

2. See Carl Dahlhaus, "Instrumental Music and Art-Religion," in *The Idea of Absolute Music*, trans. Roger Lustig (Chicago and London: University of Chicago Press, 1989), 88–102.

3. Walter Benjamin, "The Work of Art in the Age of Mechanical Reproduction" (1936), in *Illuminations: Essays and Reflections*, ed. Hannah Arendt and trans. Harry Zohn (New York: Schocken Books, 1968), 233.

4. Sontag, *On Photography*, 86.

5. Benjamin, "Work of Art in the Age of Mechanical Reproduction," 227.

6. Michael Chanan, *Repeated Takes: A Short History of Recording and Its Effects on Music* (London and New York: Verso, 1995), 20.

7. John Culshaw, *Ring Resounding* (New York: Viking Press, 1967), 26.

8. For the day-to-day genesis of *Pet Sounds*, see Keith Badman, *The Beach Boys: The Definitive Diary of America's Greatest Band on Stage and in the Studio* (San Francisco: Backbeat Books, 2004), 103–35. Some famous recording anomalies defy these categories—Captain Beefheart rehearsed his Magic Band so mercilessly for *Trout Mask Replica* that the album needed very little studio time or postproduction, and Leopold Stokowski often "played" the mixing desk as if it were an instrument for performance. But such transgressions are essential to Beefheart's and Stokowski's particular brands of musicality: their universality, that is to say their importance, resides in their manners of particularity.

9. For an overview across time of the respective roles of songwriter and sound recording in popular music, see Albin Zak, "Tracks," in *The Poetics of Rock: Cutting Tracks, Making Records* (Berkeley: University of California Press, 2001), 24–47.

10. Roland Barthes, *Camera Lucida: Reflections on Photography*, trans. Richard Howard (New York: Hill and Wang, 1981), 12.

11. "We are out to make sound photographs of as many sides as we can get during each session." Fred Gaisberg, quoted by Walter Legge, in Elisabeth Schwarzkopf, *On and Off the Record: A Memoir of Walter Legge* (New York: Charles Scribner's Sons, 1982), 16.

12. James Badal, *Recording the Classics: Maestros, Music, and Technology* (Kent, OH and London: Kent State University Press, 1996), 73, 45, 91. 130.

13. Richard Buskin, *Insidetracks: A First-Hand History of Popular Music from the World's Greatest Record Producers and Engineers* (New York: Avon, 1999), 60; italics in the original.

14. Ibid., xii.

15. Ibid., 123.

16. Ibid., 196. A similar description could apply to some classical musicians who worked in the studio, such as Stokowski and Glenn Gould, but they are the exceptions proving this division-of-labor rule. Of course it's important here that most "classical" instruments embody centuries-old, nonelectrical technology. If studios still recorded with acoustic horns, brass players could be doubling now as recording engineers!

17. G. W. F. Hegel, *Vorlesungen über die Aesthetik* (1832), vol. 1, in *Suhrkamp Werkausgabe*, vol. 13 (Frankfurt: Suhrkamp Verlag, 1970), 376, quoted and translated in Henry-Louis de la Grange, "Music about Music in Mahler: Reminiscences, Allusions, or Quotations?" in *Mahler Studies*, ed. Stephen E. Hefling (Cambridge and New York: Cambridge University Press, 1997), 123.

18. Heinrich Schenker, *Free Composition*, trans. and ed. Ernst Oster (New York and London: Longman, 1979), xxiii.

19. Arnold Schoenberg, "Brahms the Progressive," in *Style and Idea*, ed. Leonard Stein and trans. Leo Black (Berkeley and Los Angeles: University of California Press, 1975), 405; id., "Inspiration," trans. R. Wayne Shoaf, in *Tenth Anniversary Bulletin*, Arnold Schoenberg Institute (1987), 1; id., *The Musical Idea and the Logic, Technique, and Art of Its Presentation*, ed. and trans. Patricia Carpenter and Severine Neff (New York: Columbia University Press, 1995), 375; italics in the original.

20. Karajan says elsewhere in the same conversation: "When I conduct a symphony . . . I have *the impression of the complete work* in my mind." Richard Osborne, *Conversations with Karajan* (New York: Harper & Row, 1989), 97, 131; italics added.

21. Quoted in Badal, *Recording the Classics*, 130.

22. Jean Vermeil, *Conversations with Boulez: Thoughts on Conducting*, trans. Camille Naish (Portland, OR: Amadeus Press, 1996), 106, 108.

23. Pierre Boulez, "Technology and the Composer" (1977), in *Orientations: Collected Writings*, ed. Jean-Jacques Nattiez (Cambridge, MA: Harvard University Press, 1986), 486.

24. Ibid., 488.

25. Theodore Gracyk, *Rhythm and Noise: An Aesthetics of Rock* (Durham, NC: Duke University Press, 1996), 13.

26. Quoted in Vermeil, *Conversations with Boulez*, 105.

27. Zak, *Poetics of Rock*, 13–14.

28. Benjamin, "Work of Art in the Age of Mechanical Reproduction," 223. For an overview of the Adorno-Benjamin dispute over the ideas in Benjamin's famous essay, see Richard Wolin, *Walter Benjamin: An Aesthetic of Redemption* (Berkeley, Los Angeles, and London: University of California Press, 1994), 183–97.

29. Igor Stravinsky, "The Performance of Music," in *Poetics of Music in the Form of Six Lessons,* trans. Arthur Knodel and Ingolf Dahl (Cambridge, MA and London: Harvard University Press, 1947), 119–35. "It is the conflict of these two principles—execution and interpretation—that is at the root of all the errors, all the sins, all the misunderstandings that interpose themselves between the musical work and the listener and prevent a faithful transmission of its message" (122).

30. Igor Stravinsky and Robert Craft, *Conversations with Igor Stravinsky* (Garden City, NY: Doubleday, 1959), 135; David Hamilton, "Stravinsky and the Microphone," *High Fidelity,* June 1967, 59.

31. Hamilton, "Stravinsky and the Microphone," 59.

32. William M. Ivins, "New Reports and New Vision: The Nineteenth Century," in *Prints and Visual Communication* (1953); reprinted in *Classic Essays on Photography,* ed. Alan Trachtenberg (New Haven, CT: Leete's Island Books, 1980), 217.

33. Ibid., 220–21.

34. Benjamin, "Work of Art in the Age of Mechanical Reproduction," 234. Benjamin thought film was the great revolutionary medium, at the same time modern and populist. Boulez would doubtless elect recording, while Ivins clearly believed it to be photography, a medium that "brought us knowledge of art that could never have been achieved so long as western European society was dependent upon the old graphic processes and techniques for its reports about art. The syntaxes of engraving had held our society tight in the little local provinciality of their extraordinary limitations." Ivins, "New Reports and New Vision," 236

35. Barthes, *Camera Lucida,* 100–102.

36. Mladen Dolar describes such a split sense of control in psychoanalytic terms and presents the voice as aural counterpart to the visual self in Lacan's mirror stage. "So, for psychoanalysis, the auto affective voice of self-presence and self-mastery was constantly opposed by its reverse side, the intractable voice of the Other, the voice that one could not control. But both have to be thought together." Here the mirror stage is actualized when the subject hears her voice as her own or better yet hears it *acknowledged as* hers. Mladen Dolar, "The Object Voice," in *Gaze and Voice as Love Objects,* ed. Renata Saleci and Slavoj Žižek (Durham, NC: Duke University Press, 1996), 15.

37. Quoted in Glenn Gould, "The Prospects of Recording" (1966), in *Classic Essays on Twentieth-Century Music,* ed. Richard Kostelanetz and Joseph Darby (New York: Schirmer, 1996), 73. Kostelanetz and Darby present Gould's essay as it originally appeared in *High Fidelity,* that is with the multiple quotes in the margins, while Tim Page removed these for his own edition in *The Glenn Gould Reader.*

38. Marius de Zayas, "Photography and Photography and Artistic-Photography" (1913), in Trachtenberg, *Classic Essays on Photography,* 125.

39. Sontag, *On Photography,* 16, 54.

40. Susan Sontag, "Theatre and Film," in *Styles of Radical Will* (New York: Farrar, Straus and Giroux, 1966), 113.

41. Barthes, *Camera Lucida,* 82, 89–90; italics in the original.

42. Simon Frith would probably disagree. He did assume a Sontagian then-vs.-now view when he averred that "old recordings are odd or incomplete or just plain 'wrong' in the same way as old readings of literature or art," signifying in a final analysis "that the 'ideal' performance is variable." Simon Frith, *Performing Rites: On the Value of Popular Music* (Cambridge, MA: Harvard University Press, 1996), 244.

43. Lydia Goehr, *The Imaginary Museum of Musical Works: An Essay in the Philosophy of Music* (Oxford and New York: Oxford University Press, 1992), 103. For additional discussion of this Kantian notion of the work as "regulative" concept, see the section "The Biblical Paradigm" in chapter 1 of this volume.

44. Daniel Pollock, "Recreating Rachmaninoff's Pianism," liner note for *A Window in Time: Sergei Rachmaninoff Performs Chopin, Tchaikovsky, and Others* (Telarc 515607T, 1999), 2.

45. Martin Jay argued against visual primacy among the senses, however, emphasizing a general "deep-seated distrust of the privileging of sight." Martin Jay, "The Rise of Hermeneutics and the Crisis of Ocularcentrism," *Poetics Today* 9.2 (1988): 307–26, cited in Steven Jones, "A Sense of Space: Virtual Reality, Authenticity, and the Aural," *Critical Studies in Mass Commmunication* 10 (1993): 240.

46. Marshall McLuhan and Quentin Fiore, *The Medium Is the Massage* (New York: Random House, 1967), 111.

47. William J. Mitchell, *The Reconfigured Eye: Visual Truth in the Post-Photographic Era* (Cambridge, MA and London: MIT Press, 1992), 225.

48. T. W. Adorno and Hanns Eisler, *Composing for the Films* (London and Atlantic Highlands, NJ: Athlone Press, 1994), 20–21.

49. Lydia Goehr, "The Perfect Performance of Music and the Perfect Musical Performance," *New Formations* 27 (Winter 1995–96): 19.

50. Stephen Davies remarks that "the modern technology of recordings allows for a degree of acoustic faithfulness similar to that achieved by radio"; but this seems to miss the most significant and prevalent aspects of new recording technology, which are less interested in fidelity than in specific methods of "infidelity." Stephen Davies, *Musical Works and Performances: A Philosophical Exploration* (Oxford and New York: Oxford University Press, 2001), 306.

51. Bryce Morrison, "Sensibility and Bravura," liner note for *Great Pianists of the 20th Century: Martha Argerich II* (Philips 456 703–2, 1999), 9. The recording can be heard with its original wrong notes on any of the several versions in Deutsche Grammophon's Galleria series, or in DG's multivolume *Martha Argerich Collection.*

52. Schwarzkopf, *On and Off the Record*, 143–44, 73.

53. Christian Metz, *The Imaginary Signifier: Psychoanalysis and the Cinema*, trans. Celia Britton, Annwyl Williams, Ben Brewster, and Alfred Guzzetti (Bloomington: Indiana University Press, 1982), 74.

54. Schenker, *Free Composition*, 8. Writing in 1926, Schenker found all Mozart performances of his time lacking this very coherence: "The performance of Mozart's works lacks all cohesiveness. It is vapid, stiff, pedestrian, forever concerned merely with the series of notes that lies immediately ahead, thus as a whole it is lifeless and untrue." Heinrich Schenker, "Mozart's Symphony in G Minor, K.550," in *The Masterwork in Music: A Yearbook*, vol. 2 (1926), ed. William Drabkin and trans. John Rothgeb (Cambridge and New York: Cambridge University Press, 1996), 60.

55. Quoted in Trachtenberg, *Classic Essays on Photography*, 121.

56. Quoted in Badal, *Recording the Classics*, 105.

57. Glenn Gould, "Music and Technology" (1976), in *The Glenn Gould Reader*, ed. Tim Page (New York: Knopf, 1984), 356; italics in the original.

58. Ibid., 339.

59. Glenn Gould, "Let's Ban Applause!" (1962), in Page, *Glenn Gould Reader*, 246.

60. See Elizabeth Angilette, *Philosopher at the Keyboard: Glenn Gould* (Metuchen, NJ: Scarecrow Press, 1992), 22.

61. Barthes, *Camera Lucida*, 5–6.

62. Quoted in Charles Musser, *Thomas A. Edison and His Kinetographic Motion Pictures* (New Brunswick, NJ: Rutgers University Press, 1995), vii.

63. Culshaw, *Ring Resounding*, 16. For Culshaw's own account of his "SonicStage" productions before and after Decca's marketing department devised that term, see pp.9–16, 155–61, and passim; id., *Putting the Record Straight* (New York: Viking Press, 1981), 279–81.

64. Culshaw, *Putting the Record Straight*, 249–52.

65. Goehr, "Perfect Performance of Music and the Perfect Musical Performance," 2. Goehr's duality would be described in Marxist terms as the division between exchange-value and use-value; for discussion of such division in musical terms, see Arved Ashby, "Frank Zappa and the Anti-Fetishist Orchestra," *Musical Quarterly* 83 (Winter 1999): 557–606.

66. Goehr, "Perfect Performance of Music and the Perfect Musical Performance," 2.

67. T. W. Adorno, *Mahler: A Musical Physiognomy*, trans. Edmund Jephcott (Chicago and London: University of Chicago Press, 1992), 72.

68. Jonathan Valin, "The Case of the Knock at the Door," *The Absolute Sound*, June/July 2006, 104.

69. Sontag, *On Photography*, 7.

70. Barthes, *Camera Lucida*, 106, 91; italics in the original.

71. Jean Baudrillard, *Paroxysm: Interviews with Philippe Petit*, trans. Chris Turner (London and New York: Verso, 1998), 94.

72. Barthes first discussed these terms in "Sade I" (1967) and the excised and unpublished segment of the "Fourier" (1970) essay that became "Sade II"; both were reprinted in translation in *Sade Fourier Loyola*, trans. Richard Miller (New York: Hill and Wang, 1976), 15–37. Baudrillard first discussed seduction in *De la séduction* (Paris: Galilée, 1979).

73. Barthes, *Camera Lucida*, 59.

74. And yet in this particular essay, perhaps in basic contradiction to my argument, Barthes bases his discussion on a hearing of baritone Gérard Souzay's records. Roland Barthes, "The Bourgeois Art of Song," in *The Eiffel Tower and Other Mythologies*, trans. Richard Howard (New York: Hill and Wang, 1979), 119.

75. Jean Baudrillard, *Seduction*, trans. Brian Singer (New York: St. Martin's Press, 1990), 31.

76. Quoted in Badal, *Recording the Classics*, 27–28.

77. Barthes, *Camera Lucida*, 41.

78. The *Oxford English Dictionary*'s earliest citation s.v. "resolution" is an 1867 source on microscopy, where the term is defined as "the power of showing clearly minute details."

79. "High-Def Porn Has Stars Spooked," *Sydney Morning Herald*, 15 January 2007, http://www.smh.com.au/news/home-theatre/highdef-porn-has-stars-spooked/2007/01/15/1168709667041.html (accessed 10 February 2007).

80. Deutsche Grammophon advertisement, *Gramophone*, May 1984, 1289.

7. MAHLER AS IMAGIST

1. In Bernstein's view, Mahler's potential listeners stood chastened and transfigured by "the smoking ovens of Auschwitz, the frantically bombed jungles of Vietnam, through Hungary, Suez, the Bay of Pigs, the farce-trial of Sinyavsky and Daniel, the refueling of the Nazi machine, the murder in Dallas." Such accumulating horrors eventually allowed us to "finally listen to Mahler's music and understand that it foretold all." Leonard Bernstein, "Mahler: His Time Has Come" (1967), in *Findings* (New York: Simon and Schuster, 1982), 257.

2. "A remarkable Mahler renaissance began around 1960 and has lasted to this day. This astounding popularity has a number of reasons, including some practical ones. . . . Record manufacturers were quick to realize that Mahler's music was particularly effective in stereophonic sound." Constantin Floros, *Gustav Mahler: The Symphonies*, trans. Vernon Wicker and Jutta Wicker (Portland, OR: Amadeus Press, 1993), 11–12. Writing in 1969, Kurt Blaukopf offered a more synergistic account of Mahler's increased reputation, one that presages some of my own points in the present chapter: "Many diverse factors have contributed to this, but perhaps the most decisive of all was the advent of the technically perfected stereo record. Mahler's time had come when it became possible to store and reproduce spatial sound. Advances in [audio] technique played

a large part in the onset of the new Mahler epoch. One might think that Mahler could not have foreseen this. . . . Who would venture to make prosaic technique responsible for the victory of a musical dreamer? But Mahler was no dreamer. He had a very clear idea of the technical requirements necessary for the unconditional surrender of the public to his music." Kurt Blaukopf, *Gustav Mahler*, trans. Inge Goodwin (New York and Washington: Praeger Publishers, 1973), 248.

3. *Selected Letters of Ezra Pound, 1907–1941*, ed. D. D. Paige (New York: New Directions, 1971), 38; Theodore Maynard, *Our Best Poets: English and American* (New York: Henry Holt and Company, 1922), 200. Pound invoked imagism in contradistinction to the aromatic and metaphor-rich facture of symbolist poetry and differentiated it from the moralizing and sentimentality of Victorian writers. Maynard conveys an explanation from one of the imagist poets in question, Amy Lowell, whereby "imagism is presentation, not representation" (200).

4. Ezra Pound, "A Retrospect" (1918), in *Modernism: An Anthology of Sources and Documents*, ed. Vassiliki Kolocotroni, Jane Goldman, and Olga Taxidou (Chicago: University of Chicago Press, 1998), 374.

5. William J. Mitchell, *Picture Theory* (Chicago and London: University of Chicago Press, 1994), 15.

6. Christopher Collins, *Reading the Written Image: Verbal Play, Interpretation, and the Roots of Iconophobia* (University Park, PA: Pennsylvania State University Press, 1991). Mahler's score indications are taken from, respectively (1) Symphony No. 8, second movement, Fig. 89 (Doctor Marianus); (2) Symphony No. 8: second movement, Fig. 218, trumpets and trombones; (3) Symphony No. 1, first movement, 6 mm. after Fig. 16, flute 1; (4) Symphony No. 1, second movement, Fig. 8, and (among other places) Symphony No. 6, first movement, faster subsidiary B material; (5) Symphony No. 2, third movement, E-flat clarinet, 6 mm. before Fig. 30 and elsewhere; (6) introduction to "Der Trunkene im Frühling" from *Das Lied von der Erde* and fifth movement of Symphony No. 3; (7) Symphony No. 3, first movement, Fig. 45, horns and trombones; (8) Symphony No. 3, first movement, 3 mm. before Fig. 49, oboe 2; (9) Symphony No. 3, third movement, Fig. 23; (10) Symphony No. 6, second movement, Fig. 46, first and second violins; (11) Symphony No. 6, third movement, 4 mm. after Fig. 99, first violins; (12) Symphony No. 8, second movement, Fig. 136; (13) Symphony No. 7, second movement, beginning, horns 1 and 3; (14) Symphony No. 3, third movement, Fig. 28.

7. Bruno Walter, *Gustav Mahler* (Vienna: Herbert Reichner, 1936), 24. Mahler was writing the Third Symphony at the time, and Walter reports that at that time the introduction to the first movement was titled "Was mir das Felsebirg erzählt" (What the Rocky Mountain Tells Me). Different translations of Walter's book have of course come up with different renderings of Mahler's enigmatic "wegkomponiert" statement, among them "You don't need to look—I have composed all this already!" (*Gustav Mahler*, trans. supervised by Lotte Walter Lindt [New York: Knopf, 1957], 28); and the more

precise if also cumbersome "No need to look there any more—that's all been used up and set to music by me" (*Gustav Mahler,* trans. James Galston [New York: Greystone Press, 1941], 24).

8. Letter to Max Marschalk, December 1895, quoted in Henry-Louis de la Grange, *Mahler* (Garden City, NY: Doubleday, 1973), 784.

9. Ludwig Schiedermair's recollection, quoted in Kurt Blaukopf and Herta Blaukopf, *Mahler: His Life, Work, and World* (New York: Thames and Hudson, 1991), 148. Mahler was also identifying more and more with J. S. Bach's poietic sensibility at this time, and with the Bachian ethos of composition-as-craft that later came to be called Neoclassicism. He wrote to his friend and confidante Natalie Bauer-Lechner regarding the Bach influence: "It's beyond words, the way I am constantly learning more and more from Bach (really sitting at his feet like a child): for my natural way of working is Bach-like. If only I had time to do nothing but learn in this highest of all schools!" Mahler's involvement with Bach and ideas of absolute music at this time were inspired in part by his acquisition of the Bach Gesellschaft Edition, completed in 1900. Natalie Bauer-Lechner, *Recollections of Gustav Mahler,* trans. Peter Franklin (Cambridge and New York: Cambridge University Press, 1980), 165, 170.

10. Schumann praised Mendelssohn for "invariably revealing a poetic grasp" of his subject in the *Schöne Melusine* overture rather than creating a "coarse historical fabric" out of it. Quoted in Carl Dahlhaus, *Nineteenth-Century Music,* trans. J. Bradford Robinson (Berkeley, Los Angeles, and London: University of California Press, 1989), 144–45.

11. *Gustav Mahler: Briefe 1879–1911,* ed. Alma Mahler (Berlin: Zsolnay, 1924), 189, quoted in Carl Dahlhaus, "The Musically Absolute and Program Music," in *The Idea of Absolute Music,* trans. Roger Lustig (Chicago and London: University of Chicago Press, 1989), 139.

12. Quoted in Natalie Bauer-Lechner, *Erinnerungen an Gustav Mahler,* ed. Herbert Killian, rev. ed. (Hamburg: K. D. Wagner, 1984), 170.

13. This discussion naturally raises the question of just what an image is, and according to whom, and how Mahler's are to be differentiated from other composers'. For Mitchell's extensive discussion of image types described according to graphic, optical, perceptual, mental, and verbal categories, see his "What Is an Image?" in *Iconology: Image, Text, Ideology* (Chicago and London: University of Chicago Press, 1986), 7–46. Of the categories he describes, I would say Mahler tends toward the static aspect of the graphic image, with some incursion into the symbolism and idealization of mental imagery. Another significant perspective on the image is Ludwig Wittgenstein's: specifically, the "picture theory" that he proposed in the *Tractatus* (1917–21) as a way of understanding how language relates to the world and enables an understanding of it. Wittgenstein later stepped away from these conclusions, but his thoughts at this time—along with those of his colleague Bertrand Russell— offer insight into the "Mahlerian" question of how the image relates to discourse, or refuses to do so. Wittgenstein saw language relating to the world much as music does, though he didn't put it in these terms. But he presents

names as articles of language that short-circuit or evade discourse—following Gottlob Frege, who had pointed to the language "defect" of proper names that lack the *Bedeutung* that words must have. Here Wittgenstein seems to move away from the Mahlerian notion of the improper noun having greater descriptive power than the proper noun; if his argument were clothed in musical terms, it would sound like a defense of program music.

14. Norman Del Mar, *Anatomy of the Orchestra* (Berkeley and Los Angeles: University of California Press, 1981), 426; and id., *Mahler's Sixth Symphony: A Study* (London: Eulenburg, 1980), 127–29. T. W. Adorno, *Mahler: A Musical Physiognomy,* trans. Edmund Jephcott (Chicago and London: University of Chicago Press, 1992), 126. Del Mar goes on to say that the logistics of such "hammer" performance are complicated in that neither an instrument with a sounding membrane nor a boxlike construction would obtain the "deep-toned 'whomp'" that the music seems to call for.

15. Alma Mahler, *Gustav Mahler: Memories and Letters,* trans. Basil Creighton and ed. Donald Mitchell (New York: Viking Press, 1969), 99. See also Henry-Louis de la Grange, *Gustav Mahler,* vol. 3, *Vienna: Triumphs and Disillusion (1904–1907)* (Oxford and New York: Oxford University Press, 1999), 813–14.

16. Cumming argues against this long-standing presumption, of course. Naomi Cumming, *The Sonic Self: Musical Subjectivity and Signification* (Bloomington and Indianapolis: Indiana University Press, 2000), 101.

17. According to Alma, the blows are musical equivalents to "blows of fate, the last of which fells [the hero] as a tree is felled." Alma Mahler, *Gustav Mahler,* 70.

18. Roger Scruton, *Art and Imagination* (London: Methuen & Co., 1974), 173–78. Here Scruton adapts the notion of "seeing as" that Ludwig Wittgenstein had developed in chapter 11 of the *Philosophical Investigations.*

19. Quoted in de la Grange, *Gustav Mahler,* 3: 413.

20. Victor Burgin, "Seeing Sense," in *The End of Art Theory: Criticism and Post-Modernity* (Atlantic Highlands, NJ: Humanities Press, 1986), 51, quoted in Mitchell, *Picture Theory,* 282.

21. Michel Foucault, *The Order of Things: An Archaeology of the Human Sciences* (New York: Pantheon Books, 1971), 9–10.

22. Michel Foucault, *This Is Not a Pipe,* trans. James Harkness (Berkeley, Los Angeles, and London: University of California Press, 1983), 25. "The statement [*ceci n'est pas une pipe*] is perfectly true, since it is quite apparent that the drawing representing the pipe is not the pipe itself. And yet there is a convention of language: What is this drawing? Why, it is a calf, a square, a flower. . . . What misleads us is the inevitability of connecting the text to the drawing (as the demonstrative pronoun, the meaning of the word *pipe,* and the likeness of the image all invite us to do here)—and the impossibility of defining a perspective that would let us say that the assertion is true, false, or contradictory" (19–20).

23. Roland Barthes, "The Photographic Message," in *Image-Music-Text,* trans. Stephen Heath (New York: Hill and Wang, 1977), 18. To adapt Mahler's "wegkomponiert" statement to a visual context, a photographer would be more likely to "portray away" a concrete physical entity than a painter, and so Frederic E. Church must have portrayed less of the Hudson River valley "away" than Ansel Adams did of Yosemite.

24. Barthes, "Photographic Message," 19; italics in the original. Laura Mulvey offers her own take on photography's "uncodedness" when she refers to "the photographic index, the most literal, the most banal of signs." Laura Mulvey, "The Index and the Uncanny," in *Time and the Image,* ed. Carolyn Bailey Gill (Manchester and New York: Manchester University Press, 2000), 147.

25. Mitchell, "The Photographic Essay: Four Case Studies," in *Picture Theory,* 284.

26. Robert P. Morgan, "Ives and Mahler: Mutual Responses at the End of an Era," in *Charles Ives and the Classical Tradition,* ed. J. Peter Burkholder (New Haven, CT: Yale University Press, 1996), 80.

27. Carl Dahlhaus, "The Natural World and the 'Folklike Tone,'" in *Realism in Nineteenth-Century Music,* trans. Mary Whittall (Cambridge and New York: Cambridge University Press, 1985), 110–11.

28. Henry-Louis de la Grange refers here to "the ecstatic melody and sumptuous orchestral texture of its accompaniment" and calls the passage "one of the rare episodes in Mahler's music to radiate the sensuality of Strauss." De la Grange, *Gustav Mahler,* 3: 859.

29. Barthes, "Photographic Message," 19–20. Mitchell develops Barthes's notion of photographic resistance in the opening to his "Photographic Essay: Four Case Studies," in *Picture Theory,* 281–85.

30. Barthes, *Camera Lucida,* 77.

31. Walter Benjamin, "The Work of Art in the Age of Mechanical Reproduction" (1936), in *Illuminations: Essays and Reflections,* ed. Hannah Arendt and trans. Harry Zohn (New York: Schocken Books, 1968), 226.

32. "Psychically the printed book, an extension of the visual faculty, intensified perspective and the fixed point of view. Associated with the visual stress on point of view and the vanishing point that provides the illusion of perspective there comes another illusion that space is visual, uniform and continuous." Marshall McLuhan, *Understanding Media: The Extensions of Man* (New York: McGraw-Hill, 1964), 172.

33. Theorists use the term "prosthetic" to refer to technologically assisted ways of extending human perception and sensibilities. See for example Celia Lury's *Prosthetic Culture: Photography, Memory, and Identity* (London and New York: Routledge, 1998), a study that describes contemporary visual technologies and their facilitation of new ways of seeing, sensing, and remembering.

34. Michael Tilson Thomas would seem to agree, since he has come to place the hammer and its "player" on a platform some ten feet above the stage in his

San Francisco Symphony performances, with the aim of making the blows as powerful visually as they are sonically. The composer himself recognized position as a problem of his musical-imagistic language when in conducting the first scherzo of his Fifth Symphony he had the solo horn stand up near stage front and center, as if she were a concerto soloist. Another such example of prominence issues is the soloistic role of the timpani in the Seventh Symphony—again recognized by the composer when conducting in Amsterdam he experimented with an extra-large drum, an instrument that was recently rediscovered and used by Riccardo Chailly on his Concertgebouw Orchestra recording.

35. Russell interviewed by Karen Jaehne, "Wormania: Ken Russell's Best Laid Planaria," *Film Comment*, November-December 1988, 54, quoted in Kay Dickinson, *Off Key: When Film and Music Won't Work Together* (Oxford and New York: Oxford University Press, 2008), 85.

36. Gilbert Kaplan, "Adagietto: 'From Mahler with Love,'" in *Perspectives on Gustav Mahler*, ed. Jeremy Barham (Aldershot, UK and Burlington, VT: Ashgate, 2005), 379–400.

37. Donald Mitchell takes a more skeptical view of this continuing textuality with Mahler's Adagietto. As he sees it, Visconti's use of the movement was only the culmination of an arbitrary overburdening and weighing-down process that started with Bernstein's performance of the Adagietto at the funerals of Sergey Koussevitzky, John F. Kennedy, and Robert Kennedy. "The hijacking of the movement—of the supposed emotion it represented, at least—surely reached its apogee when Visconti used the Adagietto in his film of Mann's *Death in Venice* (1971) as sonorous symbol of Aschenbach's nostalgia, frustrated passion, and hopeless longing: one might think, ironically, that the singular performance history of the Adagietto up to this point had been nothing but preparation for the iconic, cult status with which Mahler's prelude to the finale of his Fifth Symphony found itself lumbered as a result of the film." One is hard put, however, to see just which connection Mitchell is trying to make between Bernstein's funeral renditions and Visconti. He most likely intimates the connection simply to support his lament over the "hijacking" and "lumbering" themselves. Mitchell certainly makes plain his disapproval of David Mellor seeing the film in the music rather than the other way around. "Every time I listen to this music," Mellor says in the quote that worries Mitchell, "I think about [Visconti's] film." Donald Mitchell, "Eternity or Nothingness? Mahler's Fifth Symphony," in *The Mahler Companion* (Oxford and New York: Oxford University Press, 1999), 310.

38. Petra Stegmann and Peter C. Seel, introduction to *Migrating Images: Producing . . . Reading . . . Transporting . . . Translating*, ed. Stegmann and Seel (Berlin: Haus der Kulturen der Welt, 2004), 9.

39. Marie wrote this in the early 1980s, before MTV changed hierarchies yet again and started a new filmic culture with editing and tempo oriented to music. Michel Marie, Jacques Aumont, Alain Bergala, and Marc Vernet, *Aesthetics of Film*, trans. and rev. Richard Neupert (Austin: University of Texas

Press, 1992), 131. Michel Chion said much the same as Marie with his declaration that there is no such thing as a soundtrack—that the aural aspect is subordinate to the shot, in other words, and there is no real continuity to a soundtrack in a way that there must be with the visuals; see Michel Chion, *Audio-Vision: Sound on Screen*, trans. and ed. Claudia Gorbman (New York: Columbia University Press, 1994), 40.

40. Claudia Gorbman, *Unheard Melodies: Narrative Film Music* (Bloomington: Indiana University Press, 1987), 5.

41. Nicholas Cook, *Analysing Musical Multimedia* (Oxford and New York: Oxford University Press, 1998), 92.

42. From Hanslick's review of a piano recital by Hans von Bülow, in Eduard Hanslick, *Concerte, Componisten und Virtuosen der letzten fünfzehn Jahre: 1870–1885* (Berlin: Allgemeiner Verein für Deutsche Literatur, 1886), 317.

43. Adorno, *Mahler*, chap. 4 and p. 55.

44. Benjamin, "Work of Art in the Age of Mechanical Reproduction," 224.

Selected Bibliography

The following represents a selection of sources cited in the text. Additional works of interest are included in the backnotes for each chapter. Many of the studies listed below straddle subjects or are taken in different directions than their authors might have anticipated, and so it would have been misleading or simply unworkable to divide the bibliography into subsections.

Abramson, Daniel. "Make History, Not Memory: History's Critique of Memory." *Harvard Design Magazine* 9 (Fall 1999): 1–6.

Adorno, T. W. *Introduction to the Sociology of Music.* Translated by E. B. Ashton. New York: Seabury Press, 1976.

———. *Mahler: A Musical Physiognomy.* Translated by Edmund Jephcott. Chicago and London: University of Chicago Press, 1992.

———. "On the Fetish-Character in Music and the Regression of Listening" (1938). In *The Essential Frankfurt School Reader,* edited by Andrew Arato and Eike Gebhardt, 270–99. New York: Continuum, 1982.

Adorno, T. W., and Hanns Eisler. *Composing for the Films.* London and Atlantic Highlands, NJ: Athlone Press, 1994.

Ashby, Arved. "Frank Zappa and the Anti-Fetishist Orchestra." *Musical Quarterly* 83 (Winter 1999): 557–606.

Attali, Jacques. *Noise.* Translated by Brian Massumi. Minneapolis and London: University of Minnesota Press, 1985.

Babbitt, Milton. "The Composer as Specialist" (1958; "Who Cares if You Listen?"). In *Classic Essays on Twentieth-Century Music,* edited by Richard Kostelanetz and Joseph Darby, 162–63. New York: Schirmer, 1996.

Badal, James. *Recording the Classics: Maestros, Music, and Technology.* Kent, OH and London: Kent State University Press, 1996.

Barthes, Roland. *Camera Lucida: Reflections on Photography.* Translated by Richard Howard. New York: Hill and Wang, 1981.

———. *The Eiffel Tower and Other Mythologies.* Translated by Richard Howard. New York: Hill and Wang, 1979.

———. "The Photographic Message." In *Image-Music-Text*, translated by Stephen Heath, 15–31. New York: Hill and Wang, 1977.

———. *The Pleasure of the Text*. Translated by Richard Miller. New York: Hill and Wang, 1975.

———. *Sade Fourier Loyola*. Translated by Richard Miller. New York: Hill and Wang, 1976.

Barton, David. "Literacy in Everyday Contexts." In *Literacy and Motivation: Reading Engagement in Individuals and Groups*, edited by Ludo Verhoeven and Catherine E. Snow, 21–34. Mahwah, NJ: Lawrence Erlbaum Associates, Inc., 2001.

Baudrillard, Jean. "The Ecstasy of Communication" (1987). Translated by John Johnston. In *The Anti-Aesthetic: Essays on Postmodern Culture*, edited by Hal Foster, 126–34. New York: New Press, 1998.

———. *Paroxysm: Interviews with Philippe Petit*. Translated by Chris Turner. London and New York: Verso, 1998.

Bazzana, Kevin. *Glenn Gould: The Performer in the Work; A Study in Performance Practice*. New York: Oxford University Press, 1997.

Benjamin, Walter. *The Arcades Project*. Translated by Howard Eiland and Kevin McLaughlin. Cambridge, MA: Belknap Press of Harvard University Press, 1999.

———. "The Work of Art in the Age of Mechanical Reproduction" (1936). In *Illuminations: Essays and Reflections*, edited by Hannah Arendt and translated by Harry Zohn, 217–51. New York: Schocken Books, 1968.

Bergson, Henri. *Creative Evolution*. Translated by Arthur Mitchell. New York: Henry Holt, 1926.

———. *Matter and Memory*. Translated by Nancy Margaret Paul and W. Scott Palmer. New York: Macmillan, 1950.

———. *Time and Free Will: An Essay on the Immediate Data of Consciousness*. Translated by F. L. Pogson. New York: Harper, 1960.

Bernstein, Leonard. "Mahler: His Time Has Come" (1967). In *Findings*, 255–64. New York: Simon and Schuster, 1982.

Blaukopf, Kurt, and Herta Blaukopf. *Mahler: His Life, Work, and World*. New York: Thames and Hudson, 1991.

Boorman, Stanley. "The Musical Text." In *Rethinking Music*, edited by Nicholas Cook and Mark Everist, 403–23. Oxford and New York: Oxford University Press, 1999.

Boulez, Pierre. "Technology and the Composer" (1977). In *Orientations: Collected Writings*, edited by Jean-Jacques Nattiez, 486–94. Cambridge, MA: Harvard University Press, 1986.

Braun, Hans-Joachim. *Music and Technology in the Twentieth Century*. Baltimore and London: Johns Hopkins University Press, 2002.

Brendel, Alfred. "Notes on a Complete Recording of Beethoven's Piano Works" (1966), "*Werktreue*—An Afterthought" (1976), and "A Case for Live Recordings" (1984). In *Alfred Brendel on Music: Collected Essays*, 16–41, 345–51. Rev. ed. London: Robson Books, 2007.

Brooks, Tim. *Survey of Reissues of U.S. Recordings.* Washington, D.C.: Council on Library and Information Resources and the Library of Congress, 2005.

Brown, John Seely, and Paul Duguid. *The Social Life of Information.* 2nd ed. Boston: Harvard Business School Press, 2002.

Bull, Michael. "The Dialectics of Walking: Walkman Use and the Reconstruction of the Site of Experience." In *Consuming Cultures: Power and Resistance,* edited by Jeff Hearn and Sasha Roseneil, 199–220. London and New York: Macmillan, 1999.

Burnham, Scott. *Beethoven Hero.* Princeton, NJ: Princeton University Press, 1995.

Buskin, Richard. *Insidetracks: A First-Hand History of Popular Music from the World's Greatest Record Producers and Engineers.* New York: Avon, 1999.

Chanan, Michael. *Musica Practica: The Social Practice of Western Music from Gregorian Chant to Postmodernism.* London and New York: Verso, 1994.

———. *Repeated Takes: A Short History of Recording and Its Effects on Music.* London and New York: Verso, 1995.

Chion, Michel. *Audio-Vision: Sound on Screen.* Translated and edited by Claudia Gorbman. New York: Columbia University Press, 1994.

———. *The Voice in Cinema.* Translated and edited by Claudia Gorbman. New York: Columbia University Press, 1999.

Clarke, Eric F. "Listening to Performance." In *Musical Performance: A Guide to Understanding,* edited by John Rink, 185-96. Cambridge and New York: Cambridge University Press, 2002.

———. *Ways of Listening: An Ecological Approach to the Perception of Musical Meaning.* Oxford and New York: Oxford University Press, 2005.

Collinson, Patrick. "Words, Language, and Books." In *The Reformation: A History,* 33–46. New York: Modern Library, 2003.

Cook, Nicholas. *Analysing Musical Multimedia.* Oxford and New York: Oxford University Press, 1998.

———. "Between Process and Product: Music and/as Performance." *Music Theory Online* 7.2 (April 2001).

———. "Imagining Music." In *Music, Imagination, and Culture,* 71–121. Oxford and New York: Oxford University Press, 1990.

———. "Words about Music, or Analysis versus Performance." In *Theory into Practice: Composition, Performance, and the Listening Experience,* 9–54. Collected Writings of the Orpheus Institute 2. Leuven, Belgium: Leuven University Press, 1999.

Cortot, Alfred, ed. *Frédéric Chopin: 12 Études Op. 25.* Édition de travail des oeuvres de Chopin [par] Alfred Cortot. Paris: Éditions Salabert, 1916.

Culshaw, John. *Putting the Record Straight.* New York: Viking Press, 1981.

———. *Ring Resounding.* New York: Viking Press, 1967.

Dahlhaus, Carl. *Between Romanticism and Modernism.* Translated by Walter Kaufmann. Berkeley, Los Angeles, and London: University of California Press, 1980.

———. *The Idea of Absolute Music.* Translated by Roger Lustig. Chicago and London: University of Chicago Press, 1989.

———. *Nineteenth-Century Music.* Translated by J. Bradford Robinson. Berkeley, Los Angeles, and London: University of California Press, 1989.

———. *Realism in Nineteenth-Century Music.* Translated by Mary Whittall. Cambridge and New York: Cambridge University Press, 1985.

Daniel, Oliver. *Stokowski: A Counterpoint of View.* New York: Dodd, Mead, and Company, 1982.

Davies, Stephen. *Musical Works and Performances: A Philosophical Exploration.* Oxford and New York: Oxford University Press, 2001.

De la Grange, Henry-Louis. *Mahler.* Garden City, NY: Doubleday, 1973.

Deleuze, Gilles. *Bergsonism.* Translated by Hugh Tomlinson and Barbara Habberjam. New York: Zone Books, 1991.

Del Mar, Norman. *Mahler's Sixth Symphony: A Study.* London: Eulenburg, 1980.

De Temple, Jeanne M., and Catherine E. Snow. "Conversations about Literacy: Social Mediation of Psycholinguistic Activity." In *Literacy and Motivation: Reading Engagement in Individuals and Groups,* edited by Ludo Verhoeven and Catherine E. Snow, 50–64. Mahwah, NJ: Lawrence Erlbaum Associates, Inc., 2001.

De Waal, Cornelis. *On Pragmatism.* Belmont, CA: Thomson Wadsworth, 2005.

Dickinson, Kay. *Off Key: When Film and Music Won't Work Together.* Oxford and New York: Oxford University Press, 2008.

Doane, Mary Ann. *The Emergence of Cinematic Time: Modernity, Contingency, the Archive.* Cambridge, MA and London: Harvard University Press, 2002.

Dolar, Mladen. "The Object Voice." In *Gaze and Voice as Love Objects,* edited by Renata Saleci and Slavoj Žižek, 7–31. Durham, NC: Duke University Press, 1996.

Dolmetsch, Arnold. *The Interpretation of the Music of the Seventeenth and Eighteenth Centuries.* Corr. ed. Seattle and London: University of Washington Press, 1946.

Du Gay, Paul, Stuart Hall, Linda Janes, Hugh Mackay, and Keith Negus. *Doing Cultural Studies: The Story of the Sony Walkman.* London and Thousand Oaks, CA: Sage, in association with The Open University, 1997.

Dunsby, Jonathan. *Performing Music: Shared Concerns.* Oxford and New York: Oxford University Press, 1995.

Eco, Umberto. "Interpretation and History," "Overinterpreting Texts," and "Between Author and Text." In *Interpretation and Overinterpretation,* edited by Stefan Collini, 23–88. Cambridge and New York: Cambridge University Press, 1992.

Eisenberg, Evan. *The Recording Angel: Music, Records, and Culture from Aristotle to Zappa.* 2nd ed. New Haven, CT and London: Yale University Press, 2005.

Ellingham, Mark, ed. *The Rough Guide Book of Playlists*. London: Rough Guides, 2005.

Evens, Aden. *Sound Ideas: Music, Machines, and Experience*. Minneapolis: University of Minnesota Press, 2005.

Fischer, Steven Roger. *A History of Reading*. London: Reaktion Books, 2003.

Foucault, Michel. *The Order of Things: An Archaeology of the Human Sciences*. New York: Pantheon Books, 1971.

————. *This Is Not a Pipe*. Translated by James Harkness. Berkeley, Los Angeles, and London: University of California Press, 1983.

Frith, Simon. "Technology and Authority." In *Performing Rites: On the Value of Popular Music*, 226–45. Cambridge, MA: Harvard University Press, 1996.

Fukuyama, Francis. *The End of History and the Last Man*. New York: Free Press, 1992.

Goehr, Lydia. *The Imaginary Museum of Musical Works: An Essay in the Philosophy of Music*. Oxford and New York: Oxford University Press, 1992.

————. "The Perfect Performance of Music and the Perfect Musical Performance." *New Formations* 27 (Winter 1995–96): 1–22.

————. "Philosophy of Music, §V Contemporary Challenges." *Grove Music Online, Oxford Music Online*. http://www.oxfordmusiconline.com.

Goldsmith, Harris. "Schnabel's Beethoven." *Association for Recorded Sound Collections Journal* 14.3 (1982): 83–88.

Goodman, Nelson. *Languages of Art: An Approach to a Theory of Symbols*. 2nd ed. Indianapolis, IN: Hackett, 1976.

Gorbman, Claudia. *Unheard Melodies: Narrative Film Music*. Bloomington: Indiana University Press, 1987.

Gould, Glenn. *The Glenn Gould Reader*. Edited by Tim Page. New York: Knopf, 1984.

Gracyk, Theodore. "Listening to Music: Performances and Recordings." *Journal of Aesthetics and Art Criticism* 55.2 (1997): 139–50.

Guerlac, Suzanne. *Thinking in Time: An Introduction to Henri Bergson*. Ithaca, NY and London: Cornell University Press, 2006.

Guignon, Charles, and David R. Hiley. *Richard Rorty*. Cambridge and New York: Cambridge University Press, 2003.

Hafner, Katie. "History, Digitized (and Abridged)." *New York Times*, 10 March 2007. http://www.nytimes.com/2007/03/10/business/yourmoney/11archive.html.

Hamilton, David. "Stravinsky and the Microphone." *High Fidelity*, June 1967, 58–62.

Hanslick, Eduard. *Concerte, Componisten und Virtuosen der letzten fünfzehn Jahre: 1870–1885*. Berlin: Allgemeiner Verein für Deutsche Literatur, 1886.

————. *On the Beautiful in Music* (1853). Translated by Gustav Cohen. London: Novello, 1891.

Hanson, Matt. *The End of Celluloid: Film Futures in the Digital Age*. Mies, Switzerland, and Hove, UK: Rotovision, 2004.

Heidegger, Martin. "The Question concerning Technology" (1954). In *Martin Heidegger: Basic Writings,* edited by David Farrell Krell, 287–317. Rev. ed. San Francisco: HarperCollins, 1993.

Heilbroner, Robert L. "Do Machines Make History?" and "Technological Determinism Revisited." In *Does Technology Drive History? The Dilemma of Technological Determinism,* edited by Merritt Roe Smith and Leo Marx, 53–78. Cambridge, MA: MIT Press, 1994.

Henning, Michelle. "Digital Encounters: Mythical Pasts and Electronic Presence." In *The Photographic Image in Digital Culture,* edited by Martin Lister, 216–35. London and New York: Routledge, 1995.

Hoffmann, E. T. A. "Beethoven's Instrumental Music" (1810–13). In *Source Readings in Music History,* vol. 6, *The Nineteenth Century,* edited by Ruth Solie, 151–56. Rev. ed. New York and London: W. W. Norton, 1998.

Hogwood, Christopher. "Hogwood's Beethoven." *Gramophone,* March 1986, 1136.

Hogwood, Christopher, et al. "The Next 30 Years: Twenty-Four Experts Speak Out on What's Coming in Audio, Video, Music, and Recordings." *High Fidelity,* April 1981, 52–66.

Horowitz, Joseph. *Understanding Toscanini: A Social History of American Concert Life.* Berkeley and Los Angeles: University of California Press, 1994.

Ingarden, Roman. *The Work of Music and the Problem of Its Identity.* Translated by Adam Czerniawski. Berkeley: University of California Press, 1986.

James, William. "The Present Dilemma in Philosophy" (1906), "What Pragmatism Means" (1907), and "Pragmatism's Conception of Truth" (1907). In *Pragmatism, Old and New: Selected Writings,* edited by Susan Haack, 273–330. Amherst, NY: Prometheus, 2006.

Jameson, Fredric. *Postmodernism; or, The Cultural Logic of Late Capitalism.* Durham, NC: Duke University Press, 1991.

Johnson, Peter. "Performance and the Listening Experience: Bach's 'Erbarme Dich.'" In *Theory into Practice: Composition, Performance, and the Listening Experience,* 55–102. Leuven, Belgium: Leuven University Press, 1999.

Jones, Dylan. *iPod, Therefore I Am: Thinking inside the White Box.* New York and London: Bloomsbury, 2005.

Jones, Steve. "Music That Moves: Popular Music, Distribution, and Network Technologies." *Cultural Studies* 16.2 (2002): 213–32.

———. "A Sense of Space: Virtual Reality, Authenticity, and the Aural." *Critical Studies in Mass Commmunication* 10.3 (1993): 238–52.

Karajan, Herbert von. "Technische Musikwiedergabe." In *Karajan: Eine Biographie* by Franz Endler, 289–94. Hamburg: Hoffmann und Campe, 1992.

Kashner, Sam, and Nancy Schoenberger. *A Talent for Genius: The Life and Times of Oscar Levant.* New York: Villard Books, 1995.

Kateb, George. "Technology and Philosophy." In *Technology and the Rest of Culture,* edited by Arien Mack, 283–304. Columbus: Ohio State University Press, 2001.

Katz, Mark. *Capturing Sound: How Technology Has Changed Music.* Berkeley, Los Angeles, and London: University of California Press, 2004.

Kirby-Smith, H. T. *A Philosophical Novelist: George Santayana and the Last Puritan.* Carbondale: Southern Illinois University Press, 1997.

Kittler, Friedrich A. *Gramophone, Film, Typewriter.* Translated by Geoffrey Winthrop-Young and Michael Wutz. Stanford, CA: Stanford University Press, 1999.

Kivy, Peter. *Authenticities: Philosophical Reflections on Musical Performance.* Ithaca, NY: Cornell University Press, 1995.

Kramer, Lawrence. *Why Classical Music Still Matters.* Berkeley and Los Angeles: University of California Press, 2007.

Kusek, David, and Gerd Leonhard. *The Future of Music: Manifesto for the Digital Music Revolution.* Boston: Berklee Press, 2005.

Leppert, Richard. *The Sight of Sound: Music, Representation, and the History of the Body.* Berkeley and Los Angeles: University of California Press, 1993.

Levy, Steven. *The Perfect Thing: How the iPod Shuffles Commerce, Culture, and Coolness.* New York: Simon & Schuster, 2006.

Lury, Celia. *Prosthetic Culture: Photography, Memory, and Identity.* London and New York: Routledge, 1998.

Mahler, Alma. *Gustav Mahler: Memories and Letters.* Translated by Basil Creighton and edited by Donald Mitchell. New York: Viking Press, 1969.

Martin, Henri-Jean. *The History and Power of Writing.* Translated by Lydia G. Cochrane. Chicago and London: University of Chicago Press, 1994.

Massumi, Brian. "Translator's Foreword: Pleasures of Philosophy." Introduction to *A Thousand Plateaus: Capitalism and Schizophrenia,* by Gilles Deleuze and Félix Guattari, translated by Brian Massumi, xiii–xiv. Minneapolis and London: University of Minnesota Press, 1987. intro

Maus, Fred. "Sexual and Musical Categories." In *The Pleasure of Modernist Music,* edited by Arved Ashby, 153–75. Rochester and London: University of Rochester Press, 2004.

McClary, Susan. "Sexual Politics in Classical Music." In *Feminine Endings: Music, Gender, and Sexuality,* 53–79. Minneapolis: University of Minnesota Press, 1991.

———. "Terminal Prestige: The Case of Avant-Garde Music Composition." *Cultural Critique* 12 (1989): 57–81.

McKenzie, D. F. *Bibliography and the Sociology of Texts.* Cambridge and New York: Cambridge University Press, 1999.

———. "Typography and Meaning: The Case of William Congreve." In *Buch und Buchhandel in Europa im achtzehnten Jahrhundert,* edited by Giles Barber and Bernhard Fabian, 80–93. Wolfenbütteler Schriften zur Geschichte des Buchwesens, vol. 4. Hamburg: Hauswedell, 1981.

McLuhan, Marshall. *Understanding Media: The Extensions of Man.* New York: McGraw-Hill, 1964.

McLuhan, Marshall, and Quentin Fiore. *The Medium Is the Massage.* New York: Random House, 1967.

Merton, Robert K. "The Unanticipated Consequences of Social Action" (1936). In *On Social Structure and Science,* edited by Piotr Sztompka, 173–82. Chicago and New York: University of Chicago Press, 1996.

Meyer, Leonard. "Toward a Theory of Style." In *Style and Music: Theory, History, and Ideology,* 3–37. Philadelphia: University of Pennsylvania Press, 1989.

Mitchell, Donald. "Eternity or Nothingness? Mahler's Fifth Symphony." In *The Mahler Companion,* 236–25. Oxford and New York: Oxford University Press, 1999.

Mitchell, William J. *Iconology: Image, Text, Ideology.* Chicago and London: University of Chicago Press, 1986.

———. *Picture Theory.* Chicago and London: University of Chicago Press, 1994.

———. *The Reconfigured Eye: Visual Truth in the Post-Photographic Era.* Cambridge, MA and London: MIT Press, 1992.

Morgan, Robert P. "Ives and Mahler: Mutual Responses at the End of an Era." In *Charles Ives and the Classical Tradition,* edited by J. Peter Burkholder, 75–86. New Haven, CT: Yale University Press, 1996.

Mulvey, Laura. "The Index and the Uncanny." In *Time and the Image,* edited by Carolyn Bailey Gill, 139–48. Manchester and New York: Manchester University Press, 2000.

Musser, Charles. *Thomas A. Edison and His Kinetographic Motion Pictures.* New Brunswick, NJ: Rutgers University Press, 1995.

Ong, Walter. *Orality and Literacy: The Technologizing of the Word.* London and New York: Routledge, 1982.

Osborne, Richard. *Conversations with Karajan.* New York: Harper & Row, 1989.

———. *Herbert von Karajan: A Life in Music.* Boston: Northeastern University Press, 1998.

Ostwald, Peter. *Glenn Gould: The Ecstasy and Tragedy of Genius.* New York and London: W. W. Norton, 1997.

Payzant, Geoffrey. *Glenn Gould: Music and Mind.* Rev. ed. Toronto: Key Porter, 1984.

Philip, Robert. *Early Recordings and Musical Style: Changing Tastes in Instrumental Performance, 1900–1950.* Cambridge: Cambridge University Press, 1992.

Proust, Marcel. *Swann's Way.* Translated by C. K. Scott-Moncrieff. New York: Henry Holt, 1922.

Rorty, Richard. "Pragmatism, Relativism, and Irrationalism" (1979) and "Pragmatism as Anti-authoritarianism" (1999). In *Pragmatism, Old and New: Selected Writings,* edited by Susan Haack, 637–76. Amherst, NY: Prometheus, 2006.

———. "The Pragmatist's Progress." In *Interpretation and Overinterpretation,* edited by Stefan Collini, 89–108. Cambridge and New York: Cambridge University Press, 1992.

Rosen, Charles. *Beethoven's Piano Sonatas: A Short Companion.* New Haven, CT and London: Yale University Press, 2002.

Said, Edward W. "The Virtuoso as Intellectual." In *On Late Style: Music and Literature against the Grain,* 115–33. New York: Pantheon Books, 2006.

Samson, Jim. "The Practice of Early-Nineteenth-Century Pianism." In *The Musical Work: Reality or Invention?* edited by Michael Talbot, 110–27. Liverpool: Liverpool University Press, 2000.

Santayana, George. *The Last Puritan: A Memoir in the Form of a Novel.* Edited by William G. Holzberger. Cambridge, MA: MIT Press, 1994.

Schenker, Heinrich. *The Art of Performance.* Edited by Heribert Esser. Translated by Irene Schreier Scott. Oxford and New York: Oxford University Press, 2000.

———. *Free Composition.* Translated and edited by Ernst Oster. New York and London: Longman, 1979.

———. *Das Meisterwerk in der Musik: Ein Jahrbuch.* Vol. 1 (1925). Cambridge and New York: Cambridge University Press, 1996.

Schnabel, Artur. *My Life and Music.* New York: St. Martin's Press, 1963.

Schniedewind, William M. *How the Bible Became a Book: The Textualization of Ancient Israel.* Cambridge and New York: Cambridge University Press, 2004.

Schoenberg, Arnold. *The Musical Idea and the Logic, Technique, and Art of Its Presentation.* Edited and translated by Patricia Carpenter and Severine Neff. New York: Columbia University Press, 1995.

Schroeder, David P. "Symphonic Intelligibility and Sonata Form." In *Haydn and the Enlightenment: The Late Symphonies and Their Audience,* 125–42. Oxford: Clarendon Press, 1990.

Schuller, Gunther. *The Compleat Conductor.* New York and Oxford: Oxford University Press, 1997.

Schwarzkopf, Elisabeth. *On and Off the Record: A Memoir of Walter Legge.* New York: Charles Scribner's Sons, 1982.

Shapiro, Carl, and Hal R. Varian. *Information Rules: A Strategic Guide to the Network Economy.* Cambridge, MA: Harvard Business School Press, 1998.

Shayo, Conrad, and Ruth Guthrie. "From Edison to MP3: A Struggle for the Future of the Music Recording Industry." *International Journal of Cases on Electronic Commerce* 1.2 (April–June 2005): 1–25.

Singer, Irving. *George Santayana, Literary Philosopher.* New Haven, CT and London: Yale University Press, 2000.

Sontag, Susan. *On Photography.* New York: Farrar, Straus and Giroux, 1977.

———. "Theatre and Film." In *Styles of Radical Will,* 99–122. New York: Farrar, Straus and Giroux, 1966.

Stegmann, Petra, and Peter C. Seel, eds. *Migrating Images: Producing . . . Reading . . . Transporting . . . Translating.* Berlin: Haus der Kulturen der Welt, 2004.

Sterne, Jonathan. *The Audible Past: Cultural Origins of Sound Reproduction.* Durham, NC and London: Duke University Press, 2003.

———. "The MP3 as Cultural Artifact." *New Media & Society* 8.5 (2006): 825–42.

Stokowski, Leopold. *Music for All of Us.* New York: Simon and Schuster, 1943.

Stravinsky, Igor. *Poetics of Music in the Form of Six Lessons.* Translated by Arthur Knodel and Ingolf Dahl. Cambridge, MA and London: Harvard University Press, 1947.

Straw, Will. " 'Organized Disorder': The Changing Space of the Record Shop." In *The Clubcultures Reader: Readings in Popular Cultural Studies,* edited by Steve Redhead, 39–47. Oxford and Malden, MA: Blackwell, 1997.

Symes, Colin. *Setting the Record Straight: A Material History of Classical Recording.* Middletown, CT: Middletown University Press, 2004.

Talbot, Michael, ed. *The Musical Work: Reality or Invention?* Liverpool: Liverpool University Press, 2000.

Taruskin, Richard. *Text and Act: Essays on Music and Performance.* New York and Oxford: Oxford University Press, 1995.

Taylor, Timothy. *Strange Sounds: Music, Technology, and Culture.* New York and London: Routledge, 2001.

Trachtenberg, Alan, ed. *Classic Essays on Photography.* New Haven, CT: Leete's Island Books, 1980.

Valin, Jonathan. "The Case of the Knock at the Door." *The Absolute Sound* 163 (June/July 2006): 100–106.

Vermeil, Jean. *Conversations with Boulez: Thoughts on Conducting.* Translated by Camille Naish. Portland, OR: Amadeus Press, 1996.

Wallerstein, Edward. "Celebrating the Fiftieth Anniversary of the LP: What Is a Long-Playing Record?" Liner note for *Mahler: Symphony No. 1 in D Major "Titan,"* 32–34. Sony MHK 63328, 1998.

Walter, Bruno. *Gustav Mahler.* Vienna: Herbert Reichner, 1936.

Wolff, Konrad. *Schnabel's Interpretation of Piano Music.* New York: W. W. Norton, 1972.

Zak, Albin. *The Poetics of Rock: Cutting Tracks, Making Records.* Berkeley: University of California Press, 2001.

Index

Abbado, Claudio, 57
Abramson, Daniel, "Make History, Not Memory," 156
absolute music, 6–12, 24–26, 60–61, 64, 67, 88, 125–27, 184, 192–93, 198–99, 216, 222, 255n24; as an expression of musical meaning, 168–71, 245–51; Mahler and, 222–27; musically absolute as a factor in recording, 207, 214; as relationship between individual and group, 101–103, 120–21, 175–82
Absolute Sound, the, 216–17
acoustic space and ambiance, 43–45, 50–56
Adorno, T. W., 85–86, 181–82, 201, 209, 216, 228; on "the expert listener," 21; "On the Fetish-Character in Music and the Regression of Listening," 181; on Mahler, 250; on "the 'We,'" 180–81
AHRC Research Centre for the History and Analysis of Recorded Music, 253n3
archiving. *See* digital archiving
Argerich, Martha, 210–11, 289n51
Arrau, Claudio, 149
art-religion, 194
Atget, Eugène, 238
Attali, Jacques, *Noise*, 22, 62–69, 85–86, 88, 89, 147, 265n6

Auslander, Philip, *Liveness: Performance in a Mediatized Culture*, 5
authentic performance. *See* performance practice
authorship, 31, 36, 40, 127
Ayers, Edward L., 158–59

Babbitt, Milton, 168–69, 171, 180, 282n18
Bach, J. S., 55, 101–102, 208; as arranged by Dmitry Sitkovetsky, 112–13, 114; Goldberg Variations, 38; as recorded by Edwin Fischer, 153–55; as recorded by Gould, 92–93, 94, 99, 112–14, 118–19, 131
Badal, James, 197
Bakhtin, Mikhail, 38
Barthes, Roland, 23, 58–59, 87, 108, 218–19; "Death of the Author," 32–33, 40–41, 189; duality of the erotic and pornographic, 218; on photography, 196, 204–206, 207, 214, 217, 232, 234, 237
Bartók, Béla, 65
Barton, David, "Literacy in Everyday Contexts," 172
Baudrillard, Jean: duality of the seductive and obscene, 218; "the ecstasy of communication," 170, 173–74, 187; on the image, 217–18, 219
BBC Legends, 153

visuality, 23–24, 194–96, 208–209, 217, 222, 223, 226, 230, 234, 247, 293n13

Wackenroder, Wilhelm Heinrich, 178
Wagner, Richard, 184–85, 225; *Tristan und Isolde*, 182, 215, 220
Walkman, 127, 181
Walmart, 131, 165
Walter, Bruno, 222–23
Wand, Günter, 87
Warrack, John, 83
Weingartner, Felix, 58
Werktreue, 91, 96, 111, 179, 191, 192, 269n3
White, Michael, 79, 80
Whitman, Walt, 235; *Leaves of Grass*, 179
Wilson, Brian, 197
Wittgenstein, Ludwig, 93, 293n13
Wolff, Konrad, 37, 96, 98, 103

work, musical, 2–3, 10, 11, 18, 26, 27–30, 35, 58, 198–99; relationship to performance, 92, 97, 120–21, 142, 212, 215–16, 272n43, 288n29; relationship to the recording, 61, 198, 204, 207–208, 210–212, 213, 214
writing, history of, 4
written transmission, 4, 10, 30, 32, 33–35, 113, 123–24

Yanagimachi, Mitsuo, *Kamyu nante shiranai*, 241–42
YouTube, 246
Yugoslav Wars, 142

Zak, Albin, 201
Zenph Studios "re-performance" of Gould's Goldberg Variations, 113–16, 134–36, 161, 277n22
Zimerman, Krystian, 124

Text:	10/12.5 Aldus
Display:	Aldus
Compositor:	Westchester Book Group
Printer and binder:	Maple-Vail Book Manufacturing Group